Renia Spiegel was born in eastern Poland in 1924. In January 1939 she began to write a diary. When war broke out she and her sister were living in Przemysl with her grandparents. Separated from her mother by the war, the next few years saw her living under first Soviet, then Nazi occupation, and the creation of the ghetto. In the summer of 1942, Renia was forced into hiding to escape the liquidation of the ghetto. A few days later, her hiding place was discovered and she was shot; she was just eighteen.

Anna Blasiak (Translator)

Anna Blasiak is a poet, translator and literature co-ordinator of the European Literature Network. She has translated over forty books from English into Polish and some fiction and poetry from Polish into English. In addition to her book-length translations, her work has been published in *Best European Fiction 2015*, *Asymptote*, *Guardian*, *B O D Y Literature*, *Modern Poetry in Translation* and *York Literary Review*.

Anna writes poetry in Polish and in English (*Off_Press*, *Women Online Writing*, *Exiled Ink* and *Modern Poetry in Translation*). She has worked in museums and a radio station, run magazines, written on art, film and theatre.

Marta Dziurosz (Translator)

Marta Dziurosz is a Polish literary translator and interpreter, and a literary curator. She was Free Word Centre's Translator in Residence 2015–16 and is a member of the ⬚⬚⬚⬚⬚⬚⬚⬚⬚⬚⬚⬚⬚⬚⬚⬚⬚⬚⬚⬚⬚⬚⬚⬚⬚⬚⬚⬚⬚⬚⬚tions and o⬚⬚⬚⬚⬚⬚⬚⬚⬚⬚⬚⬚⬚⬚⬚⬚⬚⬚⬚⬚⬚⬚⬚⬚⬚e is a

Renia's Diary

A YOUNG GIRL'S LIFE IN THE
SHADOW OF THE HOLOCAUST

RENIA SPIEGEL

Translated by Anna Blasiak and Marta Dziurosz

1 3 5 7 9 10 8 6 4 2

Ebury Press, an imprint of Ebury Publishing
20 Vauxhall Bridge Road
London SW1V 2SA

Ebury Press is part of the Penguin Random House Group of companies whose
addresses can be found at global.penguinrandomhouse.com

Englis   )19

Pro

Elizabeth I   is work
in

A CIP catalogue record for this book is available from the British Library

ISBN 9781529105063

Printed and bound in Great Britain by Clays Ltd, Elcograf S.p.A.

Contents

MAP OF POLAND 1939

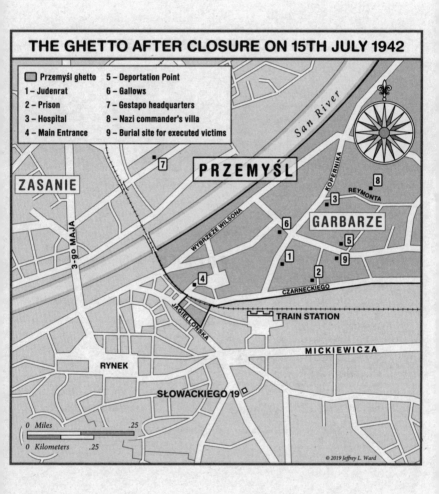

THE GHETTO AFTER CLOSURE ON 15TH JULY 1942

Przemyśl ghetto
1 – Judenrat
2 – Prison
3 – Hospital
4 – Main Entrance
5 – Deportation Point
6 – Gallows
7 – Gestapo headquarters
8 – Nazi commander's villa
9 – Burial site for executed victims

San River

ZASANIE

PRZEMYŚL

GARBARZE

KOPERNIKA

REYMONTA

3-go MAJA

WYBRZEŻE WILSONA

CZARNECKIEGO

JAGIELLOŃSKA

TRAIN STATION

MICKIEWICZA

RYNEK

SŁOWACKIEGO 19

0 Miles .25
0 Kilometers .25

© 2019 Jeffrey L. Ward

Introduction

In the past four decades, numerous Holocaust survivors have published their memoirs. Some waited to write until they reached an age at which people, in general, are more prone to reflect on the past. Some wrote because they felt the world was now more attuned to listening to what they had to say about this genocide. Others were urged to do so by their children, if not grandchildren. Since the 1980s so many memoirs have been published, that it is easy to forget that this desire to 'write and record' began far earlier.

In fact, Holocaust survivors have been writing their memoirs and giving their testimonies since the very end of the war. By the early 1960s, fifteen years after the end of the Holocaust, there were thousands of survivors' memoirs in print. In 1961, when Elie Wiesel sought an American publisher for *Night*, which had already been published in French, many rejected it because they believed there were too many memoirs in circulation. In his introduction to the French edition of *Night*, Nobel Prize winner François Mauriac acknowledged that Wiesel's was one among a myriad of Holocaust memoirs when he wrote, 'this personal record *coming as it does after so many others*' (emphasis added).* Sadly, with the passing of the generation of survivors, that trend is nearing its end.

It is sometimes hard to imagine that these recollections, now much treasured and valued, were once eschewed by historians who preferred official documents – despite the fact that most of these documents were products of the Third Reich – to personal accounts. These historians worried that personal memoirs were not as 'trustworthy' as documents. Today's historians recognize the value of these works, particularly when they are juxtaposed with the documentary and material evidence.

There are, of course, a number of methodological problems entailed in relying on these memoirs and testimonies. They are written *ex post facto*. Memory is elusive. It is impacted by more contemporary events. An individual's recollection of an event may be coloured by how another person who was also present remembered it. A survivor may recount the details of an event in order to stress a particular point, a point whose importance only became evident to her well after the fact. This is true, of course, with any memoir or testimony. We write to make a point. It is particularly true when the memoir deals with a

---

* François Mauriac, 'Introduction' to *La Nuit* by Elie Wiesel, as quoted in Ruth Franklin, *A Thousand Darknesses* (New York: Oxford University Press, 2011), p. 70.

traumatic event. And what could have been more traumatic than the Holocaust?

Moreover, memoirs are the voices of those who survived, not those who did not. It was with good reason that David Boder, one of the first scholars to systematically record survivors' accounts of their experiences, entitled his work *I Did Not Interview the Dead*. He knew that the voices he recorded were the ones who survived. The voices and recollections of those who were not lucky enough to endure were, in the main, lost to us for ever.

I write 'in the main' because we do have some of the voices of those who perished in the form of diaries such as Renia Spiegel's. Diaries are different, not only because they allow us to hear the voices of those who did not survive. They are different from memoirs because they do not pose these methodological challenges. Irrespective of whether they were written by someone who survived or someone who did not, they are fundamentally different from memoirs because they are contemporaneous accounts. Simply put, the author of the memoir knows the end of the story. The diarist does not. The diarist may well be unaware of the 'bigger' picture of what she is experiencing. For example, is the creation of a ghetto in her town part of a broader policy of ghettoisation or just something happening where she is? Whereas the person writing after an event may have a sense of how a particular German decree fitted into overall Nazi policy, the diarist generally does not. What may seem to be of relatively little importance to the diarist may, in fact, turn out to be of great significance. And conversely, what may seem utterly traumatic to the diarist may pale in comparison to what will follow.

Most importantly, diaries offer us something that memoirs do not: an emotional immediacy. And it is this immediacy that is so very compelling. I am reminded of Helene Berr, the young Israelite Parisian woman who kept a diary from 1942 through to the day she and her parents were rounded up in March 1944. Fortuitously, she begins to write just a short time before the decree that all Jews must wear a yellow star. She confides to the diary her struggle with whether to wear it or not. Was wearing it an act of compliance with a hateful regime or did it demonstrate a pride in one's Jewish identity? We read of her reactions to the comments of passers-by. Some express solidarity and others pity. She reflects on them, not from a distance of many years, but on the day she encountered them. She does not – because she cannot – contextualise this act as the first step in an array of far worse persecution to come.

In reading Renia Spiegel's diary, I was also reminded, as will many readers be, of Anne Frank's iconic work. All three of these diaries – Spiegel, Frank and Berr – are filled with the seemingly mundane musings of young girls who are transfixed by first loves and filled with hopes for the future. Renia Spiegel's diary is replete with familiar expressions of teenage angst – first love, first kiss, and jealousies that, in retrospect, may appear meaningless but at the moment seem, at least to Renia, to be momentous. It is also filled with poetry that cannot help but touch the reader.

We who read her writings are possessed of something she did not have: knowledge of the outcome. At the outset of the diary she is distraught that she has been forced to go and live with her grandparents and, therefore, has 'no real home'. It makes her so 'sad that I have to cry'. Not having a home will pale in comparison to what is to come. Had she written a memoir she would have known that fact and might have flattened this traumatic moment. She does not do so. In 1940, after the fall of Western Europe, she cries, 'I'm here on my own, without Mama or Daddy, without a home, poked and laughed at. Oh, God, why did such a horrible birthday have to come? Wouldn't it be better to die? I look down from the height of my sixteen years and I wonder whether I'll reach the end.' Were she writing a memoir, knowing what was in the offing, she might well have overlooked this moment of despondence. She might not have been so distraught when the luxury of fur clothing was taken from them. 'Yesterday coats, furs, collars, over sleeves, hats, boots were being taken away on the street. And now there's a new regulation that under pain of death it is forbidden to have even a scrap of fur at home …'

Nor does she know that what may appear to be a terrible fate might, in fact, turn out to be a lifesaver for some victims. She describes the 'fear, despair, abandon' experienced by those deported by the Soviets to Birobidzhan* and other

---

*A town in the USSR close to the border with China, administrative centre of the Jewish Autonomous Oblast created in 1934.

parts of the Soviet interior. She is distraught that 'they will travel in closed, dark carriages, fifty people in each … in airless, dirty, infested conditions. They might even be hungry … with children among them dying out.' Ironically, of course, these people had a far better chance of surviving than did those who would subsequently be forced by the Germans to travel in even worse conditions to an even more dire fate.

Yet this young girl – for that is what she really is – with her dreams for her future, recognises how the vice is closing in on her and her people. 'Ghetto! That word is ringing in our ears, it terrifies, it torments. We don't know what will happen to us, where we'll go and what they'll let us take.' Nonetheless, she continues to hope for the future. This tension between an increasingly bleak reality and an optimism about what might still be possible cannot help but break the reader's heart.

But a few days before being caught and murdered by the Germans, she senses that the end might be coming. She writes with prescience. 'My Dear Diary, my good, beloved friend! We have been through such terrible times together and now the worst moment is upon us. I could be afraid now. But the One who didn't leave us then will help us today too. He'll save us. Hear, O, Israel,* save us, help us.' Her prayer was for naught.

---

* A reference to one of the most important prayers in Judaism, Shema Yisrael ('Hear, O, Israel: the Lord, our God, the Lord is one').

Renia Spiegel, a young girl so filled with a zest for life and possessed of an ability to describe in prose and in poetry the beauty of the world around her, was denied with one bullet what she so wanted: a future. But for this diary she would have gone, together with millions of others, into the cruel oblivion that was the fate of most Holocaust victims. Those who saved the diary and those who worked to bring it to print, have 'rescued' her. They could not save her from a cruel fate. Nor could they give her that future she so desired. But they have rescued her from the added pain of having been forgotten.

– Deborah E. Lipstadt, Dorot Professor of
Holocaust History at Emory University

Prologue

My sister, Renia Spiegel, was born on 18 June 1924, in Uhryńkowce, in the Tarnopol province in south-eastern Poland. This rural town is called *Uhrynkivtsi* in English, and it is now part of Ukraine. Before the Second World War ripped apart our family, our people, and our country, Uhryńkowce was in Poland.

I came along on 18 November 1930, six years after Renia. I was happily married to my Austrian-born husband, George Bellak, for fifty-three years, taught school in New York City for three decades, and am a happy mother of two and a grandmother to three wonderful boys. My sister only lived to be eighteen. She was murdered by the Nazis in 1942. Along with a few photos, some family heirlooms, and the memories I've turned over in my head for almost ninety years, the diary you're about to read is all I have left of her.

I couldn't always face this diary, though. I hid from it and from my past for many years until my daughter, Alexandra Renata, retrieved the diary from the safe deposit box where it had lain, undisturbed, for over four decades. Realising what an important work of history and literature it is, and how it could resonate with people around the world, she had it translated into English. She's still working tirelessly to have it published across the globe, helping to make it known why this story has value, even today. I thank her for bringing it – and my sister's memory – back to me.

When I was born, my parents made a stork out of paper, placed it in the window, and told my sister I was coming. By then, my family had moved to an estate in a town called Stawki (*Stavky* in English), which was near the Dniester river and close to the Romanian border, but Renia adored it just as much as her old home. She loved hearing the birds singing. She loved the wind. She loved the forest. I sometimes think the memories of those places – far away in the country, in another time – are what inspired the poetry she wrote in this diary. Her poems were quiet, peaceful thoughts taken down while she was surrounded by war.

War isn't what drove us away from our home in Stawki. I was a child actor, called 'the Shirley Temple of Poland', and in 1938, my mum and I moved to Warsaw to promote me. She left Renia with her parents in her home town of Przemyśl, a small city in south-eastern Poland that is now on the border of Ukraine. In January 1939, Renia began her diary. That summer, I stayed with Renia and my grandparents for the holidays, and my mum went back to Warsaw.

The German and Soviet armies invaded Poland in September 1939, and by the end of that month, Poland was divided into two zones of occupation: the German side to the west and the Soviet side to the east. Przemyśl spread across both banks of the river San so it was split in two. My grandparents lived in the eastern, Soviet-occupied part. Our mother was in Warsaw, in the western, German-occupied part. We were not allowed to cross the San, so we were suddenly cut off from her. That's when Renia became a surrogate mother to me. We only saw our mum a few times in the next two years, and letters from her didn't arrive very often. Renia pined for her terribly. To this day, I wonder if this diary was a substitute for the mother she loved and missed so much.

Until my sister's boyfriend, Zygmunt, presented this diary to my mum in the early 1950s, I had no idea Renia had kept it. How she'd hidden seven hundred pages from me is a mystery, but it was her secret that she shared only with Zygmunt. Renia left her diary with him just before she was killed, and he passed it to someone for safekeeping before he was sent away to the camps. The pages here survived just as he did, and a friend – we still don't know who – brought them to him in the United States. My mother died in 1969, and when I found the diary in her things, I locked it up in a safe-deposit box in a Chase Bank near my apartment. I couldn't bear to read it. It was just too emotional for me.

I've still only read a few parts, and they've made me sick or made me cry. But I know these pages are important, so I will share them with you. We live in a time when tolerance is sometimes hard to find, but it's so important. War is also difficult to make sense of – especially if you're in the middle of it – but Renia was always so wise, and she did. I believe that her thoughts, her struggles, and her death show us why the world needs peace and acceptance. So I will let my sister's words and poems speak for themselves. At the end of the diary, I have written commentary that corresponds with particular entries and times of my life that I remember with her. I discuss history and what I recall about the last few years of Renia's life, and then I tell you how those of us who survived carried on after the war. My memories aren't as clear as they were eighty years ago, but I do my best. At some points, my thoughts and Renia's may feel scattered or not linear, but that's how a diary is. It's immediate and impulsive, and sometimes my memories are like that, too.

In the end, I know that my words are the legacy of the life my sister didn't get to have, while Renia's are the memories of a youth trapped for ever in war.

— Elizabeth Leszczyńska Bellak, formerly Ariana Spiegel

Renia's Diary

31 January 1939

Why did I decide to start my diary today? Has something important happened? Have I discovered that my friends are keeping diaries of their own? No! I just want a friend. I want somebody I can talk to about my everyday worries and joys. Somebody who will feel what I feel, believe what I say and never reveal my secrets. No human could ever be that kind of friend and that's why I have decided to look for a confidant in the form of a diary.

Today, my dear Diary, is the beginning of our deep friendship. Who knows how long it will last? It might even continue until the end of our lives. In any case I promise to always be honest with you, I'll be open and I'll tell you everything. In return you'll listen to my thoughts and my concerns, but never ever will you reveal them to anybody else, you'll remain silent like an enchanted book, locked up with an enchanted key and hidden in an enchanted castle. You won't betray me, if anything it'll be those small blue letters that people are able to recognise.

First of all, allow me to introduce myself. I'm in the third year of the Maria Konopnicka School for Girls.* My name is Renia, or at least that is what my friends call me. I have a little sister, Arianka,† who wants to be a film star. (She's partially fulfilled this dream, as she's already been in some movies.)

Our mummy lives in Warsaw. I used to live in a beautiful manor house on the Dniester river. I loved it there. I think these were so far the happiest days of my life. There were storks on old linden trees, apples glistened in the orchard and I had a garden with neat, charming rows of flowers. But that's in the past now and those days will never return. There is no manor house any more, no storks on old linden trees, no apples or flowers. All that remain are memories, sweet and lovely. And the Dniester river, which flows, distant, strange and cold – which hums, but not for me any more.

Now I live in Przemyśl, at my granny's house. But the truth is I have no real home. That's why sometimes I get so sad that I have to cry. I cry, though I don't miss anything, not the dresses, not sweets, not my strange and precious dreams. I only miss my mama and her warm heart. I miss the house where we all lived together, like in the white manor house on the Dniester river.

---

*The Maria Konopnicka Girls' Middle School in Przemyśl at 4 Grodzka Street.
† Also *Ariana, Jarośka, Jarka, Jara, Jarusia, Jarosia, Jakusia* – Renia's sister.

Again the need to cry takes over me
When I recall the days that used to be
The linden trees, house, storks and butterflies
Far … somewhere … too far for my eyes
I see and hear what I miss
The wind that used to lull old trees
And nobody tells me any more
About the fog, about the silence
The distance and darkness outside the door
I'll always hear this lullaby
See our house and pond laid by
And linden trees against the sky …

But I also have joyous moments, and there are so many of them … So many! I need to introduce my class to you, so that you can understand all our inside jokes.

My best friend, Norka,* sits next to me. Somebody might say that they don't like Nora, someone else might be delighted with her. I always like Norka, she's always the same sweet Norka to me. We share all the same thoughts, have the same views and opinions. At our school, the girls often get 'crushes' on our teachers, so Norka and I have a crush, a real one (some girls do it just to butter the teachers up) on our Latin teacher, Mrs Waleria Brzozowska née Brühl. We call her 'Brühla.' Brühla is the wife of a handsome officer who lives in Lwów. She goes to see him every other Sunday. We

---

* Also *Nora, Noruśka, Noreńka* – Renia's best friend.

tried to get his address through the address bureau, but didn't succeed because we don't know his actual name. (We call him 'Zdzisław'.) Brühla teaches Latin and we're good at this subject, which surely proves that we really love her.

The next girl in our row is Belka or 'Belania' – fat and stocky like three hundred devils! She has an exceptional talent for academics and an even more exceptional talent for earning dislike. She has a terrible 'crush' on Ms Skorska* and pulls stupid faces when looking at her.

Next comes Irka (*ira-ae* – anger). I don't like Irka and it's in my blood. I inherited this hatred: my mummy didn't like Irka's mother much when they were at school. I started disliking Irka even more when she began undermining me at school – all of this plus her unfair school report and disgusting sweet-talking, lying and insincerity made me genuinely hate her. What needs to be added to this mixture is also the fact that Brühla goes to visit Irka at home, which we investigated. And Irka's mother goes to visit Brühla at home, which we discovered peeping into the ground-floor windows of Brühla's place, where I spent many an hour with Nora waiting for her. All of that means I can't stand the girl! But since we're in the same class, we have to get on. So Nora and I just clench our fists and wait for an opportunity.

When it comes to the girls sitting next to Irka, I either don't care about them at all or I like them a little bit. On the other hand I care a bit more about the girls sitting at the

---

* Olga Skorska.

very back of the classroom, namely Luna, who sits behind me and constantly bombards my back. She thinks of herself as a very talented and unearthly creature. During parties and generally all the time she 'pretends' to be this or that, tries to draw attention to her beauty (which she doesn't possess), her exceptional abilities (which are figments of her imagination) and her importance (which she's never had). Luna is always trying to get the attention from boys, so, being short, she wears high heels, pencils her eyebrows longer and powders her face. At first she 'borrowed' Irka Łozińska's powder and did it supposedly 'just for fun'. And now she doesn't do it 'for fun' at all, but entirely seriously.

Irka Łozińska must be the most beautiful girl in our class or perhaps even the whole school. You don't even mind her dark, almost orange skin tone (powder-related, of course) and her patronising voice or harsh words spoken by coral-red lips revealing beautiful, snow-white teeth. But Irka has the worst of all flaws; she has tuberculosis ... Yes, sometimes she bleeds from the mouth and nose. I feel sorry for Irka. She has a boyfriend who loves her, but he doesn't know that his girlfriend's so seriously ill.

Irka sits at the very back of the classroom. Next to her there are two stony figures: Halina (very bad) with greatly coiffeured hair and Sławka who always pulls surprised faces, never answers and hides Halina under her desk when she wants to avoid answering a teacher's question. Then there is the third Irka, thin as a rake and very ugly. Next to her sits Elza, my former neighbour. She plays all innocent but I know

17

very well that it's just a game. She has decent marks, but her school report is always better than she deserves. Supposedly she always copies her Latin homework from the third Irka … but who cares.

Then there is the president of our class, Krzyśka. Krzyśka doesn't know anything and speaks as if she has dumplings filled with sand in her mouth, but she's pretty and always head-over-heels in love with all her Zbyszeks, Sławeks, Leszeks, Zdzisios, etc. She's friends with Luna.

In front of her the first Eda (there are three of them) bends and sways. Eda is a 'lady with claws', she's engaged, has a great figure and everything. The second Eda is Belka's former friend. She also has a crush on Ms Skorska, but she's not good at history, which makes me suspicious. The third Eda was our enemy as recently as several months ago. Just imagine, my dear Diary, some stranger, some 'stray' from the sticks arrives and wants to be the boss, tries to show us we are slow and thinks of herself as an 'all-round talent'. Seriously?

Luśka and Dziunka sit in front of Eda. Dziunka makes 'nervously tectonic' moves. I was on bad terms with her for over a year, but I got over it on Brühla's name day. Dziunka is considered the most boring person in the class and, indeed, she is one. Luśka is silly, stupid and backward. You can tell her whatever you want. But she's a fun one, she always dances the 'Andrusovo' dance with me at parties. Once Luśka yelled during a maths lesson, 'Miss, miss, I haven't been called up for such a long time and I like maths so much!' Nora's response to that was, 'Luśka, come on, don't be stupid.' 'Not at all,' Luśka answered, but then, when she realised what she'd done, she started stammering and widened her shiny eyes.

In front of them, in front of the first Eda, Luśka and Dziunka, there is a strange desk reserved for 'antiques'. Which means Janka. Janka is the best in the class at 'playing stupid' and she only survives thanks to other people's help. When she gets called up to the blackboard, she has all the answers written on her nails. If, by any chance, the teacher notices something suspicious, Janka quickly licks the ink off and plays the saint. Janka knows how to cry, wail and even faint on demand, quite like the first Eda, who suddenly feels woozy when Pacuła is about to ask her to recite a poem. Janka is generally very talented when it comes to making scenes. Next to her sits Wisia, a little creature who's not even three and a half foot tall despite her fifteen years of age. The third in the row is Frejka or Salka. She gets nervous attacks every now and then, sometimes can't say a word when too upset, walks in comical steps and skips, and often 'can't stand' sitting by her desk.

I should also mention Ninka, this unusual girl who looks completely innocent but receives poste restante letters from various 'peoples', arranges meetings in dark streets, visits lonely men and is proud of it. She's quite nice. There are more girls like her in our class, but, as I said before, I either don't care about them or don't want to hang around with them, because I am a good girl.

We've been planning a party for months now. We've fought and disagreed, but the party is on this coming Saturday.

2 February 1939[1]

My dear Diary! I have always been just average in gymnastics, so I practise at home to get better. I have just managed to pull off my first somersault. None of my friends can do it. I'm triumphant, though I've grazed my knee.

5 February 1939

My dear Diary, it's after the party, finally! I'm so happy. It was a great party and everyone, especially Brühla, had a wonderful time. But some sadness awaited me after the party. And again, for the umpteenth time, I thought, 'I wish Mama were here.' What happened was that Irka's mother, Mrs Oberhard, was all over Brühla, sweet-talking her as much as she could, which, of course, would be sure to benefit Irka and her younger sister in the near future. Oh, dear Diary, if you could only know how hard it is to want something so badly, to work so hard for it and then be denied it at the finishing line! What was it actually that I wanted? I don't know. I was given the highest praise by Pacuła, which I don't care about (she talked to us, me and Norka). Brühla was quite nice. But I'm still not satisfied.

Luna performed twice and so did I. Today I saw Brühla with Mrs Oberhard, most likely walking back from her place. I nodded politely, walked past and said to Nora, 'What do you think? She was at hers again, wasn't she?' And then I suddenly see her pulling a stupid face. I look around and see that Brühla is walking right behind us. She looks horrible,

I don't know what's wrong with her, I would like to be of use to her, to help, perhaps to advise, but the abyss between us is so huge, so very, very huge ... Perhaps even larger than the one separating me from Mama. She could help me too, she could advise. But it's much harder, oh, so much harder to bridge this gap.

8 February 1939

Dear Diary! It's been several days since I told you about my life, but actually nothing special has happened. Life goes on as normal, with a few small exceptions. Brühla attended a Latin teachers' conference, so Latin was taught by Mr Skorski. Mr Dziedzic praised Irka very much (undeservedly), Belka got a bad mark, I got away with it, but I'm worried about tomorrow, as it could be a really bad day. That's all I needed to tell you.

13 February 1939

It's raining today ... Such a sad, grey day. But I don't feel very sad, I don't know why. Perhaps it's the idea of leaving for Canada, though it might not be so good there after all. Or perhaps it's because I'm making a Greek vase. Anyway, I'm not as sad as I usually am on rainy days when I just stand by the window and count the tears trickling down the windowpane. There are plenty of them. One small one runs, then another larger one follows it closely, then the fifth, sixth ... as well as two on my cheeks. They all run down, as if they wanted to drop onto the wet, muddy street, as if they wanted to make it even dirtier, as if they wanted to make this day ugly, even uglier than it already is. But today is a mystery. Like … like a rubbish bin. Everybody thinks it's nothing much, it's simply nothing. But it's not the case. I don't know. People might laugh at me, but you'll surely understand, my dear friend. The thing is sometimes I think inanimate objects can talk. (Actually, they are not inanimate at all. They have souls, just like people.) Sometimes I think waterworks giggle. And it's not just me thinking this, so it must be true. Other people call this giggle different names, but it never even crosses their minds that it's just that: a giggle. Or a rubbish bin:

Oh, the night! Darkness came at last!
I don't like it here! I'm feeling harassed!
It was better in the city,
With its comfort, light and warmth. What a pity,
A page came clean
From a weekly film magazine.
They only bought me yesterday
and I'm already in the rubbish today!
You, at least something you've seen.
At least in the world you have been.
Your life was peaceful when at a newsagent's bound
While I had to run around
In the streets, shouting all the time.
It's better to be a weekly
Than a daily that passes quickly.

I was prepared and I'm not bitter
About ending up in the litter,
Said wrapping paper without a jitter.
I was a children's magazine, alas,
Beautifully illustrated en masse,
Full of colour and class,
The rubbish I can outlast.
I'm of a different kind,
Than a daily, I find
Or a film weekly for that matter,
Or even this ... this wrapping paper.
So let me tell you, I don't like it here.
Stay away from me or I'll disappear!
That causes a proper commotion in the bin.
What?! What cheek! Aha! There you go, you mean!
And all the papers together
Flew out of the rubbish bin like feathers.
People were surprised in the morning,
They took it as a warning
That somebody threw papers to begin
With, on the ground instead of in the bin.

Renia. I send you kisses, but now I have to sit down and cram.

13 February 1939

Can there be a worse day than Monday the 13th? Monday on
its own is usually quite bad, and now we have the number 13

added to it. Bad luck! It was definitely not a good day for me. On top of all the other little pieces of bad luck, I'm at school. It's Latin and Brühla enters, so I think she'll do a test. But no. OK, better still (I think), I'm safe. But she wants us to write essays on little pieces of paper torn out of our notebooks. Mine went as well as it could on Monday the 13th. On a bad day it went really badly. Why? Humph … Good question, why?

Only a person who's not superstitious could ask this. Exactly, so first of all: I missed school and as a result didn't have certain forms; secondly: I was laughing my head off all the time; and thirdly: the essay was written on torn-out pieces of paper which I didn't respect much, so I made light of it, not even thinking that Brühla might collect those pages. At geography we had a sudden and turbulent fight over the chairs, which I didn't take part in, but was still considered one of the castaways. We were supposed to move about the classroom. I've said many times before that I'm not some kind of a loser. So I quietly moved with Nora to the last desk. Gruca looks for me and tells me to move. I don't want to, I say I'm fine where I am. She goes on and I go on.

'Move!'

'But I haven't done anything.'

And so on and on. Finally I realise that I won't be able to get away with it, so I look for somewhere else to sit.

'There is a place there, please move,' Gruca says.

'Oh, anywhere but there. I'm so delicate, I get colds easily. I might get too hot by the stove and get pneumonia,' I reply.

It's time to end this.

'Fine, here then,' Gruca says again.

'Oh, not by the door! How can I sit by the door, being so delicate.'

The whole class is of course in stitches, howling and roaring with laughter.

I realise that I have no choice and I finally move, but it's only on her fourth attempt. Nora sits under the desk all this time and I keep knocking. I then tell Gruca that I can't see the map. And I continue knocking, pretending that a school inspector is coming. There were probably a thousand more adventures, but I'm glad that this exceptionally bad day's over now.

14 February 1939

Parent–teacher evening today. It didn't go well, thanks to the dregs of yesterday. Brühla said my essay was terrible, so now I have something to worry about.

15 February 1939

Nothing special today. Przemyśl is getting ready for a gas attack and I'm getting ready for a nervous attack. All because of last Monday! I was called up to the board at chemistry. I was prepared! Damn it, Dziedzic was trying to trick me.

26 February 1939[2]

I've been busy for the last few days. Arianka is here. We have a gathering tomorrow and I need to write my report.

28 March 1939[3]

God, I'm so sad, so very sad ... I'd just like to cry, wail and sob. How can I express how terrible I'm feeling? No ... That's not possible. Mama's just left and who knows when I'll see her again. I fell out with Nora several days ago so I need to hang out with Irka, which is not helping.

And then there are memories ... They're always there and even though they make me cry, even though they break my heart, they're the sweetest. They're memories of the best time in my life. It's springtime already! Spring used to be so good there. Birds were singing, flowers were in bloom; it was all sky, heart and happiness! People there would be thinking of the holidays now. It was so different to everything here. So tranquil, warm and friendly; I loved it so much.

On the evening of the Passover Seder, I waited for Elijah. Maybe there was a time when this holy old man came to see happy children. But if he only came to see poor people, if he never stood in our wide-open doors, if he never let me see him, then he has to come now, when I have nothing. Nothing apart from memories. Grandpa's unwell. Mama's very worried about me. Oh! I'm so unhappy! Sometimes I don't eat on purpose to avoid ...

> It waits for me everywhere
> It lurks, as I'm aware
> Its ghastly, bony hands
> Want to get me in their commands
> It whispers into my ear

In every mouthful, all I hear
It waits for me, it calls me loudly
It shakes its hands so proudly
It wags its finger
It watches and lingers …

2 April 1939[4]

The religious retreat's over. I didn't enjoy those days. I'm still angry with Nora. And Irka didn't want to leave me alone, so I hung out with her a bit. Towards the end I didn't even have a good book to read. The holidays are coming. I'm learning French now and if there's no war I might go to France. I was supposed to go before, but Hitler took over Austria, then Sudetenland, Czechoslovakia, Klaipeda,* and who knows what he'll do next. He's affecting my life, too. I want to write a poem for Arianka. I'll be very happy if it comes out well.

A little hen was feeling sickly.
She went to see a doctor quickly.
She told him in no uncertain terms:
'Help me, doctor, I have concerns.
When I'm angry, something's tingling,
Something's jabbing, something's stinging
(So badly do I suffer, it keeps me busy!)

---

*These were the territories annexed by Nazi Germany in 1938 and 1939, before the Second World War broke out.

All the time I'm feeling dizzy,
I'm not hungry, my stomach's churning,
I can't sleep at all till the morning.
Then I'm tired in the daytime.
Migraines mean I'm not in my prime.
My face is a shade of prawn.
And when my husband crows at dawn
I go purple and black,
I have a nervous attack.
And let me also add, doctor dear
That I get very sweaty, I fear.'
So many serious ailments
Make the doctor head for derailment.
He thought and thought about it hard,
He pored over many a book's card,
And finally he said to the hen:
'Go back to your pen.
I can't help you, it's time to die.'
'Die? What say you? You surely lie!
My dear doctor, don't be a beast,
I'm not ill, not in the least!'

7 April 1939

Yes … Oh yes … A bird's song
It's been oh so long
So many hours did go by
It's all the same as time does fly

It's equally sad … tearful … heavy-hearted. I don't have a new coat and this one's old and worn down. I don't have new shoes, like all my friends. And even though I console myself that I have sweet thoughts and good dreams for the future, I'm still sad. The whole of Przemyśl is spruced up, every person shimmers from afar with their new, special shoes (you can tell by looking at the underside of a shoe and by listening to voices saying here and there, 'Ooh, blisters!'). And everybody has a solemn face, as you should on festive days. I just don't know why this festive mood reminds me of the time when the air-raid training was taking place.

'Mr Sztajner, I tell you, what a farce!'

'Unbelievable! Right! They made me some kind of commandant, good sir. I keep running around like a headless chicken all day long, good sir. And I don't even know what's what!'

'Yeah, yeah. "Comediant" in the old age. Whatever else?'

You hear conversations like this one all over the city.

'Dear friend, let me tell you, it slightly stinks of war.'

'Yup. The end of the world's coming … Heard something about bombs coming down. But people say it won't be a war, my friend, just that they'll keep having a go at each other, the ones from the bottom and the ones from the top.'

'No war, you say?! But I think there'll be war. You, my friend, you don't know it, but they always put posters out before the war. They come and go and then, suddenly, my friend, war breaks out.'

C: 'Sirens?! An alarm! Turn the lights off! Draw the curtains in the windows! Kazio, grab a pan and whack it, quick,' the commandant yells.

N: 'What are you talking about, my dear neighbour? It clearly says that in case of an alarm one needs to bang on a rail,' the neighbour says.

Neighbour 2: 'What the hell? Are you mad? In case of an alarm, one needs to do nothing, just stand quietly in the gateway.'

C: 'I think I am the commandant here and I know what to do! Here you are, everywhere there are gongs going, Kazio! A pan and a rail, whack them both.'

N: 'Sir, and what about an armband?'

C: 'Excuse me?! Don't tell me what to do. If you keep opposing me, I'll immediately hand my resignation to the building caretaker. And of course you'll need to pay a fine.'

Female neighbour: 'Will you be quiet? I've only just put the children to bed and you're making so much noise. What's going on? We need order. Let decent people live their lives. You are the commandant and instead of ensuring there is peace and quiet, you make noise in the neighbourhood, keep children awake, get decent people out of beds?'

C: 'My dear lady, there was an alarm . . .'

Female neighbour 3: 'What alarm, what alarm?! Mrs Pietroszkowa, have you heard it? I've only just managed to put the children to bed. Henio is ill, the doctor said he needs rest. And now all this commotion in the building in the middle of the night. Unheard of! Have you ever heard of anything quite like this?'

Mrs Pietroszkowa: 'Yes, my dear, that's a real rumpus.'

Neighbour 2: 'Didn't I say that what we need is to stand here quietly and wait until ...'

Zosia: 'My mum has a migraine. She's said to be quiet straight away or she'll call the police.'

C: 'I'm the commandant here, the responsibility lies with me, so I do what I think is right and I don't care about any ailments. Kazio, another blow on the barrel!'

Constable: 'What's going on here? Go back to your flats. The alarm's long over. All this shouting! The racket! I'll make a note. All the residents of 13 Nieszczęśliwska Street will pay a fine for making noise.'

P: 'Some commandant!'

4 May 1939

I haven't told you anything for a while. Why? Do I know why? I study French now and I go to Jerschina*. I've written an essay on Roman painting and now plan or rather I've already started writing a German text. Yesterday, on 3 May, I took part in a march, which is why I'm unwell today. I got soaked in the rain. Much has changed since my last conversation with you. Mama and Arianka went to Łódź. I'm on bad terms with Brühla. She didn't examine me at Greek and she told the

---

* Stanisław Jerschina – specialist in Polish studies, teacher, founder and director of the Teaching College in Kielce.

Head that I just wander around with Nora all the time. That's what Irka told me, but Irka likes to spread gossip. There was a school dance, but I didn't take part. By contrast Luna was showing off as hard as she could. For some reason this idiot has imagined she's my rival! My rival! I couldn't care less about her recitation. No, I don't care at all, I just happen to know a little bit about it. I can't say I bragged about myself either. But my feeling is she'll one day become a cabaret artiste (you can tell by looking at her hair and movements), while I have different plans (I think), so our paths won't cross, so it's stupid to say that Luna could be my rival. Today I declare war – an internal war. I told her about it yesterday and I'll stick to it. What happened was she didn't want to let me into the row, where my place is. Finally the commandant arrived and told me to switch places with her, i.e., with Luna. So she says to me, 'I knew you were right, but I wanted to spite you!' She wanted to spite me! Ha ha ha, that is simply funny. She, who fully depends on me at Latin and in general. So I told her, 'You wanted to spite me, so now remember that I'll try to spite you too.' I'll do just that, until the end, because that's what I want.

7 May 1939

May. A very strange May it is. So sad ... Brrr ... It's raining. And to think it's May already, May, and I still haven't seen a tree in bloom, haven't smelt fields waking up, my fields ... It rains. It's good that it's raining. These days I like rain, because at least I know that it was like that there too, when it rained.

Yesterday I went to a party and then talked to Nora about this and that, about different goals that people have in life, about the benefits of studying. I like talking so much when I know that somebody understands me …

The moon swims out in silence
To shine in the sky, to shimmer for dreamers
While below a street rumbles shrilly
Crunching with labour, hot and weary
Loud rat-tat-tat-tat of human steps
Echoes from cobbled streets
Grey carts and their wheels
Groan and never miss a beat
Taxis whoosh ahead
And red trams smoothly slide
On their tracks of steel
Stopping only sometimes
To take in yet again
Another mass of people
Then leave without complaint
Propelled by fiery heat
Above in the azure sky
The moon's silver disc moves too
But nobody sees its flight
Below a street hums, 'Whoo'
Chains of bright lights
Illuminate the night
So strangely draped

In shop windows and posters staked
Huge electric streetlights
Stand below the silver
Of the trembling moon
No one looks up with delight
The street below is far too bright

Renia

When I look behind my small window box
I see the same rooftops, same stationer's shops
I see the same gutters, nestled snugly into walls
And only people in the street change at all
Even the road, shimmering and slippery after rain
Even the people, neighbours from across are all the same
The spectacled lawyer and his daughter
The pharmacist above, the janitor in his quarters
Two servants and the grey-haired lady on the third floor
And here a girl, a doll, a clown, a monkey, toys galore
They always open their shutters the same way
And look down at the street, every day
The houses look out too, as do windowpanes, dozing cosily
And only the people in the street change, supposedly

18 June 1939

It's my birthday today. I don't want to think about anything sad, about the fact that I'm not there ... Hush! So instead I'm thinking about all the useful things I've done so far in my life.

A voice, 'None.'

Me, 'I get good marks at school.'

Voice, 'You haven't earned it. What else?'

Me, 'Nothing. I really want to go to France.'

Voice, 'You want to be famous?'

Me, 'I'd like to be famous, but I won't be. So I want
to be happy, very happy.'

Tomorrow's the end of the school year, but I don't care. About anything … Anything … Anything.

I like Jerschina very much again, but Brühla less so. I didn't tell Nora about it, don't want to worry her. Tomorrow I'll tell you about our trip.

If a man had wings
If souls could be in all things
The world would lose its temper
The sun would shower us with embers
The people would dance beyond the beyond
Shouting, more! We want to abscond!
What we need is wind and speed
The world is dark, stifling, squeezed
Let it go to sweeping heights
Let it become great and bright
Let it cross into a boundless domain
Let it lose itself in its own vast reign
Supported by hundreds of limbs
Millions of hands, mighty wings

Let the time string go flashing through
Until the darkness of the night descends anew
This powerful realm of the underworld
Until its flight slowing down occurred
Until, tired, exhausted and all
It will have to fall

15 August 1939[5]

I haven't spoken to you for a while. The end of the school
year is long gone, my summer holidays are almost over,
and I haven't spoken to you. I went to see my aunt in the
countryside, I went to Warsaw, saw Mama and now I'm back.
But you don't know about any of that. You were lying here,
left on your own with my thoughts and you don't even know
that we have a secret mobilisation, you don't know that the
Russians have signed a treaty with the Germans. You don't
know that people are stockpiling food, that everybody's on
the alert, waiting for ... war. When I was saying goodbye to
Mama, I hugged her hard. I wanted to tell her everything
with this silent hug. I wanted to take her soul and leave her
my own, because – when?

Mother's embrace
One and only, the last
Will stay with me through all the days
Through all tears, all ill fortunes
Through all tough moments

We will both get through, you and I
And then a ray will glimmer

I can't think logically today. Supposedly they call it 'spleen'. Something flies at a rapid pace and disappears into the mist. Zigzags, circles, stripes, fog ... pink fog, greenish. No. I'm not curious about anything. One thought spins around my head, only one, the same one all the time. Mum ... war ... brown shoes ... war ... Mum.

6 September 1939

War broke out on Thursday! First on 30 or 31 August Poland went to war with Germany. Then England and France also declared war on Hitler and surrounded him on three sides. But he isn't sitting idly. Enemy planes keep flying over Przemyśl, and every now and then there's an air-raid siren. But, thank God, no bombs have fallen on our city so far. Other cities like Krakow, Lwów, Częstochowa and Warsaw have been partially destroyed.

But we are all fighting, we are all fighting, from young girls to soldiers. I've been taking part in female military training – digging air-raid trenches, sewing gas masks. I've been working as a runner. I have shifts serving tea to the soldiers. I walk around and collect food for the soldiers. In a word, I'm fighting alongside the rest of the Polish nation. I'm fighting and I'll win!

10 September 1939

Oh, God! My God! We've been on the road for three days now. Przemyśl was attacked. We had to flee. The three of us escaped: me, Arianka and Grandpa. We left the burning, partially destroyed city in the middle of the night on foot, carrying our bags. Granny stayed behind. Lord, please protect her. We heard on the road that Przemyśl was being destroyed.

> We left the city
> Like fugitives
> On our own, in the dark, dull night
> The city bade us farewell
> With the sound of buildings crashing down
> Darkness was above my head
> Mercy of good people
> Mother's embrace in the far distance
> Let them be our guidance
> Let them give us comfort and assistance
> We will walk through
> All our trials
> Until the day breaks, until it glints
> We are lonely fugitives
> Fugitives deserted by all since

18 September 1939

We've been in Lwów for almost a week and we can't get through to Zaleszczyki. The city is surrounded. Food is in short supply. Sometimes I get up at dawn and stand in a long queue to get bread. Apart from that, we've been spending all day in a bunker, a cellar, listening to the terrible whistling of bullets and explosions of bombs. God, please save us. Some bombs have destroyed several tenement houses, and three days later they dug people out from the rubble, alive. Some people are sleeping in the bunkers; those brave enough to sleep at home have to wake up several times each night and run downstairs to their cellars. This life is terrible. We're yellow, pale, from this cellar life – from the lack of water, comfortable beds and sleep.

But horrible thoughts are much worse, black as night, vulture-like. Granny stayed in Przemyśl, Daddy's in Zaleszczyki and Mum, my mama, is in Warsaw. Warsaw is surrounded, defending itself bravely, resisting attack again and again. We Poles are fighting like knights in an open field where the enemy and God can see us. Not like the Germans, who bombard civilians' homes, who turn churches to ashes, who poison little children with toxic sweets (contaminated with cholera and typhus) and balloons filled with mustard gas. We defend ourselves and we're winning, just like Warsaw, like the cities of Lwów and Przemyśl.

My mama's in Warsaw. I love her the most in the world, my dearest soul, my most precious. I know if she sees children clinging to their mothers in bunkers, she must be feeling the same way we feel when we see it. Oh my God! The greatest, the one and only. God, please save my mama, give her faith that we are alive. Merciful God, please make the war stop, make all people good and happy. Amen.

22 September 1939

My dear Diary! I had a strange day today. Lwów surrendered. Not to Germany, but to Russia. Polish soldiers were disarmed in the streets. Some, with tears in their eyes, just dropped their bayonets to the ground and watched the Russians break their rifles. Civilians took horses, saddles, blankets. I feel such grief, such great grief ... Only a small handful are still fighting. Despite the order, defenders of Lwów are still continuing their heroic fight to die for their homeland.

> The city's surrendered
> On its borders
> A handful continue the fight
> Without a command
> A handful continue the fight
> They won't surrender
> They are Lwów defenders

28 September 1939

Russians have entered the city.* There are still shortages of food, clothing, shoes, everything. Long queues are forming in front of every shop. The Russians are especially eager to buy things. They've been organising raids to get watches, textiles, shoes, etc.

---

* The occupation of Lwów began in the afternoon of 22 September 1939.

This Red Army is strange. You can't tell a private from an officer. They all wear the same greyish-brown uniforms. They all speak the language I can't understand. They call each other *Tovarishch*.* Sometimes the officers' faces are more intelligent though. Poland has been totally flooded by the German and Russian armies. The only island still fighting is Warsaw. Our government has fled the country. And I had so much faith.

Where is Mama? What's happened to her? God! You listened to my prayer and there is no war any more (or at least I can't see it). Please listen to the first part of my prayer, too, and protect my mama from evil. Wherever she is, whatever is happening to her, please keep an eye on her and on us and help us in all our needs! Amen.

27 October 1939

I've been back in Przemyśl for a while now. I go to school. Life has gone back to its everyday routine, but at the same time it's different, so sad. There is no Mama. We haven't heard from her. I had a terrible dream that she's dead. I know it's not possible. I cry all the time, tormented by bad feelings. If only I knew that I would see her in two months' time, even a year, as long as I knew I would see her for certain. That's impossible. No, let me die. Holy God, please give me an easy death.

---

* *Tovarishch* (товарищ) – comrade (Russian).

28 October 1939

School life is so strange. Yesterday we had a meeting, the day before – a march. Polish women riot when they hear people saluting Stalin. They refuse to join in. They write secret messages saying, 'Poland has not yet perished,'* even though, to be honest, it perished a long time ago. And now there is Western Ukraine here, there is 'coomunism', everybody is equal and that's what hurts them. It hurts them that they can't say, 'You bloody Yid.' They still say it, but in secret.

Those Russians are such handsome boys (though not all of them). One of them was determined to marry me. '*Pajdyom baryshnya na moyu kvateru budem zhyly,*' etc. etc. France and England are fighting with the Germans and something's brewing here, but what do I care? I just want Mama to come, to be with us. Then I can face all my trials and tribulations.

One 'auntie' died here, this silver-haired, thin, wrinkly old lady:

She lived so quietly …
She was like a shadow
One gloomy autumn, she just let go
This grey-haired old lady, all wrinkles and wobbles
Hunched, shrivelled, coughing, always needing goggles
She died … (as people do)

---

* '*Jeszcze Polska nie zginęła*' ('Poland has not yet perished') – Polish national anthem.

And away from a calendar a card flew
A new day arrived
Nothing changed in life
This life, that she held so dear
The silver-haired lady, shed a tear
For her, she was like a shadow
And one gloomy autumn, she just let go

1 November 1939

I'm so angry today. Angry, as they say. But, truth be told, I'm sad, very, very sad.

There's a new youth club here now. Lots of boys and girls have been going there, and there's fun to be had (for some). I don't have a crush on Brühla any more. I finally told Nora about it, and she told me she feels the same way. Now, according to the stages of a girl's development I should 'fall in love' with a boy. I like Jurek. But Jurek doesn't know about it and won't ever work it out. You know it, you and I, and ...

The first day at the club was fun (I mean I had fun), but today I felt like a fish out of water. People played this flirting game (some game it is) and I didn't get even one card. I'm embarrassed to admit it even to you. Some boy named Julek (not Jurek) supposedly likes me, but why? Maybe because I'm so different from my friends. I'm not saying that's a good thing – it could even be a bad thing – but I'm very different from them. I don't even know how to laugh in a flirtatious way. When I laugh, it's for real, openly. I don't know how to 'behave' around boys.

That's why I miss the old days, the age of pink ... blue ... being carefree ... When Mama was still with me, when I had my own home, when there was peace in the world, when everything was blue, bright, serene; when such weather prevailed in my heart.

> I lived among some cheerful meadows
> Among fields painted with sunlight
> I smiled at the golden stars
> To pink emergence of daylight
> My life was also all in pink
> As bright as days filled with sun
> I didn't want it to end in a blink
> Being a happy echo was fun
> Sounding with silver glee
> Reflecting merrily off the sky
> In love with all, happy as can be
> I didn't know how much a heart could cry
> I didn't know the weeping of a soul
> I didn't know it could be different.
> Today I'm filled with regret
> And though I am still so young and whole
> I look back into the recent past
> And cry. It's gone ... Shame, I'm aghast ...

16 November 1939[6]

I'm ill. I have a sore throat. But I am breathing more easily now. I know that Mama's alive, that she's in Warsaw. She'll

come and see me any day now. And I can't wait, can't wait …
Ticio* sent a postcard; they have everything in abundance in
Horodenka.† Daddy'll get a job as a farmer. He might bring us
some provisions.

We have three days off. Anniversary of the revolution.
There'll be morning assemblies at schools, young people's
marches. Such a shame I can't be part of it. I'm ill …

9 December 1939

The Christmas holidays are coming. Daddy's got a job in a
sugar refinery. I might go there. Mama's in Warsaw, not
planning to come here.

I might get a scholarship … Let's hope …

I love him, he's wonderful, just like I dream about, I love
him – but I don't know if that's in fact love. He doesn't
know about me and I only know that he's in Border Patrol.
And one more thing, something terribly 'teenagerish' –
I'd love to kiss his lips, eyes, temples, just like you read in
romance books.

Irka is passionate. She goes to Marysia's; there are plenty
of beds there, with bed linen, and each couple goes to
a separate room and … well, that makes you think. Belka

---

* *Ticio, Ticiu, Tusio* – Renia's father.
† A town in Stanisławów Voivodeship, an administrative centre of the
Horodenka district, at the time under Soviet occupation, later under
German occupation.

said one mysterious sentence while we were working (Belka knows a lot): 'Anyway look at Irka, at her broad walk …' Ugh … It's so disgusting. Truth be told, I'm not passionate. I'd like to have a pretty husband, like him … I'd like to live in Crimea in a pretty villa-house, have a golden-haired little boy, a son, be happy and love everything …

I have to write down a translation of a German poem. Oh, I've grown sick of school!

Always at work, millions of hands
For thousand centuries, many decades
And every hand, which for an axe bends
Is like an Atlas, each the sky aids

Rattling and whirring, roaring and banging
This is the sound of our land's iron call
Crunching and quaking, booming and clanging
Immortal singing of work befalls

Plenty of cylinders must go in and out
And plenty of screw bolts must stay about
Hammers must strike the anvil with might
To make the world simmer, be alight

Thousands of people must be on fire
Brains must ignite and never tire
To keep this flame always ablaze
Filling the world with warm light for years

10 December 1939

'We work!' This is the title of our newspaper. 'Work is power!' and 'Forward with work' and many more similar slogans I've heard. And I've spent some time thinking about what work is. Every time I thought about it, various images came to mind. Here is a grey working army, these are workmen, I can see students with their heads bowed, I can see pilots in roaring planes, seamen somewhere out at sea. They are all part of the powerful working army; work goes on out at sea, on land and in the air. Yes, but what in fact is work?

Everything hums and roars around
Work's going on, never breaks down
It blares, it rattles and flutters in spades
Asking for soldiers for its work brigades!
Calls everybody on land and at sea
Those in the mines and those who fly free
To grab their axes, their chisels, their trowels
To join the workforces and not throw in the towel
To conquer the world as it is wide
To build a new one with work and to do it with pride

15 December 1939

The radio didn't mention an explosion in a school in Przemyśl, the papers didn't write about it, paperboys out in the streets didn't shout, 'The Konopnicka School has been blown up with steam!' Nobody knew about anything, but 'something' did happen. This 'something' took place at a chemistry or physics lesson. It was, of course, before the war. Here's what happened: we had a guest at physics; we all shook like jelly, practised all possible emergency measures, like 'a wireless telephone line', nudging, kicking, clearing one's throat and other such methods, known only to us. Finally the new lesson started. And it was going well! But something was ticking! On the table there were plenty of little bottles, flasks, bowls, test tubes, stands, burners and other devices. It all looked rather impressive, powerful and very 'scientific'. Even more so, when it was all lined, connected – it was pretty. I can still hear this voice saying clearly, 'But please remember to leave an opening for steam, this is very important.' Of course! Certainly! Absolutely! All was going well, exceptionally well, the reactions were just like in the textbook, until … oh, what horror! In comparison to what happened next, Zeus sending a thunderbolt down was a quiet whisper and the clash of swords at Troy was a delicate rustle. Bottles, flasks, bowls, test tubes – first they all jumped up into the air and then landed on our poor tables, books and notebooks. The esteemed guest was of course outraged, etc. etc.… . But let me keep that a secret, since the papers and the radio didn't talk about it. And I've already spilt the beans, so now I ask for your discretion. Let's keep this between us.

26 December 1939

Half of the school year is gone already. The time has passed in a flash. First I was elected to the committee as the head of the drama club, then we were supposed to have a party with boys, there were many searches in the city, there were four sexual murders. And now, tomorrow night, I can go to see Daddy at Horodenka. But before I have a meeting tomorrow and I'll go for a rehearsal at Słowacy.* There might even be a party. Shame I won't be there, since recently I'm feeling kind of … I'm going through silly, childish things and thoughts, which are quite pleasant. Just silly thoughts: life, buying powder compacts, taking photos, everything, everything is silly.

The meeting's tomorrow. I need to prepare a cabaret song about our class 4A based on 'Suffer, my soul'.†

I
Suffer, my soul and you will be redeemed
Don't suffer enough and you'll be condemned
In our fourth grade
Young girls in droves
Dreaming, the whole brigade
Sitting by a cold stove
Suffer, my soul …

II
As soon as by the stove
Rogues gather and hove
Immediately the voices boom

---

*The Juliusz Słowacki High School in Przemyśl.
†Title and first lines of a folk song.

'Please leave the classroom!'
Suffer, my soul …
Even though our breaks
Loudly reverberate with sound
But during the hour
Everybody quietly cowers
Suffer, my soul …

III
Our class will compete
With such other suite
That our behaviour pales
By comparison, it fails
Suffer, my soul …

27 December 1939

I
Round the corner
At Dworski Street
Not far from the Słowacki seat
A guy and a girl walk free
Just by the Christmas tree

II
I tell you, Rena,* just listen to me
Don't be as soft with yourself as can be

---

* *Rena, Renusia, Renuśka* – variations of the name *Renia*. Also: *Aurelia*.

Grab some cash and go to school
Don't miss a party, don't be a fool

III
Józek Ciuchraj, listen to me in advance
Grab your accordion, play some Styrian dance
One, two, three, four, not a beat he misses
What a great party this is

IV
Stop sending us glances
Go and find somebody to dance with
Then run quickly home
Go to sleep, don't roam

9 January 1940

The party's over. At the Christmas party I got an award for
the best student, a chess set. Then we were preparing for a
contest, and this contest is as early as tomorrow. I'm to recite
a poem called 'The Locomotive.'* Let's hope it goes well.

Apart from that we are moving out of our school. Now
we're going to be at a school with boys. Today we took
everything from our classroom, our decorations, our ink
pots, everything. This is supposed to be a seven-year school.
Ugh, horrible. I hate everything, at first it promised to be

---

*Julian Tuwim's poem.

something completely different, but I changed my mind a long time ago. I still live in fear of searches, of violence. And this whole thing of going to school with boys! Well, let's wait and see how that works out. The torture starts on the 11th, I'll tell you how that goes. Bye-bye, my dear Diary. Keep your fingers crossed for me. Let's hope it goes well!!!

I'm so incredibly stupid, what has happened to me? I've never been like that, people used to think me quite clever. How idiotic is it to fall in love with a *komandir*, to want to kiss him? Am I crazy? How can you dream of love in the form of some *komandir*? I don't go out with boys; that's a fact. I've never been in love either, but there is still time for it, I think. Although when I was at the party, I felt sorry that I didn't know anybody and I left with Nora, while Belka and the other girls stayed behind. Belka, she stayed, I was furious. But then Belka was jealous of me, jealous that I left. And she didn't party at all, she was angry and sad, I barely managed to lift her spirits a bit. And then I was angry that one scaredy-cat turned around, the same one that I had a little bit of interest in. It's all so disgusting and stupid ... I thought I was cleverer than that ...

12 January 1940

It's all passed now. I mean everything that I've been pondering over here. I did perform at the contest. 'The Locomotive' went so-so, but the contest went very well. So well, in fact, that when I came to school, boys called me 'Four steps at a time'.

But I've completely forgotten to tell you about the boys. The Devil isn't as black as he's painted. At least that's what I think, for now. We have new teachers, but all our girls are together (I'm in 8C).

The boys are such innocent young things; they don't know much and they're very polite, they are rather great. Other girls, our former colleagues, are even jealous of our set. The 8C boys aren't particularly attractive, with the exception of one very cute Ludwik P. and sweet Majorko S. They want us to mix up how we sit, i.e., a boy, a girl, another boy, but for now it isn't so.

On the day of the contest I got a letter from some *komandir* (of the Krasnaya Armya), summoning me on a rendezvous. I've decided to hide this letter, play a prank and write a reply.

Dear Diary, I do understand how important you are. I like browsing through your pages more and more often, looking for this feeling I felt then.

You know, I go through these different phases where I choose different husbands from among the young boys around me. I must have had around sixty of those phases in my life already. Or maybe even a hundred. And of course I keep finding new husbands (I mark people). Bye, kisses, Renia.

19 January 1940

Ein Jüngling liebt ein Mädchen,
Die hat einen Andern erwählt;
Der Andre liebt eine Andre,
Und hat sich mit dieser vermählt.

Es ist eine alte Geschichte,
Doch bleibt sie immer neu;
Und wem sie just passieret,
Dem bricht das Herz entzwei.*

You might not understand it, so I'll try to translate it into Polish for you. (Oh, Granny's been pestering me since midday. What does she want from me? I'm going mad!)

A boy chose a girl as his dove
But she took somebody else as her true love
She cherishes the other one like her pearl
But the other one looks at yet another girl
He gave her his heart
And married her for a start
A story as old as time
Always a new mountain to climb
Whoever loved like this
Knows what a broken heart is

So in my case it's like this:

Łaba fell in love with Renia
But Renia is fond of Ludwik
Renia thinks Ludwik is a prize
While Ludwik to Krzysia turns his gorgeous eyes

---

*Heinrich Heine's poem.

He follows her everywhere, for her he is spoken
While Renia is deeply heartbroken
While Renia is furiously angry
But soon she'll leave that behind
A new love will capture her mind

Yes, that's the truest truth. What do I care about this Łaba, sitting there and staring at me for five hours until it makes me sick? What do I care about this or someone else who gawps at me? I like Ludwik. I turn around and look probably a bit too often, when I meet his gaze and sometimes a little smile on his face. Is it possibly a joke? Possible, likely. Why haven't I said a word to him yet? Why do I flee when he's near? Why am I glad when he messes around? He in turn never recommends me when it comes to anything, a trip to the cinema, a committee; and generally he treats me pretty badly. So why, when I turn back and look at him, why does he stare at me? A mystery. And anyway, nowadays I am somewhat flighty; I like a different person all the time, that's natural. I told Nora that I need excitement and that I need to check our biology textbook to read about the mental state of sixteen-year-old girls. And she says to that, 'Oh, if you need excitement, stop staring at books and find yourself a boyfriend.' She's mad! She's been terrible recently! Admittedly I too have a 'dirty imagination' now, according to Auntie Lusia.

Majorko is a nice, great boy, a friend. I'm impressed with Władek; I like him too. How do I know what to do?

They say spring will be hot and then they say it won't. I'm bored with those 'liberators'. It's the time for titmice now. As

Tońko and Szczepko* said from France, 'Release sparrows, keep canary birds, spring will bring titmice!'

26 January 1940

Brrr ... Brrr ... Brrr ... I can't even try to explain how terrible I'm feeling. I have troubles, like every normal human being. What on earth?! I'm no princess to feel bored, but I clearly am bored. I've been struggling with a cold for several days. I haven't left home, I've been reading a bit and nobody, literally nobody, has visited me but Eda. Nora hasn't been for a long while since the bombardments (Granny told her off once). In fact everything with Nora seems to be done and dusted. A friendship like this is good if it doesn't last too long. After all I only hang out with her because I don't have any other company, but I'll try to see her as little as possible outside of school. We don't share thoughts any more; we don't share opinions. There is nothing that connects us. And our liking for each other, as I realised, seems to be fizzling out, on her side too.

Now people seem to be only interested in material things. Which is not surprising at all, since a goose costs 100 złoty, and used to cost 4 złoty; a litre of milk costs 3.50 złoty, and used to cost 15 groszy; a pair of shoes – 300 złoty, and it used

---

* At this point, Szczepko (Kazimierz Wajda) and Tońko (Henryk Vogel-fänger), actors in the popular pre-war radio programme *Wesoła Lwowska Fala*, were in fact in Bucharest and only crossed the French border on 9 March 1940.

to be 12 złoty.* So it doesn't surprise me at all. People pay (whoever can) and wait for the spring to come. It will! It'll come, I promise you.

I have decided to have a photo taken, as there isn't much one can do with money anyway. You peep out into the street and all you see is queues, queues everywhere, people waiting in lines to buy bread, butter, sugar, eggs, thread, shoes – everything. And if you think that after five hours of waiting you might get anything else on top of bread, you are very, so very wrong. And if, by any chance, you would like to buy two loaves of bread, better be careful, you profiteer.

So listen, workmen
celebrate, do
never betray your treasure
let smiles brighten your faces
the red banner safe in your embraces
Celebrate, do!
No masters in workplaces
You can do whatever you wish
all made equal by the word *tovarishch*
the red banner safe in your embraces
Those who used to reside in grand manors
now live in poor plain huts
resigned to life in rags
and what do you have? You have your wish

_____

*1 złoty equals 100 groszy.

you have the word *tovarishch*

and the red banner in your embraces

4 February 1940

I'm so very sad! I'm singing, but that means nothing, I'm laughing, but that means nothing either. If I only could, I'd cry my eyes out. Granny took all her anger out on me. I know that they like Arianka better, they prefer her to me. I'm just a doormat. Mama loved us equally, there are others who prefer me, but she knows how to get on in life, she's like those people who know how to steal the show. And I was so happy today, wanted to write a poem, wanted to tell you something. But don't worry, all will be well again.

17 February 1940[7]

I haven't told you anything for a long while, for such a long while … But don't think I haven't been thinking about you. I wanted to speak to you at every hour, but it so happened that I couldn't. So I'll tell you briefly what happened during those few days.

Daddy came here (he brought us provisions) and now he's gone again. A letter from Mama arrived. She might be in France already. I've enrolled myself in piano classes and decided to play.

Meanwhile, I'm not in love with Ludwik any more. Which doesn't mean I don't like him, but I also like Jurek Nowak. Our class is nice, we have a class hero, Pieczonka, who lives on the same street. He walks me home, messes around, pulls my hood off my head, etc. Irka has started going after Ludwik in an impossible way. Since I sit right near them, I can see and hear everything. For example, 'Irka, stop pinching me or I'll pinch you back hard.' They flirt with each other like mad. Our class is the best in our school (though our attendance today was terrible. Only seven of us). We've already skipped out on physics three times. Pieczonka plays tricks, which makes us laugh. Łaba's still in love with me.

Mama said in her letter that she's been thinking of us constantly on her birthday. She said she was sorry she hasn't been getting any of my poems. I haven't been writing any; I'm so awful, so very awful. Granny and Grandpa are good to me. But I'm all on my own now. It's so hard being left on my own with my thoughts. It's so, so hard.

I feel compelled to draw nowadays; I find it irresistible. I keep seeing images, for example, of an archer. Begone, apparition! Ah! Ah! Ah!

A minute ticks second by second
Yet another hour beckons
Nobody knows when the end'll come
Or where it all started from
I don't know and you don't know
The world's beginning a long time ago
No beginning means no end
Earth's always sent round the sun to ascend

Millions of thousands of planets go round
Who in the world could swear it's not bound

1 March 1940

I had so much to tell you. Wednesday was a beautiful day, so our class played truant at 11.00 a.m. and escaped to the Castle. We threw snowballs, sang songs and composed poetry. I wrote a poem that's already in the school paper. Our class is really nice and sweet. We've become really close and we are good together. But because Nora and I aren't part of any gang, we've decided that I'll write verse.

I sway as if soused
with an abundance of spring incense
I'm up to my knees in water
dripping down from roofs and gutter
onto the passers-by's heads, giving them shivers
flowing out in wide, wide rivers
humming and whistling on the corners
This cloudy, cheerful flood knows no borders
Houses dance in the streets, ice breaks on the walkways
trees, cobblestones, wooden fences, alleyways
From everywhere loud shouting arrives
Everything is springlike, dancing, alive
But I'm not happy at all
I'm not laughing, I'm crestfallen
like somebody who's just left their bunk
after sickness – I am drunk ...

16 March 1940

A message from uncle in France. Mama wrote too.

Nora and I don't have much company, so we've decided to see what happens a year from today and ten years from today. So, wherever we are, still friends or angry with each other, healthy or ill, we are to meet or to write to each other and compare what'll have changed from now. So remember, 16 March 1950. We'll also write a diary together, but it won't be a diary filled with so many private thoughts, like this one here. You are and will remain my only friend.

I've started liking a boy from X class. I know that his name is Holender and he's from Zakopane. I like him very much. We've even been introduced to each other, but he's already forgotten me. He's well-built and broad-shouldered. He has pretty black eyes and falcon-like eyebrows. He's beautiful. There is a tale about a ship *Holender der fliegende Holender*.*

> You cross the wide ocean's waves
> You wander around with no home
> Known to all people on Earth
> But in fact known to no one
>
> Day and night you dash on slippery foam
> Propelled by storm, by rain, by wind that's rotten
> People talk about you often
> But in fact you are all forgotten

---

* *The Flying Dutchman.*

Deviate from your winding course, Holender
Drift into lakes, rivers, waterways
You are so close to me, Holender
You are so far away …

Finally call at some port
Tired with storm, rain and wind
You are so dear to me, Holender
I love you with all my mind

Why do you roam aimlessly at sea?
Why do you have no home?
Known to all people on Earth
But in fact known to no one …
In dark, underground dungeons
In damp holes, rotten and pungent
With eyes burning with fever and agony
They dreamed of a communist destiny.
They waited …
And waited still …
Sick, shivery, crushed, out of steam
In hospitals, prisons – all with a dream
Until their red star lit up bold
With a sickle and hammer made of gold.
Their chains were dropped down
The gates opened wide to town
They marched out, shouting loud!
And froze, the whole crowd
This star, gold-plated star

(which left their lives so scarred)
was not red by far …
They saw it and cried the most
Over the freedom they lost
Over their dreamy idea
And the grey real life.

31 March 1940

I didn't tell you anything before, even though I should have.
Our form tutor was Trelka, very learned and intelligent, more,
an angel of a human being. He always defended us; made sure
the classroom was warm; let us go home on the quiet. We got
him a cake and a bottle of wine for Christmas, sent him a
card. He didn't receive it in his office, but in the hospital. He
broke his leg and now … he's died. Today is his funeral. We
are buying a wreath; we put an obituary up. I'm so very sorry,
we've lost not just a form tutor, but a father. And now this
disgusting Józia is our new form tutor. I can't stand her.

Runaways from Jarosław* have been here with us for a
while. I'll tell you about it one day.

24 April 1940

It's been so long since we've spoken! Don't know where
to start now; I have so many jumbled thoughts in my head, so

---

* Jarosław – a town near Przemyśl, at the time located in the General
Government.

many. I should perhaps start with the fact that terrible things have been happening. There were unexpected night-time raids that lasted three days. People were rounded up and sent somewhere deep inside Russia. So many acquaintances of ours were taken away. Everybody was messed up. There was terrible screaming at school. Girls were crying. They say fifty people were packed into one cargo train car. You could only stand or lie on bunks. Everybody was singing 'Poland has not yet perished'.

Now people are getting registered to the other side of the river San. It's a German commission, so many people get through. And those from there come here. It's terrible. I've been thinking about everything, but not about that.

About this Holender boy I have mentioned: I fell in love, I chased him like a madwoman, but he was interested in some girl named Basia. Despite that, I still like him, probably more than any other boy I know.

Irka's very popular.

At this point I've decided that if I can, one day I'll write a drama about Trelka's death, about how he wasn't in the coffin, but was taken away and then he suddenly came back. 'If I only wanted ...'* After all I could have had it, but I didn't like them. And anyway ... I don't want to. Though sometimes I feel this powerful, overwhelming need ... maybe it's just my temperament. I should get married early so I can withstand it.

---

*Reference to a sentence from Henryk Sienkiewicz's *With Fire and Sword*.

I wonder if Mama'll come back here. Isn't it better for her there? I never thought it would turn out this way here. Hell, perhaps I'll put something together!

A voice on the radio rambles on
Loudly, flatly, no uproar
About what goes on in the world
About what goes on in the war

The world is not that important
Spring has only just exploded
And somewhere in faraway countries
Cheerful life has unfolded

Not much has happened at the front either
The voice on the radio says calmly
There was one single fatality
Is that such a terrible blow?
In view of many at war
In view of many thousands
Somebody cries softly some more
Somebody whimpers in pain
Somebody looks out the window
Waiting, then dying in vain
Somebody despairs even more
One victim, is it such a blow?

FOR JARKA
THE DOLL AND THE CLOWN

The Clown:
Hello, hello, pretty Doll!

I've waited for you since the balmy morn.
Are you happy to see me?
Pray, tell.

The Doll:
Daddy, Mummy.

The Clown:
You don't believe me? I liked you
as soon as I saw you that summer.
And me? Do you like me as well?
Pray, tell.

The Doll:
Daddy, Mama.

The Clown:
Come, let's have a little dance.
What shall we dance together?
A mazurka? An oberek? A waltz?
Pray, tell.

The Doll:
Father, Mother.

The Clown:
Not a word from you?
You remain so stiff, so quiet
I understand you turn me down,
You don't like the ridiculous clown …

The Doll:
Don't think so badly of me.
I do understand everything.
But I am so very sorry,
I don't know how to dance, I worry.
(she cries) Poor me, poor, poor Doll,
troubled and lonely.
How could I give you a call,
When I'm so shy and so lowly?

The Clown:
Oh, don't cry, my little Doll.
Dry your tears.
Look! One step first,
then three more, it appears
then make a turn, lean your head to the side,
then bow low and jump with pride.

The Doll:

I'll cry no more, I will dry my tears.

So one step first,

then three more, as it appears

then I'll make a turn and lean my head to the side,

then bow low and jump with pride.

The Doll and the Clown:

Let's dance together.

Let's dance around.

It'll be joyous, it will be fun.

Great will be the world to discover

Where everybody understands each other.

It'll be joyous, it will be fun!

Let's dance together, let's dance around.

(they dance)

1 May 1940

I would never have thought a year ago that exactly one year later, a long and a short year later, I would be marching not on 3 May* but on 1 May instead. Only two days apart, but those two days mean so much. It means I'm not in Poland but in the USSR. It means life; it means everything is so … I'm so crazy for Holender! He's divine, adorable; he's amazing! But what does that matter, since I don't know him? Tell me,

---

*3 May – Poland's Constitution Day; 1 May – International Workers' Day.

will I ever be contented? Will I ever have happy news to report to you about some boy? Oh, please God. I'm always so disgruntled!

Finally shimmer, the eyes
that are dark, deep, tormenting
the wonderful eyes of a boy
wonderful, loving, enchanting

Dark, hot diamonds
Fiery, excruciating
The wonderful eyes of a boy
Wonderful, loving, enchanting.

Let them even be strict
Let them be bossy, unbending
The wonderful eyes of a boy
Wonderful, loving, enchanting.

3 May 1940

They came out of a side street
from some inn or some gate,
the one they carried on stretchers
might've been ill, wounded or drunk.

Their clothes were grey, torn, worn out
Their faces dark, haggard, washed out.

And the one on the stretchers
was also dressed like that
either ill, wounded or perhaps drunk.

They moved down the pavement,
people turned their heads away
Didn't want to look. Why should they?
A healthy boy walked in the way
Healthy, lively and joyful,
with an accordion like a beast
his eyes almost saying loudly,
Look at me at least.

With his fiery music
he dazzled the passers-by.
He walked down the street, all cheery
Laughing and playing aloud.

10 May 1940

Today was a gathering of *vidminniks*, i.e., the best students.
Yes, Irka was elected. Nora went, this duffer Major went
and I didn't. What do I deserve it for? You should know,
my dear Diary, life is hardest for children without their
parents, especially for those whose mothers are far away.
Yes, know it, my dear Diary and feel my pain, because
I'm in pain too! How bitterly I cry sometimes. Let the
school get something from me! If they need an article, let

the *vidminniks* write it. Let them perform at contests too. Let's see!

Why does a child cry?
Lonely, on its own?
Why does it always yearn and is hurt, why?
Why isn't it comforted by its mother?
Why doesn't she caress it and give it cuddles?

23 May 1940

It's over … I mean the school year's over, as is my love for Wilk.* It is now busy exam time for me. It's already begun. I've already had my algebra, geometry and biology exams. I think it went well. Let's see what happens next. I'm petrified by physics. You should know that I won't speak with you until after the exams. You'll have to wait a bit. I'll sit with you on 13 June and I'll either be happy or … you'll get wet with tears. It's been a good day today. I got new shoes, which is a luxury nowadays. And also two light dresses. There is this one boy in my class who used to flirt with me, or so I thought. He's terribly ugly, but so very talented that … I like him. Let people talk, but I do like him, despite the fact that, apart from being a genius, he has few virtues. Ah, I forgot! I was made a *vidminnik*. You see, silly, how life changes? I told you once that something'll happen in the spring. It did, but it's something

*Wilk – *Wolf* in Polish. Most likely a reference to Holender.

completely different from what I thought. Belgium and Holland are occupied, the Germans have taken over France, Mum's in Warsaw. Great Lord God, please make it be all right. See you on the 13th!

13 June 1940

Done! Finally! It's passed like a dream. The exams are over. It went very well, better than I expected. Bravo, Renia! It's late now; the streets are dark. Some alarm, it seems ... Soldiers on horseback stampeding, *komandirs* getting up – there is a lot of commotion. We're going to go to Daddy's soon! Oh, who knows, there might be a new war? God save us. I might tell you something soon, wait for it!

17 June 1940

It's my birthday tomorrow. I'm turning sixteen. This is supposed to be the best time in my life. People often say, 'Oh, to be sixteen again!' And I am, yes, that's how old I am, but I'm so unhappy!

France has capitulated. Hitler's army is flooding Europe. America is refusing to help. Who knows, they might even start a war with Russia.

I'm here on my own, without Mama or Daddy, without a home, poked and laughed at. Oh, God, why did such a horrible birthday have to come? Wouldn't it be better to die? I look down from the height of my sixteen years and I wonder whether I'll reach the end. 'Quietly like a razor through butter'* ... this is death. Wouldn't it be better, at once? Then I'd have a long, sad funeral. They might cry. They wouldn't treat me with disdain, like today (Dzidziu,† 'Nobody wants to go out with this old cow'). I'd only feel sorry for my mum, my mummy, my mama ... Why are you so far from me, so far away? I'd feel better otherwise, I wouldn't ever think about it. But I cry and I cry that it won't be any different.

I walk along some empty streets
my footsteps echo from grey cobbles
the city seems to be transfixed
as if it's fallen into slumber.
Even the wind doesn't stir the leaves
nothing moves, nothing rustles or flutters
the only sound on the muffled street
is deep, sorrowful weeping that somebody utters.
I take a look, I look around
who sobs so badly in the night?
perhaps they need their mother now
perhaps they miss home, warmth, a bright light?
Why do they shed so many tears
on their own, in the midst of dead silence?
Nobody listens to you now, I fear
or perhaps I'm wrong ... someone does hear?
I roam round dark streets

---

*Most likely a reference to Julian Tuwim's '*Śmierć*' ('Death'): 'Quietly like a razor through butter / Like a stone thrown into water.'
† *Dzidziu*, also *Dido* – Renia's grandfather.

searching for the person I'm spying

on, but who do I search for?

it's me who is crying!

1 July 1940

Listen, my birthday was a pretty good day. I got two bottles of perfume, flowers and lipsticks from Nora and Irka. The three of us are now on good terms – that is my sweet, my one and only Norka, Irka and I. This idyll has lasted since the beginning of the exams. Will it last long still? I don't know. Any thought can divide us, any row or any political wind can disperse our three-way truce. And let me tell you that the political wind is getting stronger. America has joined the war.* England counts on us, we don't know what to do and so on. My mama is in Warsaw. My poor, one and only mama. You don't know it, but she's the sweetest, the prettiest, the cleverest and all the other '-ests' that exist in the world of women. Yes, I can see some flaws too, two flaws in fact, which I've always forgiven her for, which never mattered much to me. Only today, only now they affect me so badly that I need to take them as flaws, not virtues. Because, my dear Diary, what is my life?! It's just a handful of ashes of the past and some shells of the present. I hold them in my hand and I say, 'What is bad'll fly away,

---

* While the United States didn't enter the Second World War until December 1941, President Franklin Roosevelt had begun mobilising the war effort by denouncing Mussolini, increasing the US production of war goods, and appointing two pro-interventionist secretaries of war.

what is good'll stay.' And I blow. And what? All the shells and specks of ash fly away and all that is left is a whitish dust of temporary contentment such as sitting in a theatre, getting a good school report, a letter from Mum, Brühla's smile. And everything else has flown away? Yes, everything. So my life was sad? Yes, it was. And now let's be frank, let's get rid of all temporary contentment or joys, and let's classify. I've lived in Stawki. Was I happy there? No, there were worries, Mama was seriously ill, there were money issues, family quarrels and rows, first Daddy, then Mama. My home's fallen apart. Worse still. Arianka went to Warsaw, she struggled there, lost her childhood, it vanished and that was wrong. I was at Granny's and Grandpa's, I could've done something, I cried for Mama, I wasn't happy and looked like 'a motherless child'. And that was wrong too. Another mistake was the fact that Mama let us, she simply got us to get used to life here. What life is it? Yes, Granny loves us very much, she tries very hard. They pay the price and we do too. They don't live a life of normal grandparents and we don't live a life of normal grandchildren. It's been like that and it still is like that. Such is life. Mama thought of us, she tried hard, she cared, but then there was her and there was Daddy. And we were left hanging. Arianka, poor kitten, and me, even poorer (because I don't know how to make it in life). And now there's the war. Arianka and I are on our own. What does poor Mama eat? They say there is famine there, my poor Mama dear, my poor, poor sad life. My sweet Mummy, if you were here with me, there would be so much less crying, I would be so much calmer with you, why are you so far away …? Mama!!! But you know, when I finally get the goblet of happiness in my hands (even if it's short and small), I'll drink from it as much as I can, for all the happiness hidden in this tiny goblet.

2 July 1940, War

A drop slowly follows another
They'll soon form a stream together

6 July 1940

What a terrible night! Horrible! Dreadful. I lay there with my eyes wide open, my heart pounding, shivering like I had a temperature; I was all ears. I could hear the clanking of wheels again. Oh, Lord God, please help us! A lorry rolled past. I could hear a car horn beeping. Was it coming here? For us? Or for someone else? I listened, straining so hard it felt like everything in me was about to burst. I heard a jangling of keys, a gate being opened opposite. They went in. I waited some more. This was terrible. Then they came out, taking loads of people with them, children, old people. One lady was shaking so much she couldn't stand, couldn't sit down. The arrests were led by some fat hag who kept yelling in Russian, 'Sadis', seychas sadis.'* She loaded children onto the wagon. This night round-up was horrible. I couldn't wait for the dawn to come. And finally! Now! But it wasn't the end yet. Only now,

---

* Sadis', seychas sadis (садись, сейчас садись) – Sit, sit down now.

in the light of day, I could see the despair, the violence, the lawlessness. Some people were crying, most of the children were asking for bread. They were told the journey would take four weeks. Poor children, parents, old people. Their eyes were filled with terrible fear, despair, resignation. They took whatever they were able to carry on their slender backs to the place they would not reach. Poor 'refugees' from the other side of the San. They are being taken to Birobidzhan. They will travel in closed, dark carriages, fifty people in each. They will travel in airless, dirty, infested conditions. They might even be hungry. They will travel for many long weeks, with children among them dying out, they will travel through this happy, free country, the only one resounding with the song:

Широка страна моя родная,
Много в ней лесов, полей и рек!
Я другой такой страны не знаю,
Где так вольно дышит человек.*

And how many will reach their destination? How many will die on their way from illness, infestation, longing? When

---

* First lines of the famous Soviet patriotic 'Song of the Motherland', composed by Isaac Dunaevsky and with lyrics written by Vasily Lebedev-Kumach, first featured in the 1936 film *Circus*:
   Wide is my Motherland,
   Of her many forests, fields, and rivers!
   I know of no other such country
   Where a man can breathe so freely.

they finally reach the end of their deportees' route somewhere far into Asia, they will be stuck in rotting mud huts, hungry, exhausted (like those who have already left) and in this slow dying ironically called life they'll admire the happy workers' paradise, listening to the song:

Человек проходит, как хозяин
Необъятной Родины своей.*

8 August 1940

Oh! How much water has passed in the San (I say that, even though I can't see the San) since our last conversation? I've been down with a stomach bug, a headache and other horrors.

Our trip to Ticiu has been put off day after day. Now we don't have much summer holiday left, but we're still going. I'll see Lila. But! But! Do you know Lila? No? Pity! Shame! She is my wonderful, golden-haired cousin and friend. Supposedly my real friend is Nora, but it is completely different. I share everything with Lila, while with Nora ... well ... not so much. I'm not ashamed of anything in front of Lila, I don't feel embarrassed of anything. My wonderful little cousin, the companion of my childhood, the creator of the scar on my right cheek next to my nose (but only a small one). We always have something to talk about. We find out 'nice things'

---

*   A man stands as the master
Over his vast motherland.

together, we pull pranks. Lila, oh, Lila! Do you remember? And there, ha ha ha …

I get messages from Mama often. Things look good there now, much better. I'm glad. I might see Mama soon. Aha! But I'm the only one who can know this. If it comes true, I will tell you. Because in fact it's stupid: a border. What is it? People just said so, put stones along, rammed posts in and said, 'It's mine up to here!' And what does it matter that they have torn lands apart, that they have divided brothers, sent children's hearts far away from their mothers? 'This is mine' or 'The border is here' – I don't care about it at all! The clouds, the birds and the sun laugh at all these borders, at human beings, at their guns. They go back and forth, smuggling rain, blades of grass, rays of sunshine. And no one even thinks of banning them. If they so much as tried, the sun would burst out with bright laughter and they'd have to close their eyes. It'd cock a snook with its rays and cross 'the border'. The clouds, birds and wind would follow. So would (quietly) one small human soul, and plenty of my thoughts. So I might go, what do you think?

21 August 1940

And? Of course I went, I visited my auntie at Horodenka and then travelled all the way here, to Zabłotów.* So, so much has happened that I find it difficult to relay. So let me start from

*A town in Stanisławów Voivodeship on the Prut river; between 1939 and 1941 under the Soviet occupation, then under the German occupation until 1944, then again occupied by the Soviets and in the USSR.

the beginning. Auntie Lusia was supposed to take me there and that was the plan until the most important evening. On that most important evening, she was supposed to take me there, she was supposed to, and then suddenly no! Granny decided to take us there. Granny, poor Granny, suffered so terribly on the way, burnt her face and then went back. It's a pity she went back; at least we wouldn't be so alone. So alone at our own father's place.

But from the beginning! We spent three days in Horodenka. Lila was so happy to see us! Sweet kitten, she's so poor. Just think, she visits some strangers and sees her own furniture ... The same she was used to touching for so many years, which became part of her and the house. She returns to her tiny room full of remnants, she sees ... those warm, nice, cosy rooms, the mirror over the washbasin, the head of a girl deep in thought on the most important shelf of the old sideboard, a lump of salt (for rain and good weather) and shiny, decorative cushions (which today decorate some strangers' rooms). She sees it all and thinks, 'Oh, God, never again.' Yes, that's what Lila feels, but she won't talk about it with anybody but me.

Ticiu came to pick us up from Horodenka. We had to ride for four hours in a horse-drawn cart. I've missed him so much. You can't call it anything else but longing. I've been pining for somebody close, oh, yes! I'm engulfed by this strange tenderness upon seeing Ticiu, both now and all the time. Generally I'm torn between two feelings. I came here and straight away another feeling took over – some weird attitude of mine and Ticiu's to the house, and the housekeeper's towards Ticiu. And it so happened that in the evening Lila thought the same thing and we started talking about how something was wrong. Attention! If two people notice the same thing, then surely it's not just a delusion or a mishearing. Oh, no! The housekeeper tries hard to be polite, but to no avail. She knows exactly how old Bulczyk* is, she treats Tusio as if she were some feudal queen talking to her poorest vassal.

Ticio bought some fabric, but can't find it now; on top of this there is this 'intrament' plus our laughter and her folly – it all meant we decided to run away. Yes, that's the only way to describe it. We have money, we're buying tickets and going back to Auntie's. But even so, I still feel sorry for Ticiu, my poor Ticiu, but also ... what? To ... But I'm sixteen already, ha ha ha! No, it's funny! So in such circumstances this dreamt-of family home, this red velvet tablecloth and the dresser with little curtains with the pattern of dolls and all of this – God, never again. Yes, but I won't tell anybody about it. Only you ... and Lila ... and Mum. Oh, Mum! Mum! Mum! Come to the rescue!

22 August 1940

I spent half the night crying. I've decided to go. I feel so sorry for Ticiu, even though he keeps whistling cheerfully, but ... what? Children flee from him as if ... I would feel terrible.

---

* *Bulczyk, Buluś, Bunia* – Renia's mother.

I told him, almost crying, 'I know, Ticiu, that you had the best dreams, but this is not your home.' This came to me in the night:

> Will you, fantasies, all fade
> Just like the very first dreams?
> Will you flow with such small tears
> Leaving behind just weepy streams?
> Will my sun, so bright in my dreams
> And my life so full of colours
> Plunge and drown in dark themes
> And if so? Stop crying, alas,
> Stem the tear-filled stream's flow
> Even if dreams disappear
> Death will always be your beau!

> Wind, stop crumpling my petals
> I'm an orphan, can you see?
> Don't jerk me, don't bend down
> I've had enough suffering, let me be
> I'm not from these parts, you know
> But my heart is oh so strong
> Delicate, silver petals
> Not a little flower, I'm made as if of metal
> Not like the wildflowers that grow here
> Happy and playful and full of cheer
> Among the silver fields of many sisters
> Fate hurls me strangely, gives me jitters

Standing on my own is no fun
An orphan and not an orphan.

10 September 1940

Oh! So much water has passed in the Prut river in Zabłotów.
And I just sit here in peace and go to school. Beautiful Miruś
Moch is our maths teacher and I shiver in front of him as if I
were some kind of a scarecrow. We have a whole new set of
teachers. We also have a new schoolmate, Luśka Fischler. She
joined our threesome, known in the class as 'the aristocratic
three'. They call her the fourth one for the bridge. There is
one boy I like and Nora likes one too. We want to go to a
party, in part because we want to get closer to that world –
and we've already made a step in this direction – and in part
because Irka doesn't want us to come. There is very little
time. We shall see ...

21 September 1940

We didn't go to the party because there was no party. But!
But! We made a big, huge step forward. Our class is calm. But!
What do I care about the class when we are about to create
a real gang with the boys! Mine is so wonderful! Wonderful!
Wonderful! Mine, the most mine is Zygo S. Together we are
ZSR.* I've met him already today! Nora admitted that she

---

* Most likely a reference to ZSSR, the Polish-language abbreviation for
USSR, though Renia shortened it to refer to 'Zygmunt Schwarzer Renia'.

liked him a lot, but because she knew he was my type, she let go. Nora has cute, sweet Natek and Irka has Maciek. And? And I don't know how it's going to go and I don't really have much confidence in myself.

30 September 1940

It seems that our gang will not come about after all. I was terribly apathetic, but now my energy's coming back somehow, though slowly. It's all very strange. I know him, but he doesn't even say hello. Irka doesn't want to either. Nora doesn't want anything to do with Irka. There is something wrong with Nora too …

On Monday he smiled at her, so now she doesn't want anybody else. Or something, I don't know. Sometimes I feel terrible. Neither of us have it, I had more, but now it seems it's Nora. She tells me to leave him, because he's a lout … A lout, ha ha ha. And Natek's a gambler. Eh, life's nasty! Can it get better? Mum is not here. If only she were here, I wouldn't have so many worries.

6 October 1940

And another step forward. Again nothing. Before the mountaintop the heart aches, it's a time for waiting.

12 October 1940[8]

Today is Yom Kippur, the Day of Atonement. Yesterday everybody left the house; I was on my own with burning candles on the table in a huge, brass candlestick. Ah, a single moment of solitude. All memories came back and then I was able to think about all the things that get forgotten in the daily whirlwind, in the rumble, grating, splashing of the passing life.

Once again, I asked myself the same question I asked last year: Mama, when will I see you again? When will I hug you and tell you about what happened and tell you, Buluś,* how terrible I'm feeling?! And you will tell me, 'Don't worry, Renuśka!' Only you can say my name in such a warm, tender way.

Mum, I'm losing hope. How long, how long? I stared into those burning candles – Mama, what are you doing there? Are you thinking about us, too, about our torn hearts?

> Who is stifled, killed, destroyed by you
> for ever remains free
> but why do you hurt the living ones
> you furious devil, you're so angry?
> You bathe in the ocean of red blood
> livid with vendetta, seething with flames
> you'll set the whole world on fire
> and in its glow list dead people's names
> On battlefields and graveyards
> your bloodthirsty eyes shimmer with greed

---

* As before, *Buluś* is Renia's mother.

you creak, 'more' and a plague erupts
famine, misfortune suddenly freed
A new heap thrown at the feet
all fall with the same lethal wound
those who're alive have broken hearts
and the heap grows, in the sky its crown
Ah, you've had enough of revenge
a mocking laughter sounds about
you howl, you infuriated beast,
'More, I want blood to fill my snout.'

We see the boys out in town, we're close, we see Maciek almost every day. Only Zygo* and Natek are so distant. Zygo walked back from school with us today. He looked right at me. He has very powerful eyes and I went red in the face and didn't say anything. Oh, to hell with such nature! He flirts with Iśka, or perhaps I'm just imagining it. Anyway, should he flirt with me? I don't say anything. We're planning to go to a party soon – will I have fun? Nora more likely than me, since someone is in love with her. I don't believe in anything. Unless Bulczyk comes?

19 October 1940

We sat opposite each other at the Russian club this week. He stared at me, I stared at him. As soon as I turned my eyes away from him, I could feel his eyes on me. Then, when he said two

---

* *Zygu, Zygo, Zyguś, Zyguśka* – variations of the name *Zygmunt*.

words to me, I felt crazy, filled with hope. I felt as if a dream was coming true, as if the goblet was right by my lips.

But the goblet's still far away. A lot can happen before lips touch lips. So many things can happen to stop them from touching. This is the closest I've ever experienced to real love, because my victim is actually looking at me and saying two words, but then he is embracing Iśka. (By the way, Holender's getting married!! Well! Well! I'm not interested in him any more. I haven't been for a while.)

Today at the history club Nora's Natek was talking to her all the time, he was laughing and he was very polite. Oh! She's in a much better position! I envy Norka! I mean, I want Zygo to be like that too. God permitting! God permitting! Mama! I came up with such an algorithm:

Whether you love or you don't
There'll always be much crying
Your bitter tears won't be drying
Whether you love or you don't
You will send your gaze around

At times filled with longing, at times dumbfound

Whether you love or you don't
There'll always be much crying.

I've written various nice things in Norka's diary today. They announced a competition at school today, entitled

'School-free day'. My dear Diary, I want to win it so much.
Please help me. I'll try different approaches.

Appears

Like so many before, an ordinary day
Starts a bit gloomy and a bit grey
Then morning dawn shimmers and winks
The day becomes blue and orange and pink
And follows a different direction from then on
Along rumbling pavements through various town
    sections
Not rushing to school to be there on time
Not getting there just when the bell chimes
This is not an ordinary day that looms
Full of silly pranks in the classroom
One that threatens with bad marks
One that roars with alarm sirens
One that rumbles with non-stop work
Full of rushing, blurry bottom to top
Counting minutes and hours in all detail
In factories – speedy, in schools – slow like a snail
One that is cheerful and in its glad rags
On the sunny warm day outside itself it drags
One that laughs easily at ace film comedies
That brings books, stamp collections and other
    commodities

One that brightens up the lives of its fans
For whom pupils like to stop a clock's hands
One that passes so quickly and is still succeeded
By another one that rumbles to school up the hill
An ordinary day, a bit grey, run-of-the-mill …

I will also try something else. I might win.

School-free day

It slid down the sky at twilight
Rumbled down to earth all right
Filled with song, filled with twitter
Out of breath with all the jitter
A day – like a bird …
Splashing windowpanes with gold
Splashing eyes with sun and laughter
And then quickly gone, uncontrolled
Leaving just a worry thereafter
Leaving a shadow and then away
A meditation or a school-free day?

23 October 1940

This is a competition week, so I'm thinking about that more than about Zygo. Natek's coming on strong with Nora. I haven't been very lucky with him, but if all else fails, I'll always have you!

A person stares at a looking glass
sighs and says loudly,
'Wouldn't it be better alas
to have smaller lips and different eyes.
The nose also could have a resize!'
Not true, you stupid girl
Even if your beauty could outshine
that of Greek goddesses' line
Your fate will remain the same
Your life will not be reframed
Life doesn't care about your eyes
Your ugly lips
Nose the wrong size!

Mirror, mirror on the wall,
Tell me the truth you reflect and all.

24 October 1940

Why do we rush so badly
Why do we count the days
Saturday to Saturday, madly
In rain, drought, frost and haze
Fast, fast and faster still
We want the stream of life to flow
Through happy days, through tears, when ill
Day after day does go
From Saturday to Saturday, sadly

Let days leave shadows behind
Why do we run so madly
What do we want to find
Blinded and staring wildly
Into what's unknown and clouded
A pipe dream, rather untimely
A dream of a sixteen-year-old head.
We constantly speed away
Feverish, like in a nightmare
We get through short weeks, short days
Knocking them into the abyss without care
We speed ahead like crazed hurricanes
Out of breath, short-winded we race
As ever counting the days
And when we stop halfway to wait
Completely unfazed by all warnings
Life's now stepped up like mad
And runs and runs ablaze

6 November 1940

What a day I had today – I don't know if I should laugh or cry
or scream, I really don't know. Mostly I feel like crying ... It
wouldn't have happened if I'd seen you three hours ago and
told you everything, like I had already decided. 'I'm going to
a party tonight (do or die) and I know I won't dance and I
know I won't be popular and Nora might be, but I won't let
it worry me one little bit.' I was supposed to tell you this, but

no, I haven't, so when I escaped this party, I was on the verge of tears.

But *da capo*,* attention! I went to the party and, surprise, surprise, right before it I found out that I'd won first place in the competition and am to be given Mickiewicz's[†] works! My wonderful dream! Dear Diary, you helped me. My one and only, always so devoted!

So I come to the party and Maciek tells me about it in secret. Zygu congratulated me and spoke with me and only with me. Then, out of the blue, I got the award for my results, for publishing the newspaper and for my 100 per cent attendance.

Zygu was simply beautiful. All my hopes reverberated in me. Then the Head, with special emphasis, announced the winner of the competition. People clapped and congratulated me. Krela'll send it to Kiev, to *Głos Radziecki*,[‡] she'll also write about it in the school newspaper. And she, Krela, who's never happy with anything, she even praised me. Oh, what a triumph.

Then I went to that wretched party. Cukierman asked me. I said I couldn't dance, so he excused himself. Then Major. I didn't want to go, so I stood there on my own while Norka was dancing. I left. I walked through the wet streets, trying not to cry loudly. I thought, 'This evening I won on the spiritual level, but I lost in life.' I vowed I would not go to a party again.

---

* *Da capo* – from the beginning (Italian).

[†] Adam Mickiewicz (1798–1855), Polish poet, dramatist and essayist.

[‡] *Głos Radziecki* (*Soviet Voice*) – Polish-language Soviet newspaper published in Kiev between 1939 and 1941.

But no, I will! Shy or not, I need to win in this other arena. Even if that means my soul will lose, let life win!!! Believe me, this is going to be hard and sad. And again, I think for a thousandth time, I think I need to hum this sad song of my poor, orphaned heart.

Mama, why are you not here
Such a long distance between us
Far, far away you disappeared
We both cry our eyes out

Why do you sob, why do I weep
Why has my life taken such a leap
My heart follows comfort's traces
And I seek mother's embraces!

Mum! Why couldn't you be here today, to see my joys and be happy for me (as I know you are)? Why couldn't I then cry my heart out in your embrace?

I wrote a poem for the class paper, why not?

Blood pulsates and so do cobbles
Marching to big celebrations
A huge, grey crowd hobbles
Red banners … For the nation
This mass pushes through the city
Flows from suburbs, back streets, dwellings
With new people constantly swelling

Joining others in the nitty-gritty
Roads are almost overflown
Like with lava flowing down
Like with liquid iron alloy
That can set at any time
Crushing this world in deep sleep
Tearing the old world down
Those red banners ... The red sweep ...

7 November 1940

Listen, do you perhaps know if it's nice to have a lover? What do you think? I had this thought today! You know, I hate it when somebody talks about their future.

I don't want the sick ones to look for solace in me
I don't want to see hurt ones, as I'm hurt as can be
I want to live like some scoundrel, like a soul with no
  worry
I want to see good women carrying
The jobs of ministers, sailors at sea
Of diplomats, of those holding legal offices' keys
I want to see them as pilots, in action
To hear them delivering speeches with passion
I want to live with no trouble
My life to be a happy bubble
I want to write poems for ever
And I want to have a lover!

9 November 1940

I went for a walk with Zygu. Of course not on my own; it was the whole group. I might go to Irka's dance party. Zygu'll be there. I won't dance, but I'll go.

12 November 1940

Just a few words, as it's late. I got a prize, hooray! Hooray! *Children* by Jan Brzoza.* I felt so haughty; it was so nice. Pity Buluś couldn't see it. I have an essay to hand in on it on 24 December. The day of Mama's birthday … Will you be here with me, Mama? I was also selected to the Mickiewicz event committee. I'll tell you about it later. Zygu teases me sometimes, but today he was sweet. On Saturday I'm going to a dance party at Irka's. He'll be there! If I don't party, then I don't! He is what matters!!!

18 November 1940

Today I am under the spell of a film. Perhaps because I haven't been to the movies for a while or perhaps because, for certain because somehow I was in those images, people, views, incidents. Yes, some of my dreams were in it and that's exactly why I liked *Young Pushkin*.† I like Pushkin a lot, he is

---

*Jan Brzoza (1900–1971) – Polish writer, publicist, radio host, communist activist, one of the founders of proletarian literature in Poland. *Children*, published in 1936, describes the life of a Lwów paperboy.
† *Young Pushkin* (*Junost' poeta*) – 1936 Soviet film directed by Abram Naroditsky, with Valentin Litowsky as Pushkin.

my hero; I might get his photo from somewhere.* Because, you know, I'm changing my whole plan and am starting to wonder if maybe it's better to be famous than happy after all. To be a poet like (not Konopnicka), but ... like ... Pushkin!!! Now I can compare his youth to mine. It's clear he wasn't successful with women. It's a pity he died – I would shake his hand.

When Pushkin was in senior school, he didn't study at all. He went on rendezvous with the other kids, went on moonlight walks on fragrant (even in the film) nights, picked white water lilies for his lover. He pined, dreamt, loved ... Wasn't the world in his favour and could he become non-romantic? Wonderful, wonderful – ugly ape *obez'yana!*† Pushkin! And the name! One utters his name with reverence.

But I could never become famous like that. I've been like a street urchin for four years now. All I see are grey, cracked cobblestones and cracked, thirsty lips. I don't see the sky, because the sky is just a mouldy, dusty scrap of clouds. All I can see are ashes and soot that choke, that corrode the eyes, that stifle breathing. I can see people in the streets as sharp as stones steadily crushed with pickaxes and ground into sharp, stinging dust in coarse, rough fingers. No revolution will ever be able to sort this out. Nothing will ... Because those who have velvety voices and pleasant touch, those who lead silky-soft, comfortable lives, they'll always remain ...

---

* Photography was invented in 1839, two years after Pushkin's death. The author most likely means a photograph of his painted portrait.
† *Obez'yana* (обезьяна) – a monkey (Russian).

But I don't care, I detest the revolution, I, an average person (a phlegmatic) can't stand the rabid mob, so let it rather be the way it is. But you, Pushkin, what did you want?

Look, how everything is distorted
how fake, how wretched, how down-market
It's new, but completely rotten despite
red, red and white . . .

18 November 1940

My romance seems to be over. What a stupid, crude, arrogant idiot. He likes playing with me. And for all of this I could thank my dear friend Tusiek. What a rat, damn it! But you know what? He's not worth writing about. Naturally I'll have my revenge; I'll find a way. There'll be another reading evening, oh, I'd like that so much! Will you help me again?

I am coming to you
I'm on my way!
A train rumbles on the tracks
across bridges, along archways
through fields and towns, it doesn't relax
It glides ahead, it hisses, it speeds
Along the slippery steel rails
At a high speed it proceeds!

Colours are red and yellow
with some black, green and blue

The evening lights are so mellow
Scattered around each day anew
I hear the long-drawn-out toot
The locomotive wheezes and puffs
I'm coming to you, I'm en route
Following the trail on the map ...

20 November 1940

I've had my revenge today. I wrote him an offensive poem. He got annoyed. Now he'll leave me alone. I can't stand him. 'Rhymester' is what he called me today. It'll be even worse now, he'll ... I wish I were dead! You know, sometimes all of it is so stupid, and so important. No, it doesn't matter. It'll always be 'I'll never know what happiness looks like.' Miraculous God, please, don't let it be a prophecy. I'm so low, so low ... so very low.

24 November 1940

I went to the theatre today. Everybody said I looked very smart. But Zygu wasn't there. I act really indifferent now and he's surprised, angry, says this or that to me, and I still do nothing. (Nora says this is only a beginning.) All I say is, who knows!

Nora's Maciek lives on the fifth floor. She constantly stares at it.

Is it made golden with the light of dawn?
Is it surrounded by darkness?

Why are you so far withdrawn?
Why is the whole world between us?
Why does this terrible river
Divide us like a shiver?

28 November 1940, Thursday

Tomorrow is a maths demonstration lesson, I'm so terribly scared. I've had strange feelings towards Nora those last few days. I feel she's terribly fake. As soon as she notices that Z wants to say something to me, she purposefully interferes. Yes, it's all because of Waldek. And anyway she's temperamental and whimsical and I, thank God, seem to not meet her requirements any more. She was so happy that people thought she liked Z. She liked it, even though she knew it was not true. Ha ha ha!

30 November 1940

The lesson is over. It went pretty well, I was prepared. I'm in a paper. I'm falling out of love with Zygu, as I don't have any stimulation from him. Nora has sprained her ankle. I wrote an article about it and a poem too. I'll write it down for her. It's not so bad with Nora after all. I created it, so I'll write it down. I'd like it in *Piszemy sami*.* Something must be wrong with me!

---

* *Piszemy sami* (We write) – most likely a newspaper.

8 December 1940, Wednesday*

Suddenly, I love him like mad. Just think, everything was about to go dormant and today it sprang back to life. Nothing happened – but still so much! He played with my hood, stroked it, came closer! But I'm vain. I think of a thousand projects. Fralalalalala! Wonderful Zygu, wonderful, so wonderful!!! This is what I wrote once:

Hey, let's drink our wine
Let's drink from our lips
And when the cup runs dry
Let's switch to drinking blood
Wanting and yearning
Inspiration and love burning
Let them start a fire
Let rage burn like a pyre
But remember, girl, that flames
travel in your veins
that blood can burst you from inside
Wanting and yearning
Inspiration and love burning
Let them start a fire
Let rage burn like a pyre
Both wine and lips are red
One life before you are dead

---

* The author made several mistakes with dates and days of the week. 8 December 1940 was a Sunday.

Our hearts are hungry, young, on fire
Only for each other beating.
Remember, girl, that flames
travel in your veins

What is being romantic?

It's a horse that gallops through the steppes
It's a high cloud that swiftly follows
Moving smoothly, steeped in a deep red glow
Shrouding white swan's down in golden twilight
It's a Lover on the edge of a deep abyss
Sliding down the rope from the great height
A bunch of roses red in his embrace.

Riffraff, or Children of Machines

Among the rattling and grating of iron
Among the racket of collapsing chunks
Among the whirring and birring of workshops
With sharp, piercing dust that in the air hangs
burning our hearts and our dreams
we grew up, we, working children
people machines

In the roaring fire of forges
Crucibles engorged with molten metal
In the swelter of slag slurry treacle
We got tempered, we, steel people

Our hands are rough and mighty
Our hands like iron springs
Our hearts like slag – hot, flighty …
Seething, boiling power of teens
Working people – children of machines

9 December 1940

I love, I desire, I'm mad about Zygu!!!

10 December 1940

I went to the second floor today. Zygu said to me, 'How are you, girl,' or something along those lines, and he pulled my hair. You know, recently, when I see him, I have this blissful, pleasant feeling that's unpleasant at the same time. Something paralyses me. Ah, that idiot, if he only knew how much I love him. There's an invisible thread connecting us. It could break, but no … If we could really be together, it would be wonderful and terrible at the same time! 'The chocolate box may be empty, but there is a lot of sweetness in your lips.' I don't know. I have no idea what's happening to me.

Oh, age, you! When one loves like never before
The one who knows you, can't ever find peace
The one who knows you, is drunk with ardour
And life only starts when the other heart is seized.
The one in love can never wake up
Stuck in a tormenting dream, in a feverish shake

Only to fall asleep when the dawn erupts
And dream of loving and heartache.

11 December 1940

Today I stayed at home. I'm to write an essay. I'm to write for the competition. Because Krela told the Teich girl that she expects something great from me. What should I write?

Frost

The air is windy and foggy ...
The sky Decemberish grey ...
Feathery balls of sparrows, all groggy
Bounce off glassy roads all day ...

It's somewhat sleepy outside.
Snow falls softly and slides
Along invisible lines
Greyish clouds blossom everywhere
As if cigarette smoke was in the air.

*Heine**

Leise zieht durch mein Gemüt
Liebliches Geläute,

---

*From *Neue Gedichte* (1844), by Heinrich Heine (1797–1856).

Klinge, kleines Frühlingslied,
Kling hinaus ins Weite.
Kling hinaus bis an das Haus,
Wo die Blumen sprießen,
Wenn du eine Rose schaust,
Sag, ich laß sie grüßen.

Slowly cutting through my musings
This lovely, this tinkling sound
Jingle, spring song, chime your music
And travel far off, be unbound.
Fly all the way to the house
Dozing among pretty flowers
And when you see a rose there
Give my greetings to her.

20 December 1940

So what that I can write nice poems and I can say that I'm ...
well, you'll see for yourself (I'll paste a photo) and that my
couplets are so cheerful that the whole school sings them, that
girls and boys like me – I'm not happy with my school life. Jara
– ah! I always want what's best for her. I once even decided to
keep trying to convince her to practise (so that she can become
a pianist). But sometimes, almost all the time, she embarrasses
me. God! She flirts with my male friends. In fact she has this
shrewdness, this ability to win people's liking. She has a very
good heart, but not a crystal personality. She's very talented

when it comes to music, also when it comes to acting, but she's not very clever, she doesn't have this thing, this innate thing, this something. And she's a woman, oh, a real, horrible woman, like Aunt Hela – just slightly … And you know what I'm like. Mama and you – you two know! I can't fight for them because I'm dispirited, both for fighting and for life. So far my skills have paved my path for me, but now there is this terrible possibility of the two of us, poor, lonely souls, getting separated! God! Jealousy – no, I don't want, do you hear me, I don't want it, I want to love her without a shadow of resentment, I want this, I love my only little sister!!! But she, she … No, I can't. She's aware of her successes and now she's started talking to me with half-smiles, ironic semi-words. She's happy she can go with Zygu, she wants to impress me this way and when I call her, she pretends not to hear me. Once she told me, 'Rena, I'll get married before you anyway!' But it's not about that. Lord, you've separated me from my mother, don't separate me from my sister!!!

25 December 1940[9]

It was your birthday yesterday. Buluś, this was the second birthday of yours we didn't spend together. When will this torture finally end, when?! My longing gets stronger, I feel worse and worse. Sometimes it feels so terrible, I feel so empty that it's like my life is almost over – when, in fact, my life is just beginning. I can't see anything ahead of me. There's nothing, just suffering and fighting, and it's all going to end in defeat. I laugh during the daytime, but it's just a mask, it's like an oblivion (people don't like tears), but now I think that you, my mama, are so far away, that you live in a ghetto, that you are unhappy and that I can't help you, because I'm not even ready for life myself. That's what Krela says.

Today there was a rehearsal for a variety show at Irka's. I've written couplets. I also take part in the show. Krela knows so much, she knows the whole of Europe, speaks so many languages. She's very clever, intelligent and impressive. She told the boys that they're not ready for life and then she mentioned the girls too. Irka's mother said that Irka would manage all right in life. Irka is so clever! Krela said that Maryśka Filagrowicz is the sweetest girl in the school. I barely know her. And the cleverest and most well-read boy is Zygu! Him again. It's always like that – I may think he doesn't matter to me, but he surreptitiously crosses my path again and I go mad about him again. I suffer terribly. I keep crying all the time, because I'm in love.

Oh, Maciek keeps paying me compliments and saying lots of other things (which he says to everybody), but that's something completely different. And Waldek is yet another story altogether. When it comes to moments like this, no boys matter to me and I'm left with Zygu ... Him again ... 'You need to wait patiently, God willing, you will meet.' Yes, but when? God, why not now? If You want to bring us together, will it be a long time from now? Will our hearts, filled with bitterness, regret and longing, survive this? And what if one of them breaks? Then the other one'll die too. Lord God, please, help!!!

28 December 1940, Sunday

Am I a sinner? Yes! Because even when I'm supposedly close to something, my nature intervenes and stops me from going and … that's it … It just so happens – could it be any better? Zygu is going to be in the variety show! In fact, he and I are going to be in the same scene. It was so wonderful when Krela said, 'Spiegel and Schwarzer would be best for that' and … (what do I care about the rest). So we're reading from the same page. Irka says he listened admiringly when I sang couplets (I thought the opposite, but oh, well!).

Then we went to school. It so happened that Luśka dragged him out, but Irka was cleverer and as a result I walked with him arm in arm. First he waited for me to grab him, but I was too embarrassed, so he took my hand, ah! It felt like my hand didn't quite belong to me. Or it did, but it felt completely different from my other hand. Some very nice shivers went up and down it, so nice that ah …! Earlier, when he was standing there reading his part, I couldn't tear my eyes away from his wonderful red lips, I'm embarrassed to admit.

At school he suggested I should sit next to him and it would be great! If only … If only what happened today hadn't happened. Because today, damn it, I blushed so badly. (Damn it! To hell with such nature!) Then he sat next to me, mumbled something and said to Luśka that he didn't know anything about her and that we were together onstage. And I, what an idiot, I messed it all up, because I removed myself. I made him angry with me, forced him to start talking to Luśka to spite me. What's more, he threatened that he wouldn't take part in it. 'Do you hear, Rena?' And I told him that I didn't care! What can I do that I'm so stupid?!!!

29 December 1940

Today again! I've just been to a rehearsal. He was wonderful. He said that nobody sings cabaret songs like I do and that he didn't realise I was so talented. We talked and talked, he was so wonderful and lovely, my divine Zygu!

31 December 1940 [10]

New Year's Eve! We put on the variety show. I was very popular. Backstage, Zygu took my cape off and untangled my hair. When the dancing started, I quickly left. They really wanted me to stay. Poldek, Rysiek, Julek and Tusiek. But I didn't want to stay and that was that. Zygo's so wonderful, divine, so charming. It was all so exciting; I told Norka everything. But she and Maciek aren't so close any more, so she envies me. I feel sorry for her. Oh! I'm not surprised at all and I really understand her. Do you remember how terrible I felt for the same reason? Now she feels like that. She even cried, poor kitten. I would have perhaps stayed a bit longer to watch, but I left because of her.

When I was about to leave, Zygu ran up to me and asked if I would go to a party with him tomorrow. I told him that I don't dance, but he went on, something about getting an invitation, and Jara said, 'Yes, yes, she does dance.' So I'm going. I am, why not, after all I told him that I might not dance. Aha! Wait, a day before yesterday at a rehearsal he invited me to go with him to drawing lessons with the XB class. So we went, but we had to leave quickly. Aha! I am a *vidminna*,* I was the only one who had everything, etc. Aha!

What else? Today is the last day of 1940. Tomorrow is the beginning of a new year, which will bring new regrets, new laughter (perhaps), new worries, new struggles. My dearest wish is to get my poor beloved mama back. I also wish for good political relations and for 'something' with Zygu. Let it be like I have described it in the final of our variety show:

Be gone, worries, tears and upheaval
Let all be carefree and good-natured
So, goodnight and let's hope winter isn't evil
That's what we wish you, rest assured.
Just remember, don't be chancing
Start the New Year in full joy
With singing, laughter and dancing
Take the first step, don't be coy.

I want this new year to be cheerful and happy. Nice to all in the world and to me as well.

Take all in kind embraces
Let it be friendly and warm all round

---

* *Vidminna* (відмінна) – feminine form for *excellent, superb* (Ukrainian).

Paint happiness on people's faces
Call them into the future with a cheery sound
Let them walk briskly through life

With love for it and with real zest
And let my dreams come true, don't strive
That's more than gold, that's the best.

The last day of 1940. The last page in the diary. I'll greet the new year on a new page.

1 January 1941, Wednesday

I went to the party. It went wonderfully well, it couldn't have gone any better, I think. I danced with everybody. Mostly with Poldek and Zygu! Do you hear? I hope the whole year goes as nicely as today's party! Zygu talked so much; he was charming. We didn't dance too well, but it was so sweet. 'It's my fault,' 'I knew you would come,' 'Pity the lights are so bright,' etc. And when Irka said at the end that she was hoarse, he announced, 'Rena's hoarse too.' Hooray! 'The first step always matters the most.' I'll go to parties from now on.

3 January 1941, Friday

It was only the day before yesterday! And I am going mad as if I haven't seen him for a year. The closer we get the more I feel I love him. For example today I've been trembling since the morning. Every time I think of that evening, I'm gripped by something I've never felt before.

So how was the party? Everything was sweet. What was the best moment? Was it when he spoke to me while we were dancing? Or when he draped his arm around me as I stumbled in a waltz? Or when he smiled wonderfully and asked, 'Rena, why are you running away from me?' Or when he led me gently by the arm after each dance? He smelt so amazing! And when he touched me ... brrr ... ah ... so great! So sweet, so good! We sat and talked together. What an evening.

And Poldek likes me too? But I didn't know he liked me so much. He was adamant about seeing me today; he keeps walking me home, annoying me. In fact I didn't say goodbye to anybody, but Zygu approached me and made a special effort to say goodbye. I can barely contain myself.

Today we've had a terrible blizzard; it's been snowing all day long. But I'd walk through any blizzard, snowstorm, hurricane, downpour with him – as long as we were together. My wonderful, my golden boy, my lover. I have to finish an essay to hand in tomorrow, but I just want to see Zygu. I'm going mad. And at the same time I don't want to see him, because I'm so scared that something will go wrong, that this wonderful, sweet, fragrant memory will get spoilt.

5 January 1941, Sunday

And? Didn't I say it was better not to see him? I was so regretful, but tough. It always so happens that when you love somebody, you tease them. The greetings were sweet, but then he didn't dance with me, he sat there fuming, in a bad mood, but tough, after all (oh, God), love can (i.e., must!!!) sulk too. Today I'm in bed; I'm unwell. Oh, I so hope that everything pans out well!! Please, Great One! I find evidence of his liking even in anger.

A sixteen-year-old

When you're sixteen years old
you dearly love the whole world
with all its parties, pranks and jokes
and especially with your favourite folks.
When you hide your crumpled diary
from your mother's strict enquiries.
When you sing love songs
Then you are sixteen years old.

8 January 1941, Wednesday

All is well again, or even better than that. Irka insists that Zygu's in love with me. He said he would fight a duel with Poldek over me. That's because Poldek is head over heels in love with me. He came here once when I was ill.

Zygu didn't want to go to the cinema when he found out I wasn't coming. And today he said he would go and so I would, so perhaps we might manage to go together? I was planning to go to a match (because Zygu plays and he invited me and asked through Irka to come). I made arrangements with Irka, but on my way back from the post office, I turned around and somebody said, 'Rena, where have you been? Aren't you ashamed to be ill? You have really high wellington boots and you still caught a cold? Come with me to the match.' Come and come. And I couldn't go, because, damn it, I'd made arrangements with Irka. He also said this and that; he was sweet, wonderful. For example he said he'd go on the pitch first, because he didn't want me to see it, etc. etc.

Zygu won the match and I congratulated him. I wasn't able to contain my worry that he might be joining the army. And Zygu? Zygu was very happy about it. Then we walked together, cracked jokes, teased each other like lovers do (or so I thought). And tomorrow? I'll see him at the match! I'll tell you more.

9 January 1941, Thursday

Today ... Oh, I'm even scared to say it – I went to the match. Nothing special happened. (Just once a ball hit my wonderful, dear Zygu on the jaw; it was so bad he crouched down in pain. My poor darling. I was very worried.) But after the match! Ooooh! We walked together and I told him that I was very upset during the match. He asked, 'Why?' I said, 'Just because.' He persisted, 'But why?' I said, 'I was just upset. Let me be.' 'Spit it out.' He simply wanted me to say, 'Because you were playing.'

Irka was walking in front of us with Genek, but Zygu arranged it so that we split up. Finally alone! And what did fate have in store for us? Fate wanted us to see Arianka on the ice. We went down to the ice and the pipsqueak wouldn't give up and joined us. But Zygu didn't say anything. He was upbeat the whole time, mumbling something in Yiddish and asking why he hadn't seen me the other year. And he asked when we could go to the cinema and this and that.

Naturally Giza saw me in town and she pulled the stupidest face. Then Poldek saw us too and naturally he wouldn't leave us alone.

Zygu is planning to study medicine and he said, 'Rena, what are we going to do next year? You'll come to Lwów and we'll study together.' Hooray! Hooray! Zygu is a wonderful boy and he says such sweet things! If only Mum were here – I could easily count these days as my happiest so far. (He's only just slightly naughty, not like other boys, who are vulgar.)

10 January 1941, Friday

I love him, I'm mad about him! I haven't seen him all day long today. It drives me mad. If he goes to the party at the Socialist Club tomorrow, I'll go too.

Irka gave me an elephant. She blew on it for good luck for me and Zygu. Let it be so!

12 January 1941, Sunday

What shall I tell you? I feel so strange; it's all so hard and so sickening ... As if there were pawns moving around us, as if there was a pair of black eyes shining in the dark.

I saw him today, we even walked together in town, but it was because of Irka, it was her doing. Then he walked me home, admittedly on his own accord, but again, it was thanks to Irka that we were left alone. We both felt weary. He was quite polite, but it felt like he wanted to stay with Irka.

Yes, currently I am in such a state that I can barely hold a pen in my hand. I don't know what's being said to me, I forget everything, I don't write and at night I just lie in bed with my eyes wide open and think … think … Mama, I'd so like to cry my eyes out with you. Mama! Mama! Come!

> A net of interlacing cords
> A brown ball bouncing up and down
> A whistle …
> And many arms stretched out
> A rumble as if walls were coming down
> One circle full of colours
> Fans are in uproar and they scream,
> 'Not true,' 'Mad referee,' 'Go,'
> Out, service – and another whistle
> The ball bounces – that's a match, I know!!!

I can't even mention Zygu. I feel faint, it's so terrible … Mama! Help me!

14 January 1941, Tuesday

I gave a presentation today. Finally. Everybody liked it, the room was very quiet, everybody was enthralled. Krela then said something, but in fact she didn't have anything to add.

It was quite sweet with Zygu today; he congratulated me afterwards. But no matter, he said, 'Rena, what do you think? I have my call-up papers.' He read something out to me and, because I didn't understand what it meant, he said, 'Am I married?' He laughed and then we walked arm in arm upstairs. A surprise awaited me there. They wanted me to become the president of the literary club. They started shouting, 'Spiegel girl!' and one after another they nominated me. Zygu nominated me too. We voted and naturally I had the biggest number of votes. And when Krela asked who they wanted to be the president, they all shouted that it was me. But that wasn't important. Zygu was nice, pulled faces at me and when Krela was speaking we were almost in stitches ... And all would have been well, we would have been alone etc., but unfortunately one guy from IXA wouldn't leave me be. Zygu was furious and so was I. Zygu suddenly said goodbye, mumbled something and left ... What a shame! Well, let's hope there'll be another chance ... for us to be finally alone.

17 January 1941, Saturday

I've been ill for three days now. I'm struggling terribly with this poem. Oh, what a tough birth, as my sweet mama says. I have a plan, oh! I have just got two letters from my dear Mama. I'm so happy, God! She wants to come, my wonderful, sweet, good mama. She might come, I hope it will all pan out.

It's been a good day today. Today Arianka has started the fifth year. A letter from Mama. Kasia might be back. What will Irka and Norka say about … (about whom?).

21 January 1941, Wednesday

Ah, wonderful Wednesday! It was Wednesday then too. I seem to be lucky with Wednesdays.

Long live every Wednesday
good humour and fair play
Long live, in all the truth
everything about youth
about carefree laughter
about hope with no restraint
which always takes you after
to parties, no complaint
to dates and walks in town
for cakes and to entertain
and even home, when in your gown
those words you make on the windowpane
the arrows and those letters
the word that in your diary
blushes in red and is allowed
the one you always carry
the one that always rings aloud

So long live every Wednesday
good humour and fair play
Long live, above all
everything that's called love.

The party was on Wednesday and today ... Make a guess, because I'm breathless. Words want to jump out of my throat. So today ... Zygu came to visit me. He came, he was sweet, lovely. He looked at me, all the time hypnotising me with his eyes. I didn't pretend to be unhappy. He spent so much time with me and said so much. The most important thing was that when Maciek asked, 'Who has the most beautiful eyes?' Zygu went sheepish (and so did I), then he (my wonderful one) blushed and said, 'Rena.' Maciek winked at me, said loads of things in relation to love. And Zygu was sheepish.

My writing is bad today, because I have German measles. That's why Maciek, Poldek and Zygu came for a visit. Poldek, I know it, is very much in love with me. Maciek, as I know, likes me a lot too and Z is a mystery, a Sphinx.

He is an Apollo
with his stature, his skin
so brown and smooth
He is a Sphinx
with his impenetrable eyes
hiding an uncouth mystery, I think

All three of them told me that if I didn't go to the party, they wouldn't go either, so I said that I would prefer to feel better and go, and that they should go too.

They've been gossiping terribly about Nora, those brats. I'm curious what they want from her (leg, stocking, nose). They've been at loggerheads with Maciek for a while. I was angry with him and today he paid me back for this wrongdoing out in town. Maciek is as good as an angel, he could be jealous, but no.

23 January 1941, Thursday

Irka insists that I write something in her diary. In verse, of course. I'll try.

27 January 1941

I didn't finish the entry last time, because Norka came over. Then there were visits from Poldek and Maciek, and Nora with Irka. It varied; sometimes it was nice, sometimes boring (and once there was even an unpleasant situation).

On Saturday Zygu was supposed to come, but he didn't, because his mother arrived.

And me? I live off memories; I'm astounded that I remember his every word, every smile, every face he's pulled. When I remember something new, it feels like ... I don't know myself. I can't talk or think of anything else. It's becoming a real mania.

Yesterday Uncle Maciek (whom I like very much) went to theirs. He loved Zygu – himself and his behaviour. Zygu left two notebooks in the room, so he knocked, apologised and went in to pick them up.

God! Why are they telling me all of this? As it is, I can barely control my heart, which wants to jump out of my breast. Irka already says quite directly that Zygu's in love with me, but I don't believe it, no! I don't believe just yet! That'd be a miracle! And I already … God, God, God, please! And you, Buluś …

30 January 1941

Today … Today was a good day. First at school … well, nothing important. In the afternoon there was a LOPP exam (Airborne and Anti-gas Defence League)* and naturally I, not even knowing what *Osoaviakhim*† was, decided to try. Zygu trained me a bit. He came after his exam but before mine. He was wonderfully sweet and there are no words in the world to describe his eyes. He kept talking to me, laughing, paying me compliments (he's so witty) and at some point he grabbed my chin (that's his tender gesture) and he almost k … me, but I gently pushed him away (perhaps next time. Lord God! Buluś!).

---

*Airborne and Anti-gas Defence League existed until 1939.
†OSOAVIAKhIM (Union of Societies of Assistance to Defence and Aviation–Chemical Construction of the USSR) was a paramilitary Soviet organisation established in 1927, concerned mainly with weapons, motor cars and aviation. In 1951, it was renamed as DOSAAF (Volunteer Society for Cooperation with the Army, Aviation and Navy).

I said that eating hen meat spoilt my skin, to which Maciek replied that a cockerel would sort me out. Maciek is a pig. He even called Zygu over and repeated the joke to him. And I? I pretended not to understand.

During my exam Cukierman was cracking up.

I have a new rival, Dziunka. Today she noticed that we like each other (when we were cuddling on the bench). She was furious and eager to mess things up. Poor me, haven't I been in her shoes once? But now I can tell you that I'm in a better position and, God willing, if fate allows, it'll get even better? Well? Well? Well?

1 February 1941

It was a so-so day. He was sweet, talked to me, we were even supposed to go to Irka's together, but he was ready to go home and he was tired.

There is something very friendly, very intimate. But he is so proud (why wouldn't he be if everybody keeps suggesting that I'm his?). Bloody rascal, he didn't even want to invite me to sit down. He laughed, saying that when I see him in his grey shirt, what then? Ah, Buluś, Buluś, help me.

Irka has given me this to cheer me up and for good luck. It looks funny phrased like that, but what do I know?

4 February 1941, Tuesday

It was a strange day today. Nora had an argument with Maciek – she cried. Krela shouted at me. She really had a go at me.

It's all her fault anyway. He was just staring and staring, which paralysed me.

In the morning Zygo stroked my face in front of Irka, Tuśka and Ela, he took my face into his hands and called me Renusia. I just had a thought that he did it on purpose, to flummox me. Briefly everything seemed to be going well. He took me under my arm and said, 'Why don't you want to be the president? I worked so hard to get you on the board!' Then he sat down with me, pulled my hood off my head and we talked all the time. Then Krela had a go at me for various reasons but mainly because I talked during the meeting. Zygu consoled me and said that Krela told him off too. And when Krela said, 'Let's see who could be the husband killer in *Lilies*?'* he said, 'Renusia' (damn this 'Renusia'!), 'you are not good for a husband killer.' And 'I want to be Rena's son' and this and that and I started thinking that he was mocking me, which really unnerved me.

He didn't wait for me, he didn't say goodbye – as if he wanted me to follow him. But, actually, what's my problem? He was sweet after all. And if he wanted to make fun of me? God, You know how much that would hurt! He just stared and stared, which paralysed me.

5 February 1941, Wednesday

I'm so blue! I'm so low. I'm in love and mocked by the object of my love. I even cried. Such a blow. And so well aimed.

---

* Adam Mickiewicz's ballad.

I've taken offence. I've heard Zygu telling Maciek, 'Rena is angry with me.' He said that to me at school and I confirmed. Angry, is that what it is?! I'm not angry, I'm very, very sad and concerned. He told me this awful, 'Look at how she holds her leg, just like Nora does.' When he said, 'Renusia,' I instinctively turned around, immediately. And then he said that I was angry. I heard him saying on purpose that Irka was pretty. I heard it all and I cried, not with tears, but I could feel those tears inside me, stifling me, flooding my heart. Mama! I felt so bad, so very bad! But love's stronger than anything and when I went sad, Zygu laughed and said, 'Rena, what is it?' So, trying to pull an offended face, I laughed. If he really mocks me like that, if he really says it, then ...

> I will draw two tiny hearts
> two hearts linked by love
> and a wide black arrow or dart
> that pierces the red buds from above
> One heart will be true and full of life
> honest and hot – that one is mine
> the other one I'll make alive
> I'll give it love to drink like wine
> I'll feed it smiles and happy noise
> I'll feed it words, gentle touches and looks
> I'll give it silly things (the most precious joys)
> my unsatisfied dreams flowing down brooks
> It will be bright like radiant sunshine
> It will be red like a pretty poppy

And then when the other's ready to decline
The red one will whisper, 'Yes! Let's be happy.'

Pavements move, glide ahead
as do stars, tarmac and streetlights
I sleepwalk around the city
embraced by silver moonlight
I wander around, looking, looking
into infinite depths I stare
Is a tiny love seedling
perhaps hiding somewhere in there?

Don't worry, no matter, there, there
Not everything will be surely lost
'Why do you cry, silly girl?
It's perfectly normal, don't be cross.'
Oh, cry as much as you like
Perhaps sobbing'll make you weary
You might forget and sleep'll strike
I cling to hanging ropes, it's scary
to trees, wires, bells a-ringing
I cling to church bell towers
to thunder's and lightning's stinging
I go there, into the sky, into starry showers
fuelled by unearthly force, kind of
I go, I fly, I soar
Oh, I am so much, so deeply in love!!!

Strange thoughts tremble inside
cloudy, half-sleeping, dreary
jumbled into a nightmarish ride
wobbly and clumsy and blurry
spring water comes as if from a gutter
there are red, juicy berries
and this misguided, drunken thought – water
The lips' effort is a futile flurry
The effort of brain throat cracked dry lips
Words don't want to sound out
Nobody hears the lamenting apocalypse
Just those entangled thoughts all out
Splashing of water, forest-grown berries
And this unspoken out loud
Word – water – that carries!!!
For once in my life I'm surely allowed
To ride the vehicles of airstreams
To crack, to whoosh, to shine through clouds
to fly straight to the stars that gleam
For once in my life I'm surely allowed
To speed merrily through celestial expanses
To climb rainbows, moons and clouds
To roll down with the morning dawn, to take chances
For once in my life I'm surely allowed
To enjoy this thrilling ride
To jump onto a star in style
to look at the stars from the other side

> For once in my life I'm surely allowed
> To get lost in this crazy love
> To love with passion and with pride
> Even if … this love is not returned …

7 February 1941, Friday

Oh! It's so much better! It's almost good. I've had a long conversation with him in the red corner. And somehow my heart tells me that he went to town because of me (though how he walked – God, have mercy on him). And I had to leave him in the midst of it and go and study Polish. Such is life (ish). But I'm not complaining at all. I would just like it to open its wings and frrr …

Maciek tells me today, 'Aurelia S., née Spiegel … I'd like the two of you to get married, because I like you and I like him.' So I say to him, 'What's that to you? You would be a friend of the house,' to which Maciek says, 'Yes, and perhaps you might get bored in time …' No, I couldn't get bored with Zygu! Everybody likes him so much that I think I might go mad with jealousy! Lord … don't abandon me, and you, dear Mama!

8 February 1941, Saturday

Today is Saturday, 8 February, I had a sweet day. At school Zygu assured me that he would vote for me, as he's a member of the jury, and that he would give me all possible points. Later, after the match I waited for him and we walked together. Together, you hear? There was this other boy walking too, but he didn't count and left soon anyway.

When we got to the red corner, one of my numerous rivals soon left. I couldn't count all those looks he gave me. But he does it in a kind of conspiratorial way, as if not wanting me to notice. Eh! He's a wonderful boy, the prettiest in the school! Please, God and Buluś, let it continue in such manner, like this …

And now I need to get busy. I have a poem to write, praising Mickiewicz. I should write it, but am I able to? Will my words be worthy of the man? I'm not sure if I can, I doubt … but still … perhaps …

Mankind erects a shrine to your memory
It is to be worthy of you, it is to thrive
It is to look at the world with reverie
to grow, make you famous – be alive!

It is to proudly soar into the sky
fuelled by burning love and admiration
to become a symbol and a cry
of what you used to call liberation

To be a beacon for the world
To last for years, for centuries
An endless memorial is unfurled
Huge, powerful, in your memory

At its top there is a place of yours
To look down on earth below

To see what you suffered for
And what you loved even more.

10 February 1941

Today is Sunday, 10 February. The Teich girl has found out about my love and told me, 'I would prefer if you were to fall in love with Maciek. Because Zygu is handsome, wise, intelligent, but he's no good and he'll really wear you down. He's this and then that, and you'll never know why.' Yes! God, the second part rings so true. No good, oh, no! Zygu, you? You are the best, best, best, best.

11 February 1941, Monday

Lord God, my poor mama is so far away! Poor her, it's bad there, she's all on her own. I would very much like her to come to us, as I have a big problem and I'm so sad, and that terrible person is wearing me down! The Teich girl was right. He tortures me morally, he simply exercises me: contracting and stretching. Today he took offence over what? Over nothing – he pulled a sweet face and I went into the classroom first and only then approached him. And not the other way round. Naturally he didn't come to the rehearsal in the afternoon and after the rehearsal he sent me such a look that blood curdled in my veins with fear. And then he yelled, 'Leave it!' to Poldek, so that … well. God, what does he want? Zygu, have mercy, why do you tease me so much?! Stop it, I can't take it any more! Holy God, help me!

12 February 1941, Wednesday

Mama can't come; it's so bad there, famine. Zygu's angry with me, doesn't come to the rehearsals. God! God! Help me!

13 February 1941, Thursday

Hooray! I have to force myself to explain everything to you properly. There were apologies at school. But how? As if nothing had happened. He approached me, embraced me so sweetly and we had a good talk which lasted the entire break. The whole school could see us, damn it! People were pulling idiotic faces. The Teich girl was laughing under her breath. Zygo came to the rehearsal and then we went, I mean, me and him, to the red corner. Elu came too and we laughed our heads off; it was very nice. And then I talked to Zygu on my own (ah, those newspapers, what fuss), then Stela came, my number one rival. Of course I understood her mood. So then I said to Zygu to go and we went. Waldek, sweet, poor Waldek, he's a bit not right in the head, he wanted to leave us alone and go on his own, but I didn't let him. We said goodbye in town. And then I was left with Zygu. I met our Norka, Belka, Helka and other people from town. We talked about the most trivial things in the world (thank God for the existence of Kubrakiewicz). Then I met Maciek, Poldek and Julek. Maciek almost gave me a peck in the middle of the street, as a joke. Of course he was full of jibes about Zygu and me. Then we walked on our own again and again talked about nice things. In fact I don't know if that's how it's going to be till the end of the world? Do you have such ordinary conversations? I need to ask. At some point Zyguś thought I took offence. 'Renusia, are you angry with me?'

Zyguś walked me home and we made plans to go to the cinema on Saturday.

Oh, I lived today! Nothing ... but still ... Buluś, you helped me, I feel better now, even though tomorrow he might still be angry with me. And I'm so ugly – how can I be attractive? Wonderful Zyguś, don't be angry with me, be good, like today and ... even better. Mama, if you could only see him! Keep helping me, Buluś and You, God ...

14 February 1941, Friday

I'm such a stupid idiot, a moron and the rest! I've arranged to go to the cinema with Zygu. And I meant to go with him on Saturday, but I went today with Maciek and Poldek. Ah! I understand Zygu. I would take terrible offence too. God, what am I going to do? Will we go to the cinema or perhaps to a concert or nothing at all? 'I know I am worth the punishment,' but ... not quite – I wanted to know what the film was about to explain everything to him. And everything went topsy-turvy. I had good intentions, but it turned out so, so badly. Lord, I'm scared of tomorrow! Help me, God, and you, Buluś ...

16 February 1941, Saturday

I'm trembling all over today. No, it wasn't a terrible Saturday, though it didn't promise to be too good. I went to a match.

Zygu first pretended he hadn't seen me and invited Irka to sit with him, enquiring (so that I could hear him), 'Irka, are you going to the concert?' and when she asked him whether he wasn't going to the cinema, he replied, 'What good is a film today?!' And I felt so bad, so terrible, so awful ...

The first breaking of the ice took place when he pulled my hood off my head. He was still a bit angry. But later everything went well, wonderfully well! We walked together (he adjusted my hair in the street), then at Irka's and later at the concert – this was the culmination. No, not yet, no. But at the concert we sat together on one and a half chairs, ah! And we talked all the time and I realised how wonderful, how gentle, how decent he is! All the time together, a wonderful Saturday afternoon together. He walked me home, him and another one, and ... when he was saying his goodbyes, he held my hand in such a way; he held it and said, 'Bye, Renusia.' And then I said suddenly, surprisingly, as if it wasn't me, 'Bye, kitten.' And still, it was me. God! I said this, this fire which has tormented me for so long suddenly leapt out and congealed together, forming this one word. And Zyguś ... He laughed (perhaps even a bit glad?), he laughed so wonderfully ...

We were supposed to go to the cinema tomorrow, but he just said, 'Twelve o'clock tomorrow, in town.' Tomorrow, ah! Thank you, God and you, wonderful Buluś and you, Zygu, for this Saturday.

For me now nothing matters
boredom, rumpus, scandal, chatters

physics and mathematics
little Purcel's mad dramatics
Auntie Józka with meniscus
Salcia and Breit and hibiscus
Krela with her big mouth
all other creatures about
they don't matter to me now
I'm also not bothered to even look
what marks I have in the grade book
I yawn terribly in the classroom
thoughts filled with doom and gloom
Good or bad ways are not a thing
one thing that matters – is loving

I wrote this today at physics, in secret – isn't it wise?

Today I had this flutter inside
I was taken over by this strange tide
Everything pulsated and twitched
Today my heart was bewitched.

16 February 1941, Sunday

I didn't want to tell you at all that Z was out in town with his mates and I was with Julek K and we pretended not to see each other and this idiot didn't even approach me. I didn't want to tell you that this other one, the one who walked me home with Z and had already interfered once – remember? He is in love with me! What a fine kettle of fish! Wait a second, and Zygu?

I can't say either way – it's a very strange story. I just wanted to tell you that something terrible is happening to me. Some dark, crude force is seizing me. I keep looking for ambiguity in everything, I can be easily persuaded when I can't see, can't I? I'm reading Tuwim's poems, also the indecent ones. I wrote in Irka's diary.

Blood pumps, spring is about
And spring makes hearts open
It makes them grow and swell and sprout
eyes shine, the world dissolves into laughter
lips, breasts, hips enlarge
Spring is lavish, spring gives freely
Doesn't spare anything, by and large
Lips and eyelids kisses silly
Refreshes with sweet caresses
Spring's coming, be ready for its excesses

I want this power to seize me, to lift me
I want to write lopsided verses
Clumsy and savage, raunchy as can be
It simply must be so
I feel my blood boiling
I feel my heart beat faster
Spring storms are broiling
I want wind and bluster
I want my face slapped
Hit me, beat me, poison, torture

Bite me, throttle, kiss me, strap
Hellish power inside me's surging
So be a tyrant, tie me up
Curb this force that is in me
'Cause I toss and turn in crisis
my blood shouts like some banshee
You have to overpower me
Or I will overtake you

You see, just look, this is still nothing. I find some wild, sadistic pleasure in people saying, 'Rena is seeing Z.' People talk about it at school, but I'd like to write something so indecent … and then find pleasure in it … I'm ashamed … God, help me again and you, Buluś, please, make those people be right in what they say. Give me courage.

18 February 1941

Oh, what a wonderful, happy day! I don't think Z was ever as wonderful as today. I met him on the stairs. He said to me, 'My poppet, my sweetness,' etc. We spent the whole break standing on the stairs. So stupid. Ah, he really hadn't seen me in town, because he asked me where I was then. Girls from the eighth year passing by said, 'Aaah!' Zygu burst out laughing and said we should go somewhere else.

It's really hard, you have to understand that I can't even describe it in words. It should be written on a blue sky with spring fantasies, sighs and whatever ticks, whatever vibrates inside ...

He was supposed to get me *Kordian*.* And he tried. We sang something for fun at the club. He said I would be his mascot during matches. (Do I really have eyes like Valentino – big, blue, burning? What is he saying?) And even though he left early, I, for the first time, am feeling something. Touch wood, it's true. It's something and nothing, but still. I heard Jerzyk saying, 'I have a feeling that a new couple is forming at school.' Not sure if it was about us, but perhaps ... Let's hope so. God, God and my wonderful Buluś, keep me in Your thoughts, now and for ever.

19 February 1941, Wednesday

You know, I'm starting to believe. At school he behaves in such a way – I absolutely cannot describe to you how it is. We walked along the corridor together, he asked me to recite a poem, so sweet! Dziunka saw me. And when Kubrakiewicz approached us and started saying something about my eyes, something, something, Zygu added his bit too. Suddenly old Kubrakiewicz shouted, 'See how he's looking at her? He's flirting with her! But no matter. Nice couple!' If Kubrakiewicz realised that, then something must be the matter, though he's quick with those things. But if this old, wizened Aunt Józka noticed something in the red corner, even though it was

_____
*Juliusz Słowacki's drama.

nothing special … Ah, after Kubrakiewicz's announcement Zyguś went terribly sheepish and said, 'I'm embarrassed.'

Aha, and then the poem, the poem, this and that … Today I wrote in Ewa's diary on the same page as Z, the same one. And I drew a heart. Tra la la! How he was excusing himself for his untidy writing in Ewa's diary!

In the evening we walked together and this Tadek constantly wanted to be next to me, but Nora and I outfoxed him. Z and I stayed behind, walking together, just the two of us, and it was wonderful, simply wonderful!! 'Sweetheart' and smiles and looks and 'Renusia, study maths' etc.; can't even list it all. He was supposed to go home, but he walked me, and when I left for Irka's, he turned around and went straight home – he was gone a moment later. What matters is how he said goodbye – he shook my hand and held it awhile (as is typical for him), and then he did this … strangely, intuitively I sensed it … I didn't know what it meant … I asked Ariana and she knew. It means, it is, eh! – it's a calling. I don't know if he did it by accident? Have I imagined it? Have I? Because I know that Z's not vulgar or anything. Or perhaps, perhaps this is just a mask, perhaps this liking is all pretend?

Perhaps, perhaps, perhaps
Who can really tell
Help me see through cracks
Mama and You, God as well!

It's so sweet, so good, so light and strange.

20 February 1941, Thursday

I've been dreaming about Mama all night long. Together with Zygu we were rescuing her, looking for her in Warsaw. And today I remembered all those painful, burning things, so ... be quiet. When it comes to it, it's not quite working and it's partially his and partially my fault. Let's hope things get sorted by Saturday!! I'm worried about the weekend; things always go wrong then. Help me, God Almighty. Help me, my one and only true friend, my wonderful, distant and close Mama ...

21 February 1941, Friday

So far today all is well (only everybody keeps calling me 'Mrs Schwarzer'). He was so cute, shaved, handsome. Today, but ... what about tomorrow???

I have four rivals already. But please, God, and you, my wonderful mama, you love me and understand me, please make tomorrow be ... be ... be ... good. And let me tell you all about it. I have such terrible stage fright!!

22 February 1941, Saturday

I had stage fright, but perhaps it wasn't worth it. But still. A bow in the cloakroom, a handshake in the classroom and *Balladina*,* then again, after the break and then in the corridor in the morning. Exactly. The two of us stood there and I can

---

* Another drama by Juliusz Słowacki.

only imagine what we looked like – everybody was looking at us. Eda approached us (his former love) and I, stupidly, like some idiotic moron, went beetroot red! Zygu laughed his head off! Damn it! Stupid blushing …

I went to the match, I got in when he was changing, so I apologised, but he just grabbed me, like only he can, he grabbed my chin with both his hands and asked about my hairdo. Later I went to school on my own without saying goodbye. Strange enough! At school Zygu was reproachful because of my running away. During the rehearsal it got very nice, finally. It's not possible to describe it; you need to feel it in every single nerve in your body. And remember that we sat together all this time, and we walked and walked, just the two of us, and that he was hell-bent on going to the concert and this and that … at 9 p.m., and then he didn't want to and made plans to go to a party and when we were standing there, I lowered my head over my watch and our foreheads met. I think his hand trembled a bit when we were saying goodbye. He held my hand for a long time … for so long … and then he did it again (or so I think) … But it might all be just for show, oh! Perhaps it's nothing. After all he would sooner say something ambiguous in the presence of Irka and … No. Buluś, I'm going through a spiritual tragedy. Let's hope to God it ends well! Lord, please give me back my mama. Mama, come and help me!!!

It hurts like searing heat
Wild jealousy is eating me

It jerks me, it wrenches hard
Like some sharp, rough shard
Listen – spring is near
And I'm more and more jealous here
I squirm and writhe, I'm hyper
Why did you give me this viper?
to grab my peace from me?
to torment me, eat me, see?
to make me swear like a sailor?
I can taste jealousy's flavour
Oh, all those sleepless nights
All those thoughts and dreams alight
Stifling words – unsaid
Burning tears – unshed
All the teasing, taunting torments
I'm so jealous right this moment
because I love to a crazy extent!!!
Perhaps when rivers flow wide
With a turbulent and raging tide
Perhaps when the orchard glistens in the distance
Morning dawn'll embrace me, give assistance
And when clouds in pink will fly
And roll down from the azure sky
Your eyes'll shine for me
My black-eyed prince!
Perhaps when sun glimmers
With hot, blinding shimmers
Or when night descends

Filled with spring's stifling scent
And when birds' joyous screaming
In the empty valley goes a-ringing
Your lips will touch me
My red-lipped prince!
Perhaps like a flower that declined
leaving the memory of its smell behind
You will also soon be gone casually
I'll be left with longing and waiting and a fantasy …

No! No! No! Mama, no!

23 February 1941

I'm so very tired. So just quickly. At night I get up, sure that Zygu is next to me. I start shaking him, calling, 'Zygu! Zygu!' But it was Arianka, who was scared and came to me. War! Field games at war – together all the time – Zygu throws himself onto his back in the present and yells, 'Rena, down!' and then we walk together. Rysiek screams, 'Rena has a crush on you, Zygu!' Zygu mumbles something under his breath, 'Stop it.' We're having a party tomorrow! Ah, my second one. You know, I have terrible stage fright. I'm scared of everything. Will I have a good time? Will Zygu dance with me? Will 'something' happen?

Damn it, this idiot Nacek has a thing for Lidka, that's all we need. Nora is down. Poor her, I was hoping things would work out in the end, but now … Nora bet it all on the party, but Lidka'll be there too.

Norka! I hope you don't get disappointed! Z and M and the rest tease her. But this Nacek, this stupid, presumptuous, horrible brat … If it were me, I would slap him on the face angrily. What a great, smug piece of S.

Irka's Feluś is sweet and Irka is great (my matchmaker). And Irka's Feluś, though far away, keeps kissing her on the pages of her diary.

I will write when … oh, it'll be so long (or perhaps never), when … I'm worried about tomorrow's party. Mama, help me, send me your blessings, bring your little daughter back to life. God, Buluś, please, help me! Help me!

24 February 1941, Monday (second party!!!)

Oh! Ah! Eh! I'm so terribly tired. But I definitely have enough energy to tell you what I want to tell you. Mum! Mama dear, if only I could tell you everything, every single thing, and kiss you and get your advice and tell you everything. You'd surely understand me, you'd be happy for your daughter who is so … well ('let sleeping dogs lie') … contented.

At school – nothing; then – yes; then the party. I danced with Zygu the whole time, my wonderful, one and only, sweet-smelling Zygu. Roma, my rival number four, was there as well and suddenly she said, 'Look, he is dancing with her for the seventh time. If he takes it to ten, I'm leaving.' Zygu laughed and told me that Roma was still there and added, 'Now she can count to twenty.' And there were a lot of pleasantries apropos this. Then he bought me a bagel in the canteen and put it in my mouth in such a sweet gesture ... Then, when Maciek said, 'This is Zygu's love for one night,' Zygu immediately consoled me, saying, 'No, that's not true.' And he pulled such a sweet face saying this. Everybody, even a blind person, could see that something was the matter when we danced together. One thing though – I was terribly jealous (even though he danced with the others only three, four times). But he called Irka 'sweetheart' and she took him under the arm after their dance (I sometimes walk with him that way too). Zyguś called Elza 'Elzuś' and asked her jokingly to sit in his lap. When our hands got sweaty in the dance, we held each other by our elbows. Wonderful, wonderful Zyguś. Of course I'm now called 'Mrs Schwarzer' all the time. Even in front of Zygu.

We walked arm in arm from the party, with Irka on the other side. It was sweet, but it could've been better ... no! I'm sinning by saying this; it was great, thank You, God! I could see from the beginning that he wanted to ask me, but Poldek was faster and asked Nora. Oh, Nora, poor Norka, it was terrible! Nacek and Lidka flirted with each other. She was in a bad mood, didn't dance (Zygu, when he saw she was not having fun, even sent Julek – he's that nice).

Poor Nora, it was a tragic evening for her. She just told me, 'You are so happy' (no, I shouldn't sin by being jealous or anything. Zygu walked me home on his own and even though he didn't ... he was always sweet, polite and good).

Norka, I'm so sorry for her, I'm so very sorry, she left without saying goodbye before the end of the party. I've heard Nacek saying that she was sitting there on her own, so he asked her out of pity! He's horrible! Maciek also said that Nora didn't have a good time. Even this W didn't ask her, since she said no. It is better to stay on friendly terms with everybody after all.

Something's going on between Irka and Maciek again. But I don't want to be jealous of Irka, she wishes me well. Though not as much as you do, my mama, not like You, good God! Thank You so much and please keep helping me…

Around! Around! Stars shine brightly
Take me strongly by the hand
Let them play wild music, lightly
Let dance pull us deep into its land
Until death in waltz embraces
Dancing, waltzing left and right
Like at a party, at other places
All of life is fun, a delight
Let's dance lightly, smoothly, swiftly
Let's dance fiercely with panache
All life, on floors silver, shiny, shifty
Let the house be a ballroom afresh
To forget about the world that's small
To flash into the realm of night, sun bright
Nothing matters, I'm dancing with you after all
this waltz with no end, no end in sight

25 February 1941, Tuesday

Zyguś! My wonderful! Wonderful! Wonderful! Wonderful! He came to the classroom looking for me, my dear 'pet'! We stood in the corridor (while Roma was cursing me in her classroom), then I shared my wafers with him. He put a piece into my mouth. And he said to Irka, 'Rena is in the foreground,' so he lent me his copy of *Balladina*. And this and that. 'Rena, you are under a bad influence.' His, of course. Then, 'Renusia' and he almost whacked Rysiek for flirting with me. Aha! But that's not all! I still have a hum in my ears after the party – play, fanfare!! Irka told me that Zygu stood with her in the corridor and said, 'Rena is so pretty' and when she asked him if he had had a good time, he said, 'And what do you think?' and 'Who did Rena come for?' And when Irka told him, that I came to have a good time, he laughed with disbelief! I'll see him tonight at 6 p.m. Mama, dear, it's so good to be in love. Lord God, please, let things continue, please ...

> Let's spread our arms out wide
> Let's walk through life with joy and pride
> Let our song reverberate
> Let our tears dry at a quick rate
> Let's have a ring of cheer inside
> With a scarlet banner of love let us stride
> Arm in arm, together, two of us folks
> (the world will vibrate with our jokes)
> Let the world become a garden

Let spring last and never darken
Such joy in our souls, in us, ever after!
Let's walk through life with lots of laughter
Two of us, we will always cheer
We will throw the word high in the air
We will spark hot bronze and steel
Listen to love, feel what we feel

He stood in the corridor, reading the poem, and he said, 'This is Rena's poem.' Maciek told me this.

Nora's really low right now.

26 February 1941, Wednesday

I shouldn't doubt him any more. Didn't he ask me today, so sweetly, if I was going to the club? Didn't he come only because I was going, too? Didn't he carry my schoolbag and help me down the stairs? Didn't he wait outside the school? When I shared my halva with him, he said that he couldn't have it, but then took a piece without asking – it was so intimate, so nice. He took the page with the homework. But do you know what I like thinking of most? I don't know why, but I like recalling this sweet moment when my Zygu bought me a bagel and put a piece of it into my mouth. Because, you know, you understand, that apart from sweetness, there was something so … masculine about it … so husband-like. Oh, this scene, I remember it.

You know why I never draw him? Because I can't make him beautiful enough; because I'm scared, not able to. Perhaps I'll get a photo? Maybe, Zyguś mentioned it once.

For now they tease us, they make fun. I'm sorry, but ... let's hope they'll have a basis for it soon ...

God, Mama, thank you! Help! So, so much ...

I'm so happy he isn't like Nacek! No! I can't stand it any more. Even though I have homework to do, I need to tell you. I thought that was all for today, but ... Irka came with Zygu! With Zygu, do you hear me? We sat together for three hours or so, then out to town. Zygu wanted to go for a walk and Irka wanted to go home. To which my wonderful Zyguś said, 'Up to Rena.' Then we were on our own. A ha ha ha!

I have a photo, two photos – stolen, but still. When they asked him who he was in love with, Zygu said with me (he was standing behind me). Ah! Oh! Ah! I'm so happy ... I'm feeling silly, affectionate and strange. When we were finally going back, I told him I took the photo and Zygu said, 'But I wanted to give you a different one, larger, prettier. In my opinion it's disrespectful to give you a photo like this one!' Isn't he wonderful? You don't know, you can't know it, but I'm ready to burst, I'm exploding, yeah! Look! Look! Look! He's so wonderful! Admire him all day long and all night long, just like I do. Mama and You, wonderful God, lead me ...

PS When I told him that I'm scared of my rival number four, Roma, he said not to be scared and that he would defend me and that we should do something about her, perhaps send her to Kulparków.*

Flowers nearby
Stars high in the sky
It's all for you
All for you
Sleepless nights
Poems fiery and bright
Tears, bitterness anew
It's all for you!

27 February 1941, Thursday

School was good. And later it was so nice too! We met in the afternoon, I mean I met him in the red corner. Roma and Ewa were there too, we couldn't get rid of them. They followed us all the time, went to Irka's, where a farce took place – I ran away upstairs, Maciek to Zygo K's; Zygu was looking for me, etc. He then joined Maciek at K's and they were supposed to do homework. Then they whistled to me and we went for a walk. Zyguś took me sweetly by my arm and then dropped hints of this and that. But he was terribly lovely. We met Nacek who said something about the Spiegel girl and the Schwarzer boy, don't know what he meant. On

---

*Kulparków is a district of Lwów, famous for a psychiatric facility.

our way back they began an academic discussion on sexual matters. I felt a bit embarrassed. But they started explaining that if I am to study medicine then this and that. They think I'm still such a child and Zygu doesn't let them tell any vulgar jokes (I mean, to me).

We were making plans for our time at university – they'll be downstairs and Irka and I upstairs. Zygu wanted to lend me one book, 'Which you can learn a bit from.'

He generally has become very forceful recently (which I like terribly). He tells me, for example, 'Rena! Learn that German poem! Now!' or 'Rena is to go to a drama school' and he gave Rysiek a beating for teasing me. He was furious at W for his 'Can I come with you?' 'Rena, about turn, fetch the coat!' And when I took offence, he said, 'Well then, will you do an about turn and I will give you your coat?' When they were in the red corner Zygu said that as soon as he mentions me, I appear in the window. He keeps staring at me, so sweetly. When Maciek said that one needed a friend, he replied that one needed to find one then.

I could fill whole notebooks with just one conversation. That's why I'm not writing everything, just thinking … thinking … that God is good and my mama loves me very much and they'll both help me with everything …

28 February 1941, Friday

God! Saturday tomorrow already? How quickly this week has passed! It's Saturday tomorrow. What'll happen at this time of the day?! I'm so scared. Lord God, help me, and you, my one and only mama!!

1 March 1941, Saturday

School was sweet! Zygu asked if Prochaska calls me Mrs Schwarzer (so using his surname). He even says it himself. I'm not sad. It's not a sin. I turn myself over to Your care, Buluś and God.

2 March 1941, Sunday

It was such a pretty day today! Springlike! Sunny! I saw Zygu in town, walking with some ramblers, he bowed, sent me a burning look. What an idiot! Couldn't he approach me? He laughed, silly billy! But it doesn't matter; we're both in love (only me) and young. Irka wrote this and if it rubs off then … well. And it's starting to wear off already, but we don't. Oh, you know, I recall thousands of things, thousands of nice, intimate things. Otherwise I'll go crazy – and cold – and everything will go to nothing.

Irka loves Feluś. I wrote a poem for her yesterday.

Is it really nothing? This week it's Irka's birthday. There might be a dance party. Will it be sweet? Will I dance with Zygu? It's so good now, I have his photo and can stare at it for hours, stare and stare. I won't see him again today.

Goodnight, dear Diary. I'm jealous of you, because you can spend a whole day with my thoughts about him and his image … Well, let's see what happens next, Buluś. Bye …

Small, stifling flats

The day is autumnal, grey and dripping
I stand by the window tightly wrapped
Listening to the old clock's loud ticking
Watching the street in the rain trapped
It's cold and it's so deserted
My nose runs, I have shivers
I feel like many people, I'm certain
When autumn rains deliver
Everything's the same, but then not quite
Dusk sneaks in, I hear crickets chirping
I'm reading my diary in the dim light
A spring page. I'm returning

'Happy days are near
filled with sun, light, bliss
I'm so joyous, full of cheer
glad for early spring like this!
Let's open windows wide
Let's unlock doors and gates
Let's stand with spring side by side
Let's assist it, link our fates
Come! Why don't you? On our way!'
We run armed with songs and play

With flowers in many bouquets
Wait, I'm coming, with you I belong!

I'm so happy, I'm so merry
So bright, warm and so amorous
I want to open my heart, to unbury
And walk towards the glamorous spring!
I read those impassioned lines
Words filled with sun and fragrance
Sounding of carefree delight

Dirty windows cry with tears
The autumnal sky is weeping
I read and I think to myself
That something else might've happened
Sun, happiness, smiles, I bet
Now – it's so dreadful, so inapt
This autumnal day, grey and wet
I stand by the window tightly wrapped

Perhaps at some point in my life
On some sad autumnal day
When the moment is quite right
I'll read my spring, sun-filled diary!

What spell do you cast on me?
Because of you I do nothing
Like thunder you rule my eyes, me
I can't live because of you

What is it, God! Mama!

3 March 1941, Monday

Irka's birthday. Actually, Zygu's a swine, but he's so sweet and lovely that I forgive him everything. He approached me and greeted me sweetly at school, he told me he was 'dragged to a party', but that he was terribly bored. Aha! When Tusiek was trying to convince him to come along to the party, he said, 'I would rather go to town to see somebody.' See whom? Rena. They teased him terribly about me, he didn't dance and today at school he said, poor him, 'Not only do they call me Rena's husband, but also Arianka's brother-in-law.' Oh, his words were so wonderful. 'Rena, you look like you've just got out of bed.' And then, 'What about the newspaper?' and, 'You must have written something about me,' and then this look and this and that and the other.

I arranged with him to come to Irka's, but he didn't come, this wonderful boor.

Nora avoids people, even us. She holds a grudge against us, especially against me. I understand that, I'm not angry. She seems to think people laugh at her and in fact she's right. But she doesn't even realise how bad it is. This Nacek ... And today to Irka – anyway he also told her something at the party. I'd like to know what it was. What could he have told her, this vulgar lout? She might feel relieved if she were to tell me, but as it is ... poor, poor Norka ... God, Buluś, please take care of me. There is something about us like a solid relationship, like a marriage. Mama, why aren't you here with me now?

5 February 1941, Wednesday

Ah, Wednesday again! Mama, if you were here, I wouldn't be lacking for anything, I don't think! It would be so good, but ... There is always some kind of a 'but' ... When will you come?

Now there are long walks, goodbyes and meetings – I can't even describe it all. Anyway, in the morning he bought some gingerbread from the canteen and let me have a bite, in fact pushed it almost whole into my mouth. He told me about Roma, how she came to see him at 7.00 a.m. when he was still in bed. And Irka told me that he must have asked a hundred times about me during the match, etc. etc. He keeps going on about how beautiful my eyes are, these eyes, eyes, eyes (he likes my personality as well – Maciek has told me and he was right). Zygu says, 'Rena, nothing can help you, it's all in your eyes' or 'I'm under the spell of somebody's eyes.' He said something about my skin too, so I asked if he was being ironic, to which Z took offence and said ... Ah, he's so wonderful ... He stroked my hair. He said, 'Why does Irka's hair stay up so easily?' and that he won't jump higher than 1.48 metres, and that I should switch to sport. And that we'll go to a party together on Saturday. 'Rena, you'd better learn how to swing dance.' 'You are to start reading papers as of today.' It was so sweet, so wonderful when they teased us in town and he said, 'Rena, what an alliance!' and 'Roma doesn't compete with you directly because she senses your superiority.'

I really can't write it all down. He said we need to find somebody for Nora, but I told him to leave it, because she's so low. Zyguś, wonderful Zyguś ... And still so very shy ... Mama, if only you could come. God, please keep helping me. I give myself into Your care ... Ah, one part of my wish is beginning to come true, let's just hope for the other ... Oh, Lord!

6 February 1941, Thursday

He came to the classroom after his classes today. But at the break he was plotting something with Irka. They laughed a lot, I was very curious. And Irka told me what it was about. Zygu told her in secret that he was in love with me, that I have wonderful eyes (I'm fed up with the eyes thing) and teeth like pearls, eyelashes like curtains and nose and everything else and doesn't Irka by chance know if I love him too? Of course he asked her to be discreet, because he wants to tell me himself or something along those lines. He said he would be happy with me.

I'm torn, not sure if I should believe Irka, but she swears it's true ... Ah!!! If that's the case, then Zygu is a total fool! He's an oaf! He's a boor! Who deals with such a delicate issue through a third person?! Can't he just tell me? What a baby! And he still knows how to ask about my time of the month. Sweet, sweet, wonderful Zyguś! Mama, come! God, Buluś, under Your protective wings I look for shelter ...

I'm waiting and waiting, I worry
Time goes on. It's not filled with bliss
The inscription is getting blurry
And Zygu's still in no hurry to give me a ...

7 February 1941, Friday

We almost ... Today after class, he pushed me (gently) against a wall and brought his lips close to mine ... He said, he said, 'My sweet poppet,' and also, 'What shall I do with those eyes?' I told him to get me sunglasses. He asked why I was so evil? That was too much, I was outraged. 'What, Zygu? Am I evil?' He took my hands and repeated sweetly, no, no, no! And asked about the plans for tomorrow.

Tomorrow can be whatever he wants. We're going to Irka's, but will everything be the way I want it? I'm not so very scared any more ... But will I get disappointed???

I feel strange. I might go to his place. Will it all work out, at least a little bit? I pray to God and Buluś. I ask You earnestly to take care of me ...

9 March 1941 [11]

He was sweet at school on Saturday, he called me 'my sweetness' and said that he must look like a 'sweetness'. I wonder if he really likes me? But he wasn't at Irka's, he didn't come ... and I waited ... Perhaps it wasn't his fault, as he wasn't properly invited, but still. He was himself looking forward to Saturday and ...

Each moment gave me hope
Each strike and chime of the clock
A doorbell, steps, knocking – a shiver
Raised the scope of my anticipation
You didn't come. Why didn't you knock?

Today I don't miss the hum and laughter
A shame you weren't there
I'm glad it is the day after
It's all gone and I don't care
Gone are the dancing couples, quiet all the voices
And I can think sweetly
Of kissing you, brushing your hair, rejoicing
It feels so good, completely!

Something strange happened today. I kind of knew
something was the matter, but I still didn't think it was so
bad! Maciek is in love with me! So now I understand what
it all means, that he walks me home, that he constantly has
something to whisper in my ear, or a speck to brush off me,
that he raves about my lips, eyes, that he embraces me and
yesterday he even kissed me. I didn't want to tell you, because
I didn't think it was anything special. All his meaningful
hints I took as, 'Well, he says that, but it's just gossip.' But
now I don't know myself, or rather I know that Zygu didn't
come to the dance party because he was jealous, very jealous
in fact – and I so understand him. Wonderful poor stupid
Zygu! Don't you see you are the only one I love? I tell you

this with my every move, every look I send you! You! You! You! It's true, I like Maciek, I like him very much, but how can you compare those two feelings, liking and loving?!!! He is jealous. Really!

I went to Irka's today and we had a vigorous discussion about it, while Zygu and Maciek were at my place. Zygu wrote in Arianka's diary, 'For my girlfriend's sister,' so he now officially calls me his girlfriend, oh, merciful heavens! They left me a note, which I paste below. They came to my place, what a shame I wasn't at home! Zyguś was here, my wonderful Zyguś, Mama! Ah, Buluś, if only you were here … You will help me, Buluś, and You God …

11 March 1941, Tuesday

Wonderful! Divine! Good! First at school with chocolate. Then in the afternoon he came to the Shevchenko club.* It was so good to sit together and talk a lot. Everybody was pulling knowing faces. Then we left. At first Maciek and Poldek hung around, annoyingly, but soon they were gone and we were on our own. We spent maybe two, three hours walking. It was so nice. Zygu is very tactful and delicate – like nobody else! He sang, '*Du hast die schönste Augen. Mein Liebchen (Mädchen) was wils du noch mehr.*'†

---

*Taras Shevchenko (1814–1862), Ukrainian national poet.
†Should be: '*Du hast [Diamanten und Perlen] […] die schönsten Augen –/ Mein Liebchen, was willst du mehr?*' From *Die Heimkehr*, 12 by Heinrich Heine (1827).

I don't remember it all exactly. I only know I was happy. It feels so good to be with him. He was really sorry for not coming on Saturday. He apologised and promised that this Saturday we will definitely party together. Aha! And we made arrangements to go to the cinema on Thursday! Zyguś, you are so wonderful! Wonderful! Mama, I wish you could meet him soon … You will help me, Buluś and God …

12 March 1941, Wednesday

I heard people teasing him after school. Irka met him after he said goodbye to me. She said he was very irritated and when she asked him what he'd been doing for so long with me, he replied, 'What's the problem? I can't? With my Renuśka?' And he told Irka she would make a caring wife, but then he added that I would not make such a caring wife, because I like daydreaming.

I'll be such a daydreamer
A fantastic, poetic wife
I'll watch the sky a-shimmer
And count stars all my life
I'll invite butterfly swarms
I will practise playing clarinet
I will gather flowers in my arms
And make sure you never fret
Fragrant ambrosia I will stew
I'll dust with clouds, mend clothes with sunrays

I will be loving and pining and true
A fantastic, poetic wife, always
Somebody might tell you – half-witted
That it is really not permitted
To have some mad, insane wife
Don't let them talk, don't waste your life
I will fill both of my hands
With blossom of lilies, apples, cherry
I will drape them, make garlands
I'll make each moment merry
complete with a poem's amazing flow.
I'll grab the wide, seven-colour rainbow
I'll write directly on the sky's blue
That, Zyguś, that I … I love you
So hush, you magpies so outraged
With such a crazy wife
Burn piles of meat on the stage
What matters is your eyes, your life
And your brow, unclouded, under your hat
So, tell me, Zygu … Do you want a wife like that?

13 March 1941, Thursday

I'm breathless, you know?! If I only could, I'd scream with all my might, brightly, springlike!!! Just think, a whole afternoon with him! First at the cinema he paid for my ticket and he also bought a ticket for some poor child. He is so good, my Zygu! You know, I'm saying it, or rather writing, rather drily, but you should have seen it, this gesture and his sweet, wonderful face. Zygu! He's such a good person; he doesn't say anything bad about anybody, even his enemies, even his rivals.

Then we spent two hours at my place (I think he stole my photo), then at Irka's. We were, you know, like a real couple. It's better than I dared to dream! Ah, my wonderful mama, if only you were here with me now!

Then, on our way back home, Zygu wanted to find out something about Maciek. He knows a bit, he worked out a bit more ... But, you know, he's in ... I know what he wanted, here, at Rejtana Street, and then, when we were saying goodbye ... ahhh (thiiis again). I knew he was irritated. At the end he said, '*mein Liebchen*'. I won't even tell you that we walk arm in arm all the time and we are officially an item.

> *Ich bin din*
> *Du bist min**
> I wanted to punish you hard
> To imprison you in my heart
> You will stay for ever there
> 'Cause I lost the key somewhere ...

I can't even tell you what it's like ... Mama and Great Lord God, I'm so very grateful to You and I love You. And I'm submitting myself to Your care.

---

*The German translates as 'I am yours / You are mine'.

14 March 1941

It's Saturday tomorrow … As usual I await it and I'm scared … I love, love more and more … Buluś, God, You will help me!

15 March 1941, Saturday

He was wonderful today at school! And he said he would give me all of today's afternoon. And he crossed his fingers for my schoolwork. He was wonderful, wonderful, wonderful. As a result we forgot to make plans and I only saw him in the evening in town. He was with friends – he excused himself and approached me. 'You know, Irka's right when she says that we're like a "pretend" married couple.' Zygu tells me that if I don't do my hair, he won't shave, so because I'm going to the hairdresser's, Z'll shave.

There is a dance party tomorrow. Z asked if I'm going to have a good time. Oh! How could I know that? By the gate he told me, 'Rena, the gate's locked, os stel og dna yats ni a letoh.'*

He makes me so happy … Aha! We are to meet at midday, I suggested it, but he said he needed to see my hair. A 'What else do you want?' kind of provocation. Mama, please be with me tomorrow and always. I'll be happy or sad … Goodnight, till tomorrow …

_____

*Words written backwards.

16 March 1941, Sunday

It's today already. Or rather it is gone, like another stage of this beautiful, spring dream. We met in the morning like a normal couple does, i.e., he waited, I arrived and we walked until 2.00 p.m. in town. And today at Olga's picnic it was also wonderful – we danced and he pulled me to him hard, with passion. At some point we were even going to dance in a different room, but … it didn't feel appropriate.

Poldek and Maciek avoided me at first, and then Maciek said he couldn't ignore me any longer. I danced not just with Zygu, but with everybody. And on so many occasions I was stolen right from under Zygu's nose when he was about to ask me to dance (Maciek, mirror, Zygo). They kept teasing us and I kept blushing. Just imagine, Rysiek said that I must be writing poems in Zygu's honour. Zygu's wonderful!

After the picnic I walked down the street with a whole group of boys and Maciek said, 'Look, there are buds,' and Zygu to this said, 'Rena, spring!' I can feel its first waft … Of course there was a lot of teasing from Maciek, Poldek, Fredek and Julek, but no matter.

Today in fact (do you remember, 16 March?) I am to compare today with this other 16 March. Can you compare those two days at all? No! Or in fact, yes! True, Mama's still not here, but I hope to see her soon (war should be over). And I love, love this beautiful, wise boy, the best boy at school. And it's mutual. Yes! Even though Zygu hasn't told me anything, he said, 'There is something I won't tell you,' and he wants to write it all down and give it to Irka to give it to me.

I now have a so-called social life and, to be honest, I'm quite popular. Anyway, it's looking good. I go to parties now, enjoy picnics, like a normal sixteen-year-old girl would.

It's different with Nora. Her love for Nacek collapsed and I believe will be restored, but in the meantime I wanted to drag her into the youthful hum almost by force. But she wasn't well again today. I was so sorry, as I was the one trying to get her to come to today's picnic. She sat there, even though most boys were there, and later she read a book. I know she'll write an entry in her diary today and compare those two days one year apart. Even though, when we were saying goodbye today, she said, 'This isn't what matters most in life,' which is true and I say that too, but on the other hand what is more important than 'this'? Yes, tell me, what's more important? I remember that I used to say I didn't care about those things, but that's not true. Perhaps my opinion will change one day, but for now it's simple: life is worth living for the person you love, for the person you dream about and think about during sleepless nights. Living not for fame or knowledge, not for learning – these are just intellectual concepts. Living the sensual life, 'getting to the bloody core of life', snatching what's best, satisfying yourself until you're breathless. Whatever they say about me when I die, I'll die like an animal, but I can live the way I want now. To be able to say, standing over one's grave:

I got what I could out of life
a lot, but still not enough
Today my wizened body lies in the grave
I desert what others still crave
To live, live, live in such a way!
Everybody can in the grave decay
Dying is easy, but to live is art, I say

I've read Nora's diary once. I read that she wouldn't write about her loves any more, she wouldn't describe details, and it's all because if somebody were to read her diary, they could say, 'This is some stupid, vain girl who only cares for flirtation in life.'

Norka! You're so wrong! Firstly, why do you care about other people reading it? You're writing it for yourself. And secondly, is your dearest, intimate diary to be a political almanac or an almanac of your heart??? Somebody very harsh, with a stony heart, might say what you thought. Every normal human being should rather say, 'This was written by a young, sixteen-year-old girl who loved so deeply …' That's what I think, Norka, and I hope you soon agree with me. I wouldn't go back to the old sentences, the old situation. I'm in love, which is my explanation for writing all this nonsense. You forgive a person in love, you forgive them everything, and apropos the sad party I escaped.

You don't know how life can be
It's like a leaf trembling on the water

You don't know what does matter
Sometimes you win and sometimes it's me
Sun can dry it, change its form
When it suffers yet another storm
The leaf will hide deeper in
Though that will soon be a has-been
The leaf will shimmer in good weather
On the long river like a feather
It will slide on the surface
Carrying our life with no purpose

Yes, yes, yes. Buluś, if you could only read this. Thank you, thank you so much. Not sure I'll write tomorrow. You will help me, Buluś and God.

18 March 1941, Tuesday

We made arrangements today, he picked me up at 6.00 p.m. First we went to the Socialist Club, then to Irka's, then back home.

It's cold outside again.

Today it felt as if there was something hanging between us, something elusive, something unspoken. And I kept thinking this one thought, about an unfinished symphony … And I'm barely able to control myself. I'm boiling, I'm broiling, I can barely stop myself from … And I know it's a bit similar for him too.

Pity it isn't warm any more …

It's strange and wild with Mama (Leszczyńska*), I don't know what's going to happen with her now, will she come and when? When? When???

Ah, I'm so shamelessly vulgar, Z is much gentler than me and even though he said, 'I forget about everything when I look into your eyes,' I put my hand under his arm and it was so nice. He made a little pout with his wonderful lips, so, so, so sweet, but it was as if … Zygu behaves like my guardian. There is indeed something elusive in the 'unfinished symphony' … Will it ever be finished? Will it be soon? Mama, please tell me honestly, would you like it to end well and lovingly, please tell me? Anyway, Buluś and God, help me!

19 March 1941, Wednesday

I'm feeling guilty. I'm so vulgar. I can feel something powerful swelling up inside me. I need to confess to somebody or I'll go mad. I can feel all my senses are churning, I'm aware of myself boiling. For example I know I suffered terribly yesterday. Ha! What a curse.

I feel I'll destroy the old foundations
I feel they'll get smashed and crushed
by my rampant temper and frustrations
I feel so strong, so strong with love

---

* Renia and Ariana's mother was baptised on 20 January 1940, later changing her name to Marianna Leszczyńska after she secured false papers in Warsaw.

hot blood is boiling in my veins
I am so drunk with closeness,
hotheaded, dazed with desire flames
my senses send me writhing
they're tying me, entangling
I know I'm like a beast
My self-respect has decreased
I despise, I degrade myself so much
But still I understand that like a dog
like a wounded lynx I don't budge
my heart twitches, I howl inside, agog
in no time I will jump up and go savage
shake everything off and snort and bellow
the red lips will be ravaged by my lips
I'm in a frenzy, my urge and fear's not mellow
I live now, I'm not gone
and I want
I can't go on …

This is disgusting, repulsive, animalistic …

21 March 1941, Friday

I gave myself a day off today. I didn't go to school; I had a headache. Yesterday I was supposed to see Z, but he didn't come. Today I was unwell, as I've been unwell for several months now, ill with Zygu, lazy with Zygu, daydreaming with Zygu, my unfinished symphony.

My dear Diary, do you know how much I love you? Very, very, very much. I feel that I need you, I open you on one bright sunny day, read for a while – and then I know. I remember everything and all those days live in me, together and separately.

Buluś has written that there will be war. Who knows? Will it interfere again with my life, this powerful, hated enemy?

Tomorrow is Saturday. I don't know what'll happen. I don't expect anything. I shook off some of this madness. It's gone. But it might come back. And it'll be back as soon as the wind brings spring again, when I see ... I'll get terminally ill with Zygu. Or maybe it won't be terminal? Those images I pasted there, I should paste here, if I could write what I wanted.

Let some quiet song
Play a loving tune
About you living in my heart
And me living in yours too
It would be nasty, not so smart
It would be sad, teary and dreadful
If you indeed lived in my heart
And I not in yours! That would be fearful
It would be even more unkind
if cruel fate decided
to let me sleep in the heart of mine
and you in yours, divided.
Good that it is not the case

Go away, terrible nightmare
I dream of hazel eyes, your face
You dream of blue ones, of my hair
A quiet sweet spring concert
Plays us a loving tune
About you blossoming in my heart
And me in yours too.

Ah, it's Saturday tomorrow, on the one hand this is a bit too daring. Buluś, love me! Help me, Buluś and God

22 March 1941, Saturday

It was so good! Not only out in town (though that too!). I met him at the post office. I could see he was really happy to see me. It's nice of him that he didn't go to the picnic. Maciek kissed my hair and Z laughed and then kept calling me every now and then, saying, 'Do you love him? Is your heart filled to the brim with love? 'Cause he loves you, don't you know that beggars can't be choosers?' I told him he was a total swine. Z kept kissing M. When I told him to stop, Z said, 'You can do it all day long, so I can do it too.' My sweet, wonderful boy. Even though I kept saying I wouldn't go to the party, Z laughed under his breath and said that I would. What did I do? I told him the whole story with Irka and Felek. I'm so very sorry – this was somebody else's secret, but Z is discreet and anyway, I can't say 'no' to him, that's the effect he has on me. I don't know about tomorrow, as we didn't make plans. I might meet him somewhere. You would be happy for me, Buluś … God, You will help me too.

23 March 1941

I don't know why, but I'm very sad today! Very, very, very sad. Sometimes I know the reason.

I met Zygu twice today. We went for a walk in the afternoon with sweet Felunia. And suddenly! I felt this emptiness in my heart and in my life … Later Zygu said he noticed it and asked why I was so sad? We went for a long walk and had a serious conversation. Z told me he had never been like that before, but now he is sad and serious. When we were saying goodbye, Z said, 'Maybe it's my influence on you? But tough, that's what I am like. Maciek might entertain you.' He is stupid if he still thinks that I have any feelings for Maciek. But then he said, 'You will be my solid support (something, something), I will be crushed.' He doesn't know what it might be, but I suspect that Zygu is sad underneath this sweet burden. As am I.

We are supposed to go to a party tomorrow. I want to be in a good mood, even if it's fake. We made plans. And for the first time without my participation, but with his; he was eager. He reminded me about it when he was leaving.

Zyguś! I would like to be joyful, because you're sad and you want this. But sometimes a 'time of apathy' comes, as you call it, and one can't, one simply can't.

You like listening to music, you love music – and I like daydreaming, daydreaming while listening to music with you. I like to daydream and be happy when my dreams come true. But then, there are times like today. Today I am sad, even though half a dream is coming true.

I don't believe I have changed so much, that I only have expectations, no! Let's see what happens next.

I am to see him tomorrow morning, we are to go to the party, I am to be in a good mood.

Irka is travelling to see Felek, pretty much everybody is travelling to Lwów, and I'm staying with Zygu. We're staying! Spring! Seven days off! What for? To get bored? To be sad? No, to love!!! Mama, do you know it all, can you hear my heart beating with love for him and my long-distance longing for you? You will help me, Buluś and God … Great Lord God! What will tomorrow's party be like?

24 March 1941, Monday (Party no. 3!)

So nice. Zygu picked me up (even though I was supposed to come later, but he got too impatient), he paid our entry fees, bought me a cake and water, and danced with me all the time. Maybe with a few exceptions. This party was different from other parties; this was a real 'Zygu' party.

People treat us like a married couple. For example after a dance one boy doesn't take me back to my place, but says, 'I need to give you back to Schwarzer.' And then somebody else says, 'Thanks, I brought your wife back.' I even got outraged at some point. What is all this bargaining? Tusiek said, 'I will bring her back to you untouched.' He told me that, for a while, since 'this' has started, Z has not been able to think straight. Eau de cologne.

Z and I bring couples in love together. We do it very subtly. Z, 'Let's open a marriage bureau.' He annoyed Irka with Felek so much that she had to go home, but it was a revenge for Irka annoying him, as she did to Felek with Fredziu, to Julek and the whole class.

Zygu asked me how he could make it up to me, all that swing dancing. I can't do swing dance and neither can he, so we suffer and keep apologising to each other. Oh! How to make it up – I know how, and so does he. I told him he is provoking me with this alien military stuff.

We didn't make plans, because Julek was with us. Z is so good, so loving and understanding. It's so nice to have a 'pretend husband'. Tusiek was surprised that Zygu is allowed not to shave – how can I let him, how do I curl up against him? To which Z said that nobody complains about him.

Zygu was happy with the party and so was I. This was a real 'Zygu' party. I send you kisses, Renia. Please help me, Buluś and God …

PS Studying this and that with Luśka. He danced with me several times, he was completely drunk and he hugged me tight, rambling on and on. I got scared … Bye, dear Diary, see you next time.

28 March 1941, Friday

Today we went for a long, long walk. It was so good – we just walked down a half-dark street and talked, talked, talked. Now I couldn't say what he said, but I know he said a lot of pleasant and a lot of ambiguous things. He told me we would go to the Riviera together one day, somewhere far away from other people, somewhere with 'azure sky' – to which I added, 'And azure sea' – and he finished, 'And azure eyes.' Or, for example, that Mochnacki* is so passionate about mathematics, but 'I prefer to be passionate about something else, don't I, Rena?' And then a lot about hearts. 'Poor darling, I'm so very sorry for you – why didn't you come to me like you would to a doctor?' Etc. etc.

A long, friendly walk like this is perhaps even better than ... But what do I know?

We've made arrangements for tomorrow; he'll come pick me up around 4.00–5.00 p.m. Buluś, if you were here ... I'm so happy and it's thanks to you. You will help me, Buluś and God. Bye, kisses, Rena.

29 March 1941, Saturday

Our arrangement didn't quite work out, but in the end we did meet. We went to the Socialist Club and then for a walk.

---

* Mirosław Mochnacki (1904–1970) – expert in mathematical analysis, algebra, and calculus of variations. He taught mathematics at the Juliusz Słowacki Polish Grammar School in Przemyśl starting in 1934.

The walk was the nicest part, a long walk, just the two of us. We walked arm in arm and talked and talked, and apart from that we also talked with our looks. Such a walk is for me the most wonderful symphony and can replace tens of other nice things.

This walk is a force and power
This walk is immortality!*

He said that at his wedding he would want Mendelssohn's 'Wedding March' played. Fela pointed at me and Zygu also pointed at me. We talked about the future, about medicine, etc. etc. Z said he wouldn't want to have a son or children in general, because children between the age of thirteen and sixteen go through a period of rebellion and a lot of internal turmoil. I felt so good! His looks make me so warm. Not to mention that we walked arm in arm. Well, I say, such a walk is something powerful! About living in a dorm, he said, 'I don't want to look at anybody there, I would rather look at you.' We didn't arrange to meet. Aha, what antics with Maciek! Zygu was happy I didn't want to meet him. You will help me, Buluś and God ...

---

* Reference to a line from Adam Mickiewicz's 'Great Improvisation' from *Forefathers' Eve*, part 3: 'This song is force and power / This song is immortality!' (translated by Louise Varese, published by Voyages, 1956).

4 April 1941, Saturday

The entire week was bright, but for me it was empty. I feel emptiness today, and sadness, such sadness. But I found out that he came over to my place, and that made me feel better. And tomorrow? Sunday, probably nothing will happen again. You will help me, Buluś and God …

5 April 1941, Sunday

Residency – invitation. He kept saying, 'Shush, Renia!' And when I asked, 'What?' he didn't say anything.

Ah! Today! 'It was wonderful, warm, loving.' I saw him twice; we spent five hours together. We went to the cinema. He held my hand tenderly, so tenderly, and kept yawning. He pulled a sweet face when we bumped into Maciek. But, you know, I found his photo with some girl. Z was sheepish. I was too polite to ask anything. But really, believe you me, sweetie pie, my poppet, that it was wonderful. The best thing was with the sweets. Ah! Zygu, I can't even express how much I love you.

Z is supposedly angry with Irka for lying to us about Felek. And so am I. Today he said we would start going to the Castle – really??? You will help me, Buluś and God.

6 April 1941

It was so wonderful, so blissful and now it's gone like a dream, the fairy tale is over. Up until now I was still preoccupied with this Sunday, but now, you know, I'm choking with anger and I'm glad at the same time! Yes, I'm glad that I spoilt the good mood of his afternoon! I'm glad I won't turn up tomorrow at break time. I will show him, just you wait.

The Devil sent him and Irka, and, of all days, on the day when I was considering the issue of Irka and Zygo! I was just imagining the most fantastical images of Irka and Zygu in romantic poses, when I met them together in the evening. At first I wanted to run away, but we played a good trick with Nora – lucky that this building has two entrances! Ah! I got some satisfaction! Wait, you think that I'll watch you embracing Irka in my presence and at the same time watching my reaction? Go and caress her, walk with her, call her even more tender names, but I'll play on your nerves, I'll play you Beethoven's Ninth Symphony so that you'll remember me, you prat, so that you realise what it means to vex a jealous woman in love. I know that Maciek annoys you. So I'll use Maciek to get on your nerves. 'Your conscience can be absolutely clear that it is because of you that I don't study.' Anyway, none of your business. Zygu! If you only knew that I'm on the verge of tears and how terribly I hate you right now. And with what pleasure I'll take revenge on you, even if it hurts you a lot. Now, God Almighty! I'm in despair, I don't know what I'm writing and I so badly want it to be tomorrow already!!! Ah, Bulczyk, if you knew my suffering and my hatred!! You will help me, Buluś and God.

12 April 1941, Saturday

This week was somewhat sweet and hazy and I felt like that too – somewhat hazy, I was in a so-so mood. Irka kept sneering at me, but she realised that nothing came of it and she almost erupted. Anyhow she is flirting with Z. For what reasons – I don't know. And him? I don't know (he keeps criticising her in front of me). Do you remember?

On Sunday we made plans with Z to go to the cinema and Irka knows about it, because I told her and she would like to worm her way in. I'm saying no so far, but I am furious. I'm trying with all my might not to show it, but I'm only partially successful. Irka actually told him that she's looking for love, that she's missing something. All very nice, I understand, but I would prefer she looked elsewhere and not at Z. Everybody knows about us now, including the students, the teachers, even Mrs Polak who saw us from a distance, but not me.

Tomorrow we have an evening with my poetry reading. I'm not happy about it; I'm very embarrassed. And then there's a party. I'm not in the mood for a party. I don't know; I'm scared! I'm terribly scared of any party. No, I'm in no mood and I would rather go to the cinema, but – with him, thank you very much for the rest. Anyway he can bend over backwards. Do you know that today is a

holy day – holy day – holy day
not like any other day

In my despair I tried to find some oblivion in aphorisms and started writing on the subject.

What is love's worth
if you need to worry?
Bitterness, no mirth
it only carries
Each slope on earth
causes much misery
What is love's worth
if you have to worry

Do you know that everybody thinks that we have already …
ha ha ha. And I could say something about it. I understand
it myself, but, well, I'm still stupidly scared of love and
tomorrow's party, but … You will help me, Buluś and God.

13 April 1941, Sunday

There was supposed to be a party. But! Wasn't this better than
one hundred normal dancing parties? Better than swirling in
circles in a crowded room? Not letting Maciek and Poldek
keep me there after the cheering of 'author, author' and
instead going far away arm in arm with my wonderful Zyguś?
Listening to his tender words, sitting in the cinema with him
(and almost, almost, ah …) and returning home at 12.00?
Well? Wasn't it better?

I really should stop worrying about silly things. After all I have firm evidence that Z loves me (*mein Liebchen was …*). Arianka stayed at the party. A wonderful, wonderful, wonderful evening. Let's hope that this week we finally … oh! Buluś, really. Z left the party because he was jealous of me.

17 April 1941, Thursday

Actually nothing happened today, neither today, nor yesterday. Life goes on as usual i.e., we meet from time to time, walk arm in arm (I don't know how to walk differently any more), we talk, hum and we are very happy together. I mean I find it ah, blissful, angelic, sweet. And he? Must be the same, otherwise he wouldn't be making plans about going to a party on the 1st 'to belong to each other only', like Maciek has said.

I keep thinking all the time, recalling and dreaming, I daydream all the time at school. I can't learn anything, I can't talk about anything else apart from the moments when Z says, 'Don't be scared, I'm with you,' or 'We had a tempestuous night,' 'It's only half past eleven.' It's strange … Everybody thinks, nobody even doubts that we have already … But in fact we still haven't, though it's as if we have. Once it was raining and each word was said into hands, temples, with lips and heads, in whispers, ah! It gives me shivers. I don't know … I don't think … He wouldn't be so refined as to agitate me to the utmost! And why am I writing today?

Because it's raining and everybody walks hunched, and there's commotion with Mum which I can't even understand and I'm feeling wishy-washy, but still quite safe, because … Nora tells me that I 'should be happy'. To be happy I need Mama and sun and (first child). I have those shivers, but it's not because of the cold. 'Are my eyes misty?'* Ah! I'm such a little animal, well …

Sometimes those moments arrive
especially in springtime, in May
when thoughts like fine butterflies
fly far out, in disarray
They sway gently on trees
with May tranquillity elated
highly thrilled and intoxicated
look for the distant eyes these
Eyes that are misty, filled with longing
And then, as if a warning
A voice breaks your thoughts with force
Not ever reaching you, of course
You are among the clouds in the sky
clouds that are like a pink awning
strolling through green fields, don't deny
everywhere seeing those brown eyes
Eyes that are misty, filled with longing

---

*Possibly a reference to the 1931 waltz entitled '*Mały pokoik*' ('Little room'), with lyrics by Tadeusz Kończyc and music by Wiktor Krupiński.

18 April 1941, Saturday

We didn't make plans for this post office party, but we met in the street (how great) and went there together. I danced a bit with Julek B and once with Zygu. I felt faint, so we left.

Z was troubled today, but didn't want to tell me what it was about. Things got really nice during the walk. At first he was apathetic, but then perked up and we couldn't say goodbye by my gate.

I will report the broken finger at the clinic and I am to tell father that it was caused by son's sadism.

Rena, study! We've wasted some precious moments in front of the pharmacy. A very nice goodbye, aha! I'm sleepy, but I feel a bit cosy, i.e., nice, that I'll see him tomorrow at 6.00 p.m. Should I? You will help me, Buluś and God!

19 April 1941, Sunday

I was waiting on the balcony, Zyguś came, tra la la!
We went for a long walk, then to the cinema, tra la la!
My hand was so tiny
barely visible next to his
So Zyguś, oh so kindly
covered it protectively with his.
And since I don't feel pain
but have some moral distress
Zyguś promised to abstain
To never put me under duress.

He won't be in the bad husband category
Like the one in the film or worse
He will read poems for my glory
He now lives and breathes verse.
Come, poetry, let me take you in my arms
Come, pet, forget all the strife
Eyes full of yawning, ringing alarm
I'll break away from the prose of life.

Zyguś, my husband. He has a silky beard – who would have thought? Smooth hands, nice, it's so good to stroke them lightly. There's a sweet, which Z'll bite first. That's why he 'wouldn't be able to sleep beside me'. I didn't even understand the film; it was all about Zygu! Zygu! Zygu!

I'm so stupid, I was thinking of my situation – and Nora's, wondering if hers was perhaps better! But I love my beloved and we're together and I can touch him and talk to him. Just that, but that's a lot. I am to keep my fingers crossed for him and give him a mascot for his final exam. But he still needs to study, tough. Tomorrow at school. Bye, darling. Mama, if only you were here and could see it. You will help me, Buluś and God ... You will, won't You?

26 April 1941, Saturday

Some Saturday it was. Two days he wasn't at school. Maciek tried some scheming! But what?! Silliness.

Irka started flirting like mad with Waldek, so I told her that he had a crush on me. I did it like a real woman. After all I only like Waldek a bit and I don't really care about him. Same goes for Maciek, but still!

Today I saw him … And then I heard a snippet of a conversation between Julek and C G, 'I'm astonished with Zygu.' I didn't know it, but I instinctively felt it was about Zygu's love, or rather Zygu's fondness for me. It unnerved me so much that I got a headache and was in a really bad mood. I do really feel that on every level I'm not worthy of Zygu, that's the truth … But who is? Nobody! There is no girl who has as many virtues as he does and who would love him as much as I do. Anyway it worried me. But in fact what do I care about Julek's astonishment? Let him, why not. Oh, I'm being silly and that's that. If Z wanted, he could find me, but it doesn't matter. I am the one who loves the most; all I want in return is a bit of fondness, not love as big as mine. I'm happy with that – just that and so much at the same time! In fact we made plans for today last Sunday. But not exact ones. Do I know about what'll happen? You will help me, Buluś and God. I doubt we will meet.

27 April 1941, Sunday

Tearful sky and a day somewhat sombre
Somewhat rainy, slippery, scornful

Mama, on a day like today it would be good to have somebody, somebody close to my heart, dear, loved and loving. It could only be you. Mama, I'm so low. You know, sometimes I find excuses for Zygu. For example, he didn't approach me and

I said it was just because he couldn't; he didn't come to see me and I said it was just because he was feeling shy (it's true that he is easily embarrassed!). But deep down in my heart I think that he ... well, I don't know. And finally today Granny started talking about it. Yes, Granny has a fair point, but her approach is very old-fashioned. Poor, dear Granny made a clumsy attempt to help me, but instead only lacerated my already bleeding heart. It will take a while for it to heal. And will it heal at all? I know now that J and T have decided to interfere with our love. Ah! It's so nasty, this fighting and this day. I don't know why this day feels so dirty.

I don't know why today's so sad
So cloudy and so bad
Why are there so many cruel hours?
Is it because of my tears?
Everything is nondescript
It's so empty and so lonely
I would like to have somebody picked
To talk and to not feel lowly
I would like to be somebody's
Tiny, beloved child
To sit in Mama's custody
By the old fireplace and smile ...
to listen to stories, make drawings
to dream this very sweet dream
to not know how hard is longing
when a day like today gleams ...

Not to know it can be so sad
Not to know it can be so bad
Why are there so many cruel hours?
Is it because of my tears?

28 April 1941

I saw Z today. Something was telling me to play offended, so I did, but then I melted completely as soon as he looked at me. It's good. Even though those idiots made me doubt, it's a trifle.

There was a dance party at Irka's today. I mean, it wasn't a dance party, but boys from our class brought a gramophone and we danced. It was very nice; I had a good time. And it was Irka who told me that Krzyś had a crush on me! Which surprised me a lot, so I started watching him and it's quite possible ...

Major asked how many boys I have seduced already, is it half a dozen? I said only one, but it isn't true! Krzysiek is a very pretty, smart boy, but that doesn't mean anything. I have Zygu; I love Zygu. Well, he is a bit lucky too. Let's see what the next days brings ... I am waiting, Z. Zyguś, it's time. You will help me, Buluś and God.

29 April 1941, Tuesday

Tuesday! A lot of commotion at school today with Zygu, with Ewa, with the letter etc. Zyguś tried to explain himself, said it was only ten minutes. It made me want to laugh. When I told him that I danced yesterday, he was angry, furious. We haven't arranged to meet for a while now. You know how sensitive I am about it and then this terrible brat Arianka says, 'You haven't been out with Zygu for a while.' So I told her he was busy studying, to which this old person trapped in a young person's body replies ironically, 'Suppose so.' Aha!

Nobody cares about me any more in our circles. A friend from the trade college approached me today, asking if I wanted to go to a party, and if so he would get an invitation for me. Do you get it? I'll ask Z if he wants to go, otherwise I'll say no. My wonderful, good, sweet, darling Z.

We were out in town with Irka and a teacher from school. Waldek walked me home, he really does … this and that. And I'm a typical girl, why do I wind him up? It's instinctive.

Norka is feeling down. We went to visit her. She is unwell after yesterday's dance party. She's in bed, crying, worrying. Three parties like that in a row could break her. Poor Norka, I so feel for her. Some of it is her own fault, because she removes herself, but how can she not, when she's lost faith in her own happiness and popularity? I believe that it'll get better with time, that time will heal the wounds, but in the meantime I do know how hard it is for her. God, please make it all fine for her again. I'll write if anything, but so far nothing … You will help me, Buluś and God.

30 April 1941, Wednesday

I am the unhappiest of unhappy people. Why did all the troubles come tumbling onto my head in one day? Why those two postcards from Mum? Why won't I see her? Why did Zygu arrange to take Irka to a party? Why does he want to spite me (I'll tell you about it later)? You know, I am going to go anyway. I'll let myself be tortured. I can't just give up altogether.

Life is a battle
The world a battlefield
I'll fight even though
I don't believe in victory

Or perhaps I shouldn't go? You will help me, Buluś and God. Oh, if you could only speak.

11.00 p.m.!

Glad I went. As it was, Z was in a so-so mood because of me. We danced a bit; I jived with Krzysiek and a bit more.

Maciek has his own girlfriend now. Poldek is in love too and I'm left with Z, even though he is not sure of me and I am not sure of him. Ah, so many worries and troubles, but even that has its charm. There were plenty of couples dancing together, but I don't know why ours felt somewhat unnatural. Perhaps because Zygu also danced with others. Anyway I'm terribly jealous, Z is too, a bit. We both suffer (or so I think). About Irka! Even about Irka, i.e., not just about her, but I am jealous when he shows her interest. He told me he wants Irka to come on Saturday. If she comes then he will come as well?

Is that it? As he said, P and M are taken, my school back-up won't come, so I don't know about the party. Perhaps I shouldn't go ... We might meet tomorrow. Well, we'll see ... Will we meet at all during those three days off? I would like that; I miss him.

Z remembers when we last ... So he remembers too. I would really like to fall in love for a long time ... Zyguś, I want to go on a date ... Come on ... You will help me, Buluś and God.

1 May 1941, Thursday

Mama it would be so lovely
To rest in your arms and cry
To cry away my sorrows
even die.
To die or to sleep
With all the beauty of youth
And join for ever our souls in truth
And join for ever in the peace and bliss
To sail quietly to a haven
Without tears or parting ...

Mama, you poor thing, my poor darling soul. Alone among strangers ... Look, out of the window I see a small boy hugging his mother, and I feel such sorrow, because I'd like to hug someone too, and complain, I'm so upset, Mama, so very upset ... Why, why did this bubble burst? Why does the first joy give me such sadness, so many tears? You know, I cried today, oh, cried for so long – from the heart ... You know, I love him after all, and he ... I have been waiting for so many months, yes, and I've thought about this spring dream as something holy, most wonderful. And he, oh God! How foul! So this is what his shyness and modesty are about!? Today at the march ... but tell me, why was it like that? I'm not going to impose myself on you at all. No! I'm never going to take one more step, not even half, whatever for? No, Zygu, don't worry, even if I were to suffer, I will step aside. Oh, no! I won't go to the party on Saturday or any other party; I won't even try to meet you. It's not true that you're doing this out of love. Or maybe out of jealousy? And today is the first of May. The first day of the month of love and I, who had so believed in May (we'd had an arrangement after all) for those three days, must cry today. One thing, one thing bothers me: what was all this, because I don't think it was nothing. Ah, I know. I know what it was like then, and I was sweet too. If I only impress him, then ... No, I'm not saying I'm not in love, but I won't impose myself either.

Don't cry my injured heart
The arrow that wounds you won't kill
With yearning, your beating must start
Although I don't want this to happen
It will
You may now cry your helpless tears
But they won't make them pity you more
Then they'll rob you and double your fears
Since you didn't learn about people before ...

The will-o'-the-wisp will deceive you
and bend you to its will
you chase them – they run away
colourful
I found a heart
on a boundary road
a gingerbread heart
fresh, hot and lovely
a heart-shaped work of art
clapping my hands with joy
across the fields I ran
before I left the boundary road
the heart was lost and gone
Bitterly then I cried
And sighed with grief so bad
Should I look for a new heart
Or seek the one I had
I don't know
But why am I grieving
Why did my tears even fall
Before I found a heart
I didn't have one at all
I found it, I lost it – it's over
I'll visit my common sense
And say: 'Make things carefree again
As they'd been ever since …'
But there'll be a frown on my brow
Like clouds hanging over the land

Because I had that heart to heart
And felt its warmth in my hand
It smelt so alluring and sweet
I thought I felt its beat
And that's why I've been crying
That's why the sorrow and pain
For having found a heart at last
I lost it once again

Well, I'll see, I'm in love, and he ... You will help me, Buluś
and God.

3 May 1941, Saturday

God! Only you know what torment I have suffered during
these days, what torture, it can't be described or even retold,
it has to be experienced to be understood, but it's better not
to understand or experience it. I didn't go to that party, but
at what cost! And he, I don't know, maybe he's having a good
time, maybe he's dancing happily, maybe he never spared a
thought for me? You will help me, Buluś and God.

8 May 1941, Thursday

I'd like to tell you so much, so much – nothing. I'd like to speak
to you, but soberly, about the state of my soul. You know,
I'm missing Mum awfully; I feel that this emotion of mine is
intensifying, growing mightier. And I can't say how much longer
we'll be separated. I so need somebody really close, someone

who would care for me, a friend – a mother … And today I saw her, she came in the night, she was ill, suffering. Walking away, she said, 'Renuś, I will come on 25 June,' she said she'd come, so I'm waiting … I'm waiting for this symbolic dream to come true. So perhaps she will come, because Her soul was with me.

Norka interrupted my writing and I'm finishing in the evening and I won't write what I'd wanted, because on the way I met 'Him'. The lord and master of my heart and soul, the wizard whose one glance, one word or smile changes me into a different person. I succumb to the charm like one succumbs to supernatural poisonous raspberries, like one succumbs to the thorny, yet deliciously scented rose. So I take it and although it wounds me, although it draws blood from my heart, I feel I cannot give it up, because its thorns have grown into me, because if I remove them – I'll die …

I'd thought that it's already 'pro forma', like Olga wrote. That it is the end, and the ground is falling away beneath my feet. But now I feel that no, not yet, it's not even reached its height yet, so why am I thinking of the end. Today's walk and everything, was it not close – yet so delicate like the aroma of perfume in the air that one senses intuitively. I feel that I love more than any of the girls I know. Olga is in love, raving, loves with a purpose, loves an ideal. And I love a hundredfold more, to me any trifle is an enormous bleeding wound, I'm in disquiet, distress, despair … I love him and just him, an embodied ideal that I found not accidentally, and that has become my ideal … I love, I love … There's so much studying now, there's no time … You will help me, Buluś and God.

I love because there is May
in chords of bloom on Earth
the world around is pink
the soul is full of mirth
I love because he is a wonder
And has the strength and power
He took the obstacles down
And climbed my heart's tall tower
I love because I've a will
To thunder with cascades of feeling
Because I won't stop any longer
The flood of the love and the sting
I now know the reason I love
a head that is held so high
and eyes and the lips oh the lips …
I love because it is worth a try!

10 May 1941, Saturday

We went to the cinema. And for a walk, long live May! I'm feeling it again – you know. We went to the cinema and sat closely entwined, brow flat against brow, and … you understand. Z, 'Well, I'd let you go to war,' 'What will our young people be like?' 'We'll be in Lwów together …' 'Will you go to Lwów with me?' And he wanted photographs from me; he said he must take them along, because all he'll have will be memories and photographs. 'You see, I'm poor too,' with all the bullying …

Z likes to study my poems, knows the order they're in and threatens to get them published. He's generally marvellous and I love him! So much it chokes me up …

We won't meet tomorrow, but in between our examinations we'll be 'laughing'. You will help me, Buluś and God.

Yesterday …

Every time it's so similar … every time lighter, closer, and now it feels like peace, blissful peace has been sown in me. What's left are memories, something intangible, which even yesterday I would have been able to grasp in one word, in a glance, in … Funny, darling, slightly teasing memories … (he was the one who accustomed me to such views, thank you). He walked in my scarf and we haven't got a home yet, anyway everything's whirling in my head. What's it going to be like later?

13 May 1941

And what's it going to be like then …? Oh, May! How intoxicating this May is, but perhaps only to me? My whole life is swelling up in me, all seventeen years of it. All the emotions pile up into one heap of dry leaves and this May too, it's like fuel poured on this heap … And it's growing, growing, just one spark and it will erupt, flames will burst high in the sky, it will heat up and go wild like my long-imprisoned, suppressed, curbed love. Let there be a blaze, heat, fervour. Let the heart, brain, mind, body catch fire, let there be only conflagration and heat – and desire for burning, red-hot lips, desire like today, like then ... like always. Desire! Damn.

Have I lost my mind? Exams soon, there are only three days left until the end of term! And I have learnt absolutely nothing, I'm wandering around, daydreaming, ruminating ... I'm not studying for my exams at all. I just can't! Zygu's eyes are green, but his lips are the most beautiful. Such amazing lips!

The lights in the houses are all out
And all the loudspeakers are now dumb
The shops and stalls are closed again
The hot day is done ...
The footsteps stop their drum and chime
And night of silence, night of dark
upon the city makes its mark
the city finds its sleeping time
And why does May wound us all over
and tear new wounds in hearts unhealed?
why does it rouse and wake the lover
why does it burn in eyes, still filled
with April's yearning – why, at night
does May conquer our souls by might
when nights are bright with starry dust
although the mind may think 'I shan't'
the lips will whisper 'yet I must'
Why does this May with fields of green
keep getting mixed with dearest eyes I've seen

why does it swell my chest, and make me drunk and
   giddy
why, if this is such torture
do I still say I need it

Silly me, what do I care, this May won't be any good anyway.

18 May 1941, Sunday

On Friday, after school, Zyguś walked me home. On Saturday
there was a row with Irka, Zygu and Maciek. You know that
I feel something for Maciek now, I can't say I detest him, but
somehow it seems he's taking Zygu away from me. Sometimes
I think he is passable, but sometimes horrible, foul, capable of
anything. And Z is under his influence.

The school year is over. It's passed more quickly than
any other before it; it passed, it fell into oblivion, because
it was brim full of love. And the school year is over – a
pity ... Admittedly this won't change the love, but still, it
was something that connected us legitimately, something
that we shared, which concerned us equally. Well, but it can't
be said that only school connected us, well it did, but love
most of all.

Irka told me that Z's mother said that Z is in love, that he is
not looking well, that she doesn't know what's going on with
him. She was also very keen to learn something about me,
see my photograph etc. So finally, some real, tangible proof
that Z is in love. And I'd thought about it so, so many times,

about his mother. I like her, I love her for what she said, and I also love my darling mama, the best one, the only. And I'm not preparing for the exam even a little; I don't know how it will go. I'll see you on the 4th, either happy or wet-eyed. Well, until the 4th, unless … but I doubt it. Rena. You will help me, Buluś and God.

I can hardly stand it. Dear Diary, I miss you so much. I get no sleep because I'm sitting two and a half exams: for Zygu, for myself and half for Arianka. I've never known I could be so worried on someone else's behalf. Zygu is awfully good to me, and then horribly jealous for no reason.

4.00 p.m.

No, I'm not writing down the date, what for, I wasn't supposed to write until the 4th. Z is sitting his exams and I am so nervous I don't sleep at night, I don't care a whit about my own exams – am not studying. And today, God, God! Why am I so sad today, why did I do that to Z when he came? I'm awfully angry. Not angry – sad. I'm not sure why? How stupid that I stuck around for three hours, waited for the result of the task. Those girls from the boarding house were screaming, 'Ela!' What for? Because he walked me back, and Stefa from over the way was angry that Krzyś (her love) and Waldek whistled her 'Chopsticks' under my windows. But why am I telling you all this? Probably to depict the tragic state of my soul. Examine yourself, what else could have made me so – aha, perhaps that bad state of mind, I'm going through a phase when I have to admit that I'm awful, downright nasty, but perhaps it's the disappointment that I haven't done too well with my task?

> I would go far away
> and leave the people behind
> Maybe a sunny May stillness
> will soothe me
> Maybe a subtle breeze
> Will cool my mind
> No, I can't clearly meet a gaze
> I can't seek out someone's eyes?
> Go far, fall asleep in a haze
> let the time fly away
> Leave above the earth
> And follow a dream
> Become a bright fragrant shade
> a slender thought's stream
> and like a daydream's mist
> spread myself on the sky
> caressing dreamily with smiles
> to fade with a sigh
> Oh to be a cloud of thought
> pink and blue
> pale milky-watery and orange in hue
> taking the word and the gaze
> to fly away
> and to become fully one sweet dream of May ...

10.00 p.m.

I've had the most wonderful May evening. Maybe the first romantic evening in May and in my life. We climbed up high on the hills, along paths. The San was flowing beneath our feet – powerful, glimmering, red in the sunset. And the red, slightly hazy sun was slowly descending from the sky. We talked a lot, pleasantly, and I know that our spirits were so connected that I'm not sure if any physical contact could have brought us closer. It's hard to remember what we talked about. I only know that when I mentioned something about his reputation, he replied, 'So you wouldn't want a famous husband …?' and then he said something else and got very confused (passport, you don't want to come to me, you can't even control yourself, much about eyes).

Good, lovely Zyguś, although he gets angry with me about being afraid of dogs, and says that he wanted to give me a wallop, but he is perfect in absolutely every respect.

I'm really at a loss for words, so just picture silence, greenery, May, sunset and fireworks, and the two of us, in love.

But Zygu is still testing me about Maciek; does he not believe me yet? And that leaping heart? I don't believe in that power so much any more, 'is the binding of souls not worth the binding of bodies?' You will help me, Buluś and God.

Stupid idiot Belania! Those girls are shallow and trite after all! She asked me if I'm not getting bored with Zygu yet. She gets bored with students because one can't exchange two words with them – the Countess walks away.

Despite everything I see that I am more profound than they are, I really don't switch loves like handkerchiefs, I'm unable to talk about it in a cold, cynical manner! It's repugnant, disgusting! To love truly, passionately, honestly, this is what I believe in, this only! I'm terrified of chemistry.

Today's walk was – oh, nothing worth mentioning. There was company, and I always feel worse then. I will tell you I was a little jealous, but Zygu was a hundred times worse when Maciek approached, because he really had more reason to be. Anyway, I found out how they study my poems (about that explosion, about blue), aha, that linking of hands and Mendelssohn's 'Wedding March' again. And those two female neighbours that he boards with, sweet boy, tender, anyway there is something very cordial about him. The evenings and starry nights are pretty, but apart from that it's so dull, somehow empty and lonely in the world, one wants to have someone, say something. What? Why, not … Zyguś. I'm mostly interested in poems now.

4 June 1941, Wednesday

Done! I should be jumping up to the heavens! Everything went well, I passed everything, although I didn't really study too much. Well then, holidays ahead of me, three long months of holidays, and also ahead of me is emptiness. I don't know, I've got a constant feeling that something has evaded me, that something has ended. I'm in such a strange mood that I don't know what to do with myself.

Zygu was wonderful yesterday. He was so pleased when I let myself be stroked by him, but not by M! But there is something strange about this Z, something different from other boys. On the one hand that's very good, on the other – a bit bad ... You know, I keep expecting events, I keep waiting, waiting for the dream to come true, and if it fades, then – I'll leave for Horodenka – only I know, I know for sure that I would yearn something fierce ... Zyguś! You will help me, Buluś and God.

10 June 1941, Tuesday!

Zygu is sitting his last examination tomorrow! To celebrate, I'm going to wear my new navy shoes.

Today we spoke about this and that, and everything. You know, I can't write down whole conversations any more, never mind. One can't write it the way it is, anyway.

Z has a sore throat, he said I should recommend something for it or only say a word and it will get better. There was talk of Salcia and Krela. And that he's got a way of influencing me and many, many more nice things. 'Well, what am I to do to you?' he said twice. I wanted to ask if we'd go to the cinema tomorrow, but I did it so awkwardly that I couldn't manage to utter a word. Z thinks that God knows what I am to say to him? I said I'll say it tomorrow. All right, but what will I tell him, he thinks ... yes, he thinks that. And I'd also really, really like to tell him. I love you, Zygu! But no, I can't, so what shall I tell him? What shall I tell him tomorrow? He was making such a sweet, darling face ... Zygunio, I love you so much! I love you the most! That 'And whatever you prefer!' – I let it slip and got very embarrassed, but he guessed, the most wonderful wonder. I love you. Goodnight kisses. Renia.

I'm off to daydream. I will look at rooms and think about how the two of us will live there. It's a dream, a fairy tale, but one can dream. You will help me, Buluś and God.

11 June 1941, Wednesday

Zygu passed his final school exam today! He was so wonderful today! Very, very tender and very darling. I do want to tell him something after all. No! Honestly, today Zyguś was the way he's never been before. No more from me!

17 June 1941, Tuesday

I haven't seen Zyguś in such a long, long time! I do see him, but he's preoccupied with his graduation all the time. Tomorrow is the graduation and ... my birthday. I'll be seventeen. We will chat tomorrow. Actually I already know that I won't be happy, because I won't see Zygu at all. Today I translated a little Heine – this feels like a relief, some of the thoughts there are so 'mine', e.g.:

> They both loved each other, though neither
> Would love to the other confess;
> They looked at each other so sternly,
> And suffered their loving no less.

They parted at last and they met again
Where dreams would linger and dwell;
They died so long ago before,
But neither of them could tell.*

Perhaps this thing of ours will, however, have a happier ending.

I have a wonderful collection of my poems. Irka and Nora made it for me, I'm grateful for it. One for Zygu, I'll write it in, but I haven't got a rough draft. So they will be a bit disappointed tomorrow, especially that my leg's swollen and I can't leave ... tomorrow!?

18 June 1941, Wednesday

Irka and Nora got me the most beautiful leather-bound diary. I am very grateful to Noruśka and Irka and love them very, very much. Only why did she write that maybe I will be a famous poet and Mrs Zygmunt S, and if not ... then this diary will only be a very painful memory. I'm not really contemplating my life too much today, maybe I can't do it now like I used to, and anyway – it's not worth it. Perhaps the biggest event today was that I met the S family. It happened by chance, but I got very embarrassed, good thing it was dark. Z found out at school that it was my birthday. I'm seventeen. This is not so terrifying

---

*Song XXXIII from *The Book of Songs* (1827). Incipit: '*Sie liebten sich beide, doch keiner.*'

yet, but eighteen is a nightmare. I don't know why this one year means so much. So I met them, precisely on my birthday, well ... Mama, is that right? The second birthday without you. And you, are you thinking of me today? Why me ...? A new phase won't start tomorrow, no, the same one still.

20 June 1941, Friday

Today. Yes, today. I knew it, I felt it, that I'll only be able to tell you. We had another wonderful evening. The two of us alone, properly alone. The sun had set and the stars started to emerge, and the moon floated up, and we sat next to each other and talked. And it was so ... When we left, it was dark; we couldn't find the way. We got lost, yes, we got doubly lost, or rather – only just found ourselves. It was all so sudden and unexpected and sweet and intimidating. I was at a loss for words and terribly mixed up. He said, 'Renuśka, give me a kiss,' and before I knew it, it happened ... He wanted more later, but I couldn't, I was shaking all over.

Z said that he really liked this 'intentional going astray', he said, 'We can do this again now, or tomorrow.' I feel so strange and nice. It was so light, elusive, ethereal, delicate. There was much, much more, but I'm only interested in that one thing – that he has become so close to me, the dearest person in the world, and I'm dizzy all the time ... How did it happen. No more now, I need to think and dream ... We'll meet tomorrow – Z and I, and you and I. And will tomorrow also be so good and sweet ... ? You will help me, Buluś and God.

21 June 1941, Saturday[12]

I love those green eyes. First we wrote each other dedications on photographs. We used Latin grammar for this. It's a scandal, that's what Z said, that this scandal has been going on for six months already. We also went to the pines. And again it felt very good. We kissed for the second time, i.e., actually the first, because today it was reciprocal. It felt so nice too, but you know, it wasn't fiery or wild, but somehow delicate and careful, and almost fearful – as if we didn't want to extinguish something that was growing between us. Who would have thought we could talk so 'scientifically'? You will help me, Buluś and God.

Zygu wants very much to go to a party on Monday, I don't, but it seems I have to – I really don't feel like it! I do not enjoy those stuffy, crowded dances. I prefer to be beneath the stars, beneath the moon in the evening's darkness, with my grown-up Zygunio.

26 June 1941

Do you remember, on 25 May I wrote that I'd had a dream. I dreamt that Mum said she would come on 25 June. Good Lord! I didn't know this was what it was going to be. I can't write. I'm weak with fear. War again, war between Russia and Germany.* The Germans were here, then they retreated.

---

*The Third Reich attacked the Soviet Union on 22 June 1941.

Horrible days in the basement. The city has been evacuated. You remember, dear Diary, what price I paid for a short moment, today we stayed too ... Grant us, Lord God, that the same thing happens now as it did then. I begged you, Lord God, for my dream to come true and it did, you saved my mother, you gave me him and the thing I've been waiting for for such a long time, and now this war. Give me my mama, save all of us who have stayed here and those who escaped the city this morning. Save us, save Zygu ...

Today they woke me up, I ran outside and saw his silhouette. Oh, I remember that last Saturday evening well. Holy God Almighty, save us. I want to live so badly. I'm humbling myself before You and begging on behalf of us all. Save us. Tonight is going to be terrible. I'm scared, today was horrible too. I believe that You will hear me, that You won't leave me in this awful hour. You have saved me before, save me now.

Date ... I don't even know, Saturday, a week ago ... Why, why speak, why write? God, thank You for saving me.

But my heart is now so heavy
And old thoughts are torn in two
But my heart is held in a leaden fist
And the scary thoughts are new

Now maybe I'll see Buluś! I don't know what's going to happen to us. Dido, I believe nothing bad is going to happen to him. I'm terrified. Almost the whole city is in ruins. A piece of shrapnel fell into our house. These have been horrific days.

Why even try to describe them? Words are just words. They can't express what it feels like when your whole soul attaches itself to a whizzing bullet. When your whole will, your whole mind and all your senses cling to the flying missiles and beg, 'Not this house!' You're selfish and you forget that the missile that misses you is going to hit someone else.

Dear Diary! How precious you are to me! How horrible were the moments when I hugged you to my heart!

And where is Zyguś? I don't know. I believe, fervently, that no harm has come to him. Where he is, I don't know. Good God, protect him from all evil. Zyguś, my only one, because of that farewell of ours this separation feels all the more bitter. We exchanged photographs and said that we might be separated by the war after all; you were making plans for the future, mine and yours, and I was telling you, 'I don't know – there might be a war.' All of this started four hours after the moment you blew me the last kiss up to the balcony. First, we heard a shot, then an alarm, and then a howl of destruction and death. I don't know where Irka and Nora are, either, where anyone is.

That's it for tonight; it's getting dark. God, save us all, Dido, Zygu. Make it so Mum comes and let there be no more misery, God … You will help me, Buluś and God.

1 July 1941[13]

We're all alive and well. All of us, Norka, Irka, Zygu, my friends, my family. And today I want to speak with you as a free person still. Today I'm like everyone else ... Tomorrow, along with other Jews, I'll have to start wearing a white armband. To you I will always remain the same Renia, a friend, but to others I will become someone inferior, I will become someone wearing a white armband with a blue star. I will be a *Jude*.

I'm not crying or complaining. I have resigned myself to my fate. It just feels so strange and sorrowful. My school holidays and my dates with Zygu are coming to an end. I don't know when I'll see him next. Everyone is working today. No news about Mama. God protect us all.

Goodbye, dear Diary. I'm writing this while I'm still independent and free. Tomorrow I'll be someone else – but only on the outside. And perhaps one day I'll greet you as someone else still. Grant me that, Lord God, I believe in You. You will help me, Buluś and God!

3 July 1941, Thursday

Nothing new so far. We wear the armbands, listen to terrifying and consoling news and worry about being sealed off in a ghetto.

He visited me today! Do you hear? I thought I'd go mad with joy and ... confusion. He's working at the clinic, dressing wounds, so there's practice without theory. He's sweet and wonderful, as always. It's a shame he can't go to university now. He'd be an excellent doctor. But he will be one anyway, you'll see. We've arranged to meet tomorrow at the clinic. It seems a little strange, but why not? Even now that we're wearing these armbands – the thing is to be with him.

The border is supposed to open on the 7th, ah, I want Buluś to come so ardently, with my whole heart. Buluś, come. God, bring Mama, let her be with us for better and for worse. Buluś, come. Zygmunt's wonderful. You will help me, Buluś and God!

6 July 1941, Sunday

Days pass … The other day I didn't see Zygu – it was my fault, yes, my fault. Today I had work (physical, of course), one gets bread for it, I also got potatoes, that is I have had a victory in the field of provisioning. I'm very tired, but less with work than with missing Mum and Zygu. I miss them so much, I'm dying of yearning. When? You will help me, Buluś and God!

11 or 12 July 1941, Friday[14]

One loses track of time now. Today I finally saw him. It was, however, a meeting at a distance, and Maciek was there, so naturally nothing much happened.

Z's working at the clinic, changing dressings, stitching wounds and doing other horrible things; they call him doctor. He told me to come to the clinic and have him called, but I'm embarrassed again and I don't know whether I will go.

But what news I've had! I learnt from Z's cousin that he took special care of my notebook with poems and did not let anyone touch it. Comical – I ran away with you and his photograph, and he with my notebook. He said this about me (just listen, isn't it about me?), 'My woman is subtle.'

Where Irka works, so does Z's cousin and many friends from his apartment building; they all want to meet me, they know my name is Rena and that I'm 'Zygu's woman'. I'm horribly embarrassed, because I don't like such fuss, and most of all I don't like to be observed. I'll try to pop over there, but I doubt whether I can make a decent impression, usually I come across as either an uncouth barbarian or an idiot. But I shall see? Still, you will always remain my friend, and Z too. You will help me, Buluś and God.

15 July 1941, Wednesday

Today was very eventful. Namely, in the morning I met Z, and how? I was wandering around the clinic, saw Maciek and he called for Z, who was already at home. We talked and walked for a long time (and because of Z, without armbands). Our walk almost had a tragic conclusion; a policeman approached Z, asked about his nationality and passport. Z said he was Polish and had no passport, and then they both disappeared. I heard it was to the police station, so I ran like mad there and back; hard to describe what I experienced then, the despair, the fear, the guilt, etc. Everything ended well. I saw Z in a doctor's coat (suits him so wonderfully) and rubber gloves.

This event, though it's very distressing, is another brick in the mansion of our love.

In the afternoon I went to the clinic, brave as you like, and met Z (with minor complications). We went for a long walk and it was very, very good. Oh yes, I gave him cigarettes and sweets, a fortune these days! That Z is the most wonderful, the most lovable of all. Tomorrow we are to see each other in M's garden. Z is to pick me up. So I'm waiting ... for Z and for Mum (this is my whole life). Bye, goodnight and good day, Rena.

Next day, Thursday

Yes, I did meet him. He came with Maciek. M left to see Julek, and Zygu and I went for a walk. It's good to write down the details, but today I'll try to relay a few fragments and think aloud a bit, that is on paper. I say fragments, because it is hard for me to describe a three-hour-long conversation. You know, it's no use writing at all, it should be filmed, and on colour film too, so you could see how green his eyes and red his lips are, how unwell – but wonderful – he looks.

Fragments of the film: That he doesn't have anyone anywhere in Jarosław etc., thinks about his family, has no male friends either, and ... female, 'Ah, I knew this was what you meant' (well, despite everything I did not ask about the one in the photograph, but I will), later that he would certainly be able to keep me and that I wouldn't break free from him. Then that he wants to use me to learn how to make injections and that one day he'll do something about my nose and perhaps my height. He picked a fly out of my eye and do you know, it's even pleasant when flies fall into my eyes if it's Z who is taking them out. Later about the graduation exam and what 'he will do with me,' and at the end – that we can die together, holding hands, and share a grave. What do you think, it's very touching indeed, but sad. If there really was a shared grave like that, and us inside, joined in the last, but eternal embrace, and on it the words:

> here lie those …
> who were in love
> who will not be moved
> by any command
> who will no longer be parted
> who are joined together by death's hand

Yes, but not now, now one still has to live, has to strive, try, has to leave something to the world. One has to, for perhaps … one creates happiness, and then come the blessings of the world, of God and people, and one departs with the sense of a duty fulfilled. Z, you probably think otherwise – more wisely. But I think in this maternal way and because, as you say yourself, I am a little too calm. Yes, I know, I'm like a fat, stretching cat. Why do I feel sorrow now, a strange, vague and unfounded sorrow – ah, yes, Dido. So, apart from that,

I think about them all day long, and at night I also dream of them both, Mum and him. And I know that I would give them everything, and myself, and my soul, because I feel that I love those two beings the most, I feel they're closest and dearest to me. When I walk the distant streets with Zygu (such irony of fate, we're uncertain if we'll live, the city's destroyed, war, horrible uncertainty, white armbands), I'm happy, it feels good, and I'd like to grasp, to pin down 'something', something that is, and is not – but is. I walk and look at wonderfully green eyes and listen to words, ironic at times (because we are having an ironic conversation), and that normal world that I know so much about ... the horrors of war ... seems a happy one to me. And this state is not only selfishness (selfishness, i.e., Zygu and I), for example: I laugh. Z says I'm laughing at him, although he knows that's not the case, and after a minute we speak at the same time. Z, 'Laugh if it gives you pleasure, and whenever you can.' Me, 'I won't laugh, because it distresses you,' and we both burst out laughing. In such a state of mind one wants everybody to be happy, wants things to work out beautifully between Nora and Julek B, Irka and Henek, Arianka and Rysiek, and every girl with her beloved; one wants all those loves to mature and turn into exemplary, loving marriages. 'It's madness to think like this today,' do you think I don't know what you want to tell me, old friend. Yes, but lovers are always mad, because love is madness, and madness is life. So may it be good for all of us, may I soon kiss again, and may Zygu always remain the way he is now! If I could, I would sing some mighty hymn to praise God, love and the world, but I couldn't, so I hum in my heart!

Be merry, friend, and laugh
embrace the passers-by
feel good enough to cry,
'I'm living,' that's enough!
And a strange crowd crept out
From cellars hot and damp
A swarm of pale gaunt faces
eyes shone like a lamp
a starving swarm that faints and sways
crept from the rubble, and see
They all fell into a strange wild craze
and laughed in a hysterical haze
and … felt happy
see the one who sat on a pile of rubble
he has no children, no wife, no home
he poured the vodka in his mouth
and puked his blood out in wild laughter
he clung to every passer-by
and howled, 'I live, that's what I'm after!'

18 July 1941, Friday

A meeting. Again, another one similar to all the other ones, but still separately wonderful. Zygu almost kissed me in Maciek's presence, and Maciek – in Zygu's. I will point out that Z was very angry. He dismissed Arianka, dragged me upstairs (so beautiful in that white coat), and then we went for a walk.

As usual, we talked of the war, of medicine, compliments and eyes. I know we're both still waiting, this can be surmised from his various allusions. I'm an awful coward. I try to overcome it, but it is very hard. Z is sulking that I don't trust the strength of his arms and his protective wings. We also spoke about the future. We always do, and we mean by it, although vaguely (at least I do), our shared future. I blurted out one very spiteful thing, i.e., that he wants to get rid of me with his nervous yawning. Then he drew me to himself so strongly, and so close, that ... I don't know. But when I told him that my cousin was coming, well – he got very embarrassed. In the past we had a place but we didn't know how, and now we know how, but we haven't got a place; and I'm certain we are both waiting. You know, it's so idiotic, I am suffused with happy meetings, I string them on the grey thread of my life like wonderful, gleaming pearls, I string them all, equal, smooth, round, and sometimes they grow and strive, strive tirelessly toward that main one, the huge, most beautiful one. It's true what I told you, I'm incurably sick, and you know full well what with, Zygu, because you didn't ask me about it, only laughed, and how – divinely, charmingly. There is something wonderful that one can't write about, it's just what I feel and what I try to express with words in vain, because I'd distort it. Z adores children, he introduced me to this little, sweet thing he frightens with injections. I am grateful to God that Zygu exists and grateful to Zygu that our love exists, and grateful to love that she sets hearts on fire, grateful to hearts that they can love. And you see, everything comes down to this enchanted word: love. We are to see each other on Monday, 'even if there's a downpour'. Ah, if only Mum could arrive before Monday, oooh … You will help me, Buluś and God!

Next day 19, Saturday! (19 July 1941)

Those accidental meetings are rather unpleasant. Was it not better only on Monday? How much better? I wouldn't have been in this mood, there would've been no tears and the heart wouldn't have ached so. I feel better now, because I'd vented a little before I told you – but earlier, a while ago, I was squirming in the sort of pain every loving and every jealous girl suffers. And I myself broke the string I was so joyfully filling with pearls. The 'happy company' broke it, that Lidka who imposes herself on him with her sweetness, and his whole behaviour, and Maciek saying that he wants to move to dentistry on her account (you don't know her and I don't know her, but she hasn't played any part in my life yet and I hope she doesn't) and my stupid, scandalous behaviour.

Yes, I am stupid, I was punished for being so happy, for screaming happiness. It's better now and there's less bitterness in my writing, but I remember, remember how much it hurt. The whole fault lies with me and the jealousy, which I will try to eradicate. All this compensated me a little for Irka's desires and that she kissed Zygu's hand and that he is to feed her. God sent me this little creature as a consolation ... I don't know when ... I'll see you. Lida is horrible. You will help me, Buluś and God!

21 July 1941

Already a month has passed since our memorable kiss. Zygu reminded me of this. He came by with Maciek. Maciek kissed my head by way of greeting, Zygu went red. Well, but when Maciek kissed my face, Z was furious, and rightly so. He tried to make up for it all, and at the same time hide his confusion, so he began hugging me, caressing me so warmly, that I felt extremely moved and ... almost dazed. 'How smooth her face is,' he said – he remembered that once, at the house of that darling little Irusia he smelt my scent, i.e., perfume, Maciek recalled this. He held my hand tightly. When we spoke about that, er ... book, and Maciek was talking about the accident that Z wanted to tell me about on Friday, Z said, 'Maciek, stop, this is a "flower of thought", she can't listen to this,' and took as many pains about it as ... he only can.

Many more, many things I am unable to write about because I do not know how, I have to immortalise in my mind, preserve in my heart, so that I can draw on them in moments of sadness. I must surely know that Z loves me! And one has to ask God that things happen like 'our friend' said they would: after the war, after school, with Zygu, my wonderful husband – it really took my breath away – he wrote in my diary like so: '1) Happiness is the contentment man feels when he can stop wanting even for a moment, and cherish what he has. 2) The sight of something beautiful in art or nature immediately awakens the memory of a beloved woman.' How wonderful and true! I experience it in every moment, even in everyday life, in the fairy-tale life from books, and in the life of thought, i.e., in the land of dreams. Only memories and dreams live there. I love with all my heart. I'm choking on love like – he does … yes, for he also … We both want it, we make meaningful faces, and our lips tilt slightly of their own accord, M even made a remark. Buluś, come, hear me out, assess. I didn't make a date, I don't know, I'm still waiting … You will help me, Buluś and God!

22 July 1941, Tuesday

I went to the parish. I'm starting to get used to it. Z and I went for a walk. I was looking for a defence against Maciek in him. Irusia Hauser, that Irusia, is making huge progress with Fiunio. I wish her happiness and I'm very pleased. I get very confused there. Z is the loveliest, 'Have I ever been angry with you?' How those eyes peer! Bye! Goodnight, I'm off to daydream, although I'm tired. Until the next time I meet Z, when? I'll see the one from my dreams. You will help me, Buluś and God.

28 July 1941, Friday

I have already seen Zygu and had a sulk, and I missed him, 'and so it goes'. And in the meantime I live with no news of Mum. Apparently it's bad there. Poor Mama. Whatever I eat,

I think of her, I share every bite with her in my thoughts, like I do every joy and sadness. Please, God, may it really happen, that I might share everything with her. Mama, I'm writing this to you! I'm writing as if the words scribbled here had some magical power and could summon you. May they sound out so that they can be heard by the Great Lord God in heaven and you, dearest, all the way there.

Yesterday I saw Jews being beaten. Some monstrous Ukrainian in a German uniform hit every one he met. He hit and kicked them, and we were helpless, so weak, so incapable.... We had to take it all in silence. And at that moment my only consolation was the thought of revenge, oh yes, revenge is sweet, but it should not be bloody. And I want to live until I can hold my head up high, when I'm an equal, free person in a free, democratic country! I want to be happy then with Zygu, with everyone who has gone through this hell of dishonour, slaughter and humiliation. I want to be happy, I want my dreams to come true, and you will help me with this, God, because I believe in You, because You have never let me down!

Every morning whole troops of wounded Germans walk past. And ... I'm sorry for them. I'm sorry for those young, tired boys, far away from their homeland, mother, wife, perhaps children. Someone says heartfelt prayers for them too, and someone weeps for them during sleepless nights. Such is the irony of fate ...

I curse the hundreds, thousands, millions
when new recruits go to war

may they all meet their bullets
may neither of them come back to what they knew before.

May grenades' horrible hail
bring them all down one by one
may the whole cursed army fail
For the blood of fathers, brothers, sons!

Slowly he walks, harried and weak
a soldier, look, how young
wounded in hand, or in arm, hard to speak
his uniform hangs from his arm.

He walks, he limps and rests by the wall
He's sweating, he won't walk too far
His gaze is a helpless begging call
His eyes, oh how sad they are!

As if in his blackest depths
a complaint now burnt with alarm
look, see how young I am
and how they did me harm.

I learnt all life the hard way
I knew next to nothing before
my mother, my father, my house went away
I had to fight – but who for?

Now on my way back ... and again
my eyes are flashing with grief
I cry and my heart's full of sorrow
I'm weak and I can't find relief.

This is the fate, it's the life
and who can explain to me why
I curse the thousands and millions
And for the one wounded, I cry?

6 August 1941

Moods and thoughts, and words, all change ... They change, flicker from wave to wave. I'm pleased, because my heart tells me Mum will come. There will be a message from her next week.

I'm sad when I hear that they are to send us, that there's to be a ghetto, that it's so bad. And apart from this my personal trifles make me lose the last dregs of spirit.

Lida is making disgusting passes at Zygu in my presence. He behaves very stupidly. He's awfully selfish, why doesn't he think about me? Why? But I am already making solemn promises to myself that without an invitation or an arranged meeting I will not go to the parish. With Lida it's not making a pass, it's something natural, and how unnatural! Irka did a vile thing. I'm angry with Zygu, but all my worries are consoled with one thought – Mum! You will help me, Buluś and God. Mama, Mama will come??? When ... Mum. When ... Zygu.

11 August 1941, Sunday

I'm working. I have reasons to be pleased. I'm expecting Mum any day now. Each strike of the clock may bring her to me. I'm seeing Zygu, he's sweet, good, darling. He proposed that we get a photograph taken together, the two of us. I have reasons to be pleased, and yet I yearn for 'that night' …

> Such a night happens once in a lifetime
> so in memories it can linger on
> so it can be dreamt about day- and night-time
> and remembered as years are long gone
> Such a night – it's in dreams it begins
> In a girl's wishes
> Such a night turns a memory, it seems
> Like a smile, it perishes
> Yes, I remember the charms of the moon
> and holding the head I so missed
> and a bird's midnight tune
> and how you kissed

I can't write any more, but every night I miss that night so, I miss it, I miss those lips … ah, that night lives in me. Those nights exist to awaken yearning, and then an unquenched thirst. Tomorrow? You will help me, Buluś and God.

12 August 1941, Monday

It's a shame I talked about that dog. I feel better today than I have felt for days. Yes, today. Zyguś was perhaps the loveliest!

He gave me a photograph of himself and wrote: 'To darling sweet lips.' Zygmunt said, 'I see my sweet lips, so I'm thinking of lips,' and generally he says that 'this' is an understood and certain thing, and 'this' is precisely our love.

We walked far, avid for 'only sensual delights', Z said that, and we sat down, I did not want to sit in his lap, I don't know why, but I can't. I sat next to him, with leaves stuck to my lips all over. Why? I imagine it's exactly because I was choking with ... Z embraced me like he did then, and like then the scent dazed me. It was quiet again, the road empty and the field, and the pond, and when he'd finished unsticking all the little leaves from my lips and when ... two Germans came.

I can't describe everything, so I'll mention the 'alley of love', i.e., Z and I'm off to daydream, live through everything all over again.

Z invited me, he said he had a nice little room, but what of it? And you know what I wrote to him, the dearest darling? Z was awfully pleased, but that's not enough, with a whole slew of words I would not be able to say how close he is to me (and to reciprocate). Zygu, our every meeting is a priceless gift to me. Can one repay God for the sun and the sky, and life, can we speak of it? We are to have regular meetings on Thursdays. You will help me, Buluś and God.

15 August 1941, Friday

Z said that I absolutely should give you to Mum to read, I should not keep secrets from her. Mama! Come, and I'll open this diary to you, and my heart at the same time!

I'm ill. I have a temperature and a sore throat. Yesterday I wanted to tell you that this makes me inordinately happy. Zygu came to visit, sat by me, and was, well – as always. He wanted to examine me. I was happy, but I always talk myself down. Yes, I told Norka and Irka about it, and talked myself into sadness.

Z came today too, he was sweet, but whenever he comes to me, the whole 'esteemed company' gathers, and I'm upset, Zygu is too. Apart from them came Rena F, Lunka and Lidka, but more on that later. I will have a photograph, but I had to give him the one from the graduation anyway, he asked me.

Apart from my illness I don't really have anything on my conscience – but still, how many worries weigh down my heart. Mama, when will you come? I haven't heard anything about that, or from Lila ...

You know, Z held you in his hands today, he wanted to read you, I got very nervous, and in the end he asked, 'Well, but when I become a doctor, will you let me read it?' Zygu, do I know what will happen before you become one? But may God make it happen. That you are a doctor and that I can give it to you. I miss ... You will help me, Buluś and God.

16 August 1941

It's a normal, grey, wartime day. It's like those sixty-three days that have already passed, and like the days that are to come. It's a neurotic day, drizzly, cold, unfriendly ... What do I know? I reply, 'I don't know,' in advance to all the questions I desperately want to ask. Why is Mum not writing, why is there no sign from her? What has happened to her? Why do we live in fear of searches and arrests? Why can't we go for a walk, because 'children' throw stones? And why, why, why? I'm overcome by some infectious fear, no, I feel no foreboding, but still – I am so afraid, so very afraid. Miraculous God, keep and save my one and only mum.

Maybe one day the sun will shine again …
maybe one day we'll walk, me and you
through a world that has awoken
from a long winter's dream
to have our students' rendezvous
as the memory holds what's dear
maybe one day yet, one day
we will sit there on the bench
forget and remember what we may
maybe once more we'll get 'lost'
in an alley lined with pines
with a scary premonition
it may well have been 'on our minds'
maybe a green blade of grass
when we face the final day
and maybe for real this time
a flash of sun – a golden ray?

You will help me, Buluś and God.

9 in the evening!

Something's bursting within me, choking me! One wants more, endlessly more. Oh, how good it is to be kissing lovely red lips, how good to be caressed 'like that', talk about the taste of kisses, about love. About obstacles to our love, etc. All that hurt has already been erased, a kiss wiped away the reason why … why I cried on 1 May. Oh, how good it is to kiss … kiss … kiss. You will help me, Buluś and God.

25 August 1941, Monday[15]

On Friday there was the first letter from Mama, then a second, then third, and then dread, a horrible fear for her life and ours, and everyone's. My heart's been so heavy since this morning and now and always I'm calling to God and placing our fates in His hands. He's the only one who's never disappointed me; He will hear my voice. I want Him to protect Mum and return her to me from far away. God, protect her and all of us from everything that is evil and protect my Zygu from the evil that can happen to him. I'm suffering today, but I thank You that in those horrible days of the turmoil of war You have sent me a bright ray of light. I'm writing down what I feel, and I feel gratitude, deep, sincere, immortal.

Zygu talked to me like nobody else apart from my mother … He said he felt sorry for me and that I deserve happiness in the future for the things I am suffering now, and know, Zygu, that it is for always! He said that the hearth and home is only necessary in childhood, but I know he wanted to console me.

Good, darling Zygu! I am not worthy of you even in part. You wanted to substitute my mother with those caresses and console me, that's what you said. Zyguś, my mama will give me those maternal caresses, and these ones, they console me very much. You will help me, Buluś and God. God protect Mama and us all. God and my entreaties will help you, Mama.

27 August 1941

War! War! No end in sight. I would like to write something, but I can't. I'm dreaming, dreaming, dreaming. All that's left are dreams, hope, and what … what's left to you, Zyguś, yes, and me too. Oh, to see my mother just for a moment. You will help me, Buluś and God.

28 August 1941, Thursday

It's no use moaning, 'Don't cry, don't cry, it won't do.' It's what must be, it's necessary for us to walk with our heads lowered now, to run along streets, to shiver. For the meanest streetwalker to provoke and insult me in Zygu's presence and he can't help me, or I him. Trifles, really, but it is very, very hard. I've felt a little confused since Zygu's lecture about Nietzsche, Werne* and their ideology, about how he's for young marriages, 'childless for now'. You know, my attitude to those 'serious' matters is awfully silly and childish. For

---

* Renia possibly means Werner May, the author of *Deutscher National-Katechismus*.

example I completely do not understand that Rena who works with Zygu and says that I have 'a unique face', but do you understand me? Well, yes, you know! No, this has nothing to do with her. What is it really that makes me feel indignant, or worried, or bored?

Rejoice, rejoice
this is your feast
oh gutter, cellar, tavern, inn
the world is yours, we are your toys
streetwalker with a nasty grin
today you bully, yell and curse
you bring me low and make me worse
you, flowing here on gutter's scum
from what is lowest, rotten, vile
the only homeland you have got
is a pile of rubbish and a lustful smile
Your day – remember
you'll see the day
when I will spit, not turn away
you and 'your' lover, vermin both,
will travel back to swamp and sloth
in which you brood, cavort and sway
And I will … no!
Although I hate
My contempt and disgust are too great
Your kin, your sins, you cursed one
Mean that to you no harm is done

Like snakes and worms that live in filth
Because they would not be killed – just despised

You will help me, Buluś and God.

1 September 1941

A year ago … Oh, a whole year has gone by. I've experienced so much good and bad. But perhaps more good. Maybe Mama will come soon after all. Today Z came and I felt some sort of thing when he said, 'Well, talk as if we're married.' With that Hala – a trifle and that thing, you know, with the one from the photograph, also a trifle. Generally everything is a trifle, apart from my mad love. Oh, God, how I love him, how much. Even though he thinks I'm the opposite of dynamite, still … ha ha ha! I gave him a photograph to whet the appetite. I haven't seen Maciek in a long time. Despite everything, I like Maciek. Why do I give away that I'm jealous? You will help me, Buluś and God. And you, Mama, come as soon as you can!

10 September 1941, Sunday

And sometimes it's like it was today. And today it's – I don't know – today it seems to me that everything is stupid, love, and him, and life, and all the daily matters. Everything in reality that is stripped of its romantic ornaments and flourishes is odious. No! Not odious, just genuine, just how it truly is. And on days like today it feels that this can be soothed by music, light, resonant … Yes, on those days all that's left is music and dreams. But not the dreams related to reality, those that are pink, but still connected to life, no! Detached, fragrant, colourful dreams – like poetry. Ah, I would like to know how to play beautifully. One can conjure the soul's every state with music – to only know how. Today I feel an aversion towards love, no, not for the first time. It is unfair, I know, but I don't understand that today, I can't believe in anything. Today it's good to listen and think …

> My chiming song, keep sailing so
> Across the Danube's deep blue flow
> Through waves that glitter like a star
> Carry on, song … far

So I'm thinking, and thinking, and dreaming, and mocking life's worries, gossip, jealousy and love, I don't know …

> Life is some ugly, worthless stuff
> stripped of its charms, it's bare and rough
> so calculating, hard and dry
> dirty and daft, though you may try
> it's lewd and boring and it's weird
> with stuff you cried at, hurt at, feared
> it's cruel, noisy, and it's mocking
> two-faced and empty and so shocking …
> J. Strauss*

---

* Poems inspired by the waltz 'The Blue Danube', composed by Johann Strauss in 1867.

My chiming song, keep sailing so
across the Danube's deep blue flow
through waves that glitter like a star
Where tears and grief no longer are
in a land of dreams
wind and the clouds swap poses
and there's a sea down below
of orange flowers and roses
and dusks and dawns are pale green
and the dreams are just like mists
coloured ... and nothing's felt or seen
but ethereal and full of shimmer
ever so light and unreal
fragrant and dreamy in feel
slow, dizzy and lazy
careless and hazy
dreams
fragrant, bright and ever sweet
loveliest, when senses never meet ...

11 September 1941, Thursday

4.00 in the afternoon. I need to leave the house. I am simply escaping Zygu. If this had happened, let's say, a month or two ago, I'd have cried my eyes out and screamed that he's foul! Not today – nothing at all, as if nothing's happened. It's strange ... and yet I can't even say myself whether I'm at least a little sorry. I don't know if it's over, but this is exactly what I've been suspecting on the 'subject'. A woman senses it, oh, yes, she has a well-developed warning system. You know, I don't even hate 'the other one', I will admit I find her somewhat attractive, like Natasha does Katya. But this whole thing is a little different, although I've also been hurt – but never humiliated! I'll see you again today, I'm going to Norka's. To my only Nora I've got left. I've also got you, Mama, and you, dear Diary, and it's almost like it used to be. Only there is no yearning left for something close ... unknown ... To be clear-headed about what I feel, I'd say this: I very much want to impress them with something, I very much want to take my revenge in the same way, but for the sake of revenge itself, for – pleasure. I used to despise this attitude and today I admit it's awful and when I perhaps become such an easy girl, it will only be your fault, Z, and my jealousy's, that sacred feelings, sacred rules and sacred love have been desecrated ... You will help me, Buluś and God.

14 September 1941

But still – it's sad, so very sad, so utterly, so horribly ... I didn't tell you that evening about him coming – what for, anyway? I didn't want to tell you anything because I felt that I loved him the most then. And now – I do not. I'm waiting. Waiting's tired me out. And I'm afraid of tomorrow and I want it to come now, and I feel aversion, and doubt. And sometimes I don't want to say anything, only think and be

Bernard and Róża Spiegel on their wedding day, 1923.

Renia (*right*) and her cousin Lila, *c.* 1937.

Renia and Ariana playing in the Dniester River
in Zaleszczyki, *c.* 1935.

Renia in a boat on the Dniester
River in Zaleszczyki, *c.* 1936.

Renia, Róża and Ariana in the city of
Przemyśl, *c.* 1937.

Ariana, Róża and Renia in a vineyard in the region of Zaleszczyki,
1935 or 1936.

Ariana and her grandfather,
Markus Finkel, 1936.

Grandma Anna Finkel and Ariana
in Przemyśl, c. 1935.

Renia, Róża and Ariana near the Dniester
in Zaleszczyki, 1935.

Róża, Ariana and Renia eating
ice cream, most likely in Przemyśl, 1935.

Ariana, Renia and Róża (*all standing*) in Zaleszczyki, 1936.

Ariana (*far left*), Róża and Renia at the Lesieczniki grape farm in the region of Zaleszczyki, 1937.

Róża and Ariana in Skole, 1936.

Róża and Renia in Przemyśl, *c.* 1939,
before the start of the war.

ARIANA
Polska Shirley Temple

Słodka sześcioletnia dziewczynka umie wszystko.
Śpiewa nie gorzej od niejednej artystki operetkowej,
tańczy jak Ginger Rogers, recytuje niczem dobry ad-
wokat...

Widzieliśmy krótki film, gdzie Ariana pokazuje
wszystkie swoje talenty.

I nie dziwimy się wcale, że zachwycają się nią reży-
serowie Lejtes, Waszyński, Tristan, Adwentowicz i inni.

Młodzież polska przestanie wkrótce uważać Shirley-
kę za jedyne cudowne dziecko, gdyż Arianka bije ame-
rykańską gwiazdeczkę pod każdym względem.

Szkoda, że film „Granica" w którym nasza mała ar-
tystka gra w epizodzie, nie jest dozwolony dla mło-
dzieży.

Szkoda, że „Gehenna" i „Kariera Nikodema Dyzmy"
w których Arianka weźmie udział są także tylko dla
dorosłych.

Ale cieszymy się, że nasza rodzima przyszła gwiazda
daje się coraz lepiej poznać publiczności i realizato-
rom filmowym.

Po występach w radio Arianka wystąpi na swoim
poranku scenicznym, gdzie grać będzie na fortepianie,
śpiewać, tańczyć i „robić" artystkę filmową i recyto-
wać.

Zobaczycie wtedy wszyscy, jak wiele prawdy kryje
przysłowie „cudze chwalicie, swego nie znacie, sami nie
wiecie co posiadacie".

Ariana 'the Polish Shirley Temple',
in Warsaw, *c.* 1936.

Norka and Renia, around
sixteen years old, 1940.

Norka and Renia in Przemyśl, *c.* 1940.

Ariana and Róża, who were now known as Elżbieta (Elizabeth) and
Marianna, in Warsaw at the Hotel Europejski, where Marianna worked, *c.* 1943.

Elizabeth and George Bellak on their wedding day, New York City, 1965.

Elizabeth's children, Andrew and Alexandra Renata Bellak, at Jones Beach, 1976.

Alexandra and Andrew at Alexandra's twenty-fifth birthday celebration, 1995.

silent. And sometimes I want to be evil and hated, I want to spite everyone, I want to torment and hurt everyone – no, not everyone, not him, and not her either. But really I'm only sad, utterly, horribly sad … Sad, but I can't cry, I simply do not have the strength. So I look at the wild ivy, how raindrops stream down its leaves, and somehow it feels like I'm crying.

> Springtime – fresh and green
> a wild vine climbs
> rises full of life
> onto the balcony glass.
> It reddens in the summer,
> pales with the autumn winds
> and hangs its head, in sorrow,
> sad for what now must pass.

> I like sun and the flowers in spring
> When I also feel a joyful thing
> when the laughter's in me and nearby
> When around me life can abound
> When the earth is all joyful all round
> like me!

> And when I am both angry and sad
> then I like a grey day, wet and bad,
> and a cloudy and tearful dark sky
> crying just like my heart, full of rain,

quiet, full of tiresome pain
like me ...

That's when I like a mist on a hill
and a sadness that wants yearning still
and the voids you can't calmly pass by
Polish verses, of autumn, of tears,
that are filled with the sadness and fears
like me.

No, I didn't mean to write that, but I'm very, very sad. Ah!
What a rainy, nice day. You will help me, Buluś and God.

18 September 1941, Thursday

How good that I didn't write throughout this week. I didn't
write or I would have blasphemed. I suffered, that's true, and
a lot too – but now it's fine again, perhaps even better than
it had been. Because every time there's a bit of a worry and
some crying, and hours spent thinking, I am more convinced
that I love my wonderful boy very, very much. And an
apology – although one can't really talk of apologies if one
were not angry – confirms this conviction too. So it will be
even better than it has been, because Arianka is at Mama's
and she's to bring her here, and maybe I'll finally see her. Ah,
I've let it slip; it was supposed to be a surprise. Everything at
once, oh, God – really, how can I thank You? Now I believe
in happy endings ... I believe and trust You, for You have

given me what I asked for. I love You. You will help me, Buluś and God.

22 September 1941, Monday

Now the dream has practically come true. It's the New Year*
today and the dream has come true? Actually not completely,
but in 99 per cent it has. And I wish all dreams came true
like this. It feels so strange. To think that Mama is so close,
that she's in the same city, that she's thinking about me
now, that she'd like to embrace me as much as I her ... to
think there's a horrible river, a river people have made
horrible. A river which has been separating us for two years –
and now again. Why, it's unthinkable that I can't see Mother
when she's here so close, so close. Arianka, I'm so jealous,
she is with her. And now she will leave again and I won't even
kiss her. I won't say anything and again – but for how long –
and again this question, when? But still, there's a weight off
my heart that it's not so far, that You have brought her closer
to me, Good Lord God. How good would it be if I could
tell her everything, tell her about today and these past two
years? You know, Mama, I am who I have always been, your
reticent one, all 'yours', but maybe I feel somehow more,
oh, I don't feel that well. All because of Z. I don't know
why I'm abashed by this thing I've dreamt of? Why do all

---

*The year 5702 of the Jewish calendar started that day.

those kisses only burn me up after he leaves? I start to feel everything, I writhe on the sofa, I don't sleep, my senses are stimulated to their limit. And when 'this' happens, when it lasts two hours, then Z doesn't have to threaten me with bromide injections, etc. Why? I don't know ... but I know, that is, I feel instinctively, that much has changed about Zygu, I can't say whether for better or for worse, because I 'generally have no firm opinion about anything, damn it', but the changes are surely there. It even seems that, er, well, I don't know ... In any case there is a distinct influence of that 'freethinking and free-doing' woman. And I have a stupid, odious, irritating feeling, aah! I am an idiot of the highest order that I can even say something against the prettiest boy and besides, I know that I love him very, very much anyway – but still, I am horribly upset, and I think I already know why, namely! Because I am stupider and uglier than he is, and I stand lower in every respect. 'What can I do apart from writing poems?' Well, but do not try to persuade me that you have to teach me everything, because you don't know everything yourself, you have no idea. Blind leading the blind. But I feel much better now, I love you so much now, dear Diary! Phew, what a relief. I'm not telling you the silly details; it's better this way. Although they're not so silly, they're sweet, but always, well ... the secretiveness. It's much better now, oh, almost good. So goodnight, Mama mine, I can say this to you for the first time in two years. You won't hear me, but I know that you're thinking about me too and wishing me a good night. Mama, come to me.

Come, my only Bunia. You're the only one who always loves me steadily and you don't laugh at me. Bye, Mama, sleep well; may you dream that everything I prayed for yesterday comes true. Today I wish for a favourable end of the war, for my parents to reconcile, Zyguś for me only and good things for everyone. You will help me, Buluś and God.

29 September 1941, Monday[16]

I'm on this side. You know, I'm here with Mama. Just think, I have finally found myself beyond the river and met with Mama. How did I get here? It's a secret. Know only that I've been through a lot and was very scared. I am still afraid of Wednesday. The dream has practically come true, I'm seeing Mum and I've got a letter from Zygu. I'm still waiting for something in politics and I know it will happen, like that other thing did. You will help me, Buluś and God.

5 October 1941

For Buluś (letter to Mother). I love you so, so much, and 'I love the eyes that are green.' Yours, Renia.

> A ship sails for a haven after a gale
> A bird that's scared away returns to hide in its nest
> A child, in trust, chooses its mother's arms …
> to cry its grief away, and soothe the pain as it knows best.

For Buluś:

When pain starts burning
Or you feel the hearts' frosty chill
When you feel ground to dust
By the turning wheels of life
Shelter under her wings
She'll hear you out and understand she will
You will feel good again and free from strife.
There's sadness for those who are in grief and pain
Pity for those whose hearts were broken again
Shame on those who face both contempt and fear
But you're really unhappy without your mother dear
I suffocate in small rooms
And feel crowded in vast halls
They won't bring down the sadness
Even if it tumbles and falls
In life's vast, great expanse
The winds of life blow wild
They'll blow away all sorrows
For one sweet moment mild!

     6 duvet covers
     8 pillowcases
     2 small pillows
     3 sheets
     2 tablecloths

9 October 1941, Thursday

I haven't seen you for such a long, long time. I've missed you. I was unable to talk, to write. So many thoughts have gathered in my head, they have made it heavy, although this little head of mine is usually light and empty. And now I don't know where to start? So much has happened ... So maybe I'll tell you briefly. I've dreamt through the dream. I was with Mama and it seemed so wonderful, so extraordinary, this thing which for others is so wonderful and natural. But then also my mother is different. She is a friend, a peer. And now I'm back on the other side, yearning and wanting again. But listen, my dearest Diary, listen and listen, because it seems to me that you're praying for me, that your prayers are being answered, you sweet little notebook that contains the depths of my soul. Mama writes me letters, so long, heartfelt and loving that I must cry. But that is nothing, I still believe! I believe in God, in you and in Mother. I believe it will be like Zyguś says. We'll survive this war somehow, and later ... ah, will it really be as he says? Anyway, we'll both see, you and I, and either we'll be disappointed, or perhaps we will be happy after all, you and I. Because if I laugh, how could you be sad, you 'little looking glass' of mine (this is what Buluś called you)?

My own diary can be just as cheerful
Or nasty and mean as me
After all, we went to school

Together, and on dates, and a game
to see ...
So it has just the same wild ideas
the same laughter and yells and tears
there's more bad and less good there to see
because just like me, it's hard to bear
sometimes shy, sometimes with a lewd stare
sometimes trusty and the one faithful friend
or a grump on whom you cannot depend
my own diary is really just me
But on days when I'm really in trouble
it becomes my own soul's little double
there inside – both in dreams and in verse
in the yearning and each moment that hurts
every word is as sad as can be
where it's poor, and afraid, and it's shy,
where it's sad with no tears left to cry,
there my diary really is me.

Yes, yes, this is what I'm like. I'm just one of millions of
girls walking through this world – uglier than some, prettier
than others, but still, different from all of them. Zyguś, he's
also different from everyone, he's so good and wonderful, and
subtle, and sensitive ...

They came over with Maciek once, Zyguś got angry with
me, because I behaved as if I didn't know him. I didn't do
it on purpose; I didn't want to distress him. Poor Zyguś
couldn't sleep. But he's no longer angry. Mama, why do you

say I shouldn't drown in those green, deceptive eyes? Can you not see, I have already drowned, but those eyes are not deceptive?

I really like it when Z talks seriously about medicine, the future and so on. It makes me want to laugh a little, but it feels very good and blissful, as if Buluś was wishing me a good night. You know, I told him about that whole affair with RK, that I was distraught, that I went through hell. What for? Although I might tell him as much as possible, for now I've packed it into a separate suitcase and left in the 'lumber room of the soul'. In fact, it doesn't even hurt any more, and I don't think about it.

Z became my guardian, he said he would take care of me. As a matter of fact Buluś asked them to, all three of them. But Z must tell Maciek that he doesn't need to do it. All in all, Zygmunt and Maciek are friends, real friends, but ... but. It's good that I can write it all out. I feel the load in my heart and my head lightening. I can't describe 'it all' with Zygu, and you know why, because now it's much more than when it could still be described. No descriptions, but it sinks deep into the heart and surrounds his image there with a beautifully warm, golden halo.

Mama, forgive me that I can't heed your words. You see, I can't, I can't do it any other way, it is always like this – whole heart, whole adoration, whole being. I really can't, not even from the outside. Maybe, maybe I will love somebody else in my life, but if so – it will be the same. It's this or nothing.

Zygu wants to read you and he said, 'You'll see, we'll be reading it together when I'm a doctor and I will laugh and you will laugh.' I hope he said it at an auspicious hour. I thought about how I've put in new pages which may last until the time when, when ... well, anyway, it can be later or much earlier, and you will be my friend no matter what, even if you're scandalised and red with anger, so what of it?

Zygu wants me to remain what I am, Buluś would like that too – and me? I am very curious ... anyway, let them be happy! But 'everything in the world passes slowly'. I love all three of you, each one differently, and you too. I think it will be like in my dreams, grant me that, Lord, and you, Buluś, give me your blessings. You will help me, Buluś and God.

10 October 1941, Friday[17]

It's so sad at home. Today the piano was taken away, so the flat is empty; today Arianka went to Mama, so the soul is empty. It's cold and dark, and lonely, and somehow ... aah, I'm left all alone and all I have is a letter from Buluś, or rather letters. I'll write a poem here. Actually I've put everything I feel and experience in the letter to Mama. And now I'm cold and my eyelids are drooping, and my fingers are numb. I'll go to bed, but not to sleep, no! I'll daydream a little, maybe I'll feel lighter. I'll think about being with Buluś, that the world is so good and warm and sunny, we open the windows and the lovely scent of the full carnations from Stawki enters the house. Or that it's a cloudy, rainy autumn and I've got a cosy room with a fireplace. It is this little house that Zyguś and I live in, working there in the evenings in the glow of the fire. And I write, write a lot and my legs aren't cold like now. And then I go to another room and our children are sleeping there, the wonderful angels, none sweeter. But it must be warm, must absolutely be warm, because my fingers are awfully cold.

It's stupid what I think about when I'm so alone and they leave, when the cold days will be full of yearning again. Buluś, but you'll come back soon. I'm off to daydream, after all God remembers about me, perhaps He will really make those dreams come true ... Renia. You will help me, Buluś and God.

17 October 1941, Friday

I'm alone again. I have already had a letter from Buluś, from Warsaw. Jarosia is away too. Bimba* is ill, Dido nervous and tormenting me especially – and I am alone. But am I really alone, no! I've got a whole guard of dreams, lovely, delicate, shy, and I've got you and Zygu and Nora.

Meetings with Zygu are so pleasant, ever more pleasant. He's even more wonderful than I thought, this 'guardian' of mine.

Norka is teaching me English now. I'm learning eagerly, but I would learn French even more eagerly, and I will! Learn with all my might to speak French. After all, nobody can take

---

* *Bimba* – Renia's grandmother.

knowledge away from me. I must learn, I promise myself that. All that I can. Maybe one day I will really go to the faraway France of my dreams – no, not I – we will go. Yes. 'Z will be driving a Buick, and I'll be sleeping with my head on his shoulder. And then he'll enroll me in Collège de France. And he'll buy me the sort of bedroom I frequently travel to in my thoughts.' Zyguś can dream aloud so beautifully, like a big child. And in the meantime Z is preparing bloody revenge against me for those Sanok influences. I have some regrets perhaps, but he'll have his revenge. I can't help it that he's so tyrannical and firm, tough luck. His character is absolute. But I'd rather agree to everything than finish this, and that's that! Maybe we'll see each other tomorrow. You will help me, Buluś and God.

25 October 1941, Saturday

You're pretty now, handsome, bound … I've started missing you, being able to write. I want to write a lot, a lot, so many confused thoughts linger in my head. Zygu says he absolutely must read you, and I don't want to think about it, because then I'd write dishonestly (as it is, there are places where I'm not delighted with my honesty), I'd write for him then, and at the same time not for him, because this diary would not be genuine. Still, your sad pages are the sweetest, at least they're not so banal – he said, she said. But so it goes, when one's pleased, delighted with something, one's words get all confused in the enthusiasm and there are only cries of oh, ah, this and that!

And now, now I should study, after all I'm no longer at school, after all I need to do something for the future, after all I'm already seventeen! And it's just now that some lazy, awful apathy grips me, brr, I can't be bothered to do anything at all now … Now I stand at the window and watch the wild ivy getting wet, look at various people moving in the street and think about their worries and how they feel. Or I look at the women and think about which one has already had intercourse and what did she look like then? Yes, this one is old and wrinkled, but she used to be young and then … and this one, how strange, and that one … it's all laughable … poverty in its rags is laughable, people pinched with cold and hunger are laughable, and how laughable is the man afraid of the soldier, talking to him, smiling, standing at attention, bobbing … ? An old man in front of a youth. And prisoners? Those swaying, blackened skeletons, how funny the way they rock on those spindly legs, and how squeaky and quiet their voices – they're also laughable, laughable – it makes me feel faint. I go to the stove then, lean against it and daydream … Because what else is there to do? And even if there was, I can't be bothered about anything anyway … I somehow, strangely, can't be bothered about absolutely anything … Or maybe I can, yes! About dreams coming true … You will help me, Buluś and God.

29 October 1941, Wednesday

All day yesterday and today I've wanted to talk to you. Yesterday I felt so bad, so sad and empty … I had this awful feeling of an 'inability to act'. I thought about learning mathematics and shorthand writing, and a language; I wanted to do it with all my soul, but at the same time I knew that I wouldn't raise a finger to do it, I knew my hands wouldn't obey and I myself would turn out to be powerless. Mama is right. Someone always has to give me directions, order me around, force me into things, even if I myself want them. And now Mama's far away again with Jarosia, and 'the one for me,' in Buluś's words, he can't, because he has no power over me, and generally it's not that ... Now I'm sinking into some sort of stupor and what is it? – an aversion? I don't think so. I was thinking yesterday and I said this to Nora, 'You know, Norka, I'm tired of life.' This sentence coming out of a seventeen-year-old girl's mouth amuses me, and it's not accurate. It's not life I'm tired of, because after all I haven't really lived yet; I'm tired of anticipation, idleness, and maybe precisely the desire for life. Because not so long ago there was a time when I was intoxicated with sensual love, kisses, caresses, touches, and all this was enough for me, so much so that I forgot one can desire something more. Now? No! Now I have come to my senses. Have I rejected that? No! It's just as important as what is now.

Don't look for solace only in the senses
they burn bright as a flame, fade away just so
If you look to your comfort in learning, then hence it's
where your thirst will be quenched, where your soul
did go

Yes, that soul's lying there, and not moving at all, though I myself often move away. I will give you an example, proof, or maybe not, not proof, well, judge for yourself. Yesterday at 5.00 p.m. I was supposed to go to Nora's for an English lesson. It took me ages to set out, I was putting it off (anyway, Nora couldn't have been at home yet). So I was all the more still, just watching the pretty, colourful, carefree film scenes. My dreams made up this film. And any moment would break the plot, so although the hands of the clock were rushing onwards mercilessly, I didn't leave my chair, what for? It would be like leaving the cinema during a screening. Still, I went. I went, but ... not to Nora's. I went, of all places, to Belania, to Helka, to Giza, those girls one meets most frequently, just those completely normal girls. I wanted to listen to their conversations, their thoughts, their plans; I went 'for a bit of gossip'. The whole 'gang' wasn't there, only Belania. That was enough for me. Belania is, after all, the life and soul of the group, she's the cleverest and most intelligent of them all. I came, I sat down, I listened to some news, then I told her what I knew, and I asked, 'All right, so what do you talk about every day?' 'Food,' says Belania. 'What do you dream about?' 'About once eating so much I can't stand up.' Well, I knew everything then. Was I disappointed? Maybe not, to an extent I'd been prepared for it. I knew, and even agreed with Belania that it's best to have four 'sweethearts', each of them of a different nationality. So I returned to my interrupted film. I really do prefer that to baked potatoes. It's good that there's something to tear me away from sorting out breakfast, lunch, dinner and breakfast again. I am glad, after all, to have my colourful, faraway film. Nora dreams too, but differently, in a more real, logical way. My fantasies are unrelated to everything, except, perhaps, my vivid, very vivid imagination. Maybe I never properly appreciated Nora. She is admirable. She's eager to learn and there's a readiness about her, but not just readiness – she does learn, she reads all she can (but never worthless books). Nora is a well-rounded person, the sort of girl you don't meet any more. She says she's matured this year. I would say she's even more noble now, because 'suffering ennobles one', and she's been through so much – she even 'didn't dare to dream'. And here, again, a difference between our dreams. Norka, she's so brave, after all she's got nobody, she's all alone (with that faraway 'pretty boy'), and me, if I'd been alone, without Zygu? God forbid, maybe I'd break down, and maybe I'd do what she does ... But no, I don't want to! I just don't have the strength. I would have to walk alone, and otherwise I can at least imagine that I'm supported by someone's arm, by 'His' arm. Will the war end soon? God grant us that. Tomorrow I'll probably see Zygu, perhaps chat to you too. You will help me, Buluś and God.

3 November 1941, Monday

Since we last saw each other I've often felt like sitting down with you and crying. I've felt so bad at times. Dido and Bimba are nervous and vent their whole anger on me, keep reminding me how they've deigned to let me stay with them etc. Parents would never say that to their own child, but they're not my parents after all. So sometimes (when I wake from my fantasies) I am terrified by what's happening around me. But this only lasts a moment and then I fall asleep again.

Buluś is there with Jarusia. They will come here to me. I'd like her to be with me, I want her to leave Warsaw (typhus), but I'm afraid of this stay. Buluś is so sensitive. She'd be very hurt by a statement like that. It hurts me too. I am strangely sensitive about it and I feel like great, great harm is done to me ... In fact I don't cry often – but I always cry when it happens. I'd like to snuggle into something warm and nice then, and settle into a comfy armchair, and throw those worries into a roaring fireplace, and soar again. Such is my catlike nature that I need warmth (yes, Buluś, you know), much, much warmth, all the more for how little I've experienced it in life. Because apart from you and Jarosia nobody in the world can give it to me. Maybe you'll think – him? No, he gives a fire that explodes and dies down. I feel it, I feel it all, because I'm sensitive.

Guess who paid me a visit today? Ludwik! I've actually been thinking about him lately. Today he came over (by chance); we had a very lively two-hour conversation. He is perhaps prettier than last time and very handsome, dashingly stylish and well mannered, not especially educated and conceitedly vain. He talked of his victories and popularity, flirted with me from time to time and had the pleasant feeling that I was impressed. I was pleased with him, etc. He probably noticed that I blushed when he came in, but that doesn't matter, because it's in my nature to blush and that's that. Well, but Ludwik doesn't know this. Anyway, it was nice to chat. I'd like to have some company already, ours, kindred.

I'm learning French now and reading books (quite good) and Nora and I are studying ancient history. Apart from that I do nothing, I don't listen to what people say, I prefer to listen to 'birds in the bush' chirping.

When Ludwik was casting coquettish glances at me, I didn't react, don't think some other eyes have overwhelmed me, I've just got used to it. Ah, if only they could come as soon as possible!

Zygu hasn't come on Thursday or today. I wonder what is stopping him, but really I don't. Today I myself forgot that he was supposed to come. But on Saturday ... I think he came, yes, wearing a winter coat, brr ... He brought such a chill ... So, Buluś, when will you come to your poor, lonely orphan and non-orphan? You will help me, Buluś and God. A fireplace is the pinnacle of my dreams? And how!!!

There's a blizzard raging outside
All you see is a white cloud of snow
All the world, all the people, each soul,
Snow and wind are beginning to hide ...

Someone weaves all their dreams in a shawl
Or remembers, and then smiles sweet and wide
There's a fire cracking warmly inside
You can wrap up in tales, stay, don't go

This is my tiny little dream home
where my soul always yearns to find rest
a home full of pale yellowing memories
a hearth full of motherly warmth

A cold night, there's a big blizzard on
In my home it is cosy and bright
from old dreams, little lives being born
I can put them to sleep, rocking light
Fetch some wood so the fire's not gone
And my worries can fade in the night

This morning our grandma
sat herself today
reading a thick old notebook
she can't put away.
She's been reading squiggles
filling page after page,
nodding and then grumbling
'foolish, youthful age'
she's been turning pages
crossed out, scribbled on,

with faded hearts – which could be red
but the ink's all gone
from all long ago,
a time since so great ...
Our grandma's been sitting,

reading date by date.
Sometimes she would smile,
take another look,
say again, 'oh, the youth'
and smile at her book.
The grandchildren wouldn't know it, but the book's not
    done
Among these old pages
A former grandma lives on
They won't know that from that page can waft, flow,
    or spurt
tears that don't turn bitter
griefs that do not hurt.

4 November 1941, Tuesday

I'm glad that's what I'm like
Little, round, and stout
because if I were slender
I'd fly up like on a cloud.
I'd fly up far away

Chasing dreams around
Then what force would there be
Pulling me back to ground?

Buluś …? Zyguś …? Life …?

I like it when a wide road is rocking
Under the weight of the lorries
When a shrill street-side silence
Is pierced by a klaxon's blast
As the steady rhythmic shocks
Shake a line and a house and a lamp
And the hum and the speed hang above us
Like a current rushing past
Till the trucks press the tarmac and shove its
lazy flow to each side till it spreads
And flows off the road and it sweats
In this frost

6 November 1941, Thursday

I have such pangs of conscience, and I'm so upset! It's all because of Bimba, anyway the fault is entirely mine. I was actually only five minutes late – such a short time – and yet so long. It's been a whole week now. God, let me make it all right on Saturday. Will I, will we meet? I am to copy poems with Nora now. You will help me, Buluś and God.

7 November 1941, Friday[18]

Again a day came when all former worries faded. Ghetto! That word is ringing in our ears, it terrifies, it torments. We don't know what will happen to us, where we'll go and what they'll let us take. God, I believe in You, that wherever we'll be, You will not desert us. Last night everyone was packing, we were ordered to leave our apartments before 2.00 p.m. with 25 kilogrammes of possessions. Maybe there will be a ghetto, but it seems that we will definitely have to move out of the main streets either way. God, I know You heard me a moment ago, when I was petrified and my heart was fluttering so!

At 10.30 last night, suddenly the doorbell rang, and who was there? The police! I pressed my hands to my face then and I called You, oh God, and You heard me. It was a policeman from our old village, from Torskie,* and he let himself be bribed. I reminded him of the good times, the friends, the revels, and somehow it worked. And now I'm asking You, oh, Great One, I'm asking you – I, a speck of dust, I without father or mother here, a poor one ... If those lonely, desolate voices have any power, then listen to my call, too!

Today I got a postcard from Mama. It touched and moved me strangely. Because in all the turmoil of the day I felt that I have someone who loves me, who cares about me. At the same time I felt the powerlessness of that love; my poor

---

*Torskie, a village near Zaleszczyki, now part of Ukraine.

faraway Mama can't help me at all. Mama, I know what you're going through there, but know that I'm suffering here too and going through things that can make one's hair go white. But I believe in you and God. He has saved you from so many disasters, led you through so many dangers, because I was praying then and begging Him: save her, save my mother! He listened to me then, so He will help me, help us now too. Ah, if I only knew what's better?! For you to be with us, or over there with Jarosia? I don't know, I don't know, I don't know! 'I'm sending Renusia a package' – so God has not forsaken me yet if someone out there is saying this, because the world is alien and cold, and this is heartfelt, like my prayers are heartfelt. My Beloved Mama, I never think you're hurting me, even if you said as much to me, I wouldn't believe you. Because your letters, postcards, your words exude love and concern, and something as warm as – I don't know. God, listen to my prayer, solve the puzzle You have given to people. I hope Zygu comes tomorrow, so that I'll have someone to complain to. Help us, God, and bless us.

8 November 1941, Saturday

First and foremost thanks be to You, and secondly I shall deliberate over an issue brought up today by Zygu. I need to consider it carefully, mull it over and understand. This is how it started! It started with him saying that I'm childish, that I've got a child's mentality, that I have not matured psychically to the level of my seventeen years.

Actually at first he said that it's usually the boy who's not mature, doesn't think about the future or marriage, only the girl does. And in our 'relationship' it is different, i.e., the opposite. But I don't think it is opposite at all – I do think seriously. So I told him he doesn't know me at all. Then Z took the offensive and accused me of being like a doll that he plays with and if he presses a button, it makes me react; he said I'm passive, that he didn't know this until our first 'real' meeting. He kept adding that it's not an accusation and that I shouldn't consider it a reproach. Finally he said I'm like the North Sea, or the Arctic Ocean, or ice, that I have no initiative, in a word – I lack temperament! He said that his friends had already mentioned this to him (ridiculous, but I've known that since the beginning). He set, say, Rena K (whom he apparently finds attractive) as an example, or rather didn't set her as an example but compared us, said that it's impossible to talk to me seriously about this, that it would be easier with Irka. He asked whether I have anything against him or if there's anything I don't like. I told him that yes, indeed, but I can say that to everyone else, but not him, and that he's right – there are many things he doesn't know, but I'm not to blame for that, at least not for all of it. Why? And how do I explain that I've gone through various periods ever since we first met. You know it best; you know them all, dear Diary. Wouldn't you agree, then, that I've been crazy for ... love, that I sometimes clutched at the table so as not to fling my arms around him, that I had sleepless nights, tortured, tormented by the senses?

But you see, this has passed somehow, at first it was hard to hold back, then it got easier, and then not at all. And then, back then, couldn't I have told you all that you blame me for today? Couldn't I have accused you of the same thing? Be fair, Zygu! It is possible that back then those old rules stood in my way, those great-grandma-ish opinions about love and a girl's attitude to it. But May came and I was, again, ready for ... anything, and you were 'passive' again. Then I waited for it impatiently, partly in desire, partly in curiosity. And then (on that first June night – it can't be called that), when you judged me, I judged you and ... I was disappointed ... Know that it was you who made me timid with your timid kiss. But it's true that I've unearthed this piece of information from the unconscious and only now too. Or maybe even when Belania asked me, 'But the question is whether Zygu is a good kisser,' and I said, 'I don't know.' But that doesn't mean I didn't love you then. I loved then and now, and always, only I had to cast off what overwhelmed me after you left, and anyway I am not reproaching you either, just telling the truth, to clarify misunderstandings, as you say yourself. But it needs to be said that you are not a good psychologist if you want to achieve a better result by what you said. In fact, in order to understand each other we'd need to talk seriously, unashamed by anything, we'd need to reach back into the past, etc. etc. And I can't bear to do that yet, maybe in two to three years, as you say, so perhaps you're right after all when you say I've got a childish mentality? That is the whole misfortune right there – you are usually right, and even when you're not, you somehow end up being right after all. And as for me, words are definitely not my forte, at most I can write everything down, and this happens only after you leave ... Naturally you'll tell all this to Nora, as you'd guessed she will say I'm right. Ah, if Buluś were here too, she'd understand me. I could also show this ... What had been written here absolutely does not stand any more, so I've erased it. I'm going to the Teich girl's tomorrow with the latest poems. Here's to feelings. You will help me, Buluś and God.

10 November 1941, Monday

I got a parcel from Buluś. My darling Buluś and lovely Jarosia! I'll write them a thank-you card. We have reached an understanding with Zygu, it wasn't the way I interpreted it last time, after all. It was supposed to be friendly advice. So finally we're on the right track, although Zygu is to tell me many more things still. So now it's all right, but before it was – God have mercy! Zygu was irritable and sweaty with the effort; I was on the verge of tears. I wanted to say everything that I'd decided on during those past two nights and ... I couldn't. The situation was so tragic that the phrase 'break-up' even came up. Now I'm smiling when writing this (even though I've got terrible menstrual cramps), but I really was worried and didn't know how to resolve the situation. I'm glad it ended well. I'm feeling strangely light, oh, good. I've got a very pleasant feeling, how – and I actually owe it to Zygu. By the way, nobody has ever taught me such a lesson before. Well, but he was right, I have to give him that. When things get better, we'll meet.

Open your hearts your souls out wide!
living is easier with less to hide
few things hurt more or bring more sorrow
than a grudge you choose to bear till tomorrow
until a thought you could nearly forget
awakes again, and brings more regret ...

Maybe the bells should suddenly ring
and rouse a half-healed, half-buried sting
Open your hearts your souls out wide!
living is brighter with less to hide
Why choose the grudge, the guilt, the moping?
Open your hearts – to hearts wide open

14 November 1941, Friday

I should've written much more, really. But you know, back then ... I couldn't, then I didn't want to, maybe I'll write more tomorrow. Know only that much has changed in life, in friendship, and in this (I don't know what to call it?), moods have changed, and maybe even ... I have. Have I really changed? Or have I just poured out my feelings to myself and you? In any case I will write all the poems now, I've decided;

at worst I won't show them to anyone. I was terribly angry yesterday at again being told I'm childish, so I announced to her that by now I have definitely matured and I do not want to hear it ever again. And tomorrow I'll tell you something interesting, something really interesting, you'll see. I was going to tell you today, but no … tomorrow. So you will help me, Buluś and God.

16 November 1941, Sunday

We only met the day after tomorrow, because today is the day after tomorrow. And I haven't really wrapped up that issue. Zygu read all that I have written and … that's that. Now thanks to everything I've been through myself, and to what Zygu told me, I'm closer again to this life, the real one. Speaking out was necessary. Because if all those unspoken matters had accumulated, one day a flood could happen, destroying the bridge, yes, the bridge that connects us. And we've just built dams and reservoirs, and pools, precisely because we've been open with each other.

It's the same with Nora. Our long friendship has also had its stages. At times we would be close, cordial, and then we'd grow apart for long months even. And was that good? Was that heavy silence right? Why didn't she or I say to the other, 'Listen, I don't like this, don't do this, that hurts me'? And there would've been an explanation, and it would've been fine. Why did we never, ever behave openly? We were friends after all! But it always somehow worked out that we found each other again. Because we were and are (it seems to me) made for each other, because we are kindred souls and I doubt, very much doubt whether we could find a third one who'd understand us (Irka – and Irka, I do not even want to mention her, that would be a profanation of our friendship). For now there's nobody like that in our circle We are, in every respect, in the same situation and we can truly understand one another. And Nora is growing up now, growing through me, through my growth. And me? What do I know? And even if I do know, I can't write it down, because there's so, so, so much of it.

The thing with Rena K, although I was aware of it – or rather sensed it – after all I didn't know what it really was. And it was 1 millimetre more than I thought, or 1 millimetre less. But Maciek is to tell me all about it. I was only wrong about one thing, the first one.

I can't write. My thoughts are just flying away somewhere far and I can't focus even for a moment. It could be called laziness, yes, outstanding laziness, e.g. I take people from my environment and I transport them somewhere into the spirit world, create thousands of contradictory situations and completely new persons, all of them talking, laughing and moving, like in life. Ah, if only one of those unreal, faraway dreams came true … But tough luck, it is those more real, vital dreams, those related to life, which rather ought to come true. Although tell me – a girl with ash-blonde curls, blue eyes with dark eyebrows and eyelashes, red lips just so, lovely and sweet like my dream – is she not possible? I keep writing in snatches. Again. My senses have awoken, but not as strongly as before. Still, they've risen and they want to rebel. But no, the world is too sad for them to take off completely – and fly. Although 'everything' also has its limits, this is what it was like in May.

It all took place one May
left that spring and did not stay
before it even began …
It melted away into nothing
There was no pleading, no gloom
but there is no need to feel pain
What once was may come back again
When the lilac again is in bloom …
When (grant this, God) the world around
can resound in green glorious May
May all be drowned in a flowery flood
and heart and body will blush with blood
and it will shiver in newfound might
in May each and every night

I can't write about it now because … Because I can't! How can I write about it when the world is cold and sad. We don't leave the house now, it is forbidden from 10.00 p.m. until 5.00 in the morning. At 5.00 the street looks almost funny, everyone rushes out of their houses and white armbands gleam everywhere outside.

Nora's house was searched.

I don't know when I'll see Buluś, maybe at least Jarosia will come. O God! Let us somehow survive this war. But it is true I'm awakening again, although it's not a torment to me any more – a pleasure. Goodbye ... how? You will help me, Buluś and God. As usual. It's actually not that I've been thinking for a long, long time about writing a poem, I'm just haunted by the thought of it, it's to be a description of one of my dreams, my 'little beauty'. 'You're like a golden royal whim.' I can't again, I know I can't now.

I was always shy and meek
never cheeky, always weak
as if always trying to seek
safe places from the hurtful world ...

Goodbye ... how? Here's to feelings. You will help me, my only Buluś and God.

24 November 1941, Monday[19]

Buluś came on Friday and left today! Jarusia went with her (but will come back tomorrow) to take something. She was here for three days and this feeling is left:

with a flutter and a squeak
rubbed soft down on sharp small beak
left the whole bush rocking

She came and moved the whole house, and left, and I don't know when we'll see each other again. Whenever Buluś comes, she talks to me and I feel that she's the only person in the world who is truly most sympathetic to me. Buluś is actually against it. She doesn't like Zygu, maybe because she'd rather he were Aryan. She warned me not to take this relationship too seriously and says I won't be happy, because ... etc. It's strange but after those lectures, I feel that I'm growing apart from him, that I just don't like him and am afraid of him. And then some other hazy figure appears, that old one, indistinct.

Sometimes Buluś is wrong, and she doesn't know him. But sometimes she's right! Because, listen, won't his assertive nature – which I find so attractive now – torment me one day? Won't he do whatever he pleases with me and with himself? Won't some Rena, Halina, Lidka poison my life? It would be all over then. Hope would be impossible. I'd only have one more home to look forward to: the grave.

And I, how would I behave? I think I would either be completely indifferent to everything, or horribly jealous, so much so it'd cause me physical pain, and then – no, I wouldn't argue or make jealous scenes, but I'd systematically, with full satisfaction and calculation, repay him in kind. This feeling has gripped me at times, precisely that. In fact, no, I still owe him. And when I'm able to do it with pleasure!

Why am I so angry, really? Is it because of what Buluś said? No, I do still want him to be my husband. And I said, 'Maybe it's not the husband I want, but the children, yes, definitely, "You're like a golden royal whim."' Mama says you mustn't want anything that much, because you might not get it. I think perhaps God will listen to this heartfelt, girlish request. Yes, may it happen!

Jerschina might give me lessons. I'm nervous about it. Ticiu and Lila are living in the ghetto.

God, may my dreams keep coming true like that. I'll be so appreciative of it and I'll give thanks … You will help me, Buluś and God.

26 November 1941, Wednesday

After Buluś left, I dreamt I had an all-night argument with Zygu, I really did. I don't even know what I was angry about and why I felt hurt. It would seem it's because of those old issues and thanks to suggestion. Only due to that, only because of that. Jara, she hates him and keeps teasing me by wanting to provoke suspicion and jealousy, and only provokes anger directed at her. Because I am really not jealous. I mean I am, but only about the things I see, and if I don't see, then I'm not, I'm not angry or jealous at all. Close your eyes; that's all, that's all.

Z was very sweet and tender today and I was annoyed with myself for those unpleasant reproaches. Or maybe it's like Mama says, maybe I will be unhappy? That would be bad, it would mean not making the most of life. But am I ready to give up on my dream, even for such a price? Maybe … I don't know … I'll see … You will help me, Buluś and God!

29 November 1941, Saturday

I wanted to write yesterday and this morning, but I couldn't get round to it somehow. I wanted, that is, I planned two poems (about girls and school). But now we've seen each other and as always I won't start where I wanted.

I told Zygu that I always defer to him, that he's tyrannical. Why did I even tell him that? I think because of Mum's suggestion and that dream (the row about the swimsuit). Anyway, I've told you and Nora about this. No, not in a negative sense, on the contrary. You do remember, 'Let them even be imperious, even commanding ...' Yes, and I've told myself that, although I've given it a lot of thought. And Z, as usual, immediately started arguing and saying that he actually enjoyed the role of the 'listener'. It's ridiculous, no, it's impossible. Either he doesn't realise or doesn't want to admit that he is the kind of person who exerts influence, imposes his will on others. But he doesn't think he's a tyrant because this word is completely negative. So a tyrant is someone who imposes his will on others regardless of whether he is right or not. So there, I'm changing my opinion about the word tyrant. It is negative. All right ... I reject it. But what, then, do you call it when someone unknowingly exerts influence on others, who – also subconsciously – submit to it? Someone may not like this influence. There are people who would in fact break away from it, but it actually appeals to me and it's precisely what I like, maybe only that! It is not because, as he says, 'I like it because it can't be changed'; it's not true. I liked it before I met him, and I remember that since I was about fourteen, heroes from books, films and dreams had exactly this imperious quality, I won't say tyrannical, because I now consider this word to be negative! And we signed a contract, that is Z wrote it, so that I didn't change even a sentence later, it says, 'I used to like and still like conduct which I used to call tyrannical, but do not call tyrannical any more (due to the change in the definition of the word "tyranny").' And? And nothing. That is Z all over, made demands of me, I'll try to satisfy and have already done so in part, while what I demand – actually, I demand nothing … I only said it. So Z remains as he was by mutual agreement. So why the whole discussion, when I feel good in this role and he wouldn't change his even if I wanted him to, and it seems this is what I'm looking for in the excess of words, what hurts me? Anyway, he'd like even me to impose my will. Or maybe what hurts me is this and I won't say anything else. I don't know, but there is something that hurts. There is some discontent – I don't know. Maybe the reason is that I can't accept him, that something is always in the way. Or maybe I lack interests. Yes, if I had other goals, it would be different. As it is, I think about it too much, I deliberate, I contemplate, it's the whole content of my life, and it's too early for that! Today, for example, I felt such a yearning for the school that adults talk about. And I'm due one more year of school, of learning. I would really, really like to go to a Russian school like that. I felt so free there and it felt good, and strangely I'd already realised this during the school year. I would like another year, yes, and then to go far away, to acquire life, learning, pleasures – but to return. To return and to make the dream come true. To return to him and for him! Yes, those are my most secret subconscious dreams. In anger or in spite, whether I love him or hate him I always think that and believe it will happen.

I think it could be really great
To go to school again
Come back to any previous year

I can't write now, I can't, all of me is preoccupied with that issue. If all men are selfish tyrants, he's also a selfish tyrant – because he is, after all, a man. Oh, life, life, stupid life.

Like a bird sprung free from a cage
like a colt that was bridled too hard
I would fly away from my nest
and jump over fences and start
crossing valley, river and ditch
I would run free and mad like the wind
somewhere far where no eye can reach
I would dance in a mad whirlwind
and sway as if in a haze
I would drink down my bliss
and thunder down my ways
I would rumble and shake
with laughter and freedom and joy
and move from bloom to bloom

flashing like a star, like a blast
of dawn
and at night
I would fly back to my nest

In any case, let Renuśka stop crying now. Because, really, Renuśka is a very poor girl, so poor and wronged. Rena is a teacher, there's a loving Rena, there's also such and such ... but the one from the dreams, the loving one is the poorest and the saddest ... Really? No! Not from the dreams at all, but the wretched Z's one. What is going on with me? And what will happen to me? You will help me, Buluś and God.

31 November 1941, Monday

A letter from Mum. She arrived safely, no adventures. The letter again mentioned 'it'. But it's lost all its power now: firstly, she's not with me; secondly, it feels good. It, and he, feels good. So apparently this is how it must be, that for this (some caresses and warmth), I'm committed and ready to sacrifice myself, that when it's cold and dark outside, there's goodness and light in my soul, and ... I cannot renounce the dream. In the morning I thought I'll be unhappy in the evening and thought this:

I started to build
A building tall and proud
Wings and floors built from sighs aloud

In my dreams, I was so skilled …
In the dream-light, all looked bright
Dark ebony, marble white
Claws of columns there to hold
A head of domes and towers bold
Raised so high and held so strong
Lasting solid, lasting long.

If it came down quick! It wouldn't
Cause me so much pain
But look, the walls now crack with strain,
Crumble, begin to fall,
every fragment of my soul
Melts and slips, goes slowly bad
that's what's weary, that's what's sad.
I started to build
A building tall and proud
Wings and floors built from sighs aloud
it melted, with my tears filled …

One must forgive the spring
all rains and storms and gales
the pranks one forgives and forgets
the clouds will be chased by sunshine
and roses and nightingales
and a bright day awaits as a grey dusk sets

You will help me, Buluś and God.

8 December 1941, Tuesday [20]

8th or whatever of December 1941, Tuesday. Actually nothing happened today that was happy, or sad, or worthy of description. Just a normal December day. But I've decided to finally tell you what's going on in the world. Cannon shots are going on, muffled detonations from the south and the east. The Germans are fighting Russia at the huge Eastern Front, fighting along with Italy against England in Africa in Libya outside Tobruk, where a new front has been created. Hungarians from the Eastern Front are riding towards the Heimat. Nobody really knows why. America is fighting Japan. And … so we've lived to see the Second World War in this century. For me it's the first, but for others it's also more horrific than the previous one. Blood is flowing, cities are ruined, people are dying. There is awful poverty among people, cases of typhus (Ticiu and Lila in the ghetto). God, make this terrible war end! Make it so that we survive and keep our health until a peace treaty! Everyone is praying now, everyone believes that only some higher power can protect us from evil – it's God!

In rowdy dancing,
in a wedding, a feast,
where the crowds make the floorboards creak
they don't ask for him, they don't call his name
God's name is silent and weak.
Drunken, they spout more vodka forth

They drink and shout, then the blood will spurt
'Come on, come on!' let the world all tumble
here's to you, if you drink too!
In drunken fun – pick anyone
life strife with a knife.
Let there be a gush
of blood. Let cheeks flush
with golden sweet champagne
let there be a screeching orgy again
of tinderbox moods of those with 'no pain'
God is not needed
maybe the sad ones will silently pray
he is not with us
in laughter or play
in scenes or fights
in wine in glasses!
But when the unhappy hour comes
when the sky bleeds with fire and fear
they fall, and wish God was near!
when their lives waste away in sickness
when through poverty their bodies decay
when fear makes them dumb and hunger takes a toll
all they can ask is, 'Won't God help at all?'
Then from barred windows of every jail
and from damp cellars you hear the wail,
You hear complaints from wide and far
Lord, won't you save us! Lord, but you are!
(You are the only one who can save)

If only our God forgot and forgave!
That's when they turn into your humble slave.
You're there again. In a loaf of black bread,
In clouds that darken over each head,
under each summer of heavy drought,
under each conscience guilty with doubt
in tears of comfort, in hope and need,
You're there again and called indeed.
And when the sun returns to the sky
And things get bright – from that day on
You won't be called
they will keep sinning, you will be gone …
as it was before

So it is. Jerschina came over. Actually I didn't know that I would care so little. Might be because I hate them. Forgive me, God! Zyguś is very good and lovely, and argumentative. Maciek came. We'll talk another time, when there's some news. You will help me, Buluś and God.

11 December 1941, Thursday

No! … war, who knows? Maybe in two years … But Zyguś, so wonderful, tender, sweet and good, and lovely, that he exceeded my dreams. I felt so good today. I would like to tell someone about the happy moments I'm experiencing within this misery. The way Zyguś was, it would be a sin not to love him like I love him … I've got many poems in my head, but

I can't write. See you later … You will help me, Buluś and God, until dreams come true.

15 December 1941, Monday morning

Today I'd like to talk and write, and talk, and talk, and I don't even know where to start … I think with the fact that Nora doesn't understand me. Yes, she herself knows it and told me I am a step ahead. She's behind, where I was, well … more than a year ago, or a year. And I would gladly reach out to her, but she … why? She's hindering herself. I'd like it if you could understand me completely. Why, Noruś, when I'm telling you something, I'm not complaining, I'm just saying, and you don't understand me and make it into an accusation yourself. However, we do understand each other in other matters, something always remains.

If only you knew, dear Diary, how many poems live in me, but I don't even know if and when I'll commit those thoughts to paper. And even Nora doesn't understand me any more. Oh, I must have changed a lot. Well, perhaps I'm really not myself any more, maybe I'm the lining of Zygmunt's soul. I've transformed awfully, but after all my old self is still there! And life, life is anticipation now. For do you know, there are moments in life without sad or happy experiences, without storms, without streams of happiness, and one doesn't count those moments later. And while they last, they plunge one into a blissful state of calm and indolence.

No, it's not because I wore a hat that I've become unfamiliar to Nora, not at all – but for some other reason, why, why has my sensuality faded? Because it has been replaced by a monotonous caress, an almost 'marital' one. However, I realise now that I need it very much; I need this gentle, delicate tenderness as much as the outbursts. And do you understand now, Noruś, and perhaps it'll be: 'How much one should prize you, only he who has lost you can tell,'* but you and I are similar, so I don't know … but maybe you'll need it too?

I've written an idiotic thing, I probably won't send it to her. And those poems crowd in so much, but I won't write either. Bye, dear Diary, until … I don't know. You will help me, Buluś and God.

16 December 1941, Tuesday

Bulczyk's birthday is coming up, as is the date of writing the birthday letter, the traditional letter. Because I always send a letter, and only very, very rarely can give my wishes in person. And now what in the world can I send her? No, I can't send wishes, greetings – no. Buluś, what can I give you? I've been thinking about this all day. I will send you, then, a bright, silver, winter memory, a memory from a time when we didn't know we were happy. Only I don't know if I can re-create it so vividly as it was. No, I can't do it at all now. And such is the illness I am suffering from now. You will help me, Buluś and God.

---

* A paraphrase from Adam Mickiewicz's *Pan Tadeusz*.

20 December 1941, Saturday

For Bulczyk's birthday. Do you remember?

Horses galloped at a steady pace
A sleigh raced on just like a lightning flash
Snow and frost laid kisses on our face
Frosty hair, and snow-kissed winter blush
The wind blew panting, right across our eyes
Hooves struck up snow fountains from the ground
Riding in a sleigh felt so nice
With the bell's laughing sound!
Snow and pine cones fell on our heads
Which our passing there would shake and stir
Both of us went on, deep in our sleigh,
Wrapped up warm in a lovely coat of fur.
Silent trees around us stood in wonder
Morning silence shaken from its thoughts
We went riding, like a laughing thunder
With the bell's laughing sound!
Our tracks with fresh new snow are filled
The horses' silhouettes were drowned in fog
the driver and the sleigh, the wood, the field
all you heard still was the bell's sweet sound …

Know that when the dusk begins,
and the tower bell tolls for evening prayers
and the December day has spent

all its power – curled, and shrivelled
in a ponderous hour – I will come to you
I'll come in yearning that flows
or in a sparkling star that glows
or in a silent holiday breath
or in a sigh instead?
I'll come …
In a grey winter's hour,
when the windows sparkle with ice,
I'll say one word, just one word,
frank like tears, but soothing and warm …

Yes, we'll be with her then, so that she's not lonely in that crowded, rumbling and empty capital. Bye, dear Diary, we'll go to her together … You will help me, Buluś and God.

23 December 1941, Wednesday

Nothing, days pass. They are all alike. Oppressed with thoughts, waiting, idleness … They pass, I sit at home and think, think, go crazy with thinking. I'm gaining weight. I'm as big as a barrel. Disgusting. I wrote a birthday letter to Mum. I've seen Jerschina; he has two sons. Well, is this even thinkable? We're making an album with Norka, i.e., Norka is making it, I'm helping and it brings me such delight, such pleasure, that I could spend whole days doing it. I wouldn't even want to see Z. Just keep making this beautiful album. And then … who knows, perhaps it can be published like this?

There is something I would like to say about Zygmunt. Something that worries me. Namely – I don't hate him, but I don't love him either. Maybe it's not true, maybe it's only temporary, and I did swear, did make solemn promises. And I did promise to last throughout the war, but I don't know how it happened and where it came from, but here it is. Can I deny it? I can't even tell him this either, that – what, I'm not attracted to him, I'm fed up with all 'that', and I'm left, again, with poems, you, Mum, Nora, such ethereal beings. And you know that at times there's something and then all the shortcomings come to light and create something like aversion – weariness. Why? Whence? I don't know. Oh! If I hated, but not that, I don't hate, I'm indifferent to it. So why, why do I pray every night for the dream? I don't know either. I only know one thing: I need work, physical or intellectual, work away from home – an occupation! I've got many 'poemy' thoughts in my head. You don't know that this question accidentally turned into a most genuine compliment.

I can wake the day
and spread around the shadow of the night
I can scatter blackest clouds
with golden flashes of light

I can stand around the deepest snow
and call forth spring
and I know where treasures hidden lie
and where fairies dance and sing

I can find my way on city streets
in taxis, in trams I can ride
Light bulbs – I can light the spark inside
Wrap a village deep in muffling snow
Soothe the pain – I know
people who dwell in cities and towns

I can spread silvery cheer
wrap trees in warm moss, both far and near
I know where tiny dwarves reside
and blow forth bubbles with dreams inside
I can make starry skies appear
right in the middle of the day
And I know a magical world
of elves and princesses, castles in air
I know a whole world that isn't there

But that's something that I never knew
and I never thought of that before
Someone asked me with reproach, 'And you,
you write poems, but can you do much more?'

The album is coming along beautifully, ah, it's come in handy, the way he is … no, no, I won't say. You will help me, Buluś and God.

24 December 1941

Ah, I feel like writing poems so much, I want to write and write for ever.

Windy, cold, and icy
Wind is in a mood, not nice, he
blows on since the dawn
Gusts and gales, they swerve and sway
People wonder at the wind, and they
don't know what's going on
Why's the wind so raving mad
Was it crossed by some brave lad
as it blew about?
Maybe gnomes or dwarves awoke it
with a woodland shout?
or it had a dream in which
a rival wind blew through, and each
leaf in the woods blew out!
It blows and wails and paces
falters, picks up, races
snow or no snow,
sand or no,
roofs get blown,
branches caught
Burnt-out dust it raises up
makes a mess and will not stop
through the swamp and through the hollow
where the streams flow, it must follow
It sits on the windmills' wings
and flings clouds through the sky
then it jumped and swayed away
shook around a pile of hay

Messed a branch about
and it flew right out.

28 December 1941, Sunday [21]

Or maybe because I didn't submit myself to Your protection. Think and believe, although it's hard to believe. Yesterday coats, furs, collars, oversleeves, hats, boots were being taken away on the street. And now there's a new regulation that under pain of death it is forbidden to have even a scrap of fur at home. I feel so sorry, actually for Dido the most of all of us. But then what is there to be sorry for – the furs or that warm, cordial relationship which dissipated and disappeared.

I didn't see Zygu for a week and I can admit I was pleased with this, it cured me of this persecution mania a little. But ... but he came after a week, i.e., paid me an official visit (in a coat), and generally made the impression of slaving through some duty. That's not what's awful, he came because he had to, but he'd rather not have come and it'd have been a hundred times better if he hadn't. I'm not going into any details, but it's only my instinct which tells me that ... well, you probably know.

Another thing, which abashes me slightly, is that he lies. I have never imagined a person I respect would lie. It's disgusting and I really do not understand it. They were all little, meaningless lies, so? So nothing. But this morning I choked on tears of anger. I know only one remedy for those miseries;

perhaps I'll apply it! Yes, yes, but wait a bit. Oh, it hurts – so I love. You will help me, Buluś and God.

30 December 1941, Tuesday

So it's been a year since I wrote: 'Be gone, worries, tears and upheaval.' And today, today it's completely different, today I'm a year older, a year more experienced, maybe a bit more mature, but not worth much more. There's not much more I can do.

I remember it was a variety show, it was fun, Rysiek was in excellent spirits. Today I met Rysiek too, how different from last year's. He's huddled, his fur's been plucked, he's disinfecting some sick people from typhus, but he still chats and tells his tall tales.

I saw Poldek, he was carting along some corpse.

I had a letter from Nora, so cordial and warm. Oh, yes! Everything's revived in this area, everything fell into place, we've become closer and understood each other, and we're united in friendship. One year, how everything's changed, I don't know what the next one will bring? And how can I know what I will come to write next year? Next year and a year ago ... And now I'm standing on the border and ... I'm grateful to the one passing for listening to my pleas and I'm asking the new one to be favourable. Oh God, let all dreams come true like that! I saw Mama, there was something with Zygu and something started in politics. So this year, which will end today in an hour and a half, will disappear and pluck one flower from my life. It was a year overflowing with love. Everything, tears, sighs, explosions of anger, jealousy, all this stemmed from that one emotion. And you, New Year being born, will you be sympathetic to Cupid's hearts? You are young after all. You too know how to love. And if you want to be loved as well, for people to say goodbye to you with regret and not a sigh of relief, if you want your date to be entered in golden numbers into the world's history and in a flowery garland into people's hearts, become worthy of it. Bring a branch of peace into this howling, fighting world and quieten it like a rough sea with a magic wand. And let me still love the one I have fallen in love with, and let me be loved. Make it so that people who were separated by the war are joined in a blissful calm. And return parents to children and my mama to me. Actually, it's a continuation of my dreams. Let them continue, each of them is a little part of the fireplace, of the 'royal whim'. You'll understand and I will too. And tomorrow I will greet you on a new page, although maybe only ugly things will happen tomorrow, but the Year will be New, it'll be full of hope for the long twelve months. So farewell, old year, with thanks and gratitude for those first love's kisses, for motherly caresses, for friendship, for everything good and bad. You will help me, Buluś and God.

1 January 1942, Thursday

I promised, so I'm writing. It was a day like all the others, in the morning I went to Norka's, then I was at home, then

I was sorting out a birthday present for Zygu. And when I came home, I found Zygu there. He was very debonair and pretty. His wish for me was to endure and survive. It was very ordinary; we sat at the table and talked.

Z left soon (angry that I didn't want to show him the previous New Year's Eve in the diary). But it's not true! I know that although by all appearances everything was all right, things were subdued somehow. It seems that Z had the best of intentions, but they slowly cooled down, and … I don't know, but I feel there's something. It can't go on like this! If we had decided to act openly, it must be done. The truth must be revealed! Because I know that all aversions, contemplations, enquiries, suspicions are just another form of love. Because there are no dreams in which he doesn't appear. And now my spirits have lifted, because maybe I've just convinced myself. And I'd felt sad, oh, how sad. I was crying and thinking of Bulczyk. I wanted to write a letter, which would have been a cry of yearning! I feel so lonely, like I have nobody, nobody. There is only Buluś, but so far away. I've realised that mother and child are the closest beings after all. I understand that I am to Mum what my child would be to me. I feel like crying, I'm unutterably sad. God, make it so that it gets better now. I'm yearning for something warm … You will help me, Buluś and God.

5 January 1941, Monday

The letter from Mother was warm. But I wrote nothing, I was waiting, always waiting for a warm embrace, a look, but only a cold, frosty wind blew. It chilled my heart, it brought tears to my eyes. I wanted to write a letter to Mama, but changed my mind. This letter would've been such a painful cry, it would've wounded a mother's heart. No, I'm lying to the world that I'm indifferent to it; it's not true! I am hurt, I am simply writhing in pain. I don't know, is it that unknown girl who won him over with her father's position and nationality? Or that he never mentioned a word about it, or that he practically stayed away for two weeks? What? – Everything!

I talked about this with Jarośka. We talked like two women friends. But there is a difference between us (not even of age), but of emotion, I love despite everything, she hates. But we agreed about one thing: I need entertainment, I need somebody, urgently; I've written to Norka about this already. If this doesn't heal the wound, it will make it scar over. And then … Who knows what happens then? Times are such now that one should think about something else, about life worries, but well, I can't. Maybe I am sinning. And do you know with what disgust I'm making an album of poems for his birthday? Because Maciek told me that he's asking for it. Well, but one has to be magnanimous when saying goodbye. Next time I will try not to fall so hard, treat it lightly, from hand to mouth, and not go into the depths. But this one has deeply affected me all year round. Just think, 365 days and not one when I didn't think of him, so few nights when I didn't dream. And now will all this dissipate in such a pedestrian way? Actually, it should have already collapsed because of this a long time ago, after all he always had a roving eye for every skirt, excuse me, not every one – those who looked him in the eye. It is typical for him that he's attracted to girls who are attracted to him. In fact, he told me once that he reciprocates feelings excessively, apparently he reciprocates coquetry too. That I don't know, but surely, have I not experienced it myself? But in this album I'll write what I feel. I have to. Maybe he'll understand me.

How

A butterfly loves every flower
on the meadow, plain, and hill
lily and chamomile
plain bloom and bower
When it's not chasing scents
But yearns for nectar still

Leaves

The leaves in May they shiver
play with the wind impatiently
Is it strange?
To me it is not strange at all
Through August nights
they burn
with a blissful might
of loving, maybe
in autumn they turn yellow

shrivelled and pale
this must be envy
They're dead in the winter
and frozen right through
onto a snowy forest floor
they fall
they rustle, and don't sing
and instead of caressing, they sting
Is it strange? To me it's not strange at all

And I don't know, is he worth it or not? Rather yes. I had
more joy than sadness after all. Goodbye ...

I dreamt, a sweet
and wondrous dream
I moved my feet
in clouds, it seemed
a land of colours and scents
and bells
and bells
of laughter
which echoed after
repeated again
until it spread
wide and away
until a whisper
of a sunny golden laugh
what a day

then in a cloud of white
a flock of butterflies flew in
with a name across the sky, so bright
a name as sweet as my dream
and just as wonderful ...
then the awakening
not as eventful
with a prod in the side
my eyes open wide
it's dark, day wakes
the shade's about to stop
a lovely dream
a springlike dream
but not worth the waking-up

A very sad and teary day. Noruś, I wanted to write to you today. Not – although I know this belongs in the past – 'that I'm your friend for crying', but you see, this is how it works out, strangely. But have you ever thought about the meaning of those words? When someone is having a hard time, yes, a hard and sad time, when they need consolation, they turn to their closest person, to their mother – and I didn't have a mother here. I wanted to write about friendship, but I know that my mood has changed since the morning. And? And it's my lot to cry again. Oh God, but my heart is heavy! Words are only words and they say nothing. This burden won't be shifted either by a letter to Mother, or to you, dearest Noreńka, or even by poems; this burden was imposed by his words. So humiliating! Why did I ask about that? Noruś, just think, I've got a sword in my heart, when it's there, it hurts, it hurts very much, but when I try to remove it, it hurts even more. And the thought of our friendship seems to me such a quiet haven that I consider it sacred. Can you believe that he sensed it back then? But still, I am better. Can it be said that I have two faces? You will help me, Buluś and God.

19 January 1942, Monday

Birthday! Dear Diary! Mama! Noreńka! I feel so good! I feel so light. It was his birthday today. I gave him a collection of poems (granted, it is rather pretty and I almost fell in love with it when making it) and he was so happy! I didn't know it would please him so much. He was touched. I asked him what he'd like me to wish him. He said for us to survive this war without splitting up. Do I want that, too? What a question, do I? I don't want us to ever split up at all. As Z put it, the poems connect us. How good that he understands this. Poems are something extraordinary and unique, they connect souls and ennoble, elevate love. God, thank You and may my dreams come true … You will help me, Buluś and God.

24 January 1942, Thursday

I feel so good! We understood that we've understood each other completely. And I opened your depths, dear Diary! Are you angry? I opened them to someone close and very loved! I gave all that's deepest, most precious, most honest – all the worries and thoughts enclosed in poems. 'When we are like water lilies,' Zygunio. The way you are honestly makes me feel at a loss for words, it's better to lie down, close one's eyes and dream. Only Jarośka keeps ruining the image for me with her comments, 'He looks like a real Yid in that hat.' Let her talk, maybe she's right, I'm unable to see it, and even if

> The heart will take no orders gladly,
> it is wiser than you are*

Generally I've been wanting to write something, but I've not known what all day.

> First, 'he' was on
> a golden throne
> a castle, horses, knights
> and wings, like on a ghost
> a true crowned prince – like most
> sweet dreams on sweetest nights
> He runs, jumps, flies
> the dragon dies
> and golden horseshoes gleam
> and gleaming so

---

*An allusion to the verse of a song by Julian Tuwim (lyrics) and Henryk Wars (music) performed by Hanka Ordonówna in Mieczysław Krawicz's film *The Masked Spy* (1933).

he jumped to glow
onto the silver screen
Again, it was 'him'
a girl's true dream
He captured towns and hearts
so lovely and unique
He tore down walls
scored hockey goals
The suit showed off his physique
Then new ones made a start
heroes from books
the soldier and the guard
with aeroplanes and with rank
And it was due to them
your heart sank
And then, a – who?
A figure on the street
Someone with lips so sweet
Someone with eyes bright and deep
Someone you dream of and would keep
Someone like a daydream in May
who won't disappear or fade away
Again, it was 'him'
a girl's true dream
a star of some repute
He tore down walls
and scored hockey goals

A talent beyond dispute
His suit was well-tailored and clean
and he vanished on a bright silver screen

And sometimes it's exactly like it was with this poem. First it gained speed, winged out and stopped, and I'm struggling, struggling, struggling and I can't finish. But maybe I will finish it ...

He sulked and lay in wait
then with one leap
he gushed a stream sharp and deep
He spread dark wings
and in a flash
he scrawled a streak of poems
across a page at a dash
Each feeling and each thought
he pressed through signs of black
He moved in narrow scribbles
which gleamed behind his back
He spat verse after verse
and coughed up rhyme, and then
he brought forth inky tears
from a poor old fountain pen
Then he stood
his back against the script
on a clear blank page, as dark
as a stubborn mountain goat

as an arrow through a tree bark
he clammed up with a frown
and looked around in fear
and the ending of this poem
will never draw near

Maybe I will finish it after all. You will help me, Buluś and God.

26 January 1942, Monday

Today was such a strange day. My poor darling Noruśka. She came over this morning at a run and said, crying, 'My grandpa is dead.' And ran off. My heart gave such a squeeze and hurt so much. Later I was anxious about her, I thought they rounded her up to sweep snow. I know how sensitive she is and what it means to her. And when I was wondering whether the poor thing isn't freezing somewhere and what she's doing, I felt how dear this little friend of mine is to me. Her diary is a story of our friendship. It could be entitled 'How a friendship strengthened'. Oh, but it must be said that she should be given the more noble position, the one of more respect. And now we're so close that I feel her pain like my own. I would like her to come to us. Her most recent letter was something so warm that one really has to be very cordial to be able to write it. It is so terrible, Irka lost her grandma, Norka – her grandpa. Oh, God, preserve the lives of everyone else and stop this war. Buluś hasn't written. Ticiu hasn't written. Oh, this whole family of ours is also a body torn to shreds. Will it come alive? Will it ever come together? I've come to doubt the term 'family home' – I can only have my own now. Oh, make it happen, God. The grandparents are to us all that's protection and care, and everything. Oh, good, darling, saint Bimba! It's somehow warm and sunny with them in this freezing weather. I'm experiencing moments which are rare in life. I'm seventeen and when I look into his eyes I forget everything that's sad in the world. And I'd inscribe them in my heart in golden letters. Because I'm at that age and in that state when words, glances, caresses give joy. When I'm happy at the mere sight of my sweetheart. And now perhaps the poems have introduced this clarity. Mama, write how you're doing! Your silence is such a burden. I say 'goodnight' to the young and happy, 'goodnight' to the sad and worried, 'goodnight' to you, my faraway mama, and you, my sad dear friend. Goodnight ... You will help me, Buluś and God.

> May this night bring relief
> some sweet respite
> to those in pain
> and grief
> a hopeful, joyful
> sprite
> to those in happy love
> May its cool hands lie
> across the temples burning
> with heat of day

To the world
may it bring all the help
it might
and may it knock on doors
to hearts barred shut
goodnight ...

29 January 1942, Thursday

Well ... She hasn't written, no. It weighs so heavy on me. And, as is my wont, I immediately start imagining – and I don't want to think. I am so sad. Z stirred such concern in me too. He says I'd like to live lightly, that I don't care much about anything. Does even he not notice this mask I put on (with difficulty), or maybe, maybe it's true, maybe always trying to 'mock the world' I now mock unwittingly? But I can't say I think like that about my only mama, my dearest, and about our affairs, which are a difficult, oppressing experience to me. My whole youth has been like this. You know. I have never lacked for anything materially – but morally, sometimes. And I couldn't show it, and I didn't want to care much about anything, and it's stayed this way. And now, Buluś, write and visit. Such are my most ardent wishes. You will help me, Buluś and God.

30 January 1942, Friday

No, there's been no letter, not a word ... only my head is thumping, why? And I'm thinking of writing a novella. No

content, no so-so moods, no more. And in response to you,
Buluś.

> If I was just like you are now
> I would have all the boys in tow
> I'd be surrounded by many a lad
> and let them kiss me!
> let them go mad!
> I wouldn't mind, I wouldn't care
> the young girl's shame would not be there
> I'd fling my arms wide open, then
> I would deny it all again
> I'd kick back those who are a drag
> Then I would show a lot of leg
> And hike my dress up high enough
> To let the blinding light shine through
> With so much grace
> who could ever face
> so much temptation and resist?
> The righteous ones would not be missed
> The chaste old souls could let tongues fly
> against my body, till they die
> against my lips, and all my hair
> I'd keep all boys so sweet right there
> I'd make them choke on bliss – and how!
> if I was just like you are now ...
> But I am not, and that is why
> I'll love no other, even if I try

> my love is young, ashamed, aware,
> and so unhappy, so full of care …

I'm happy with what I've written about myself – I'll refresh it a bit. You will help me, Buluś and God.

6 February 1942, Friday

Such an ordinary Friday. Because you don't know that on Fridays too, and, well, generally always, every day. I've had a letter from Buluś, Jerschina brought it. I've studied nothing for him. I am so sorry, so ashamed – horribly. And I really want to learn now. I want to, so much, I think about it. Mama, forgive me, please, forgive me, you've experienced this too once, after all – I … I can't.

Zygmunt wanted to come more often, I agreed. But this is something I've experienced since the very first stages of love – I don't like to see him that often. It is as if I'm worried that it'll become commonplace, that I'll get bored, run out of energy (but it's not so, right, Noruś?). So why blubber? Because it was the way it was today? After all, yesterday and earlier, and before that, it was different. So it has to be said how it was. Was or wasn't. It got me very excited and caused pleasurable unsettling shudders. Everything was sweet: kisses, glances and words, and all that wasn't so ethereal, yes, that too. And today it was like that at first too – not at the end. Because really, who's to blame that I started thinking about the honest and clear way Z has of telling things. I told him things too and perhaps it was this telling of mine that humiliated me so much internally. 'Renuśka! You're so silly!' Mama would say. Because you didn't experience another love before this one? Because your dream was so undreamt? Because that first kiss, as Z says, was like freshly picked cherries? Yes, because of that! Because when he (after all quite honestly and in good faith) told me about all those flings of his, the casual flirting and little romances, I couldn't impress him with anything like that, if it could impress him at all? Or maybe not that ... I must touch my heart like this, bit by bit, to see where it hurts. Maybe the impassioned speech about that first Jadzia, no, not that either, and not the fact that those experiences were much more romantic than ours, or perhaps the comparison? Yes, yes ... you compared me loving you to yourself loving her. I was nothing, nothing at all in your life; you didn't even pay attention to me. But what do I really want? I've always known this after all, I didn't even (at times) demand reciprocity. Still, why are you surprised that I was 'consumed by reticence'? Why, I was embarrassed, humiliation was ravaging my eyes anyway. Whatever I said and did always seemed too much to me. You were free to do anything, but girls have their own special 'blessed' rules. And why, Z, why did 'it' happen? It was not because you found me attractive ('Because I didn't even try to make interesting conversation'), not because I found you, is that it? Or perhaps the row with the variety show and the contest? Perhaps that was unimportant – quite unimportant? Those rivals I conquered, that didn't make me happy (or did it?) (I know now – the variety show). After all, each one of them could have done it. I knew all this, but never, ever, suspected that hearing it in such a nice, 'accessible form' would cause me such pain, well, not as much pain as a spasm. You could only love her, although later no longer. And there was no name for our relationship – it was something between a friendship and exactly that – and then it took on a more distinct character. But I can phrase it differently. To me, you were immediately more than a friend (although I hated you at times), maybe precisely because of this. Maybe I would have withdrawn and closed the front if ... ? Oh, there's always been an 'if', and that's why I stayed and would stay. But even today I'm sorry I was wet behind the ears, a novice, a goose; I'm sorry that I can't say, 'At least I know I didn't live tediously.' But one promise will be kept, even if I loved most ardently – like today. Now it feels better, it feels good, now I will leaf through the old, those disarmingly naive pages. You will help me, Buluś and God.

Let us then sing
let us then sing
until the dream
of youth lives on
till it can thrill and thrive and spring
let us then fill
the sky with song!

8 February 1942, Sunday

I'd like to start a story. A story of our love. Written completely independently. But one has to, it's hard maybe, when ... I don't know. You will help me, Buluś and God.

16 February 1942, Monday

Tomorrow I'm going to Noruśka's. For the whole day. We'll talk to our hearts' content. We'll settle everything and build, at least theoretically, our future company. We have to do it. At all costs, we need to. I went to Irka's, she's paid me a return visit. And again a cobweb of relationships is starting to be spun. But I don't want this web to wrap itself so much that spiders suffocate me. I need to see my own one, we must meet.

It is disgusting, this life which starts with staring at his lips and ends with looking at his fingernails. I try with all my might to remove myself from this influence. But it's very hard, because I dream of throwing my arms around him. If I had some occupation, or someone else, I wouldn't think so much about it. It's strangely amusing that I always know it in advance.

Yesterday I told Jarośka the story of my revenge. Jarośka says, 'Stupid, you are making up stories!' And today, today there's some truth to it after all.

Sometimes one has rivals; that's the way it is. In some cases their very name can make one see red. What am I if she's my rival?! I never thought of it, but he, apparently, did. No.

It's nothing. It will heal, that is certain. Either it will heal, or break for ever! Perhaps only for some time. Because I find it hard to renounce the dream. The dream I've brought to perfection, cultivated in my most secret thoughts. Endure moods – already? No, I've given it the wrong name. It was a good mood, but I immediately know, feel it at once and change, ah, adjust myself. And I'm angry! But it's best to hide a bad mood in the best mood.

We wrote portraits of each other. Zygu was more open, so I wrote an even more 'adoring' addition. How strange it is that I always prefer to say more, that I like to give as good as I get? I know a frame changes a lot, it's like a stage set in the theatre. Bye, goodnight. You will help me, Buluś and God.

18 February 1942, Wednesday

Why did such a nice day end like this? Why did this particular day, filled with friendly conversation with Norka and light, radiant plans from our world, close up and hunch down, like – me? Why am I not brightened by that day of 16 March and the beautiful dream of being together, being in the mountains, only for each other? Why is my own, my beloved, worse than all the others? Why is he so odious!? Odious, yes! This is not a cry of an effusive girl, no! I fully realise that all the letters of that word are odious little worms which comprise an odious whole. How shallow, low and mundane it all is: circles, gossip, circles, gossip, circles … to infinity. Mama, my only, my dearest, take me away from this stifling disgusting atmosphere in which I'm suffocating. And Jarośka, she's making my life impossible too! You see, I wanted to give love wings. I put all my soul into it, but the wings broke off and it fell, earthed, turned grey. Well, why am I surprised? It all boils down to this. Or perhaps we never, never really understood each other? And I am in such need of warm words. Oh, Mama. And I'm reading a book about love. Great, pure, although 'earthly', and I think that such a love can exist only in books, or maybe … Maybe great, beautiful love exists out there? Maybe one can receive what one gives? But not here, I have knocked at the wrong heart, I was wrong, oh, how horribly, horribly wrong I was … You will help me, Buluś and God.

24 February 1942, Tuesday

Me. I make myself laugh. I've got fatter like some old, pudgy, chubby auntie. I have a triple chin. What is there to write about? I'm alive again. Plenty of errands to run. Plenty of things shared with Noruśka. And you know what? We might have an official celebration of our friendship anniversary. 16 February 1942.

Today started just like any other day lately. He told me I've been nasty recently and this and that. And everything was kept at a distance etc. etc. until we looked at our bet (and counted the poems). Zygmunt took the photo away from me, the one that entered the arena of our lives so many times before. He wanted to keep it, I begged him, I asked,

I started crying. Nothing. Zygmunt was relentless, though I cannot say he was uncaring, on the contrary. Jarośka makes me cringe with embarrassment. As a gesture of peace I will let Zyguś have a copy. But I resisted with all my might, even his caresses and looks didn't tempt me – no! And why? Zygmunt asked me this and I couldn't, I didn't know how to explain. After all, this photo is part of a dream. The great, golden dream I carry with me through life, a dream that is stuck in me, that lives, that pulsates. So I said – whatever it takes. The price is peace and quiet, an incomplete album entry, perhaps even tension in our relationship or even a break-up ...

But this dream is unbelievable, nothing will make me withdraw, nobody will wake me up to reality. I think that one day it will be in the album and I will tell one little poppet, 'You know what ... it's not my tears flowing. A dream cannot be conjured up before it is realised.' So Zygu might be cross, even though I thought he reached out. Zyguś, I love you so much; whatever I've done, you should forgive me. But when I thought that it might not happen on Thursday or on Saturday or ... ever, it broke my heart, I felt such longing ... again. You will help me, Buluś and God.

28 February 1942, Saturday

It was good and it was bad and then good again. Those feelings spill over in me. But I wrote a letter to Mama, a long letter, which gave me some relief. Oh, if I could only get away from here. It feels as though every person I meet is my enemy. Perhaps it's those stories.

Zyguś is so sweet, but I am not able to dance, I am languid, nasty, terrible. I don't want anything else but ... to go to Mama. Go there and have some respite for a while. I am so awful for saying all those things about him in a moment of weakness. It's wrong, it's low and it's true. Mama, I'm so unhappy ... You will help me, Buluś and God.

6 March 1942, Friday

This week has been very eventful. It was Irka's birthday. We spent the day with Nora; it was very pleasant. We had some pictures taken with Nora and Jarośka (they will probably be terrible, by the way). There might be some photos taken on Sunday and Mama wrote and sent two parcels and this and that.

I haven't seen Zygmunt all week long. Yes, and now I will have a nervous breakdown, I will vent my anger, I will explode! Yes, because I don't care that he goes on his little visits. I understand – and he even told me this himself – that he likes company. But he is too embarrassed to go with me; he is simply embarrassed and ill at ease. He actually told me this, i.e., he didn't want to go with me and said he would go on his own. Whatever, I will absolutely spare him the displeasure of my company, he might even be embarrassed in the street too. Well, tough. It is difficult to describe how bitter I am, I can taste the bile in my mouth. And just think, just think how I felt when Lidzia asked sweetly, 'Why didn't you come with Zygu?' New disappointments all the time.

Letters to Mama are the only things that calm me down the most. I don't mention anything about 'the issue', but I do say, rightly, that I would like to get away from here, to find a different world – I know it wouldn't be better, but it attracts me because it would be new. I have had enough of this tête-à-tête. And it's all because this roast is lacking gravy. 'I'm angry, because I turned my heart inside out like an old pocket and shook all the crumbs out. I know, I know I'm a stupid cow, you don't need to tell me.' This is what I wrote for Binka. Do you remember 'open your hearts'? I'm angry with this poem now, I contradict it; it convinced me only temporarily and now I negate it with all my might. I was biased. Indeed, 'open your hearts – to hearts wide open' is the right thing. But only to the ones that are wide open. And if there is no sweet secret left there, it will be empty.

Purple light trickles out thin
illuminating a ruby red urn
showing some visions within
enchanted spectres that churn
You can see some deep trances
hidden in the ruby tone
resting foreheads, sending glances
You can see the crown of glimmers
Mystery queen deep in fantasies
on her throne of twilight dimmer …

Then somebody opened the canopies
Letting the light inside
into the dark secret
looking for something that hides
Checking dressers, corners in sequence
Peeping into a vase
Looking, rummaging with both hands
To conclude, 'Empty, she's an empty place.'

A secret stops being itself when somebody finds it out. My
heart is empty because I said it all.

I will never be angry, my darling
when your cheeks go bright red
when you find a question alarming
when you say softly, 'It's a secret.'
You'll put a finger on your lips
Your hair will fall onto your brow
Your eyes'll look up and eclipse
Filled with mystery, surprise, disavow.
I know you would like to say
I know you would like to call
it's tough, so tough, but hey
You want to know it all?
It's boring and it is fruitless
Yes, I'd like to hear about it
but I won't be angry, my sweetness

because then it would be unfit

it wouldn't be your secret sweet ...

So he is embarrassed. Well, till tomorrow. You will help me, Buluś and God.

(On Saturday)

The wound has not healed, how could it have? Irka was there and Waldek and Zygmunt. And it was nice. Quite nice. I'm sending kisses ... You will help me, Buluś and God.

11 March 1942, Tuesday

Again he reached out to me and he was like he used to be. And again I rejected him. I can't say I wasn't tempted. Indeed I was, but the wound has not healed just yet and I think it'll never heal. This anger will resurface elsewhere, while it's all about me wanting to get the other part of the portrait back. Why? Because now the most intimate issues – not of the heart, but of the soul – lay shamelessly on paper and bare their teeth; they are in somebody else's hands. And it's not about him possibly showing it to somebody else, now or later, when 'this' is not there any more, or about him reading it himself, or not. It's about the fact that another 'I' exists, lives. That I'm split in two, that I expelled something and that it now exists. It doesn't mean I'm stupid. It rather means that I love this idiot who doesn't love me back, that I believe, strongly believe in a dream which will never come true, which is just a phantasm. And I feel so very sorry for myself that I'd like to curl up in some corner and cry. I feel so sorry for you, stupid girl, because I can see how much suffering you have ahead of you – it won't end any time soon.

So, so many worries are piling in front of me. I'm glad that Mama is coming, I'll tell her. But I'm afraid she might not understand me, she might tell me to laugh it off, to stop caring, while I still feel the love, I love so much. The slightest whiff is enough to give me heartache and it goes on and on, until I tell Nora or you. But ... Nothing ... Is it true that ...

Yes, exactly this!
I think spring is not a bliss
It doesn't fit my mood
I'll revolt, I will be booed
I'll defy those hard constraints
grab my old, leaky umbrella
put on black galoshes, no complaints
my scarf and autumn jacket.
I'll sniffle, oh how yucky.
And in all this gear
I'll walk through town all mucky
saying for all to hear,
'What foul, autumnal weather.'
I'll bump into some moron.
Passers-by at the end of their tether

will stare at this rubber phantom
speaking now of autumn.
'It's autumn where I am, really,
I promise you, you have my word,
I bring autumn to the fore pretty freely
as spring is not in step with my mood!'
Nobody seems to get it.
Nobody says I'm right.
So bored, tired, unhappy
I stay at home, I hide.
I draw the curtains, shut doors
Put lots of wood in the stove
guarding myself from the spring
Rubbing my hands in the alcove
until snowdrifts are here again.
I will return to the autumn
unless it changes from the very bottom!

I really wouldn't want it to be nice and for thousands of 'couples' to come out into the streets. I am selfish, terribly selfish, but, really, what for? I don't need it; it just yanks at my heart. Sometimes I get rebellious. I want to raise my head (after all spring is coming) and fight. Yes, fight against my love, against him and against my own helplessness and my own stupidity. I want to forget everything and write a novel. I'll start soon because I feel that everything has to find an outlet. Bye, goodnight … You will help me, Buluś and God.

12 March 1942

There is no way to express this. No way at all. I only think about my parents who, even though they are alive, made me an orphan. Why don't I have my own place today, why am I at the mercy of people who, at any moment, can say, 'Go away! We don't have to feed you'? That's what Granny said to me today. 'Go away!' Why didn't she say that earlier? Why did she let me live with them? Why didn't my parents send me to go into service somewhere or even better, why didn't they kill us both when they split up? And now I have to think about it. I have to think about a way to leave this life in a quiet, unnoticed way. To remove myself. Everybody would be happy then, my parents wouldn't need to think about what to do with me, Granny and Grandpa would have plenty of food for themselves, they wouldn't have somebody else's bastards to take care of and I . . . I'd be the happiest of them all. But I know it won't come to that. I don't have the courage. Why, why do I tell myself this, I don't know. I only know that the hope of tomorrow keeps me together. But if tomorrow is . . . I'll try.

Bye, dear Diary, I love everybody, but my raw nerve, my only goal in life was home. It's not my fault that I don't have a home; it's everybody else's fault, not mine, but it's not them who suffer because of that, but me, only me. So I suffer without any fault on my part. Bye. You will help me, Buluś and God.

We'll compose a living poem
we'll drown it in a happy flood

by all it will be softly spoken
among spring, by all young
it'll be made of hot promises
with bloody laments of affection
adorned with our sweet caresses
linked and framed by our lips' attention
It will pulsate with our blood
taste of our kissing, our tears
smell just like jasmine or lilac
be sweet as old song in our ears
it will be fresh like a fierce river
whoever reads it, he will say,
'I know it, it could be my verse ...'

16 March 1941*

The third year of the war. But Renia! What do we care about the war today! We celebrated the second anniversary of our friendship, just like we planned.

You didn't let me finish at yours, so I have to start from the beginning. The old-fashioned clock's hands have moved just a few hours forward, but so much has changed in that time. The morning was wonderful, it was as good as one can only imagine, it was familiar, delightful and at the same time unusual. We triumphed over Irka, we felt we were heading for something better, we felt we had a great day to celebrate! It's been a while

---

*This entry has been written by Renia's friend Nora.

since I was in such a good mood … And it was all gone the moment Zygu appeared. He brought with him something alien, something stiff, he pushed me into the state I am in now.

I'd like to write something cheerful, to thank you, Renia, for all your efforts to make this day a pleasant one, but I can't. In the morning I radiated joy, now I sit here, cold, hunched over a page from your diary, completely broken, and I can't even think of anything any more. It is all Zygo's doing. He made me feel like some small, stupid, unimportant person who at best can smile idiotically, or rather laugh, and nothing more. Renia, don't hold it against me that I spoilt this day filled with warmth, sweetness, delight. We need to remember one thing: satisfaction is never creative. I'm grateful to Zygu for bringing me back to my senses (I'm sure absolutely unintentionally). I sobered up, I don't know for how long, because there is somebody else who can affect my state of mind again.

We could actually start our novel now, the mood couldn't be more appropriate, but there's one problem, Renia, I'm simply not able to. I don't have even the slightest bit of a writing talent. You have so much more imagination. To you writing comes easily, you have panache. And my knowledge is way too limited to undertake the writing of even the smallest novel. Renia, start writing on your own, I might join you or not, that remains to be seen.

But now I'm thinking of something new, Mila's idea. 'Organise a day of truth,' she told us and, 'Put it all on the table.' Yes! We need to fulfil this plan. It might change my attitude to Zygu, it might even bring me closer to you two.

It's strange, after all we don't need any new circumstances, because I don't think we could be any closer to each other than we are now. Because, Renia, we are very close, but I am distant from you and Zygu. I always feel it when you are together and I would really like that to change. So chin up, all must end well. We have achieved so much, Renia, we'll achieve this as well. Vivat 16 March! Vivat our dear friendship! 'Be gone, worries, tears and upheaval ...'

17, Tuesday

I didn't write yesterday because you were at Norka's. Pity. I felt so good. And all that joy, this blissful calm, I transferred onto the pages of Nora's diary. I felt like this even in the afternoon. We were together, the four of us, and I thought we were so close. Shame that you, Nora, didn't feel the same way ... (ah, you don't know anything about Julek). Strange that I wrote so little about Julek. I'll write some more now, since he's become my ... let me say it ... my 'brother-in-law'.

In fact I like Julek a lot, especially that he disappointed me in a nice way. I expected him to be rather experienced, to like girls, to be idle, a pleasure-seeker, superficial, talented and very smart. And now I see that there is something very straightforward about him, that there's nothing artificial about him, nothing unnatural. He's very good and not at all bigheaded. So I'm glad that Norka said the words, 'I love.' Admittedly she said it as a question, 'Do I?' but she's loved him without being aware of it for a long while. And I wish her all the best in love. I'm waiting impatiently for it to happen.

Yesterday I felt that everything we dreamt about came true. We won over her, that awful cow, we have our shared 'baby' (the album), we have our friendship and … we take photos. Yes, this (for those in the know) means a lot too. And then, i.e., yesterday, when we were finally alone, it was sweet and it smelt of spring. Zygmunt said that we would never argue again. But I replied it was not possible. True, I knew it and I admitted that I was angry and when I'm angry I invent outrageous things about him and I have already forgotten what it was about and I felt bad about it, until this wound stung again. Until I remembered that he was embarrassed to go with me to Irka's. And today this story with the photo unnerved me again.

And you know what, today I looked at him terribly unfavourably. Krela was indeed right when she said he was vulgar – I could die of embarrassment. But Norka made it all disappear, she presented it somewhat humorously and gently and as a result one could be sympathetic. Good, dear Nora, it's so nice of her. I'm curious about the photo and what he says. I'm sure we look like Antek and Margośka.* You will help me, Buluś and God.

19 March 1942, Thursday

Sweet Thursday, which tastes of kisses and tears! I have expressed my worries and now I feel better. And Zyguś was

---

*This might be a reference to Antek from Władysław Stanisław Reymont's *The Peasants* and the title character from Józef Birkenmajer's *Opowiadania Margośki* (*Margośka's Tales*).

also so good and loving. But something still bothers me. I don't know what it is. Some conversations leave me with an unpleasant feeling. But I still love him very, very much, even though I don't find him as beautiful as I used to. I like this tender atmosphere, full of caresses, warmth – I would give everything for it. Yes, my dear mama, I long for, I crave what I didn't have, because you were far away. You will help me, Buluś and God. Goodnight …

21 March 1942, Saturday

Irka is supposed to come. It's all trifling; she is meanness incarnate. Mila called it as it is …

But today's a special day for me, because Norka … I tremble with curiosity and contentment. Finally, phew! I can breathe now.

I am so very sorry
for spring, for love, for myself
I'd like to drown in the sky's expanses
in blueness, following my gaze
or into the unknown take my chances
I feel so lonely, oh so poorly
I know that by all I'm forgone
I struggle in my helplessness, sincerely
my heart'll stay here even when I'm gone

I will do nothing, my dear madam
'cause I can't fight against myself

though I do know, though I do want
though I push for it, I say it myself
Stay, I'm dying with you
I know this is not true
Mock me, why don't you?
I will not die, I'm not in line
I'll keep on living, I'm not yet due.

I'll finish later.

We've won. Or rather Nora has won. She pushed for it and today it (didn't happen) but manifested itself. We felt we had each other and that we have them.

Julek went with Nora, Zygmunt stayed with me. She was somewhat deflated, disappointed and lonely. I could see she wanted to make me jealous and then show me pity (like she once did), but she trapped herself. To a large extent it was Zygmunt's doing. I was so grateful to him for it. I could kiss him to death. Zyguśka, I feel such an urge now that I haven't felt for a long time. By the way you were in a bad mood.

The best thing is that now I feel sorry for Irka, I'm torn with regrets when I think about her almost crying when she was leaving. I'm very, very sorry, but it has to be that way, such is life. If she went away smiling, I would be the one crying now. Buluś, now you can laugh. Bye, I'm sending kisses to you ... and not to you. You will help me, Buluś and God.

23 March 1942, Monday

Thank You, Lord! Many thanks that I'm not alone now, hungry and locked away in prison, but at home with my dear ones – that I can appreciate. I can still remember the face in the helmet and again I'm terribly scared, so terribly scared like I was then and I badly want to cry. It was really a miracle, an extraordinary miracle – thank You, God Almighty and my dear mama who prays for me somewhere far away. Compared to this, everything else is trivial and pale, a walk, kisses, photos. So what that Z, so what that I was worried that I didn't like him any more, that he seemed ridiculous, that in my thoughts I turned his face in my hands. But that's not even funny, how can I even say that, what a terrible cow? In the face of his tenderness I have forced myself to get over it somehow and then I didn't need to force myself at all, which was the best. I'm glad today is over … and it's a pity too. Because I crave something again. You will help me, Buluś and God.

25 March 1942, Wednesday

It's so ironic. They are closing our quarter (I won't be able to see Norka); they are moving people out of town; there are persecutions, unlawfulness. And on top of that – there's spring, kisses, sweet caresses, which make me forget about the whole world. Bye. You will help me, Buluś and God.

28 March 1942

Somebody stays at home, because they must. Somebody has a mirror on the desk and looks into it and can see that they've gained weight. Thoughts rush through somebody's head like water through a mill wheel. I've been interrupted and haven't finished, bye. You will help me, Buluś and God.

The following day

It's a pity I didn't write yesterday. Spring longing engulfed me yesterday. Zyguś is so good to me, so tender, so affectionate – like never before. Even in company I feel good about it, i.e., I have felt good about it, it's not the case any more, no, it isn't. I simply can't stand all those 'hunters'. There are plenty of them; I'm surrounded as if I were in a cage. Some try their openness and honesty, others bad-mouth me behind my back, others still try through a brother or a cousin, still others … eh, it's not worth writing about.

Shame we didn't take any photos. Did you know? And what did you think? Nasty world. No, not the world, just our little world. And anyway why is Z telling me all this, it seriously puts me off our relationship and at the same time gives me a kick, I start 'feeling' that I am on earth. 'If the sun only shines for the bourgeoisie, we will put the sun out.'* That's right! Yes, yes, this is what I've learnt.

---

*Leon Trotsky's words.

Julek disgusts me. I feel bad about not telling Nora, but I can't. She seems so happy, so self-contented. How could I destroy it with one word?! No, I won't do it, I can't. And anyway nobody is perfect. Nobody. I don't even know what is better. But when Z was telling me this, I was glad; I was glad that he exists at all, that we exist, and our miss.* I felt that what we had was somewhat bigger than what she had. That Z is more permanent. But nothing's certain. Nothing at all. I'm going through a strange period, I want to write poems and I can't – I really don't have the energy.

Hello, listen, hi
you funny passers-by
you dreamers, rhymists
and incurable fantasists
walking the earth
always looking up
what do you search for
among the stars high up?
Who do you sigh to
on a silver moonlit night?
There is life down here
It rumbles ahead with might
it bubbles over, boils, brews

---

* This term appears several times throughout the diary, but its meaning is never clear. It might be Renia and Zygmunt's inside joke, a metaphor for their love or relationship.

First the wave needs to be pacified
You must not follow paths untrue
on the map of the endless sky, its guide
Stop staring at expanses
with your daydreaming eyes
unless you want to take your chances
be jostled and well chastised
Gather your powers don't think twice
look what's here, take a look around you
or else you'll pay the price
and plenty of bruises will come through!

Yes, that is true, but it's so nice among the clouds and so ugly down on the earth – there is no point in it. Now for something for the club, a little gossip.

D'you want to?
We will climb the mountains
I used to say, 'I do'
But now I ask you
D'you want to? Can you?
You crave it? Know it?
That is all my affection
It's just one big question.
Do you know …
Yes, yes, our affection
is another question
What do you want?

Yes, yes, our affection
is really a question.
How dare you!

I will ponder on things in bed. You will help me, Buluś and God.

7 April 1942, Tuesday

That's that ... We fell out and ... I've decided to stay angry. But Norka came to persuade me. And she did. I'm easily persuaded. And in fact I'm happy that Norka talked to Zygu. I've wished for it for a long time. I'm also glad she is coming to the picnic tomorrow and that she loves her Julek, that she's going through this spring with such a 'flourish'. I keep thinking of my spring last year. Let Noreńka be happy, she deserves it. Everybody needs to experience the first spring. Our 'springs' are so similar, just like the two of us are. But there is also a different 'something', as you know.

I'll fight Irka with ... every available weapon. I had this silly, indifferent feeling and now – it doesn't matter ... You will help me, Buluś and God.

9 April 1942, Thursday [22]

All's well already, all's well. Things are good ... and that's good. My adorable, adorable Zyguś! My dear, dear Nora! I'm so glad you got to know each other. Zyguś, your soul is as delicate as a sprig of mimosa. It dwindles with every gust of wind. It dies. I'll never be different. I'll always be a dreamer and that is that. I still soar high, I still live in the realm of dreams. Buluś, today, even though I don't love you any less, I have a grievance, and it is not the first time. I feel so good with him now, I would like to cling to him, hold him tight and … already. Mine, mine, only mine! Good, better than me. Bye, Zyguś … You will help me, Buluś and God.

10 April 1942, Friday

This morning I thought a lot about our yesterday's conversation. The sun was so bright and (it seemed) loving. I sensed the spring and I can tell that this was my first proper spring day. Today I wasn't annoyed with 'couples'; actually it's been like that for a few days now. Today even kissing couples could evoke only friendly and warm feelings. But even today, yes, still, in the morning, I was planning to go far away, high up, deep inside and, as I've planned for a while, I wanted to take Zygmunt with me. I think the beginning went like this:

What do you say? Give me your hand
Let's go away, let's leave this land

Yes, this was the beginning for sure, I wrote it down exactly as it was, but later I gave up on it, I wanted to travel on my own, but then I thought we were walking together. Something like that came out of this jumble of thoughts:

I ride on each dragonfly
I gallop on the bright sunrays
I climb every cloud that goes by
I make circles all day.
The old wind knows me well
It warmly shakes my hand
And asks, 'Are we going, pray, tell,
my fare dodger, oh, so grand?
'Where to?' A snowdrop wants to know
which grows by the big bush of blackthorn
'Far, my friend, so far I want to go
where the sky kisses the earth at morn.'
Worldly news won't catch me there
Even if they speed like light
But if you want to track my flight
Look for me, but there, not here!

Yes, but that's not all. In the morning I felt this rush, I
wanted to write a poem made of pure absurdities.

Everything is twisted
Everything is wrong!
The earth is too slow unassisted
Giving birth to days too short
The sun creeps in too quickly
Into the sunset's dying might
The moon is looking sickly
Against stars in the sky so bright

Silence is too loud
Distance is too near
Spring unusually dowdy
sorrow is too drear ...
But if you want ...
we will get the world going
we'll move the sun to the sky's crust
the moon will be glowing
If you want, then you simply must!
The hum of silence must be quelled
Close distances – pushed away
Spring must be less dowdy, sorrows curtailed
No, let's get rid of the sorrows, if we may!

I've finished and I feel good! Today Z solved me like you solve a riddle. It's true that I run away from this world only because I'm not in a good frame of mind. He said that this is not a regular romanticism, but it's more something like symbolism. It is an escape from an oppressive life, which I don't know how to enjoy, which I don't love. He was terrified that this might be quite abnormal and that I might drag him with me. Yes, he is right, 100 per cent right (as usual), because I wanted to do it. But now I see that I had no right, that I must not do it! I can't hijack a person who passionately loves life, who knows how to seize it and lets life seize him, just because I feel bad here. No, I don't feel bad, I feel unwell. Yes, he needs to stay here, play, have fun and ... nothing. And I? I'll try to fall in love with life, with the 'earthly' spring and people. Falling in love with life is my new task. Adjusting to its requirements, becoming a regular romantic (if I must) to a high degree. The other option is what I thought of so many times, shedding all those dreams, never writing poems again, never analysing anything – and instead becoming a regular 'earthly' seventeen-year-old girl, learning to dance, going to parties, enjoying it and everything else. Becoming like, you know ... like Rena, but this other one, like I wrote. Then there would be no issue of developing a complex; I wouldn't even know that something like it exists and I'd ask, 'What's that?' I know it'd be good, but that means dying and being reborn. Perhaps I can become the first one. I'll try, anyway.

Anyhow I'm full of good intentions and cordiality, I reach out. Let's see how the world receives me, no, not the world, our little world. But let me admit here that I'm only doing it under Zygmunt's influence and because of him; otherwise I'd never do that. Aha! Just in case I wanted to defect (it might happen), just look at me, Zygu, like you did today and ... all will be well. See you soon.

Until spring betrays you
until it gives you pain
until false thoughts hurt you
get some hugs while you can.
Until you buckle under
the heavy weight of the moments, years
laugh out loudly, don't ponder
love the world, give it cheers.

7.30 a.m.

You will help me, Buluś and God.

11 April 1942, Saturday

I've missed Zygu, I've missed him so much. All night long I kept thinking about it and the day seemed to go on for ever. All day long I waited to see him. I was as excited as I haven't been for a while. And I was in such bad luck! I barely had him to myself for a moment. But I'm very contented, very happy! Zyguś, darling, you were so, so sweet and good, I was really touched. I can appreciate your behaviour. My dear, good, wonderful boy! I'd like you to always be like that. That would make me happy. And what I'd like the most in the world is to have you by me now. I'd like to be with you, because this is no relaxation, it's a torment of waiting and longing, but! I'll just imagine in detail that we are together! Yes! Help me, Buluś and God.

13 April 1942, Monday

A sweet day. There were parcels from Mama, and in those parcels there were sweets, sweet sweets. But ... It wasn't the only reason it was sweet. Somebody's lips were much sweeter. Whose? You can work it out. I don't feel like writing it, what for? I would spoil 'it' with words. 'It' needs to be experienced to be understood. You can envy me, all of you who have never experienced spring, the second one with a subtle fragrance of April fields or love so hot, though earthly, which sometimes travels across my skin like shivers. Ah. You will help me, Buluś and God!

16 April 1942

Can you hear me? I call you over the world
The wind catches my every word
I command it to carry them across
This is my song, my response
My spring mating song!
I shout, I gush
taking air into my lungs
this chuckling rush
Listen to the wind when it comes
Listen to the hum, the chirp, the whisper
I call you, Mum, I summon
It's a cheerful call, the song's my whimper
It'll land by your feet, Mama
It might've seen blood on its way
It might've been scared by some graves
It might've met a cloud of grey agony
Or maybe hot tears in waves
And now any sound it doesn't deliver
It is pale, it curls up and shivers.
It was dawn
fragrant and vivid
in the orchard

wind
shook blooms
off the trees
We just sat there
daydreaming, in oblivion
forgetting the world that looms
Sweet gazes
and sweet verses
(d'you remember my blushing face?)
so very shy and cautious
the first ones, the very first
I loved, I dreamt, I longed.
All was quiet, bright and fresh
snow of apple blossom on the ground
we just sat there in the flesh
pale with happiness
white with flowers.
Sun took mercy on us
and covered us with dew
Not true, that didn't happen!
But it might happen anew.

You will help me, Buluś and God.

20 April 1942, Monday

Today is the Führer's birthday. And more. I want to scream
with all my might. And I keep thinking of the words, 'Vodka

is cold and lips are hot!"* And ... No, I can't say this; Zyguś is right, can you express just how much? No, there are no words to describe it.

How can you be in love for eighteen months? What an idiotic question! Only now you can really love. I am ... Well, I lost my mind, I think. But no, everything is real, pulsating, seething with life and love and youth. I feel as though I were riding a chariot or racing into the wind and rain. And about Zygu, about my most wonderful one in the world, I can't write. I can't catch my breath, I can't find words. I might dissolve in my own tenderness, my affection. Today I was really ready to strangle him, but what would I do then? Zyguśka, I'm really writing this for you and you only! I've opened my heart to you and you're so very dear to me! I'm happy, happy and light and ... Dreams! Stupid, mad, wonderful dreams! Everything.

> I'll jump onto the windowsill
> No, higher still
> Onto the roof I'll go
> Climb a very tall tower
> I'll strike a blow
> Hit the bell's clapper on the hour
> I will shout, I'll bellow
> In a voice that is not mellow

---

* Quote from a popular waltz entitled '*Gwiżdżę na wszystko*' ('I Don't Care About Anything'), with lyrics by Krzysztof Lipczyński and music by Jan Markowski, performed by Mieczysław Fogg.

The clapper ding-dongs
Bell-like, d'you hear?
Joy, bliss, life all along
Crazy love in the air
Which can't wait to be in the world
Quivering soul's a-ringing
I'm sweet eighteen years old
It's all brimming
It's way too much to hold in
Perhaps then I will tell you
Perhaps I will begin
And it will be true
As if everybody knew
As if the whole world knew
What it doesn't in fact know
That in the spring breeze that cuts through
In every bit of sun aglow
Your little miss is on her way to you

You will help me, Buluś and God.

Beyond today. Tomorrow

I'm scared. I'm really scared for myself. I kept thinking in the night to write, write, write, but I couldn't write. Because I know my thoughts were focused. Just think, spring and the dreamy stuff that used to wander over the moon and the stars and in the world, was now combined into one strong embrace! And now it's not enough to imagine ♥, now I want to have him with me. It'd be best for me then, as it is I'm only well. But yesterday, I won't forget it, Zyguś, yesterday it was spring!

I'm just shocked that flowers
don't sprout at your feet
you, my bird, angel empowered
you, May, paradise, you spring sweet

I stifle this scream in me. I would run out to the fields, spread my arms wide and scream like mad. May! Paradise! Spring! Spriiing! And then ... One more embrace like this. Which would contain everything. God! I'm so terrible!

I've received postcards from Mum and Ticiu. Sad cards, horrible! And I, their child, feel so bright and singsong?! This is a terrible sin. Forgive me. Because I ...

I don't care
in the attic, in the cellar
on the Aryan side, there, there
as a ghetto wretched dweller
my heart warmed with a flame like this
makes the world a happy place
my heart warmed with a gaze like this
I'll go to the bottom of the sea with grace
I can even wear an armband
and not just one
but bands in abundance.

No, this is still not what I want to write.

Listen to my news
Wait, I will tell you something
At night spring rain oozed
And out of my head violets are sprouting.
Don't know how it came about
but when I was woken up
the world was pink somehow
And my head … green like a buttercup!
I saw countless gloomy faces
heard sighs full of black despair
and the lament, 'what's with her
this girl! She whistles and leaps, oh dear
like a street urchin.
Incredible, something new is occurring here!'

Aunts, cousins and distant relations
Discuss how to bring the sinner back
Such disgrace for the family, such sensation
the whole clan is under attack!

I know, I should cower, make a sad face
I should crouch down a bit more
lament the world and the human race
busy darning old stockings, what a chore.
I should sigh over hard times
over endless human stupidity

I should worry
But why should I? What pity?
I promised myself long ago,
to chuck worries and sadness out.
Begone, what's distressing and full of sorrow
There's only space for love in my heart.

My buttonhole is adorned
With a pretty blossom
I paint hearts all over the world
I draw hearts all over the heavenly parts
Write your name in each of the hearts

I am to do physical work. You will help me, Buluś and God.

24 April 1942, Friday

You were at Z's place. Zyguś knows you! Oh, paradise! Oh, May! Oh, springtime! Enough … You will help me, Buluś and God.

26 April 1942, Monday

I don't know where to start! I need to collect my thoughts and myself; I need to force myself to express everything. In fact this exclamation about paradise, May and springtime was the final one. At first I felt terrible. I wanted to tear you apart, burn you, crush you for giving my secrets away. How could you? After all, you promised me in the beginning to stay faithful! By what right did you reveal your pages so shamelessly? When I thought that somebody had forced (well, yes, forced) their way into my personal, most intimate realm, no, I didn't feel emptiness, but a terrible, burning shame. I don't any more and I stopped feeling it soon afterwards. You know, I thought he could understand me more than anybody else. In fact, I thought he was the only person who could understand me. He knows me terribly well, scarily well. And he's good, loving, understanding and … Didn't he kiss me today like a father, a husband, a mother?

Ah, I don't feel like writing at all. I have some terribly sweet dreams to think through. But I have to write to make my soul lighter and brighter, to make everything clear. True, I'm not describing the details now, but I can't. (Zygmunt, after all you wanted me to grow up one day.) My writing's honest, that's true, it's fiercely heartfelt, but … (so there is a but) I think I lost a little, just a tiny bit of trust in you. In the past I entrusted you with my thoughts, those thoughts I didn't even think yet, but today I don't want to, I can't … Not that it's your fault, my dear Diary, it's not you, it's me and … no, it's just me. I'll forget about it now. I want to forget, I want to give you a verbal hug and say, 'Thank you, my dear friend, for letting Zygu have a glance at my soul.'

We came to an understanding today. I know we have understood each other for a long time now, but those words were not gathered together. I also know that I'm looking for a job and I know why I need this job. After all I'm me and I know why I'm doing something. But think, Zygu knows it too! This is outrageous and wonderful at the same time. And how does he know it? As I said, he knows me terribly well. Ah! Do you know that in fact this was the first time?! So did it come true? Do you know that Zygmunt's cousin came; she lives with them and I am to meet her? But I've saved the sweetest, the dearest bit for the very end. Do you know that we talked with Z about children today? About my, or rather, about our children? When he mentioned it I was very upset that he read it here (you spilt the beans again), but it was true. Zyguś was so loving when he asked me, 'Boy or girl?' I almost went mad with happiness. So now our secret has a third accomplice. This is so dear. I can't even … Even now I feel strange. Norka understands everything, but I know she doesn't want it as much as I do, that she finds it a bit surprising, because she's a modern woman. I, too, am not a thousand years old, but if the price of modernity is relinquishing a dream, I would go centuries back … Just to tenderly stroke my beloved child's head. And Zyguś understands it. Zyguś is a wonderful, good husband, the best. I'm still a bit shy writing about it, but it'll happen soon, very soon. You will help me, Buluś and God.

30 April 1942, Thursday

What do I have to tell you? Ah, there was something. It's almost May. But this May is not fragrant, green and fresh.

I laugh my head off when I think that this bad weather is my doing. Indeed it's quite autumnal. I can feel this devilish temptation. So I won't say yes or no. But knowing that it might have happened because I wanted it so much pleases me, amuses me, delights me! Well, I don't need this wet weather for anything, but it also isn't in my way. And it serves to spite so many people. Ah, sometimes, like today, I'm tempted to be a malicious goblin. Yes, because Z said today that the little world consists of all people, while the world is Nora and me. He said it as ironically as he could. Well, because this is how it is. Aha! 'But I'm sensing something.' What? Something unpleasant must have happened to Z. Tough. I imagine he feels like a woman who has given herself away. I have also given myself away spiritually, i.e., I have given you away and now I'm not ashamed of anything (perhaps that's why I stopped blushing), but from time to time something flashes to remind me that it's happened, that it's done. I'll always be left with something, because I have thoughts even more secret than the biggest secrets, more secret $+ - \infty$. What Z showed me today about Brilliant People was very wise – that there are people who are proud but also sensitive, weak and touchy and that is what makes them big-hearted. He's really got it spot on. Even though I still sighed with relief when Z told me he would never read you again.

It's so nice to run a pen on a page. I'd like to write everything. That's why I create such a mess. But I'm still a bit worried that Z might have made me believe that I am

somehow different. Will I not get manic, like Klim Samgin?*
No! I will try to be normal (if I'm not already; and 'average'
too). Ah, excuse me! Perhaps all girls write diaries, ponder
over everything, analyse everything? How do I know this isn't
the case? My God, they do think after all. What do they think
about? Perhaps they dream just like me?

Do you know, Z's mother said he doesn't look well when he
comes back from my place, because he doesn't have an erotic
outlet. I like that very much. Do you know why? Because it's
serious and grown-up. This is not child's play, this is not about
drawing hearts and staring at the moon. I can say that 'an
animal has awoken in me'! And again I get lost in myself or I
annoy myself with my own thoughts, with what I say. I either
exaggerate or there is more than I think.

No, today my writing's quite sober. It's horrible and cold.
I can't smell the fragrance of daffodils or lilac. Not now, now
there is nothing. But I know that as soon as I go to bed, it'll
come; no, not today. Today I'll daydream; I'll imagine things.
No, I'm taking it too far (or at least I think I do today).

It's natural that it's so incredibly nice to lie next to Z.
Today we lay on the sofa. In fact all intimacy is delicious and
I constantly feel the need for such closeness. Yes, yes ...

Anyway, I'm looking for a job, I don't have it yet; I don't know
where I'll work. I don't want it to be at the Castle. But when

---

*Protagonist of Maxim Gorky's series of novels *The Life of Klim Samgin*,
describing the life of Russian intelligentsia at the turn of the nineteenth
and twentieth centuries. Its Polish translation (by Karolina Beylin) was
published in the years 1929–1930.

I think that Z has read the diary, I can't believe it sometimes. But still … I'm generally sleepy, but I know that I'd happily drop all my complexes and shyness and analysing and (oh no, not my dreams, I'm sorry, no, my angels!) and I'd give a big sigh like somebody who's removed uncomfortable clothes or shoes with some difficulty. In fact Z doesn't care that much about children, how can he? I haven't met a person yet who would want to ponder on this subject. The other day I thought that he did. But he didn't even mention it. I know that if he'd talked about it, I would have been moved and happy. Ah, I'm such an idiot. I really am abnormal. It needs to be said. Bye, Zyguś, bye, Diary, bye, Mama … You will help me, Buluś and God.

2 May 1942, Saturday

I feel heavenly in my blue shoes. Zyguś made them for me! What deliciousness! I'm touched when I think that he had me in mind while making them. And I'm so glad that it takes my breath away. I generally like everything and then this commotion with the clogs and all the fuss …

I'll write a letter to Buluś in a moment and tomorrow I'll invite Noruśka over for the whole day. Tra la la. Waltz and love and … May! Do you know it's May already today? It doesn't look like it outside the window, but you can sense it and you can kiss its sweet lips. Ah, how we caressed each other today! How delightfully! I simply can't write, because I float up in the air with euphoria.

Maciek came later and this and that, and Z, my love, was angry because of it and he said something (I stopped writing,

I was having a bath). You know, I haven't felt so great for a long time, I can barely keep my heart in, it wants to jump out. When Z told me today that it's May, I felt completely different, more love-like. But I calmed down a bit and I have to say that … well, despite everything I was a bit jealous of Maciek today. I was in such bliss today that I stroked Maciek. (Don't be angry, I'm trying to explain myself.) Well, whatever. Whenever something unpleasant happens to me, it's enough to look at those azure shoes and think that he's made them for me and … I feel somewhat azure-like too, i.e., heavenly. My life's filled with 'this' again.

Aha, this cousin, Zośka, came today. I was terribly embarrassed because I felt she came to have a look at me and she did it with a curiosity that only women have. I don't know what to say about her, because I don't know her. But it seems she's quite like Zygu has described her … I don't care at all.

May has its own rights, especially for me. Zyguś is May-like too. This year he's more mine, not so mysterious, but affectionate and sweet. I think he loves me a bit more, while I love him the same, always the same, with all my might. 'You cannot love less or more – you can only love' (*Anna Karenina*). It's the beginning of May.

Welcome, May … love
illuminate our whole family*

---

*The first two lines refer to Rajnold Suchodolski's '*Śpiew*' (Singing), written during the November Uprising: 'Welcome, May dawn / illuminate our Polish land.'

you will only come and visit in May
but you will never cease to exist

Bye, Zyguś … You will help me, Buluś and God.

Today is Sunday. But I can't wait any longer and so I write.
I wrote a letter to my dear mama. And I told her everything.
And, in the spirit of honesty I also revealed what I didn't write
down. I felt my joy was great – limitless, but somewhat stifled.
And when I was writing the letter, I thought that I could hug
her and show her my blue shoes and tell her that all is well;
or perhaps it's this longing that I tend to always feel in May,
this call of fields, trees in bloom, singing woods. Shame. If
not for him, I wouldn't have even known it was May. But
perhaps if Buluś were here, she wouldn't understand me. But
Zyguś does understand me. I love her and I am writing to
her. My wonderful Zyguś! I can feel this warm, heartfelt wave
flooding my heart. In a moment I'll imagine myself hugging
you, in your embraces and … much, much more.

Zosia L came today. She's a lovely, very well-educated
girl. Nora and I like her a lot. One can simply rely on her.
I talked about Zyguś. Do you know his father asked if we
were engaged? I like that very much, I like playing a pretend
married couple. I like our 'marriage'. Indeed, you know, there's
something very charming about those shoes, too. You have to
feel it. How he brought them! Ah, he was such a darling. Can I
write about it? No, there are no words for it, you can never tell
how much. Why the mind? Why? And about May?

It tosses, it wants to break free
It's locked away, sort of
May … May, crazy as can be
so green and so in love!
It jolts, it jerks, it lurches
'It's stifling, let me go
out in the fields, where sun marches'
It looks around feebly, but no
It punches hard with its fists
It fights with tears too
It calls for help, it twists
And opposite, is that true?
Another grave of the same kind
Among those walls so sombre
A hundred Mays cry out
Asking to be freed to wander
in fields, in meadows, in the sun

You will help me, Buluś and God.

6 May 1942, Tuesday

Norka's somewhat low-spirited. I think I've found a job; I might get it tomorrow. But no, I didn't want to write about that.

Today I was engulfed by this laziness, this delightful feeling. I wanted to laugh, to cry, but first and foremost to write. I didn't have time, I couldn't. But this May is more beautiful than the one last year. I mean, it's completely different. When

I think about how close we are to each other, how honest with each other, I feel very moved. Just think, you can say what you think. I think 'My dearest' and I say it. I want to kiss him, so I kiss him. I can tell him about my joys – and my pains, too. And he understands. Isn't that beautiful? Ah, it's so good. So good.

Today I fantasised, like before, that we are on a train. I sit in the corner, leaning against Z's shoulder, embracing him tighter and tighter. The train rumbles and speeds somewhere ... Where? I don't know. I shout out the name of some station – I don't care which one. We travel together; we leave the old world, its worries and regrets behind, we move towards a new, better one. That's why I always imagine us travelling. To make even one single step in life, you need to travel. So it's a pity that when I think 'stay' (or even when I say it), he doesn't stay and then I miss him ... We both miss each other. But this is the most beautiful longing, the most wonderful, because it's not hopeless. I would be embarrassed to write heresies. I'm sleepy. I send you such big kisses. You will help me, Buluś and God.

8 May 1942, Thursday

Ah! I love our miss so much! I love her, herself and her manifestations. Now I don't need to be told it's May. I can feel it in every muscle and every drop of my blood. I can feel something swelling in me, something growing to the absolute limit. It's nothing else but this love of mine, which became so 'marriage-like', so bright and simple, direct, honest. It really is like that. Not only does it have its spiritual side, but also ... the very tangible one too. Well, what shall I say, after all I'm not embarrassed in front of people – I simply feel that I can't get away from Zygu, that it gets more and more difficult to part with him. I never have enough caresses, I could bite him to death ... you know, I can't ... The memory itself has exhausted me. I don't know what happened to me. Just think, I am contented now that I'm not 'flat as a board'. I don't know what I need it all for, but I feel my own body. In fact this is the first time in my life that I am experiencing this feeling. I feel that my legs exist, I feel it all too well, I (cover your ears) would like to ... well ... I wanted to sgel ym neewteb mih ezeeuqs.* That's monstrous. No! Not at all, in fact it's pleasant! Why should I be shocked with something that seems to be delightful? Zygu's not so innocent either. It was him who stirred me up today so much I trembled, and then, then he gave me one more kiss and left as if nothing had happened, left me alone with my burning heart, my trembling soul, with my pressing thoughts and my simply sick, 'nervy' imagination! No, it can't be like that! I don't write poems any more! I'm going through a period of not writing. And I don't want to force myself. But if I could, I would write! Rebellion! I'm rebelling; can you hear me? I don't want to lie there half the night with my eyes wide open; I want Zygu as close as is possible ...

---

*Words written backwards.

Phew, I got it out of my system. But even if I filled this diary to the last page, I wouldn't extinguish all of this fire raging in me. That other May was so very different, so much more subtle and romantic. This one, this one is wild, but it's this one, the untamed, wild one, the earthly one, that's the most true and most delectable! How do I know?! Do I? I can't stop writing. Just like I couldn't part with Zygu. So much, so much … love overflows in me.

Tittle-tattle
What a chatter
about love, spring, May, some other matter
About colour red and green
in somebody's eyes shimmering
About the morning dawn's hue
Listen, Renuś, it's all for you.

You will help me, Buluś and God.

9 May 1942, Saturday

This morning was so sunny, like a proper spring. The sun woke me up and as soon as I opened my eyes, I thought about seeing Z. And the sheer thought made me so happy that I wanted to see him then and there. I got dressed an hour too early … Doesn't matter. Finally we were walking together, holding hands like 'two well-behaved children'. No, it really was sweet and when I write this, I don't want to write the rest. Because when I started ruminating, a thought came to me that he's a bit patronising, that he kindly allows me to love him (I didn't say he doesn't love me, I didn't say that at all), but sometimes he looks at me as if he wanted to say, 'Let the child have fun.' And when he notices that I'm all ... well, springlike, then I have a feeling that he thinks himself better and wiser. For example yesterday he said, 'I will give you one more kiss and off you go.' And it came to me that this is something a girl usually says. But whatever, let's assume that I love him the way a boy loves a girl. And anyway, when I said that our miss is so direct, why didn't he want to look me in the eye? Perhaps it's only on my side? Ah! I must shake it off. I must! This stumbling is terrible. I know what it did to Anna Karenina and Anna Fülop.

I felt so fantastic in the morning and he said, like he hasn't for a long time, he said, so sweetly and brightly, 'Bye, poppet.' Aha, this was the so-called (self-) confidence that the sun shone for me! It must be because of the war, but the war'll surely end soon. Zygmunt says there'll be an offensive from the west, in France. He said that a long time ago, but he's convinced it'll happen now. Well, let's see if he could be a diplomat. Springlike bye-byes ... You will help me, Buluś and God.

9 May 1942, Saturday

The spring appearance materialised. But I know what I wanted to write about. Something's bothering me. It was terribly delightful. We started talking about a complex and again I felt small, unimportant, helpless. I felt very sad. Good that Zyguś put it down to unusual times.

I'm sad about not seeing anybody, I'd like to invite Norka for the whole day, but I can't and it's not up to me. I feel she's angry with me.

The job's not working out either. I have to go there the day after tomorrow and I'm very scared.

Zyguś is lovely, but … Listen, Rena (just between the two of us), aren't you by any chance jealous of this Zosia? No, why would you think that?! But something's the matter. Perhaps I'm envious of her self-confidence or the fact that she has him all the time, always, all day long and I'm left with such emptiness, like now … I got so attached. His condescension is still apparent, even more so now. 'You are already thinking of a little house,' and in general he says, 'More and more.' And he thinks that I … He doesn't even imagine how bad this longing can be, this longing for the person closest to one's heart. One can pine like that, I pine like that – but not all the time. And then I feel bad. I have decided to get it under control, not to say it. Not to say that I miss him so much, so as not to make him look down on me the way he does. Whatever happens, not to say it all. It is annoying, even to me, that he knows. But he knows how to mitigate it. He's so becoming when he says that we're children after all.

I wrote it all down, but I don't feel relieved. Maybe a bit. I'm still so-so. I can't even daydream, the way I did in the morning. And it was so good to daydream in the morning! I'll write after work, which scares me so much. I believe in You. Surely You will lend me a helping hand. You will help me, Buluś and God.

I have also been thinking about the insignificance of life in the face of eternity. It calms me down. I didn't write down the date, as I was supposed to write tomorrow. But I have a terrible urge to write today, or to speak to somebody.

This morning I did some thinking and I wrote a letter to Mum, but neither calmed me down, on the contrary. I feel as though it's terribly cold and stifling at the same time.

Today I thought about working incognito in the countryside, for example as a farmer, about experiencing only physical labour and not thinking at all. About feeling the work in my bones and muscles, about understanding the carefree calm of peasant life. What am I supposed to do? Something torments me all the time. Recently I've been tormented by the idea of Zygu loving me more than I love him and I was feeling guilty about it. Now I think that I love him more and somehow more fiercely than he loves me. And so on, and so forth. And life's so simple. I just complicate it terribly. You will help me, Buluś and God.

10.00 p.m. I need to write again. Earlier I worried unnecessarily, now I have a reason. Ghetto again. Oh, God! How much can we take? Who knows where we'll live and how? You have to pay through the nose for everything. We used to sit here in this room with Zyguś and caress, hug each other, and now it's all getting ruined again. But I believe, I feel that nothing bad will happen. Lord, listen to my pleas that I bring to You every day.

I went to Nora's, on my way back I bumped into Julek and Lidka. They were walking together. This really unnerved me; I was disgusted and sickened. It was so insincere. I don't know whether to tell Nora. I think I will. I'm glad it's Monday tomorrow, I want to share my worries with Z. I can't live without it.

I will give you all the flowers
Just love me, my dear child
Nightingales' musical shower
Will meet you by your hut
My tears' stream will emanate
Meadows in bloom by the forest
And my deep sighs will create
Nightingales' nightly chorus

Bye, Zyguś, bye, Mama, I'm so scared of this job. Lord God, help me tomorrow and always … You will help me, Buluś and God.

11 May 1942, Monday

Thank You, Miraculous God. The job isn't so terrible. I spent the day with Nora today. We talked all day long. We understood each other, we always understand each other easily. But her attitude to love is different, light, while mine is serious. She says that will make me unhappy. Perhaps, but I know I can't do it any other way. About the complex too.

Yes, Nora, if we learn to dance and if we dance well, all will be well! After this conversation, I was exhausted and had a headache.

One shouldn't think or talk about it, Z is right. Z, my heart, has read you. I'm angry! This truly is the end. But we need to talk about this issue; it isn't our fault, but spring's. And this ghetto, this situation, this war ... Bye, I will be working and I won't write often. You will help me, Buluś and God.

12 May 1942, Tuesday [23]

Recently when I've felt bad, I've written, and when I've felt good, I've written. I must write. Listen! Listen to me and understand. Some kind of fever has taken over the city. The spectre of the ghetto, already forgotten by everybody, has returned. And it's even more dreadful than before, because it knocks on the doors of petrified hearts and it's ruthless, it doesn't want to go away. Yesterday it scared me too, but today – no. Nothing can touch me today. I'm glad I'm crying now, when nobody can see me. I shouted today, 'Oh, God, I want the moment to come when they take me away!'

No, I don't want that! Lord, forgive me. But my soul was so embittered that I felt as though maybe that would be for the best. Mama writes to us saying that children are being taken away into forced labour. She told me to pack. She wants to be with us and at the same time she wants ... ah! They are splitting up for good. Mum wants to send Ticiu an official letter asking for divorce. And us ... well, what's the point of writing about it – it makes me blubber terribly and turn on my waterworks. In this terrible whirlwind of the war we have neither mother nor father. The turmoil of life has taken us to some terrible crossroads. We are left on our own. They'll never patch it up. Mama will remarry and I will never, ever again come to the door of my parents' home. My mother … Her husband will be a stranger, a foreigner. And Father, oh! He wrote to me that he was not sure if he would ever see me again! Ticiu, you are an unlucky Jew, just like me, locked away in the ghetto. Holy God, can You save me? Can You save them? All of them. Oh, please, work a miracle!

Such a heavy mood at home. Bimba is stressed, overworked and exasperated. She torments herself. She suffers because of children, because of her husband and relatives. One can't even laugh in the house because of that. And they keep reminding me that I'm at their mercy.

Life is so miserable. Miserable, ugly, evil, but my heart still fills with sorrow, when I think … will I die? What awaits us in the future? Oh, God Almighty! So many times I've asked You and You've listened to me – please bring an end to our misery. I feel better now; it's so good to have a cry. What hurts the most is them. Indeed a long time ago already, indeed always, but … still. People say now that food's the most important thing. I've had a good, filling dinner – and I feel so terrible. I'm not hungry, but I'm hungry for somebody's caring protection.

And Zyguś? Yes, that might be why I don't want to say goodbye to life. Mama, don't hold it against me. I know it would be a terrible blow to you, but you are going to have your own life now. You might even have more children. And my grandparents are old and tired, they deserve a better old age. Sometimes I just want to ask why we were forced onto them? But now I am so exhausted. I didn't really count on us having a home together in the future; I just had this timid, naive dream. I'm not really disappointed, I just looked around at the world and it scared me with its emptiness. Nobody! Is there really nobody close? And Mama, so dear, is always so far away, and will be with some man who is a stranger to me. I'm not crying any more. The man I will be with will be a stranger to her. Life brings people together and then separates them.

> With passion they squabbled and scuffled
> feathers got ruffled
> they tore their little nest
> to pieces and still didn't rest
> down was scattered around
> quill, blades of grass and chaff,
> hay too in all this riff-raff
> they told each other words that were sorest
> and flew into the forest
> to look and roam
> for new homes
> forgetting, both of the birds
> about their two chicks
> left on their own in the sticks

15 May 1942, Friday

Today is a memorable day. I've received the first money I earned. I'm very proud of it and I don't know what to spend it on. I'd like to send it to Ticiu. I'll see.

Imagine, he came today. I was so happy. So, so much. It was my dream to see him today and he came. My beautiful Kokośka, my Zyguś. He's the sweetest. My daddy. He was my shoulder to cry on for a bit. Oh, he understands me so well, like nobody else in the world. And, you know, indeed he understood, as I knew he would. He told me that he can't worship me all the time like some goddess, that he's not a perpetuum mobile and this and that. And I think sometimes, for example today, that I am indefatigable and that this miss doesn't show herself in her entirety at all. Great Lord God, You know how much I like hugging him, snuggling next to him, being cuddled by him. It's so lovely, so delightful, so sweet. Everything is easier and cosier when I'm with him. Bye-bye, dear Diary, so many new sensations, good ones, I think, thanks to you, who 'leads me into the unknown'. You will help me, Buluś and God.

Saturday

For you I waited
in the evening with bated
breath, with the door ajar
by brightly shining stars
their colour was the sweetest

and the flowers' caress was the deepest
their fragrant grace
gave the cosiest embrace
May breeze whispered to the moon
that my beloved will be here soon.
The evening's hum was gone
its wings slid across the nightly sky
the flowers and stars withered in front of my eyes
You didn't come, unfortunately.

Sorrowful is the last gaze
into the distant haze
sorrowful is longing
for love and bonding
and somebody's extended hand
to say goodbye in the end
Sorrowful is such a long, futile wait
like today at the gate.

Everything was so pretty
flowers and all the sweeties
goodbyes and handshakes
like the words of a banal song
out the window as if wrong.
A platform, noisy and busy
then the rattling and wheezing
of an arriving train
a window open again

in a carriage
a heart broken in the chest
tears barely swallowed at best
and the train and me and YOU …
Golden oranges were beautiful
as were words of farewell
and pleading looks and a sigh
The most beautiful was this one word,
an ordinary word – goodbye.

I'm so very sad. You will help me, Buluś and God.

18 May 1942, Monday

'The world is so lovely and I'm feeling good' – this is what I wrote to Buluś. Oh, so so good! Today made up for the Saturday waiting. It was so delightful, so May-like, so springlike! May is such a wonderful month! Zyguś is divine and love's beautiful! It's hard to part. And those caresses … Ooooh, I might see him tomorrow.

It's nice at work. Norka has a problem with Julek. I feel very sorry for her. Z'll see her tomorrow. Bye-bye, dear Diary. I send you kisses, just like I kiss and hug Zygu. You will help me, Buluś and God.

19 May 1942, Tuesday

My mama has written a letter. So heartfelt, so lovely. I'm feeling so good and I'm so moved. She says she loves Zyguś.

Oh, it's so so so good, Mama. She has called to me from afar in such a sincere way, with such warmth. I need to respond to this cry of the mother's heart. She told me about her worries and joys, about her hopes. Poor her. Lord God, please protect her and carry my blessing to her. Sleep well, dear Mama. God is looking after us.

Noreńka came today. She's in a terrible state. Irka and Lida are getting back to themselves. I can't write about it, it's disgusting. When my beloved Zyguś mentioned him, I felt sick. Of course it's fear. He sometimes jokes about it too. But, you know, we talked about Julek's 'involvement' (it's all because of the involvement) and then I thought that Z, as lovely, close and real as he is, is also afraid of it. He's afraid of words. He either doesn't want to say too much or is evasive. And I still blush. For example today, couldn't he say to this stranger, a soldier, '*Das ist meine Braut*'?* I'd say it for sure. But there's something else here; this is an emergency.

In the meantime I fall even more deeply in love with him. If I can, I'll rekindle the relationships with my girlfriends, otherwise I'll become a recluse.

I feel very sorry for Nora, it must be so hard for her to see us together. But truth be told, 'The replenished understand not the pain of the starving.' And perhaps I don't feel as sorry for her as I'd like to. I don't know why, but I do think it's her fault too. Well, what matters is that Mama stays safe and

---

*The German translates as 'This is my fiancée'.

I and Zyguś remain in love and … I can't, I'm blushing, this morning was so wonderful. Goodnight. You will help me, Buluś and God.

20 May 1942, Wednesday

I'm so selfish, it's unbelievable! I have to write every single day. Even if it's just a few words. I have to repeat that I love him, because I don't know where it ends and where it starts. Yesterday I was a little bit angry. But think, Z came to pick me up from my job at the factory and we walked holding hands. Orchards are in bloom, May is shining with its blue skies and I'm shining, too, with joy. That's how I feel, I really feel like his little daughter and I like it oh so much!

Zośka works for the regiment. I told Malka about miss, but only in general terms. She's a very nice, sweet girl. I was really happy. Bye-bye, we might talk soon … You will help me, Buluś and God.

21 May 1942, Thursday

Oh, the dream, the dream, the dream of youth! I'm tired, so very tired. It's a wonderful, May night. So fragrant. The sky's navy blue, but I'm not allowed to get too emotional, because when I think of … Grrr …

Zyguś was terribly amused today, he was laughing and ready for jokes. Sometimes I think he jests on purpose, because he's ashamed of himself. But I get embarrassed when he reminds me that I … well. He said that he was quite serious about it; that he'd like to put me to bed, to take me with him (it was on the platform). Why does he say those things? Well, let him, I actually like it very much. Let him say it, let him kiss me, let him love me, love me, love me! After all! Is it true? Ah, how lovely Klaus* is, really, how about it? I think it would be the height of happiness. I'm so silly. But still I want and that is that ...

> You tell me that you love me terribly
> that you miss me unbearably
> I know it isn't very modest of me
> but I want it and that is that

> You will help me, Buluś and God.

23 May 1942, Saturday

Always on Saturdays. It would have been easier if I'd written several days ago. Now I don't know what to write, where to start? Something has been bothering me terribly the last few days. I talked to Nora and in the end I told her that this other trait of Zygmunt is bothering me. This and that. But still, once, not so long ago, I asked Jarośka why the whole world was against us, why they all thought it funny, stupid, absurd? Not Mama, not any more. And I'd like to give her a big hug for it. But Nora too, even her. I know that she is thinking

---

*It is not clear who Renia is referring to here.

about what it's going to be like when my romance ends. She's accusing me of taking it too seriously and (does she have a clear-headed view of it?) she makes my heart ache. I know that she's not sure, she doubts whether Z really loves me. I know it; I can feel it. And it pains me; it bothers me perhaps. Those tiny, unimportant details …

Because you should know that I am jealous, terribly, madly jealous. And I think it's this jealousy and not my complex (which is gone now) that makes me hate. It annoys me. Constantly, it annoys me constantly.

And Zyguś sometimes says something without realising it and it hurts me so badly. Sometimes, when it bothers me too much, I think about running away. To run away, to run away as far as possible, to be away from him but also to not see it all, to not suffer this agony. But there are times when I know that it is not possible. When I hold him tightly, when he's near, so very near, I feel that I wouldn't be able to part with him for all the treasures in the world. That would mean giving up my soul, the most important part of my life.

Nora, you are wrong. You're different, but I'd be left with nothing.

Studying, nature – that's all good when love is fulfilled or when you've never experienced it. One thing perhaps – poetry. Poems would flow in a wide stream like tears, like longing, like despair and suffering.

I knew that Zygmunt's parents were part of the hostile atmosphere surrounding us, but I wasn't aware how much against it they were and how important it was. Because of his late returns? What else? And what if Irka ... What then? But I do know, because I take a bit of him away from them. Who ever heard of such a young boy getting so seriously involved? I understand and I don't resent them for it, but I'm a bit sorry about it, yes and no. It can be something very important or not important at all.

I love Zyguś the most in the world. He is my dearest and he is most mine. I don't want to bother him with my issues, but I know that nobody in the world understands me like he does. It's always so that when your heart aches, you can feel this pain in all your limbs. Which is why my worries hurt me more then.

When Z is good to me, everything is good and bright and full of sunshine. It's May, 23 May – such a shame the month is about to pass. The nights are filled with stars. They're so intoxicating and I dream so much, I dream, I dream. You will help me, Buluś and God.

24 May 1942, Sunday

A morning like today can happen only when you're young, when you're in love and when you're loved back. Oh, my God, it was so amazing! We were so close and ... no, nothing can change that. The world's so cruel! I always knew it too. But it's sweet that Z has various adventures and that he tells me about them ... In any case I like to know. I'll come up with something. But why would I care that they are evil, insincere, jealous, when Z is the best and the sweetest? After all I am not in love with them, but with him. And I know that my dream will come true, like all my dreams, because it is fate. And it'll be so, if we persevere, we'll survive and we'll be a happy couple. And I won't be stupid any more; I'll just smile when looking at silly things. Oh, Mama, my mama! You and Zyguś, please love me! You will help me, Buluś and God.

25 May 1942, Monday

He picked me up from the factory at noon. And it was (oh, Dido is so annoying!) wonderful. All young, all May – that should be enough for you and anyway:

> When I hear those words so sweet
> those dear words, oh, my Good Angel
> each is a precious treasure at my feet
> each says more than many pages.
> But if I wanted to say
> how wonderful is this night in May
> words would become meaningless
> words would be laughable, I guess.

It is a wonderful May night now! With a smiling moon. Oh, if only Z were with me. I place my invisible hands on Mama's temples and on Ticiu's. Good Lord God, take care of them and of us. You will help me, Buluś and God.

26 May 1942, Tuesday

I'm writing by the light of the moon – literally. The story unfolds. I know, or rather I feel, that it's all Zośka's fault. And I know why she does it – it's not about the other girl, but about the change, about separating me from him and … Not tomorrow, on Thursday. I can't even tell whom I hate more – her or them. It's been like that from the very beginning, grrr. You will help me, Buluś and God!

28 May 1942, Thursday

I love Z very much. He is so athletic and I'm so impressed. I can take cover by him, I can simply cuddle against him – it's so great, so snuggly and …

But let's start from the beginning. After all it wasn't a nice day today.

First thing in the morning – the meeting, going beetroot red and then discussing work; then the conversation with Zyguś. Then there was Maciek and finally this disgusting plot, which evolved into something of a horrible size and nothing of it. Because this whole adventure with Z is rather pleasant. But also strange, oh, so strange! I didn't realise it could be like that.

Z says that I am languid and inflexible, and this and that, and he constantly probes me about the reasons why I don't like dancing. And I don't like dancing because I don't know how to dance. And when I feel like today, when I feel so strange, it's like a shiver, like I don't know what, and I'm against it. Hell, am I the biggest swine on planet Earth? Oh, it's so good to get it off my chest, I feel relieved. I'm glad he feels comfortable mentioning me so openly, but at the same time it hurts, I feel like I'm stuck at a lower level and I can't soar. But then I forgot about everything in the world. When I hugged him, when I clung to him with my whole body …

The most difficult part is always saying goodbye. Somehow I love him with my whole body and having him close is like having a personification of spring by me. And spring can be intoxicating! Is it true that women are dangerous in springtime? Yes, wild females. But not me, I only like the most innocent caresses which then make me go into a strange state and if it wasn't 9.00 p.m. I would probably go wild just like them, but … Well, girl, don't go mad – ah, I'm taken and that is that. You will help me, Buluś and God.

2 June 1942, Tuesday

Probably – but it's difficult to write. You know, now I know what the word ecstasy means. I almost understand it. It's indescribable; it's the best thing two loving creatures can achieve. For the first time, I felt this longing to become one, to be one body and … well … to feel more, I could say. To bite and kiss and squeeze until blood shows. (And then there's this other symptom.) And Zyguś talked about a house and a car and about being the best for me.

Lord God, I'm so grateful to You for this affection and love and happiness! I'm writing these words differently, whispering them in my mind so I don't scare them away or blow them out. To write a poem, but a bloodthirsty one, a springtime one. Mama is on her own, even H is not there. I don't want to think about anything, I just want to desire so badly, so passionately like … you know. You will help me, Buluś and God.

6 June 1942, Saturday

Days and moods have shimmered. Not many days have passed, but many thoughts have flown through my mind. One morning I woke up and I thought that something had happened. Two aerials stuck out of the roof opposite, piercing the blue sky. I could only see those aerials and the snippet of the sky between them and nothing more. Why am I writing about it? Because I want to show you that it wasn't some symbol that brought this thought. I simply woke up from a dream, which told me not to believe in my great, cherished fantasy. Why? I don't know. I just felt grown-up and found this fantasy childish, stupid and unfeasible. So this is how it is when you look at the world dispassionately – two aerials and the sky. And me, so wise, I could smile with derision, but I have no energy and no courage for it … So my belief lessened now, but it came back and is increasing bit by bit. I still pray with the same zeal as before. Not now. What I want the most is the dream. I want the desire, yes, because I desire with every tiny bit of my body, my thoughts, my imagination. Even the most innocent book stirs me up, as does the closeness of other people, and us. Ah, I struggle with such horrible dreams, disgusting dreams. And I ... and you. A swaying ship, I'm running, gaining speed ... and ... and ... should I jump?! I would jump if ... I'd jump a thousand times if he existed for ever.

I haven't seen Zyguś today, he's overworked, tired and weak. And it's good, it's very lucky, because right now I'm brimming with energy. My greed for life makes me fierce. I'd like to use my power in an honourable battle. You will help me, Buluś and God.

7 June 1942, Sunday [24]

I'm at peace. Nora and I went for a long walk deep into the quarter and we talked. She was the first person I told. I realised that burden was what was tormenting me. We browsed through the sweet album and I felt good and most of all – at peace.

Zygmunt was there too, he was there and then left, I shouldn't have written it down.

We also talked about Waldek. It's strange. Sometimes I wonder if I'm not in l ... e with him. I could choke on this word. And only half an hour ago my heart throbbed with fear.

Wherever I look, there is bloodshed. Such terrible pogroms. There is killing, murdering. God Almighty, for the umpteenth time I humble myself in front of You, help us, save us! Lord God, let us live, I beg You, I want to live! I've experienced so little of life, nothing. I don't want to die. I'm scared of death. It's all so stupid, so petty, so unimportant, so small. Today I worry about being ugly; tomorrow I might

stop thinking for ever. Yes, yes, war is terrible, savage, bloody.
I feel I've become like that because of it.

> Think, tomorrow we might not be
> A cold, steel knife
> Will slide between us, you see
> But today there is still time for life
> Tomorrow's sun might eclipse
> Gun bullets might crack and rip
> And howl – pavements awash
> With blood, with dirty, stinking slag
> Pigwash
> Today you are alive
> There is still time to survive

> Let's blend our blood
> When the song still moves ahead
> The song of the wild and furious flood
> Brought by the living dead

> Listen, my every muscle trembles
> My body fumbles for your closeness
> It's supposed to be a choking game, this is
> Not enough eternity for all the kisses.

I was interrupted. But this thought absorbs me. Is it worth
making an effort? No! I'm telling you, something'll come up.
What? Don't know. But it will. Or perhaps already has. Can't

get it out of my head. Now is the time to think of other things. Lord God, forgive me, save me and protect me. Great One, end this war now. You will help me, Buluś and God. I believe in you!

9 June 1942, Tuesday

I'm ill and slightly grumpy. I fear so much for Jarośka. She's coughing, she needs to be taken to the doctor's (her lungs are so weak). Granny refuses. I tell her that she should do it, Granny thinks that 'should' is a relative thing to say. So what now? She's a young child. Ah, Granny herself never goes to the doctor, she has this rule, but should it apply to a young child whose whole life is ahead of her? Maybe she should simply be helped, saved? Perhaps she's really ill?

These are ordinary and stupid words – but tell me, do you understand the despair they contain? This child is really poorly. Bimba nags her terribly, but she never holds back. This situation's not her fault after all, it was others who did it to her, why is Bimba so unfair?

I really felt like crying today. Granny thinks I should revive my poetry-writing ambition. I yelled, 'Granny, you don't understand!' Mum wanted to turn me into a writer, but can one be 'turned into' a writer? Oh, these people don't understand anything. And I'm being told this now, when I'm trying to stop myself from writing verses. Because I don't want to write when I have something to write about and I want to, but when I can, when I have to. They don't know how much it hurts. And the killing goes on, the murdering. Zyguś is the only breath of spring and sunshine. You will help me, Buluś and God.

14 June 1942, Sunday

It's dark, I can't write. Panic in the city. We fear a pogrom; we fear deportations. Oh, God Almighty! Help us! Take care of us; give us Your blessing. We will persevere, Zyguś and I, please let us, let us survive the war. Take care of all, of mothers and children. Amen. You will help me, Buluś and God.

15 June 1942, Monday

I'm restless and drunk. I spent the whole day in a terrible fright. I was tired, exhausted, in despair. And I've longed so badly … I long. Just think, two days and two nights. Dark nights, thick with darkness, just think, I burnt so badly, I longed so badly.

In the daytime I was choking with the heavy, threatening atmosphere of the dead city. Oh, days are so hard. Nerves are engaged, they jerk with tension, senses are engaged too, dying with longing.

Was Zyguś sweet? I don't know if he was particularly sweet, but he was somehow deliciously manly. And at the end I felt that he was first and foremost a man. It was the second time I felt it. I compared it to a book. I surprised myself that I could. I want to laugh out loud, ha ha ha, laugh myself sick. This feeling is worthy of gods and people in ecstasy. One would like to let go. No! No! We'll persevere, won't we? Yes. My wonderful springtime head, we'll persevere!

He was delightful and when I'm with him, I feel so small, like a child, I feel safe. It's completely dark now. I'm writing in the darkness, but I still know what I'm writing.

The conversation about lips was not pleasant, but it didn't spoil anything. Nothing and nobody could spoil this.

God Almighty, please let it go on, keep on saving us. Only You can protect us and my faith is so powerfully strong. You will help me, Buluś and God!

I devise you, my amorous tremble
I devise you with my thoughts alone
A bloody spring fruit you resemble
My body embraced by hips, I groan
My chest billows restlessly, I moan
Veins pulsate angrily, with danger
with a holy act, holy pain, holy anger
blessed be the sense that feels.
I will grab you, smother, crush you, peel
Take you between my hips
Oh! I will be generous and giving
I will be happy, I will be living.
I will absorb you, I will writhe and adore,
I will kiss you like a lithe whore
A real one, real and alight.

The pinnacle of crudeness! I will smack my own face for it, but I'll still write it. In the evening! I haven't written down a prayer. I wrote about silliness and I was thinking about it. Forgive me, Lord. Who will I raise my hands to, if You abandon me? Whom will I trust? Holy God, please protect me, put Your hand on the heads of those who believe, who need Your protection.

My dear mama, today, in this terrible, horrible moment, you're with strangers and perhaps it's better this way, perhaps you're safer ... but if you were (God forbid) ... if we were ... I don't want to say it. And again, for the umpteenth time when children cuddle up to their mothers, you're far away. All of the important, dangerous, crucial moments in life divide us. And you, my dear mama, pray for us, pray for us wherever you are. There is one God. He will listen to you, pray for your orphaned children. Our God is the only one, people died saying these words, believing and I am still alive, alive and faithful.

You will help me, Buluś and God.

18 June 1942, Thursday

Today is my big day. I've turned eighteen on the 18th. I'm an adult now, but I don't know much. There has been plenty of sadness and worry in my life already, plenty of joy and love too. But I don't know much; I don't even know what I should know. Right now I'm feeling good, I'm not so bad, thank goodness.

Nora is a sweet, good creature. She suffers because she doesn't know much. I find it strange how we all attract each other, we who are so 'self-critical'. She likes Maciek. That would be great, wouldn't it?!

What's the day today? I smashed my head. Then everyone gathered and it was quite nice. Norka has given me the album, a complete one, beautifully bound, wonderful! Oh, there's something so sweet, so lovely, so good; something that lifts us, makes us better. Yet another fulfilled dream. Nora, I believe and you know that it's not the last one …

Zyguś has given me chocolates and two gingerbread hearts, Irka flowers and perfume, and Maciek sent me roses and a card, wishing for all my dreams to come true.

And I? What can I say, sometimes I dream about being famous, about reaching heights and flying across the world, and not just in my mind. And yet sometimes I just want to be an ordinary person – a townswoman, a mother. I want, I want so very badly to have children, happy and good, righteous, noble and honest children. Who knows which of those tasks is nobler, which one is harder?

Oh, I feel so good, Mama, and I know that you're sending many dear words through the air. Do you know that I am already eighteen? Yes, and I believe, and I love those whom I loved.

I have decided to work on myself from now on. There's still time, one can still become somebody. The one who has a spiritual life, who can have such a life, has to have something to build it upon. Not all lives rest on beautiful legs. And yes, yes, yes … Should I say it? Well, yes, I will, as it's like a grain of sand stuck in a shell, which becomes a pearl. Suffering is the pearl of love. I was angry with Irka and Zygu. I can't even imagine good moments not being poisoned by something. But he was so sweet, that's true, so lovely. He's coming tomorrow. If it's not a dream, then we'll soar high …

This goodbye has made me angry.

Tomorrow I go to Nora to get Kiciek.

Good night. Mama, I send you a kiss, I embrace you, as always. You love me the most in the world. Your wishes are my road to follow and my life's blessing. You will help me, Buluś and God.

19 June 1942, Friday [25]

And God saved Zygu. Oh, I'm beside myself. They were taking people away all night long. They rounded up 1,260 boys. There are many victims, fathers, mothers, brothers. The sea of our blood is red, forgive us our trespasses, listen to us, Lord God! This was a terrible night, too terrible to describe. But Zyguś was here, my sweet one, sweet and loving. It was so good; we cuddled and kissed endlessly. I almost forgot about yesterday, though it was my birthday, so he could have spared me this. But that's the way he is. That's his disposition, his nature. He likes 'women'. Zośka, this 'red-haired fog', was here as well. I was so stupid to show that poem. Even Z said so. Well, tough, that's exactly what matters. There are times when one can speak and write, but not act. And it really was so delightfully pleasant that it was worth all the suffering. But sometimes I think it isn't worth it, that a loving woman has to pay too high a price.

June night
pregnant
with dense darkness

night ... stretches
above my head.
Night of solitude
Came. The irresistible one stood
at the end of the bed
with a tormenting face
dug its claws
into the sticky brain
and I dream ...
My naked thoughts
stripped of clothing
stretch under my skull
in silence
and for mercilessly long
the night goes on.

Heavy black shroud
dropped and clings
to the body
silent and stubborn
I shuddered.
The flower opens
in quiet
open lips
whisper words
fragrance of jasmine
of maturing buds.
Moan

exasperation slowly easing
senses sigh with relief
sweet fantasy
Dawn ...

You will help me, Buluś and God.

23 June 1942, Tuesday

Again words mean nothing; again words are ridiculous. Yesterday we experienced one of the wonderful symphonies of youth.

There was a kind of pogrom in our quarter. Buluś wrote and told me to leave the city for Tłuste* with Zyguś. She wrote 'together'. 'Together'! It would be so delightful, so sweet! Though it's absurd for now. But nowadays even the biggest absurdity can become true.

Oh, my dear Zyguś, we'll go away together, tra-la-la-la-la ... aaah! Bimba says hello and I send you a kiss, Zyguś does too. Rena. You will help me, Buluś and God.

25 June 1942, Thursday

Where to start ... Well. I'll just say it how it is. A wave of good and bad came. It's all right now, because it's all right to dream, to kiss. But today I don't 'burn', I'm not like a dog trying to break free from its chain, even though I'm still full

---

* A pre-war town in Poland (near Zaleszczyki), a district during the German occupation.

of longing. That's because Z has said a terrible thing today. He's said he wanted to read my diary, because that arouses him; it provides him with stimulation. Listen, my dear Diary, I love you, I love you, you're my soul, you're alive in a thousand of my bright memories, you cry the tears of my old worries, but I never ever wrote you for you to become stimulation in love! Am I to constantly tear the deepest parts of my soul apart, am I to make my heart bleed so that he can believe me and so that he can find pleasure in it? What about me, why do I love without any stimulation? (I find my stimulation in daydreaming.) I don't think life's so idyllic. Life is full of bitterness; one doesn't even need to look for it. And that's why Zygmunt was like that, exactly like that. It was because there was too much sweetness.

When your worry goes to sleep
don't wake it up
there's so much bitterness in life
it's the source of the worst evil
when your worry goes to sleep
don't wake it up.
Be happy, laugh and smile
it only lasts a short while
When your worry goes to sleep, don't wake it up
there's so much bitterness in life!

I think that even though Z is good and affectionate and sweet (today he was really sweet), there's something strangely calm about him. It's not the first time I've thought this. I'm writing and thinking, and I'm angry, like today, but as soon as I curl up next to him, as soon as I hug him, I walk on air again. What am I going to do? Fantasies are the most wonderful too. They'll come true; they have to! Can one love somebody and dislike them at the same time? You will help me, Buluś and God!

The following day

Most likely one can. No, I can't write about it today, because I'm angry. Z, the one who can be so dear, as warm as my own heart, can also be so distant. Yes, yesterday he was distant. It was hard for me, and strangely gloomy. I'm so glad I have my poetry! My poems. I love them so much.

It's not true, Z is not good for me at all! He says things, for example about my taste changing. He says that on purpose, he says that to hurt me and when one loves somebody, one doesn't want to hurt them. Life is overcast, but our tiny bit of sky was blue. Now there is nothing left. On days like today I think that we would be unhappy together. But this thought hurts so much. Oh, Lord God, why does it hurt so badly? It's terrible, it's so very hard; I wish it were Saturday already. You will help me, Buluś and God!

27 June 1942, Saturday evening

Good, peaceful, quiet, blessed Saturday evening. My soul has calmed down. Why? Because again I curled up against him, he caressed me and made me feel like his tiny little daughter. I forgot everything bad. It's a shame that Zyguś is gone now. I could lie curled up against him for a long, long time. You will help me, Buluś and God!

28 June 1942, Sunday

It's quiet and peaceful now; I'm well. I would like to curl up again, just curl up and sleep. It was something beyond words. He was. I don't know what I'm writing. Because it's dark. Oh, such a balmy night. This was a wonderful flight, devilish and heavenly at the same time. We took a big step forward. Towards this Z who is adored by people! Why, oh, why only in five years' time? After all today, already, already today. My legs couldn't cope. It was so very sweet what Z said – I am mature. And it was also very sweet with Marysia, because I really like this Daddy–Mummy sweetness. Perhaps I even prefer it. All of it is so wondrous. Divine and very human. Oh, how much I'd like to curl up against him again and say, 'Oh, Daddy dear!' Off I go now to dream sweetly and in peace. You will help me, Buluś and God!!!

29 June 1942, Monday

So tell me, Zyguś, how am I to survive those two days, those two nights? Each hour lasts ten times longer. Oh, they go so slowly, they are so horrible, so excruciating, so oppressive. How did it come to that? How did it spill out, what was piling up, growing and growing? And will it always be like that from now on? Will we ever want more and if so, when, oh, when? Because today I don't want it, but my body does, it asks for it, it demands it. Won't it be like that every day from now on? Strange that I don't seem to be able to go back to what it was like before. I have ripened; I've gone overripe. It's good to think, to want and to complete – but how? It all scares me. Because it's a sober thought. Too sober. How can I think about it as a done thing or being done, but not about how to get there? No! No! I simply can't be bothered to think. And that's why this letter hit me like a sledgehammer. My lovely Buluś. My good, dear one, I know now that you have good intentions. I know, because I want it too, because it's my destiny. But do you know that it's highly absurd, it's the biggest illusion under the sun. Now, only now, when I read your letter, I thought that there are no real, serious reasons for it. You are a woman who's lived through a lot. You know a lot. And you tell me to be practical. You are such a child. Do you know that the way you presented it to me, I found it, well (to avoid committing a sin), simply in bad taste. Think, two young people and …

Zyguś tells me bad things, he tells me sweet things too … He reckons we must part, he says that in five years' time I will be 10 centimetres taller and I will be prettier. But I won't be either of those things. I'm always prettier afterwards – with shining eyes, with burning lips and flushed cheeks. Zyguś is also at his most beautiful then. I prefer to clear all obstacles and dream that it is already, that it is … You will help me, Buluś and God.

5 July 1942, Sunday

We feared it, it threatened us and then it finally happened. What we were so afraid of has finally come after all. The ghetto. The notices went out today. We might stay here; we might not. Oh, Lord, You gave me so much hope, so much comfort – thank You for it.

It's so terrible. You don't know how terrible, you know nothing. You will come with me, because, of course, I will take my soul with me, my little looking glass. Just think, what remained in some old, yellowed books, in vellum scrolls covered with writing, what lived in legends, what one learnt with surprise at school – has now come true. The truest truth of all. And it's so terrifying.

We fear deportation, supposedly they're planning to deport half the people. Oh, Dido, oh, Bimba. Great Lord God, have mercy. My thoughts are so dark, it's a sin to even think them.

I saw a happy-looking couple today. They'd been on an outing; they were on their way back, amused and happy. Zyguś, my darling, my love most sincere, when will we go on an outing like theirs? I love you as much as she loves him. I would look at you the same way. But she's so much happier, that's the only thing I know. Or perhaps – oh, Holy God, You are full of mercy – our children will say one day, 'Our mother and father lived in the ghetto.' Oh, I strongly believe in it. You will save us, oh, God Almighty. My mama prays so hard for us. You will help us, Buluś and God.

6th of I don't know what, Monday

There is so much worry and concern, so much bitterness that I feel ashamed to write about our little nest. But ours is sweet, charming, wonderful. It's so good to talk about the nest. You will help me, Buluś and God.

10 July 1942, Friday

Goodbye, my little Diary! I will miss this abode. Let's hope Good God will let me see you here again. Give me your blessing from afar, Mama, and You, Lord God. Bring me back home soon (not in the ghetto). Our home … I've lived so many happy moments here, I'll always have fond memories of this flat where my love blossomed and matured. I'm in the middle of moving out, it's a terrible mess, I have to get going. You will help me, Buluś and God.

15 July 1942, Wednesday

Remember this day; remember it well. You will tell generations to come. Since 8 o'clock today we have been shut away in the ghetto. I live here now. The world is separated from me and I'm separated from the world. The days are terrible and the nights are not at all better. Every day brings more casualties and I keep praying to You, God Almighty, to let me kiss my dear mama.

Oh, Great One, give us health and strength. Let us live. I feel horrible, Bimba is sick. Hope is shrivelling so fast.

There are fragrant flowers in front of the house, but who needs flowers? And Zygmunt, you know, I haven't seen him yet. I mean I saw him from a distance today, but he hasn't come over yet. Lord, please protect his dear head. But why can't I cuddle up next to him? Pity ... Perhaps he ... God, let me hug my dear mama. You will help me, Buluś and God.

16 July 1942, Thursday

You probably want to know what a closed-off ghetto looks like. Pretty ordinary. Barbed wire all around, with guards watching the gates (a German policeman and Jewish police*). Leaving the ghetto without a pass is punishable by death. Inside there are only our people, close ones, dear ones. Outside there are strangers. My soul is so very sad. My heart is seized with terror. Such is life.

I have missed Zyguś so much today, I thought about him all the time. I haven't seen him for a week, I've missed him so much and I still miss him, because his visit today wasn't a real visit. I longed so much for some caress, nobody knows how much. After all we face such a terrible situation. Let me get some caresses. But it ended up being strange and cold, probably because there were other people in the flat and there

---

*Within many ghettos there were Jewish police units, set up by order of the Germans. They guarded the ghetto, collected money and taxes, gathered labour forces, and more. While they were officially part of the Judenrat, they were often eyed suspiciously by them, as well as by the Jewish inhabitants of the ghetto.

was such a mess. Perhaps Saturday'll work out better ... Yes, it must. We need a week's worth of caresses. I'll now dream like before. You will help me, Buluś and God.

18 July 1942, Saturday

Days go by. They're all the same, like drops of rain. Evenings are the most pleasant. We sit in the yard in front of the house, we talk, joke and – breathing in the fragrance of the garden – I manage to forget. I forget what I want to forget. That I live in the ghetto, that I have so many worries, that I feel lonely and poor, that Z is a stranger to me, that despite all my longing I cannot get closer to him. It's not a relationship that other couples have, after all.

Here, in the yard, doves coo. The moon's crescent silently floats into the sky, flowers give a sweet fragrance and when I look at it all, I ask myself why. I was on the verge of tears three times today. I blamed the living conditions, but that's not true! Love can flourish anywhere, dear love, full of warmth ... And yet, shadows always flit on my path. What is it? Where do those shadows come from? Are they shadows of clouds floating above? No, unfortunately not, these are shadows of a clouded face or, well, it's not worth mentioning. My heart aches so badly.

I don't want to ask God for anything else, only for our survival. But one can dream, why not? I dream about putting my head on Mama's bosom and crying so sweetly, it's good, just like now ... Mama's not here, Norka is, so I'll go to her and cry my eyes out. She's a dear soul, she'll understand. I'll go. I don't want to see any other friends. Irka said she would call in. What for? I can't stand her. I don't want to renew our relations. It's all stupid, calculated, contrived. Sometimes I just want to say that I don't care, but all I say is that I wish for the war to end! Bye-bye, dear Diary, my heart is heavy, like it's made of lead. You will help me, Buluś and God.

> What scares me most are the shadows
> When in the morning
> a shadow flickers without a warning
> on the road ahead of me
> My heart trembles inside
> and I look around
> petrified
> you can't look a shadow in the eye
> you can't grasp it by its elbow
> you can't touch it, ask it questions
> you don't even know who casts it
> This crawling, slithering greyness
> That shimmers and strangely twists
> What scares me most are the shadows.

> You will help me, Buluś and God.

19 July 1942

Tomorrow is Norka's birthday. Irka is coming, so it won't be the way it could be. But it'll still be sweet, because Zyguś, my beloved Zyguś, is again my beating heart; he's so delightfully sweet. The world's good to us, even in the ghetto. It's just that I'm always a bit silly, I get embarrassed about going there. But Z is truly the most beautiful and curling up against him, seeking his protection is the best. So today I'm much calmer. In this apartment 'it' is wonderful as well. Now I will have sweet thoughts about everything!

Tomorrow Norka will be eighteen. I'd like to give her some of our dreams, something more than an album and flowers, something that nobody else will give her. I promised to buy her a wonderful camera when we leave here and to go hiking in the mountains, to make my friend happy. That would make me happy too.

in a little house
with green blinds
where flowers will bloom
where it will always be just the two of us

Zyguś, my beloved, the best. I send kisses to everybody and I thank Good Lord God for this and my dear mama for praying for us. You will help me, Buluś and God.

20 July 1942

Nora's birthday. Well? I knew it was going to be like that. But now I have talked to the neighbours and I feel a bit better. Holy God, protect us and save us. You will help me, Buluś and God.

22 July 1942, Wednesday

I have to write to silence the pain, to open the wounds and let worries seep out. Such a terrible, grim time. We don't know what tomorrow will bring. We expect families to be taken away. Bimba's sick and exhausted, Jarośka's terrible, not a word from Mama or Daddy. It's not good with Zygmunt, either. I didn't, I really didn't want to admit that I'm seething with venom. But I couldn't stop myself. Also because I'm right. I have tears in my eyes from grief and the tips of my fingers are tingling with anger.

I don't want to write about the details, as I might write surly, clamouring words, and what's the point? It will always be the same. It's his fault. He is right, I'm resentful and helplessly in love. One thing has to be changed though, just one expression – after all 'the mug' might not tell anybody and … no! When I think about it, I get so furious that I don't want to see him ever again. I've had enough of it all. I cover my ears with my hands and close my eyes. I'd like to use my suffering to create suffering, to make myself ill. And he's right, he's the wisest of them all …

But in my dream it's completely different. My dreams are sweet … You will help me, Buluś and God.

23 July 1942, Thursday

Well, Noruśka, my dear, dear child. I admire this world of yours, I love it too, but, you know me, one word shatters everything. Noruś, I'd like to study too and improve myself, but everything comes down to one word. I already know who is worth what, I know love and I told you the truth (although it's the first time I thought it) – he's not worth it. But it's not a question of him being worth it or not, one needs to love, one needs to go on loving, one can't say no!

I know, my dear, that you understand everything, but you don't understand how weak I am and how hopeless when faced with ... this word. What I told you is true, even though he didn't say no, I know. I know he regrets it and is embarrassed. And (that's funny) I'm exasperated. If only hearts could be healed of love! But I don't even know myself if I'd like that. What I want, Noruś, is to go back to life and go hiking in the mountains with you. You will help me, Buluś and God.

24 July 1942, Friday

Dear God, help us. We need to pay our contribution by 12 o'clock tomorrow. The city is in danger. But I still have faith. My faith is deep and I beg You. You will help us, Buluś and God.

25 July 1942, Saturday

The following day in the morning! Ordners* came last night. Dido hasn't paid everything yet. Not enough money. Oh! Why can't money rain from the sky? It's people's lives, after all. Terrible times have come. Mama, you have no idea how

---

*Members of the Jewish Ghetto Police (Jüdischer Ordnungsdienst).

terrible. But Lord God looks after us and, though I'm horribly frightened, I have faith in Him.

I trust, because this morning a bright ray of sunshine came through all this darkness. It was sent by my mama in a letter, in the form of a wonderful photograph of her. And when she smiled at me from the photo, I thought that Holy God has us in His care! Even in the darkest moments there is something that can make us smile. Mama, pray for us. I send you lots of kisses. You will help me, Buluś and God.

In the evening!

My dear Diary, my good, beloved friend! We have been through such terrible times together and now the worst moment is upon us. I could be afraid now. But the One who didn't leave us then will help us today too. He'll save us. Hear, O, Israel,* save us, help us. You've kept me safe from bullets and bombs, from grenades. Help me survive, help us! And you, my dear mama, pray for us today, pray hard. Think about us and may your thoughts be blessed. Mama! My dearest, one and only, such terrible times are coming. I love you with all my heart. I love you; we'll be together again. God, protect us all and Zygmunt and grandparents and Jarośka. God, into Your hands I commit myself. You will help me, Buluś and God.

---

* A reference to one of the most important prayers in Judaism, Shema Yisrael ('Hear, O, Israel: the Lord, our God, the Lord is one').

Zygmunt's Notes

27 July 1942, Monday

It's done! First of all, dear Diary, please forgive me for wandering into your pages and trying to carry on the work of somebody I am not worthy of. Let me tell you that Renuśka didn't get the work permit stamp she needed to avoid being deported, so she has to stay in hiding. My dear parents have also been refused work permit stamps. I swear to God and history that I will save the three people who are dearest to me, even if it costs me my own life. You will help me, God!

28 July 1942, Tuesday

My parents were lucky to get into the city. They are hiding at the cemetery. Rena had to leave the factory. I had to find her a hiding place at any cost. I was in the city until 8 o'clock. I have finally succeeded.

29 July 1942

The Aktion *was prevented for the second time, because of a dispute between the army and the Gestapo.* I cannot describe everything that*

---

* Most likely it refers to the attempt of stopping the destruction of the ghetto undertaken by the Wehrmacht lieutenant Dr Albert Battel *has gone on for the last three days. I have no energy for it after twelve hours of running around the city. These events have shaken me to the core, but they haven't broken me. I have a terribly difficult task. I have to save so many people without having any protection for myself, or any help from others. This burden rests on my shoulders alone. I won't last long and I will share the fate of my three doomed ones. I have taken Arianka to the other side.*

30 July 1942

Today everything will be decided. I will gather all my mental and physical strength and I will achieve my goals. Or I will die trying.

5 o'clock

Skrzypczyński will give me the final answer at 5 o'clock. At midday they took away our cards for stamping (along with the wives' cards). I decided to risk my document, because I thought it was my last chance to save Renuśka. No luck! They threatened to send me to the Gestapo. After a lot of begging, they finally withdrew that threat. But that forgery cost me my job at HUV.* At 8 o'clock, I'll find out whether or not I'm going to stay. I set off.

(1891–1952). For saving about one hundred Jews from the Przemyśl Ghetto, he was recognised as one of the Righteous Among the Nations by Yad Vashem in 1981.

* Heeres-Unterkunft-Verwaltung was responsible for managing military quarters.

In the night

Oh, gods! Such horror! It was all for nothing! The drama lasted one hour. I didn't get my card. Have I just slaughtered myself?! Zosia is gone! Now I am on my own. What will happen to me? It's a great question. I wanted to save my parents and Rena, but instead I just got into more trouble myself. It looks as though the end of the world is here. I still have hope.

31 July 1942

Three shots! Three lives lost! It happened last night at 10.30 p.m. Fate decided to take my dearest ones away from me. My life is over. All I can hear are shots, shots … shots. My dearest Renusia, the last chapter of your diary is complete.

Epilogue

I only spent about two weeks in the ghetto, which was in a poor, run-down quarter called Garbarze, north-west of our grandparents' apartment. The Nazis had given every Jew twenty-four hours to move there and allowed each family to carry only twenty-five kilogrammes. My grandparents, Renia and I gathered together our most practical clothes for summer and winter, our sturdiest shoes, and a few coats in case we never got our furs back. My grandfather taped as many gold dollar coins as he could in a corner of his suitcase, hoping the guards wouldn't find them. The silver was safely buried in the basement; Granny and Grandpa would be back for it after the war.

On 27 July, an *Aktion* began within the Przemyśl Ghetto; unless you could prove you were employed in an essential labour or administrative position – and then get a stamp from the Gestapo on your work permit – you were going to be forced out of the ghetto to the camps or to your death. Only 5,000 Jews were expected to receive this stamp, and Zygmunt and Maciek were luckily among them. Unfortunately, my sister, my grandparents and I weren't.

Just one day later, the Gestapo surrounded the Przemyśl Ghetto and began rounding up the people who lived there; 6,500 Jews were loaded into cattle cars and shipped off to the death camp at Bełżec, about 100 kilometres north-west of the city. Another 2,500 – who were deemed to be too old or frail – were taken by truck to the Grochowce forest, which surrounded Przemyśl. There, they were shot in the napes of their necks and buried in a mass grave.

My sister and I were not in either group. Somehow – I don't know how, and he never told me – Zygmunt smuggled Renia and his parents into the attic of a three-storey tenement house at 10 Moniuszki Street, where his uncle, a member of the Judenrat named Samuel Goliger, lived. I wasn't with them. Zygmunt had escorted me out just before them, and we'd sneaked towards the check point to try to get out to my best friend Dzidka's house.

I think I left in the early morning, but I say that only from a place in my mind where I've replayed every memory a thousand times. This is the same place I've searched for my last memories of my sister, though those have come up blank. How have I forgotten saying goodbye to her? What was the look on her face? What did she say to me? I'd give anything to remember our last words to each other. I'd give anything to know that I told her how much I loved her.

I do remember the last time I saw my grandparents. They were trying to be brave as Zygmunt motioned that it was time for me to leave, that I had to get out, that time was running out. My granny, whom I loved so much, turned away, raising her hands to her face. My grandpa knelt down, placed his hands on my shoulders, and looked me in the eyes. Then he handed me a small, colourful box with a chain-link handle. It was the kind of compact suitcase perfect to carry lunch in, as if I were a little girl about to walk to school by herself for the very first time – not a child fleeing for her life.

'I've taped twenty gold coins inside,' he said. 'It's all I have. Wherever you're going, you can always sell these and get some cash.'

My grandmother approached me, carrying a thin, blue coat that I only wore on summer nights. She slipped my arms into it, being careful not to wrinkle the pink dress I was wearing, and then buttoned it up. Granny and Grandpa pulled me into a quick hug and then guided me gently out the door into the garden, where Zygmunt was waiting.

I don't know what happened to them, but I'm sure they ended up in that mass grave in the Grochowce forest. They were just too old for the Nazis to want to take them to a camp.

I'm not sure how Zygmunt got me out of the ghetto, but somehow, he took me directly to the Leszczyńskis' home. It was a first-floor apartment near the tinned coffee factory that Mr Leszczyński owned, but in another part of town from my grandparents' shop, my school, and the ice-skating pond. Dzidka, my closest friend in the whole world, was there to greet me, along with her parents and her two sisters.

I didn't know how long I'd be there. I don't think I even understood why I was there. All I knew was that, even though I was with Dzidka and her family – whom I loved and trusted

– I was terrified. A few times a day, someone pounded on the door, demanding to search the apartment. Mr and Mrs Leszczyński would motion for me to hide under a bed, whispering, 'Do not say a word. Do not breathe. We'll be back for you.' Then they'd close the door.

I crouched under the bed in a little ball, my chest heaving as I tried to choke back tears.

'Just a minute!' Mrs Leszczyńska would call to the person on the other side of the door.

Then Mr Leszczyński would open the door and say a few words, and silence would follow. The door would close. For the next two hours or half a day, I was safe.

I trusted Dzidka's family, and more than that, I trusted Zygmunt. I knew he'd do whatever he could to keep Renia safe – whether she was still in his uncle's attic, or whether he'd moved her like he'd moved me. He loved Renia, and he had promised our mum he'd protect her.

Of course, you know the rest of Renia's story. As hard as he tried, Zygmunt couldn't save her. My beautiful sister was murdered on 30 July 1942, alongside Zygmunt's parents.

It was several weeks before I found out what happened to her. Crouched in a ball in my best friend's apartment, I had no idea that someone had told the Germans that there were three Jews hiding in the attic of Mr Goliger's tenement house, and that when the Gestapo forced their way in, Renia and Zygmunt's parents had been taken outside and shot.

The Leszczyńskis might have found out right away, but I don't know for sure. All I remember was that, as I hid in their apartment, desperately afraid that the Gestapo would come in, grab me, and take me far away from my family, my protectors, my best friend, and a life that had become increasingly bleak, I missed my mother desperately. It was a stabbing ache, like Renia had felt every single day since 1938.

After a week in the Leszczyńskis' apartment, Mr Leszczyński told me it was time to leave.

'We're going to the railway station,' he said.

I didn't ask why. I just slipped on the same pink dress I'd worn when I left my grandparents, wrapped my blue coat around myself, and grabbed the small lunchbox that my grandpa had taped the coins into. I remembered his last words to me, his moustache, the kind twinkle in his eye, and I thought about how he must have felt giving it to me. He must have known his life was over and that the lives of his two granddaughters might end soon as well.

I have no memory of the walk to the railway station, nor do I recall where I sat on that train – or even if I did. It's been almost eighty years since I left Przemyśl, and I've cycled so many smells, visions, meetings and conversations through my mind that it's sometimes hard to tell one from the other. I've also never returned to my grandparents' city. I can't. It's just too emotional for me.

We had to transfer in Krakow, and Mr Leszczyński and I exited the train cautiously. He held my hand tightly, and we started to walk right towards a few Gestapo officers, dressed in their familiar grey uniforms with their ranks on their shoulders. They had Alsatians by their sides. Seeing the Gestapo wasn't unusual, especially in a public place like a train station, but this was different. I didn't have papers, so there was no way to prove that I wasn't Jewish. If Mr Leszczyński was caught smuggling a Jew, he'd be sentenced to death.

We kept walking as my heart pounded in my chest. As we got closer, one of the Germans glanced at Mr Leszczyński, seeming to miss me entirely, then turned back to the other officers and continued whatever conversation they were having. I let out a deep breath as we made our way past them, and then we waited for what felt like hours for the train to Warsaw.

Today, the train from Krakow to Warsaw takes about two and a half hours. In wartime Poland, it must have been twice that. I don't remember the ride – what passed me out of the window, whether I slept, what Dzidka's dad said to me, or even if I knew where I was going. But we arrived in Warsaw at some point, and as the train came to a stop, I felt more anxious than I ever had in my life. Here I was in a familiar city, where I'd stood on the stage reading poetry when I was only eight, yet my mum – the person who made me feel safer and more loved than anyone else in the world – felt thousands of miles away.

When the train doors opened, I picked up my little lunchbox and looked around. There were no Gestapo officers or dogs on the platform. Instead, there was a crowd of people rushing from one train to another, and it seemed as though no one was looking at the little girl in a thin coat carrying a tiny lunchbox. But someone was. As Mr Leszczyński and I walked down the platform, a young man in street clothes stepped forward and raised his hand to stop us.

'You came here with a Jewish child?' he yelled. 'I'm turning you in!'

Mr Leszczyński put his arm around me and pulled me close as he moved towards the man, towering over him. 'Get the hell away from me, and if you don't, I'll kill you right here,' he said.

What felt like five minutes of silence followed, but Mr Leszczyński didn't move. He just stood there, looking down once to make sure I was OK. The man stared at him just a little longer, then turned and ran away. I don't know who he was. I don't know how or why he believed I was Jewish. All I remember is that Mr Leszczyński and I walked off the platform, out of the station, and into the busy streets of Warsaw, my old home that was very much changed.

Mr Leszczyński took me directly to my mum's friends, the Beredas. They lived in a nice building on Ossolińskich Street, close to Saxon Garden State Park. I had never met Mr or Mrs Bereda before, so their smiling, tear-streaked faces were scary and unfamiliar. I trusted no one. But suddenly, I saw the face that had haunted my thoughts and my dreams, and I felt the longing I'd felt for months explode inside me. I dropped my tiny lunchbox and fell into my mum's arms, sobbing. Then my heart broke, because I knew I was experiencing something my sister wasn't. My mum had probably found out from Mr Leszczyński that day that Renia was dead, but she didn't tell me until she'd confirmed it herself weeks later. With the help and accompaniment of Mrs Bereda's niece's husband, a Hungarian aristocrat named Von Anderle, she gathered together her papers and took the long trip to Przemyśl. That train ride must have been the hardest of my poor mum's life, hoping against hope that her elder daughter might be alive, but knowing, deep down, the horrible truth.

She didn't go into the abandoned apartment where her parents had lived, so she didn't see that the piano was missing or that the cupboard in the living room didn't have any crockery or cutlery in it. She didn't see the blank desk, where her father had signed all his contracts. But while she was in Przemyśl, someone gave her a small amulet that Renia used to wear. I think it was then my mum accepted that my sister was really gone.

Mum came back to Warsaw and retrieved me from the convent where I'd moved temporarily. Together, we took a tram to the room she rented in an apartment in Żoliborz, a very nice neighbourhood adjacent to Warsaw. Over the next few weeks, Mrs Bereda's connections got me papers that gave me a new identity, and I was baptised by the same priest who'd baptised my mother. Just like that, I was Catholic, with a new birthday and a new name: Elżbieta Leszczyńska. Just like that, the Polish Shirley Temple disappeared.

Even though Mama and I lived outside the ghetto, disguised as Polish Catholics, we still saw and felt the war every day. Because my mum had to work, I lived and studied at a convent school during the week, and at weekends, she picked me up and took me home. On Sundays, we went to church, embracing the religion that had saved our lives. We took a tram to the church and back, just the way my mum did every working day. During the war, tram cars were divided in the middle, and in the front sat the Germans. In the back, the Poles.

One day after church, we planned to have supper at the home of my mum's boss, whose name was Kosiński. The tram we'd boarded was moving along, with us seated comfortably in the back. It slowed down, then stopped, on its regular route, which took it next to the tall walls of the Warsaw Ghetto. There, a German army lorry sat with its engine idling. Suddenly, the passenger-side door of the truck opened, and a Nazi soldier exited and walked up next to the tram. He was holding a gun.

'Everyone out!' he yelled in German. 'Germans on this side, Poles on this side. Exit!'

My mother grabbed my hand. At the time, there was something we called *łapanka*, which meant 'to round up people'. This practice, which had been around since the Germans first occupied Poland in 1939, referred to the act of removing people from somewhere – like a tram – separating them into groups, forcing one group onto a lorry, and taking them off to a labour camp. There, these people would assist with the German war effort, digging, shovelling, paving roads, operating machinery in a factory, or, likely, being beaten, starved and killed.

I'd witnessed this in Przemyśl, and my mother had seen it in Warsaw. It was nothing new. My mum was having none of it, though. She was *not* going to lose another child.

Thanks to an education at universities in Berlin and Vienna and her work at the Hotel Europejski, my mum was fluent in German. Her head bowed, she grabbed my hand and started speaking to me in German, a language I couldn't understand. But I played along, nodding at everything she said. Holding his gun, a guard approached us, overheard my mum talking, and motioned for us to stand to the side with the Germans. As we turned around, I was sure I was about to be shot in the back.

But we weren't loaded onto a truck or killed. We were allowed to walk away, toward the Kosińskis' home, which was at the hotel. We walked for what felt like hours, hiding in different doorways when we sensed danger. Passing lorries full of people – more than I'd seen at any other time during the war – we arrived at supper late but before the 8.00 p.m. curfew. After we ate, I collapsed into one of the Kosińskis' beds. I lay there all night long, sweating from a temperature, and the next day, my mum called the doctor. After he examined me, he told her that I'd developed yellow jaundice, and he believed it was brought on by fright.

After that night, Mr Kosiński allowed my mum and me to live at the hotel. For weeks, I recovered there. When I was feeling better, we ate supper with them. We went to church. We celebrated Christmas and Easter. My mother became friends with the girlfriend of the owner of a restaurant across the street, named Ziutka, and sometimes she fed us for free. She loved my mum. I went to *komplety*, which means I studied school privately, in secret. And day after day, my mother and

I watched the Jews and Poles get trampled under the boots of the Germans. That's how we lived.

I didn't come to America immediately after the war. Some time between the summers of 1942 and 1944, a German officer who lived at the hotel fell in love with my mum. He wanted to marry her. I don't think she loved him back; it was simply a very beneficial arrangement for a woman who'd used every bone in her body becoming resourceful enough to survive. But as the Soviet army advanced towards Warsaw in early 1944, an underground movement plotted a rebellion against the German occupiers. The Warsaw Uprising started in August 1944, and Germany fought back with everything they had. In sixty-three days, almost 250,000 Poles were killed, and half the city was destroyed by bombs.

The German officer begged my mum to leave Warsaw when the violence was at its worst. 'It's too dangerous here,' he said. 'I love you, and I can help you get out.'

My mum agreed, and the officer prepared papers for us. In the summer of 1944, my mum and I packed a few small suitcases. Before Warsaw surrendered, we escaped from there to Germany. Travelling through Germany was highly dangerous; we passed Berlin and Dresden before finally crossing into Austria. Then we made our way towards a famous spa – where the officer told us wounded German officers and soldiers went to recover – via a Red Cross ambulance.

It was a dangerous trip. Fighting continued all around us as we travelled through the Austrian Alps. But when we arrived in the resort town of Bad Gastein, I realised the officer had been true to his word; there were thousands of wounded German soldiers there, and the hotels were all decorated with red crosses, signalling that they'd become convalescence hospitals. My mother soon got a job as a desk clerk at one of the hotels, called Straubinger, and we lived there from September 1944 to May 1945, when the American army arrived. Germany had been defeated by the Allies, and Europe was about to be liberated.

I'll never forget the first time I saw American soldiers. They were standing in a line, handsome men with smiles on their faces. I liked them straight away, but there was something about them that seemed strange.

'What's going on with them?' I asked my mum. 'Their mouths are moving, but they're not talking!'

My mum laughed. 'They're chewing gum,' she answered.

I was a teenage refugee who'd barely survived the Holocaust, and I'd never seen gum, much less chewed it.

My mother got a job with the American army and tried to secure papers that would let us move to the US. But she also knew someone in New York, and through the Red Cross, she located her. That woman helped my mum find a cousin of my grandfather, who wrote us an affidavit of support, allowing us to leave Austria for the United States. But we didn't go there directly; with the help of the Catholic Church, we ended up in a displaced persons' camp in Munich. Then we were sent north to Bremen. My mum had re-established contact with her brother in France, and he wrote to her, begging us to come to France to live near him. When she wasn't responsive, he sent a car for us. It rolled up to the place we were staying, and when it stopped, a man named Major Zaremba, who was in the Polish army, stepped out. He was holding papers that gave us permission to settle in France.

Right then, my mother faced a decision.

'I've gone through too much in Europe,' she said to him. 'I've lost everyone. I want to start a new life, and that life is in America.'

In December 1946, my mum and I gathered together our suitcases, plus $500 that my uncle Maurice had sent. We boarded a rickety boat called the *Marine Marlin*, and with the winds whipping and rain pouring as the boat tipped on its side, we sailed for five or six days across the Atlantic Ocean. We landed at a pier in Manhattan and were greeted by my grandfather's cousin's son, Dr William Dubilier. He took us to New Rochelle, north of the city in Westchester County. We only stayed there for a few weeks, because my mum found a job in Greenwich, Connecticut. She worked there about a year, and then she moved us into a tiny room on West Ninetieth Street in Manhattan.

Apart from a conservatory I'd attended in Austria some time in 1944 or 1945, I hadn't gone to a real school in about three years. My mother valued education above all else, so she found me a Catholic boarding school called Nazareth Academy in Torresdale, Pennsylvania, and I moved there. I hardly spoke any English, and I had maybe two skirts to my name. I felt dirt poor next to all the other girls, but I couldn't tell them why. I didn't even want to tell my new best friend, who was a Polish girl named Ewa. The truth was too much for me – let alone another teenager – to digest. I told myself, *This is my new life. I'm in America, I'm Catholic, and I'm Elizabeth.*

I graduated and went to college, first in Manhattan, then in Missouri, and then back in Manhattan at Columbia University. But one day in the early 1950s, while I was home visiting my mum in her tiny apartment, Zygmunt Schwarzer came to visit. This handsome, green-eyed man who had loved my sister more than anything in the world hadn't just survived the Holocaust; he'd become a doctor, just like he'd always wanted to be.

'I have something for you,' he said, extending a thick, blue-lined notebook towards my mum.

It was Renia's diary, all seven hundred pages of it. My mum and I broke down in tears.

Zygmunt stayed for a little bit and told my mum and me how he'd survived after he'd smuggled me to Dzidka's house. In late July 1942, he had avoided being taken to the Bełżec death camp because he'd finally got his stamp from the Gestapo, confirming his employment. Between July and November 1942, he worked as a forced labourer at the German military base on the right bank of the San river. When the base got busier due to soldiers coming back from the front, Zygmunt became a carpenter, and he was assigned to building barracks where the newly arrived were disinfected before they left to go home to Germany.

In November 1942, there was another displacement *Aktion* of the inhabitants of the Przemyśl Ghetto. By then, Zygmunt had lost his work permit, and he was in hiding with a few other people in the attic of one of the ghetto's buildings. Somehow, they managed to survive until the end of the *Aktion*. I never confirmed it with Zygmunt, but I think this was when he left Renia's diary with a friend outside the ghetto walls.

After the final destruction of the ghetto in September 1943, Zygmunt was sent to the labour camp in Szebnie near Jasło, and from there – two months later – to Auschwitz. In October 1944, he was evacuated to the Sachsenhausen camp and worked at the Heinkel bomber aircraft works in Oranienburg. In December 1944, he was sent to the camp in Landsberg in Bavaria. In January 1945, he came down with typhus and only managed to survive thanks to the help of a doctor and a Lithuanian girl working in the kitchen. If you can believe it, that doctor was Josef Mengele, the death camp physician who's famous for having conducted horrific experiments on Jewish prisoners.

On 30 April 1945, the camp was liberated, and Zygmunt was finally free. He met his wife, Genia – who was called Jean in America – at a displaced persons' camp, and, that autumn, he started studying medicine at Heidelberg University. He graduated in 1949 and left for the United States, where, some time in the early 1950s, he tracked down my mum and decided to pay her a visit.

Getting through college had been such a struggle for me. My mum and I had no money, and we lived in a fifth-floor walk-up on Third Avenue, where the rent was only $55 a month and where the elevated train line went by till 7.00 at night, every single day. I worked as a waitress when I wasn't in class, and I was always so tired. My mum was, too. It wasn't like her, but she even said to me once, 'Why do you want to go to college? You're just going to get married.'

'No,' I answered. 'I want my degree.'

I finally got it in 1955 – with a major in German and a minor in Russian – and I was so happy. I'd *finally* done it.

One day, just before I graduated, I got called into an office at Columbia by a man I'd never met. When I sat down across from him, he offered me a job.

'What kind of job?' I asked.

'Well,' he said, 'it's a job where you can't tell anybody what you're doing.'

It was the CIA. They wanted me because I could speak and write Russian and German fluently. I didn't have to think for a second about what *I* wanted, though.

'Thank you,' I said to him, 'but I can't take it. I've lived all my life in secret. I don't want to do that any more.'

But it's hard to give up a secret life when it's protected you for so long, so my mum and I still didn't talk to people about who we were. Even when she married her second husband, Clyde, in the early 1960s, she never told him about her past. I didn't talk about where I came from to my friends at Columbia, where I stayed to get my master's degree in child psychology. I made myself forget the films I'd been in, and I didn't even see them until 2014, when Tomasz Magierski, a Polish film-maker who's been researching Renia's and my story, found them in some archives and showed them to me. At the primary school where I started to work in 1963 as a German and Russian teacher, I didn't tell anyone I'd once been the Polish Shirley Temple. I just laughed when my students called me 'Miss Niska' because they couldn't pronounce *Leszczyńska*.

One day in 1964 – after I'd left a job teaching business at Newtown High School in Queens and settled into a sixth-grade teaching position on Staten Island – I got invited to a party for the United Federation of Teachers, a teachers' union. The party was at a friend's big house in Queens, and she had a piano in her living room. It might have been thirty years since I'd acted, but I was still a performer, so I decided to sit on the piano bench and start playing and singing my Polish and Russian repertoire songs. When I finished one, a tall, handsome man who was a few years younger than me approached. He was George Bellak, a teacher from Newtown whom I'd always thought was very nice. He'd been born in Vienna, so we'd sometimes spoken German to each other, but I'd never considered him more than a friend.

'You play very well,' he said, then smiled. 'How are you getting home from the party?'

We talked all night and got on the subway at 2.00 a.m. When we got off, George walked me back to my apartment. That's how our romance started.

Everything happened so fast after that. We got married at City Hall in June 1965 on a weekday that we both had off. We laughed when the officiant stuttered my name, 'L ... L ... L ... shhh ... ka,' and we celebrated that night at the Russian

Tea Room. Within a few months, I was pregnant with our son, Andrew.

It took a long time for me to tell my husband who I was. Even though George was so much like me – he was Jewish, though his family had fled Austria in 1939 – I wasn't sure I could stand to face the pain of talking about my past. I also wasn't sure he'd accept me. The war was over, and I didn't want to think about it. I had spent years trying to forget that I was the little girl who'd made it out of Poland alive but whose sister had not.

That's why, when my mother passed away from cancer on 23 November 1969 – just a few months before my daughter, Alexandra Renata, was born – I placed Renia's diary in a safe-deposit box at a Chase Bank in Manhattan. 'The past is the past,' my uncle Maurice had always said, and that's the way I treated it.

It wasn't until my children started asking questions that I told Andrew and Alexandra the truth.

'I'm Jewish,' I said to them, 'and it's time I told you my story. I think you're ready for it.'

The past still makes my heart race and my stomach sick, and reading Renia's diary gives me panic attacks. George, Andrew, Alexandra and I visited Poland in the early 2000s – the first time I'd been there since I'd fled – and I couldn't make it as far as Przemyśl or to my family's old estate on the Dniester. I saw Maciek after I got back in town and told him about the trip, and I mentioned that I was still anxious and struggling to breathe well. He looked me up and down, then shook his head.

'If I'd known you were going,' he said, 'I would have stopped you.'

I can't imagine the pain my sister went through in her last moments, seeing me leave for a new life while she was left to her fate. I can't explain why I was allowed to live, and that's why I've tried for so long to turn my mind away from it.

Before his death on 1 April 1992, Zygmunt had learnt to process the past in a different way. He'd retired from his successful paediatrics practice on Long Island, and he'd created a space in his basement for Renia's diary. He'd photocopied all its seven hundred pages, and he'd laid them out carefully as though they were treasures. Every few days or nights, he'd wander down to his basement, and he'd read and study the diary near a photo of Renia he'd hung on the wall. His son, Mitchell, said spending time down there was almost a spiritual experience for him – as if Renia was his muse.

In one of the very few times I saw him, he opened the pages of Renia's diary and wrote:

Another month of May is coming, the month of love ... Today is 23 April 1989. I'm with Renusia's sister – Jarusia. This blood link is all I have left. It's been forty-one years since I have lost Renusia. When I think about her, I feel so small and unimportant. I owe her so much. Thanks to Renia I fell in love for the first time in my life, deeply and sincerely. And I was loved back by her in an extraordinary, unearthly, incredibly passionate way. It was an amazing, delicate emotion. Our love grew and

developed thanks to her. I can't express how much I loved her.
And it will never change until the end ... Zygmunt.

I think all of us – and I especially – can learn from Zygmunt's example. The past isn't long gone; it's present in our hearts, our actions, and the lessons we teach our children. For Renia and Zygmunt, the past stood for love, and I will thank Zygmunt till the day I die not just for saving my life, but also for opening that chapter of my life again. Facing what you thought you'd put behind you may be painful, but learning and growing from it is the only way I can live now.

I hope my sister's diary teaches you to do that as well.

Notes

[1] Renia was only fourteen when she started this diary, and she was pensive, thoughtful, sentimental, and everything else a 'good girl' in school usually is. She was innocent. I think we all were. You could be at the beginning of 1939, before the Germans and Soviets invaded Poland.

Back in those days, I wasn't living in Przemyśl with my grandparents and Renia. I was travelling around Poland with my mum, acting in films and on the stage. I was in a movie called *Gehenna* and one called *Granica*, and I had a steady job at Cyrulik Warszawski, a famous theatre in Warsaw, singing, dancing, and reciting the poetry of famous Polish poets like Jan Brzechwa and Julian Tuwim.

Renia had lived with our grandparents since some time in 1938. Our dad, Bernard, whom we called Ticio, still lived at our family's estate in Stawki. Our village was tiny, but it was near a bigger town called Zaleszczyki, which was in a bend in the Dniester about 300 kilometres south-west of Przemyśl.

Being separated from your dad wasn't strange in those days. Ticio had employees to look after, wheat and sugar beets to grow and harvest, and acres and acres to manage. He provided for us like any good father should, but he didn't have enough time to devote to us with my mum away. Besides, fathers were more removed then; mothers were the ones who brought up the children.

My sister and I loved to read poems in public, so when I was five, my mum took us to try out for a radio show based in Lwów (called *Lviv* today), a large city about 200 kilometres north-east of Zaleszczyki. The producers thought we had a lot of talent, so we got a spot reciting poetry. Renia soon decided to devote herself entirely to writing, but my mum took me to Warsaw for more auditions. Within two years, I was a tiny star on the stage and screen. My mum became my manager, and I became her shadow.

Unlike Renia, I was always with her, and when we weren't on the road, we rented a room on a beautiful street in Warsaw. I thought the city was so big and grand, with ancient cathedrals, synagogues, symphony houses and museums – almost all of which were destroyed during the war. Because I was on the stage so much, I didn't go to a normal, Monday-to-Friday school. Instead, I had a tutor named Mrs Arciszewska, and she taught me how to read poetry. I also studied at a dance school, and every week I saw a lady who taught me how to play the piano. When I think about it now, I was so lucky, like a little celebrity. I was in magazines and on film posters. People recognised me on the street. My mother had cute dresses made to order for me, and one of them had a row of six buttons down the front that read *A-R-I-A-N-A*.

Our mum was tall and elegant, with dark hair and bright blue eyes like mine. She also had these beautiful, straight teeth. People used to stare at her and ask, 'Who made your teeth?' and she'd laugh and answer, 'They are my teeth!' She had a tremendous presence, and she used to wear fancy shoes that made her long legs look even longer. Even though we'd lived in the country for most of my childhood, I never saw her wearing trousers. She was always in dresses, suits or coats, with a corset underneath that Renia and I loved pulling tight in the back.

She wasn't an aristocrat, but her friends called her 'the Baroness'. There was a very exclusive shop in Warsaw called Telimena that employed a team of tailors, and my mother once commissioned them to make her a green wool suit with leather buttons. She wore it with a silk blouse. Even when she went out to run an errand, she'd look like a lady. 'Dress for yourself!' she'd always order me. I still say that to my own children.

Renia also had my mother's bright blue eyes, but she looked less like Buluś (the name we called our mum) than I did. Renia sometimes got a little plump, and our mum never did. Renia was smart and thoughtful, but she wasn't a big personality the way my mum and I were. The differences didn't matter, though. Renia just adored our mum.

While I wouldn't call Renia beautiful in the classical sense, she was gorgeous and lovely, inside and out. She had a sweet smile that made everyone comfortable, and people always wanted to be around her. She wore her hair in plaits that she clipped up at the back of her head and, in many of the photos I have of her, she has on button-up shoes that go up past her ankles. She sometimes complained that the other girls had nicer clothes than she had, but I did that, too. After all, by the time I got stuck in Przemyśl, our mum wasn't there to buy pretty dresses and coats for us.

I'm sure none of the other girls cared or even noticed what Renia was wearing, though. I think they were jealous of her because of her accomplishments. She excelled at everything she put her mind to at school: maths, geography, Russian, Latin, French, Polish and German. She also studied Polish at the house of a professor named Jerschina, and, under him, she learnt to write beautifully. At home and at school, she read all sorts of famous Polish writers and poets, and I think they inspired her own poems.

Her high school – called *gimnazjum* – was on the corner across the street from my grandparents' apartment, and it was a huge place with a big garden surrounded by a high metal fence. In those days, a teenager's life outside the house revolved around school. Kids today either go out at the weekends – like to the cinema or the mall – or they stay inside and play on their phones. In 1939, it was more black or white. If you were in for the night, you were writing in your diary, drawing, playing an instrument, reading, or doing something else that was solitary. If you were out, you were at school, where there were always activities and parties. When Renia wanted to connect, she went to school – and it seemed like she was forever going there.

Renia had lots of friends, and everybody really loved and respected her. I know she writes about having problems, but I think that was just silly, typical teenager stuff. We've all had that, right? Her best friend was named Norka, and sometimes Renia would take me to her house. I liked it there, and I liked Norka. Our grandfathers worked in the same business, painting houses and doing construction, so we had a lot of history in common.

Around 1942, after my sister died, Norka wrote a two-page letter that she sent to my mum. She said that my sister was the most wonderful, deep, exquisite human being she ever knew and that they were devoted to each other. I know Renia sometimes fought with her, but Norka was her best friend, so she saw past that. That letter breaks my heart, and I cried when I read it.

Then there was Irka Oberhard. Renia complained about her, and I know why. She was a very snippy girl, with a lawyer father who I always thought was a very ugly little guy. Her mother had gone to *gimnazjum* with our mum – I believe at the same school Renia attended – and they were so-so friends. Irka's mother had a very caustic way of talking, and I thought she was always trying to interfere in Irka's and her sister Fela's lives. They came from a nice home, but they didn't have the talent my sister had. Renia was president of the literary club. She won all the awards. She wrote beautiful poetry, which all her friends and teachers always wanted to read.

[2]Before the German and Soviet occupation, my mother and I visited Renia in Przemyśl when we weren't in Warsaw or on the road. I don't remember how much we went there, but I know Renia loved it. I did, too. I'd missed my sister constantly, and being in my mother's home town was magical. Przemyśl was a lovely, ancient city built at the place where the Carpathian mountains and the lowlands met. The San river slowly wound its way through it, and the Przemyśl cathedral towered above it, the focal point of the city. It wasn't a big place – before the war, there were about 60,000 people living there – but it felt busy, with a big market in the centre of the Old Town, which was on the eastern bank of the San.

I wish I'd known how much it broke Renia's heart that Buluś and I weren't always with her; if I had, maybe I would remember more. Maybe I would have shown her more how much I loved her. But I wasn't even ten, and who remembers day-to-day events before they're eleven or twelve? I recall the big things and the general impressions, like how the room in which we stayed in Warsaw was on a fancy street and how it was full of Biedermeier furniture. I remember how my mum and her big smile and fur coats seemed right at home there. I remember her dragging me around Warsaw from place to place, appointment to appointment. I had a performance a few times a week, and I had to be there on time! I remember studying poetry at night with Mrs Arciszewska. She had smooth, porcelain skin and lived in what looked like a castle, with a gorgeous bed and jewel-covered walls inside. She had a butler, a cook and a cleaning lady. She owned a big dog named Rex and a small dog called Toja, which means, 'This is I'. These are some of my major memories before the war, and Renia missed all of them.

I'm not sure what was happening with my dad then. I'm sure he was busy doing what he'd always done – growing and harvesting wheat, tending to his sugar beets, and overseeing the peasants who worked for him, many of whom were Ukrainian and lived in the little town of Tłuste (Tovste), which was a few miles from our house. We had horses and cows, and my father – who was tall and handsome, with green eyes and wavy, reddish hair – used to wake up early, put on his riding trousers and leather boots, and walk out to check on the animals and workers.

I know my dad was a bit older than my mum, but I have no idea how they met. I only have one picture of them together, and it's framed and sitting on my kitchen counter next to my favourite photos of my children, husband and grandchildren. The picture is from their wedding day, and on the back, someone has written *1923*. This was one year before Renia was born.

But that's all the information I have. I don't know where my dad was born, and I don't know when. My daughter, Alexandra, has tried all kinds of ways to uncover something about him, but when you don't have birthplaces and birth dates, and almost every piece of paper your family owned was destroyed in the war, finding your family's history is next to impossible.

[3] We were Jewish, but we weren't really observant. In Stawki, we'd celebrated the high holidays, and when I got stranded in Przemyśl in 1939, we did the same. I remember my grandparents' synagogue was down the street from their building, and in the congregation, the ladies sat upstairs, and the men sat downstairs. But I wasn't there much – just the holidays.

My grandmother had a stationery shop on the ground floor of the building that she and my grandpa owned. They lived above it. In that shop she sold books, pencils, notebooks and cards. She'd collect food for the poor on Fridays, and our maid would cook chicken for Shabbat, when we'd light candles. My grandma also closed the shop on Saturdays. But as far as being religious, that was about it.

I didn't think all that much about being Jewish, in fact, until the Germans came. We never felt different. My father's workers were Polish and Ukrainian, and so were my grandfather's. Those men might have been anti-Semitic – at least a little bit – but I never witnessed it. In Przemyśl, my friends weren't only Jewish. My best friend, Dzidka Leszczyńska, was Catholic. And when I was on the stage, no one talked about religion. My name was Ariana and nothing else. No one was interested in the fact that my last name was Spiegel.

All that changed during the war, of course.

[4] My mother had one sibling – a brother named Maurice, who was a few years younger than she was. Maurice was such a

good-looking man – very dashing, with the same blue eyes as my mum, and a big, thick moustache. Some time in the 1920s, he went away to school in Caen, a city in the northern part of France. He stayed in France, became an architect and an engineer, and married a French lady from high society. She was Catholic. I don't know if he even told her he was Jewish – I suppose he must have – but he got married in church; I believe he converted.

Hitler annexed Austria in March 1938, and Sudetenland, the German-speaking part of Czechoslovakia, was taken over by Germany soon afterwards. By March 1939, the rest of the country fell. Although some of this takeover was peaceful – Sudetenland's annexation was agreed to by the major European countries in the Munich Agreement – everyone knew that Hitler was a threat to all of Europe. The agreement had just been a way to try to get him to settle down for a little bit.

Uncle Maurice must have been worried about Hitler and the Nazis even before the Munich Agreement, because he came to Stawki around 1938 and tried to convince my mum to move to Paris. I remember he brought her a beautiful watch as a present. But it was no use. My mum's life and family were in Poland, and she didn't want to leave.

Clearly, Renia did, even just to get away to see the world. She was so curious and interested, and she wanted to study in France, just like my uncle had. She never did; the war got in the way of all her dreams.

[5] Officials from Germany and the USSR met together secretly all during the summer of 1939, planning to form a political alliance that laid out each country's sphere of influence throughout Europe. By 15 August 1939, the beginnings of an agreement were in place, and by 23 August, the Molotov–Ribbentrop Pact – also known as the Nazi–Soviet Pact – had been signed. It promised peace between the two countries and sealed their top-secret arrangement to split up Romania, Poland, Lithuania, Latvia, Estonia and Finland between the two countries. Poland would be divided in half along the Pisa, Narev, Vistula and San rivers. Germany got everything to the west, and the Soviets got everything to the east. On 1 September, Germany invaded Poland, and sixteen days later, Russia marched in and began their occupation.

Our lives were never the same after that.

Mummy dropped me off with her parents one day that summer, when the talk of war was just that. She then went back to Warsaw, most likely to promote me. Our separation was never meant to be for more than a few weeks or months; I was her little girl, and I had films to star in, lessons to take, and poems to recite. I was building a career in Warsaw. But August turned to September, and without warning, German troops marched towards Warsaw, bombs fell from the sky, and Warsaw fell to the Germans. Then the Soviets invaded Poland, and the half of Przemyśl that was on the east bank of the San went to them. The other bank became Nazi territory. The Germans destroyed the road bridge that went from one side to the other, but it didn't make much difference to us; you couldn't cross the river without official papers. We didn't have those, so we were cut off from our mother.

It took some time for me to understand that I wasn't going to see my mum any time soon. I was just a little child, and the idea of not having the person I loved more than anything in the world around was impossible. But Renia understood – she'd felt that pain of being without our mum for over a year – and she decided to tell me the full truth one day.

'Now, stop crying,' she said, holding me tight. 'I know you miss Mummy, and I do, too. But we have to get used to it. This is the way it is now. Life has changed.'

I don't think my grandparents had had the heart to tell me. They were good, kind, hard-working people, and they always wanted to protect us, especially when we weren't with our mum and dad. My grandmother was named Anna, and my grandfather was Markus. My grandma had been born and raised in Jarosław, a town about 35 kilometres north of Przemyśl on the west bank of the San. I'm not sure where she met my grandpa, but at some point early in their marriage, they settled into a home on the first floor of a two-storey building near the main street in Przemyśl. That's where they brought up my mum and Uncle Maurice. That same apartment – located at 19 Słowackiego, just down from a major plaza – was where I lived from 1939 to 1942.

Their apartment wasn't very big. Renia and I slept in a corner in the living room, near the big, wooden desk, where my sister did her homework. That desk was also where Renia used to write the proposals for my grandpa's work, drawing up estimates that he'd then give to potential customers. People didn't have closets like they do now, so in that same room stood a large cupboard that stored their crockery for Seder. I remember, one day, a cat crawled inside and had kittens. It was mad! I still don't know where that cat came from.

Their building sat on the corner down the street from a synagogue and near Renia's school. My grandma's shop occupied half of the ground floor, and in the other half was an apothecary. Her brother's wife had a cheese and milk shop that took up the spot next to that. I never worked out that relationship; her brother and his family lived upstairs in the apartment next to ours, yet they never talked to us.

My grandma's other brother – who'd been president of a bank – had passed away before 1939, but his family ran away from Jarosław when the Germans came. His wife, his two lawyer sons, his daughter – who'd headed a school – and their families stayed with us for a little bit until they could find their own place. One of the sons had a small child of about six named Marylka, and she had flaming red, curly hair. We practically slept on top of each other till they left, but it didn't matter. We were just happy they were safe.

Granny was taller than my grandpa, and she was in her mid-sixties, which in those days seemed and looked much older than it does now. Like me, she'd been on the stage when she was young, and I wonder sometimes if she identified with me because of that. Or maybe she just knew I was a motherless child who needed extra attention. Sometimes at the weekend she'd get dressed up in one of her nice fur coats and take me for a walk to Zamek, a castle on a hill just outside the city. She held my hand tightly the whole way, and I still remember how safe I felt with her leather gloves wrapped around my little fingers. I loved my granny very, very much.

Grandpa was quite short, with big, piercing, blue eyes the same as mine, Renia's and our mum's. He was bald and had a small, neatly trimmed moustache, and he had a nice fur-lined coat like my grandma. Like most men back then, he wore a hat when he left the house. The people who worked under my grandpa loved him, and I know why; he wasn't well educated, but he was kind. He treated his employees with the same respect he treated his family

He also did everything in his power to protect us.

On 7 September 1939, bombs started to fall on Przemyśl. The shopping centre, Pasaż Gansa, caught fire, and as the Germans advanced, thousands fled – especially the Jews, whom the Germans began threatening, arresting and killing. Many of them crossed over to the Soviet side looking for refuge.

The Polish army tried to fight back, but it only took a month and five days for the whole country to fall. The Germans and Soviets were well armed, coordinated, and much stronger than our foot soldiers, horses, bombers and volunteers. We were targets – under attack and not safe in our own home – so my grandpa decided to take Renia and me out of Przemyśl when it went under siege. With no real plan, nothing except the clothes on our backs and a little money, we left the apartment and started to walk towards Lwów, which was about 100 kilometres away. Lwów was where I'd gone with my mum and Renia to recite poetry on the radio, and I knew it wasn't close – at all. But I kept my mouth closed because I trusted Grandpa. He and Granny and Renia were all I had.

My grandma stayed at home with the maid, whose name was Pelagia Paliwoda. She didn't say why she refused to go, but I suppose she was just too old and tired to walk that far. Pelagia would be good company, though. She and my granny were very different – Pelagia was a simple Polish woman who slept on a bed that folded down from the wall in the kitchen – but they were close. Pelagia had devoted her life to my grandparents.

As soon as we stepped onto one of the major streets leading out of Przemyśl, I remember seeing crowds of people fleeing with as little as we had, and those who could were running. There were more horses and carriages than cars where we lived, and we may have got a lift in a buggy at some point, but I can't recall. All I remember is that it was pitch black, I was hungry and terrified, and nobody knew where we were going. Even to a naive little girl, it seemed as though we had no direction. All we understood was that the Germans were here, they were bombing our homes, and staying put wasn't safe.

As we fled, we could hear German planes circling near us, the steady whirl of engines roaring and the *bang-boom* of bombs falling on the ground. But we assumed that the enemy would bomb a town rather than outside it. People lived in towns, in buildings, and if your goal is to kill as many of them as possible, the city is the place to bomb. We assumed we'd be safe in the fields or forest, so that's where we headed.

September was harvest time for wheat, and wheat is rough when you cut it. As my sister walked through the fields, she sometimes fell or brushed against a stalk that had been missed, and she scratched up her arms and legs, which started to bleed. We couldn't stop for her, though; we had to keep moving away from the firing and bombing we could hear behind us.

We walked out from the wheat, passing the forest as we headed into another field. I looked around and noticed row after row of cabbages, round and ripening and almost ready to be picked.

'They look like heads,' Renia said. 'I mean, like human heads, not just cabbage heads.'

Then Grandpa stopped, looked at us, and whispered, 'Run to the forest, girls. Run! We can't be here, because the German planes will see the cabbages and think they're people. They'll want to bomb right here.'

So we shifted directions and ran for our lives through the forest and towards Lwów.

[6] I don't remember this postcard from my dad. In fact, I don't remember anything about him during the war. But it's clear he'd lost our estate. The part of Poland where I'd been born was occupied by the Soviets, and they were Communist, so our land was now the government's. Ticio had moved to

Horodenka – a town just to the west of our old home – to find other work.

We weren't aristocrats, so we didn't have huge collections of art that the Soviets could steal the way they did from so many other Polish landowners. We'd lived in a manor house, not a mansion. But we'd been comfortable. We'd had nannies and employees. We'd owned a hen house and a place to store bushels and bushels of wheat. We'd grown sugar beets that we sold to the factories for sugar. But most importantly, we'd lived on acres of fertile land, and that's what the Soviets wanted.

[7] I don't remember this visit from my father. I wish I did. I think it's shocking how someone so close to you – your own blood relative – can fall so far away from you in such a short period of time. Now, after all these years have gone by, much of my understanding of him is constructed from things other people later told me.

For example, Renia had a nanny named Klara when she and my parents lived on the estate where she'd been born. Apparently, Klara was a very skinny woman and wasn't beautiful like my mum, yet I heard later that my mother believed my father had had an affair with her. I don't even remember who told me this; it was just family gossip, passed along from person to person, and now it feels as real as any other truth I know.

I was also told my mum lost a baby between Renia and me because she'd caught a venereal disease from my dad. Everyone suspected him of having had an affair with a woman who worked on the farm and that she'd been the source of it. Was my dad a womaniser? I'll never really know, but I still believe he was just because of those two stories.

Regardless, my parents clearly had problems, and it must have been part of the reason Buluś moved to Warsaw with me. Or maybe my father just didn't take much interest in us girls. Maybe he wanted a boy to help him on the estate, which was what good sons did in those days.

[8] I never would have guessed that Zygmunt Schwarzer – or Zygo, as Renia sometimes called him – would play such a major role in my life. That he would change my life, really. But he did, and, more important than that, he made the last two years of my sister's life better in so many ways. With Zygmunt, she knew the strongest, most romantic love she'd ever experienced.

Zygmunt was born in 1923 in Jarosław, where my grandma was from. I didn't know his family well, but I understood that my mother had gone to *gimnazjum* with his mother, and that his father, Wilhelm Schwarzer, had been a respected doctor in Jarosław. When the Germans invaded Poland, the Schwarzers fled to Przemyśl, just as my grandma's family had. In Przemyśl, Dr Schwarzer picked up his practice right away, even though he had a brand-new home and the country was in the middle of an occupation. That kind of toughness is what Zygmunt also possessed, though I wouldn't realise it for a while.

I always thought Zygmunt was so handsome, and that drove my sister wild. 'You're such a flirt!' she'd yell at me, and

I'd say back, 'He's your boyfriend, not mine!' I promise you I didn't have a crush on him. I was just a dramatic little girl who loved to follow my sister around and make friends with her friends. And Zygmunt was so easy to be friends with.

Zygmunt had black, curly hair, bright green eyes, and dimples on the sides of his cheeks that got deeper every time he smiled – which was a lot. Zygmunt was two years older than Renia, which made him eight years older than I was, but despite our difference in age, I always felt warm and comfortable around him. So did Renia. My sister liked him very, very much.

Zygmunt's best friend was named Maciek Tuchman. Maciek was about the same age as Zygmunt, and he was jolly and kind of plump. He always had a crush on my sister, and even though she loved being with him, Renia only had eyes for Zygmunt. Though I know there was some playful competition between Zygmunt and Maciek, they really were a team. 'We were tied to one another and living each other's lives,' Maciek – who was called Marcel when he got to America after the war – once said in an interview.

I don't know exactly how Zygmunt, Maciek, Irka and Nora became such close friends. It must have been school, since my sister was now going to school with boys. But Zygmunt occupied all her thoughts. They fought sometimes, but it wasn't serious; their little arguments were just the ups and downs of young people in love.

⁹ Between October and November 1940, the Nazi German government created the Warsaw Ghetto across 1.3 square

miles of the northern part of the city, right at the centre of the Jewish quarter. Immediately, the entire remaining Jewish population of the city – many of whom were refugees rather than Warsaw natives – were forced into it. About four hundred thousand Jews squeezed into a space that held about nine people per room, and a giant, brick wall encircled them. A train line ran just outside the ghetto walls, with several stops to load passengers and take them away to the death camps.

The formation of the ghetto wasn't a surprise to anyone; the Jews had been persecuted ever since the Nazis invaded Poland in 1939. Starting that November, Jewish businesses had been forced to display the Star of David, Jewish bank accounts had been frozen, and Jews around the city had been ordered to wear armbands. All of this – plus a real fear of deportation or execution – was why so many Jews had fled the German-occupied portion of Poland.

Mummy was Jewish, so of course Renia assumed she was inside the ghetto walls. But she wasn't; she'd avoided the ghetto by securing false papers with a Polish, Roman Catholic name. Some time after the Germans arrived, my mum had connected with an old friend named Halina Bereda, who was also Jewish but had married a wealthy Polish Roman Catholic and converted. One of Halina's husband's great-uncles was a cardinal in the Polish Roman Catholic Diocese, in fact. Halina and her husband knew people who could arrange for Polish papers, so they paid them to create some for my mum. In January 1940, my mum was baptised by a priest named Fajecki into the Roman Catholic faith. She later changed her name to Marianna Leszczyńska and – just like that – she blended in.

Renia and I knew none of this at first. If we were lucky, we received letters from Buluś maybe twice a year because it was almost impossible to send post from the Nazi-occupied zone to the Soviet-occupied zone. All outgoing mail was read and censored by the Gestapo. That didn't stop my mum from trying, though. Around the time the ghetto went up, my mother paid a Polish man from Warsaw to cross the river San with a letter for us. When he turned up at our door, we were so excited! Then he went back to Warsaw, found my mother, and threatened to report her to the Gestapo if she didn't pay him more. She fled her apartment and moved to escape him.

My mother was charming, capable, intelligent – and fluent in German. She'd gone to university in Berlin, then Vienna, and she'd learnt the language there during her years of study. Some time after 1939, she became the assistant director of the Hotel Europejski, a gorgeous historical hotel with a grand staircase, a ballroom, and a large terrace that spilt out onto Piłsudskiego Square. During the German occupation, three hundred Wehrmacht officers lived there, and the German government had renamed it Europäisches Hotel. Mummy was dedicated to her job, and she was so good at it that she worked there several years during the war.

I know now she rented an apartment in Żoliborz, which was a neighbourhood just north of the city centre on the western bank of the Vistula river. She'd got the place thanks again to Mrs Bereda. But other than Mrs Bereda and her husband, I'm not sure who her friends were. Apart from working, I don't know how she spent her time. When I had lived with her in Warsaw, she'd had a male friend who I now assume was her boyfriend, but I don't know if they stayed together after 1939. Regardless of who she was with, I know she must have been lonely because the few letters that made it through to us said she missed us terribly. Imagine being a young mother separated from your children for two years because of war. I have two children, and my heart aches just to think about it.

[10] As I've said before, a teenager's life in Przemyśl revolved around school, and there were constantly parties, dances and get-togethers. I know I went to at least one event with Renia – and I loved every single second of it – but most of the time, I was more interested in being with my own friends. The best of those was a little blonde girl named Dzidka.

Dzidka Leszczyńska – whose real first name was Zosia – was the youngest of three daughters in a Roman Catholic family that owned and ran a small tinned coffee factory at 41 Mickiewicza Street in Przemyśl. Her dad, Ludomir, was tall, slender and aristocratic-looking, with a thick moustache and a confident way of walking and talking. I didn't know it till much later, but during the German occupation, he was in Żegota – a member of the Council to Aid Jews – and that gave him some influence. Mr Leszczyński was devoutly religious, but he didn't see barriers among people. In his business and his life, Jews, Roman Catholics, Ukrainians, Poles and more worked together for the good of society and their families, and for that reason, his youngest daughter's best friend might as well have been his own. Or at least that's how he always made me feel.

Dzidka was skinny, fair and a little taller than I was. One of her older sisters – either Ludomira or Janina, I can't remember which – went to school with Renia, and they sometimes spent time together creating poems in their little leather-bound notebooks. Renia would write them and her friend would illustrate them. Dzidka and I were probably off together while they did. She and I used to sing songs, play with dolls, and walk hand in hand around town after school. We were inseparable.

Dzidka's dad saved my life, and I talk about that in the epilogue that follows Renia's diary. But, even though I never saw my best friend again after I escaped Przemyśl, being close to her is the single greatest bit of good fortune I've ever had. I don't know how Dzidka made it through the war, but I found out, thankfully, that she did. She moved to Krakow, married, adopted children, and died a few years ago from Alzheimer's. My dear Dzidka, I missed all those years.

[11] I had a diary? I don't even remember it! But I knew Maciek Tuchman for over eighty years, and if he had a crush on my sister, I am sure it was harmless. He and Zygmunt were the best of friends, and Maciek would never try to steal Renia from him. He was a joker then, and he was for the rest of his long life, too.

Maciek and I were friends in New York until he passed away in 2018 at the age of ninety-seven. When he came to America, people began calling him Marcel, and I usually did, too, because it became his identity in the same way that Elizabeth became mine. But in my memory, he's Maciek, and in Renia's world, that's who he'll always be.

Like Zygmunt, Maciek secured a work permit before being sent to the Przemyśl Ghetto in 1942. He lived there with his parents until the ghetto was swept clean, the Nazis shooting the people who still lived there in the back of the head. His mother was one of them; she was taken out of the ghetto and murdered in the Przemyśl Jewish cemetery. Maciek and his father were hiding in an attic, listening all night to the sound of gunshots.

Some time in 1942, he and his dad were shipped off to Auschwitz, and there they were ordered to work in a Siemens factory that was just outside the camp. Along with a hundred other prisoners, they laboured as slaves until the SS forced them out in a death march in 1945. They made it – alive – from Buchenwald to Berlin, where they were liberated at the end of the war. At a displaced persons' camp in Bergen-Belsen, he met his wife, a Czech woman named Shoshana.

Like Zygmunt, Maciek wanted to be a doctor, yet there were few opportunities for a survivor in Europe to get an education. Maciek and Zygmunt applied to and were accepted by a special programme at Heidelberg University, and they, their wives, and eight hundred other survivors lived and studied surrounded by former Nazis. Maciek graduated with honours in 1949, then moved to New York City, where he became an internist at NYU. He was there for fifty years.

In 1963, I was working at NYU's medical school, and one afternoon, I walked into the cafeteria. Suddenly, I heard a voice yelling out. It had the same Polish accent I have.

'Arianka! Arianka!'

It was Maciek! Smiling, jolly, warm, familiar Maciek from Przemyśl, who had made it through the ghetto and the camps and had lost half his family just as I had. He was alive, and he was in a New York City cafeteria with his arms wide open, ready to embrace me.

Maciek was my internist for many decades, until he retired after he'd been diagnosed with Alzheimer's. I visited him at his home after he left his practice, and he didn't remember recent events, like the death of his son, Jeffrey, from cancer in 2017. But he could recall things from the time of the war. We held hands and sang a few old, traditional Polish songs, and he said each word perfectly. He could even recite Pushkin in Russian.

Maciek died on 10 November 2018, and I attended his funeral on my birthday, 18 November. Afterwards, my family and I went to my favourite Italian restaurant, where we toasted Maciek's ninety-seven years – and my birthday as well. What a miracle to have made it through so much and to have lived for so long.

[12] It's been almost eighty years since I last saw my sister. That's a lifetime since I heard her laugh ringing out from the kitchen, saw her looking up from one of her leather notebooks, her bright blue eyes shining, or felt the familiar touch of her hand holding mine. Yet her presence is one of the largest in

my life. A photo of her hangs in the entry of my apartment, looking out over the centre of my living room, and it's a constant reminder of the past. Seeing Renia's smile every day, I remember the good times, but I also remember how the world shifted suddenly and spared me, while it sacrificed so many others, including her.

I'm not sure I fully realised how traumatic my childhood was until I was well into adulthood. War is too big and too scary for most children to understand, and I was no exception. But in her deeply poetic way, I think Renia grasped what was happening around us. She just saw the world differently. Her fatefulness, her carefulness, her subtle, perceptive observations about the pace and meaning of every moment show me how she processed the passage of time. She realised she was witnessing the calm before the storm, and she captured it. She savoured it, knowing it was fleeting.

The shaky sense of security we had in Soviet-occupied Poland slipped away on 22 June 1941, when war broke out between Germany and the Soviet Union. Nazi Germany decided it wanted to take over all of Europe and that the Soviet Union was the biggest thing standing in their way. That summer, German troops invaded Soviet-occupied territories on three separate fronts. The code name for this assault was Operation Barbarossa, and it was the largest German military offensive of the Second World War.

This German assault was what our secret, forbidden radios had warned us of, what the Communist propaganda we were taught in Russian class had put into verse, and what Renia had

had nightmares about. At the end of June 1941, bombs fell fast on major cities in Soviet-occupied Poland, and Przemyśl, unfortunately, was one of the first hit.

[13] Just like that, the German army came, bombs fell, lives were lost, and the Soviet army retreated. Then the Germans pushed east. To Lwów. To Kiev. And eventually, in the bitter, cold winter, to St Petersburg.

Przemyśl was just a stop on the way for the Nazis, who'd been across the San river for two years, waiting for the order to attack. Almost immediately after they invaded, they began to suppress the Jews. First, they forced all employed Jews to register their names in the local labour office. Then they ordered all Jews over the age of twelve to wear armbands with a blue Star of David on them. If you were on the street and passed a German soldier, you had to show your armband. If you resisted, you could be imprisoned or killed on the spot.

I was not yet eleven, so I didn't have to put one on, but when I first saw one, something in me died. My family and friends and neighbours who wore them weren't people any more. They were objects.

[14] When the Germans came, getting work meant everything if you were Jewish. Maybe your work was dirty, unpleasant, or far below what you'd been trained for, but it didn't matter. Doing anything that proved you were strong and capable enough to support the war effort might save your life.

At first, Zygmunt worked at a clinic, as Renia described. I'm sure this was happy work for him because he wanted to be a doctor, but that was the last intelligent job he had. The next summer, when all Jews were ordered to move into the ghetto, he and Maciek found work in a German storage depot that was located just outside Przemyśl at an army labour camp. They both sorted and organised uniforms there.

In his book, *Remember: My Stories of Survival and Beyond*, Maciek writes that their time in the factory almost got Zygmunt killed. Knowing that there were hardly any supplies in the ghetto and that he could trade a good pair of trousers for food, Zygmunt decided to take a chance. He looked around and realised that no guards were watching him, and he put on six or seven pairs of army fatigues under the trousers he'd come to work in. As he started to walk towards the door, looking like he'd put on two stone since that morning, he was stopped by a guard.

'What's going on there? What are you trying to do?' the guard asked.

Zygmunt knew he'd been caught and that he was going to be either beaten, jailed, or executed immediately, so he kept silent.

There was a young Jewish woman working in the administrative offices, and she liked Zygmunt. She also knew that the German soldier who'd just caught Zygmunt had a crush on her. Seeing that Zygmunt had been caught, she stood up from her desk and intervened.

'Please let him go. I can give you something.'

It's unclear what she gave him – and, I hope, for her sake, it wasn't much – but she saved Zygmunt. Just to be extra careful, Zygmunt also slipped the German soldier a gold coin.

That incident was the first of many things Zygmunt survived in the war. Between getting work, making connections, and being resourceful, he and Maciek had more lives than almost anyone I grew up with.

[15] After the Germans took over all of Poland, my mum's letters came more frequently. As Renia wrote in her diary, it was one after the other after the other. I suppose this was because post didn't have to pass from one occupied zone to another any more, but it could have been something else, like Mama becoming friendly with someone at the post office. I didn't ask at the time; I was just glad to hear from her.

With her new papers and name, my mum also had the freedom to travel to see us. It would be difficult and dangerous – she had to take time off from work, she had to travel through a war zone, and, most likely, she had to lie about who she was seeing. The train trip was also over ten hours, with one transfer in Krakow.

But my mum hadn't spent a significant, uninterrupted amount of time with her children for two years, and she had to. She missed us terribly. And we missed her!

[16] In 1939, the Germans had bombed the bridge that connected Zasanie – a part of Przemyśl on the left bank of the San – so people crossed on the railway bridge instead. But by September

1941, Jews were forbidden to use that bridge. The secret Renia writes about died with her, so I have no idea how we got over the San. Nor do I know why I went to see our mum before she did. Did our grandpa or mum bribe a German soldier? Did we walk with Dzidka's father, who lied by saying, 'These are my daughters'? I wish I remembered, but I don't. All I know is that when I mention to people that I saw my mum a few times during the war in Przemyśl – and that she returned to Warsaw without me and Renia – their only question is, 'Why didn't you stay with her? You could have escaped!'

It wasn't that easy. Death lurked around every corner, and it was an expensive and dangerous endeavour to start a new life. We didn't have papers that would allow us to do it. Yet a new identity was the only way to get out, like Buluś had done.

[17] Soon after the summer of 1941, the Nazis began seizing the Jews' valuables and household items. If you didn't open up your door when they knocked, they forced their way in, and you were taken away and beaten or put in prison.

My granny and grandpa's upright piano stood next to the balcony Renia was on when Zygmunt blew her a kiss before the Nazis arrived. For two years, we'd played that piano almost every day, and practising never felt like a chore. We liked playing, and Granny liked helping us. For my grandparents, my sister and me, that upright piano was a symbol of something strong and permanent. It stood on solid ground, as it had since my mother and my uncle Maurice were babies.

But the Nazis took whatever they wanted. Your money, your china, your clothes, your cutlery, your children, or your life. The first thing they stole from us was my grandparents' piano, a few soldiers entering the apartment one afternoon while I was out. They hauled it down the stairs and out the door, leaving a small pile of dust in the space where it had stood. When I came home, Granny was a different person, as though her heart had been ripped out.

Not long after Germany invaded Przemyśl, they also forbade Jewish children from going to school. This policy wasn't new for the Nazis, just to those of us in Przemyśl. In April 1933, the German government ordered that only 1 per cent of the population within German universities could be Jewish. The problem was that 5 per cent of the German population *was* Jewish. Then, in 1938, Jewish children were barred from enrolling in any German public school. Although Jewish teachers – all of whom had been fired from the state schools – were allowed to form their own Jewish schools, many mothers, grandmothers, older siblings or neighbours chose instead to tutor their children at home.

Renia and I had always gone to state schools, and during the Soviet occupation, nothing had stood in our way. Our friends and classmates were Jewish, Polish and Ukrainian, and we didn't distinguish among them. Our teachers didn't either. But when the Nazis came, I was forced to stay at home. During those long days, I daydreamt or made up stories with my dolls. When I was so bored I couldn't stand it any more, I'd put on my coat and go outside for a walk, counting the minutes until Dzidka was home from school and I could run over to her house.

Renia wrote in her diary, made up some poems, sent some letters, and looked out the window for hours, feeling nothing. Sometimes she'd sneak away to Norka's house to study French or ancient history, relying on books rather than teachers. Luckily, Jerschina still came for Polish lessons, and Renia always looked forward to that.

In 1944, I still hadn't gone back to school, but I enrolled at a conservatory in Salzburg, which was as close to an education as I could get. I thought about my grandma the whole time. With my fingers stretched across the ivory keys, Granny would have been so proud of me. Today, I have an upright Steinway in my apartment, against the wall and near a large window just as my grandparents' was. When I'm feeling nostalgic, I play the Polish and Russian folk songs my teachers taught me in my youth, when patriotic music was hopeful and defiant. The Nazis might have tried to take everything – our identities, our passions, and our education – but they couldn't steal the music in our hearts.

[18] The process leading to the creation of the Przemyśl Ghetto was slow, careful, and well thought out. In late autumn of 1941, the town quarter of Garbarze – which was bordered by the San on the west, north and east, and on the south by the railway that connected Krakow and Lwów – was proclaimed to be a Jewish residential area. The quarter's establishment took until the summer of 1942, and up to that time, Jews

were allowed to walk freely through the streets, but with their armbands on.

This area wasn't called a ghetto – yet. It was a residential area for Jews, and when a policeman came knocking at our door in early November 1941, he wanted us to move there. I don't know who bribed him, though I'm sure it was my grandpa. Maybe he appealed to the fact that he was Polish like us and that the Germans might be able to take our possessions and homes, but they couldn't take who we were. But I bet my grandpa didn't say much. He probably rummaged around in his desk, grabbed a few gold coins, and muttered, 'Here, take these. Just please let my family stay. Please, just for now.'

But I know my grandpa realised that the next time a soldier or policeman came knocking at the door, he might be giving final orders to go, now, with only 25 kilogrammes of our worldly possessions packed in a suitcase. Maybe my grandpa could attempt to bribe this next person, but you can only do that for so long. We were going to lose our possessions and our homes, and we had to prepare.

At some point during the autumn of 1941, my grandparents packed up all the silver they'd stored along with their Seder china in the large cupboard in their living room. Lining a big, wooden box with paper and cloth, they placed spoons, knives, forks, serving platters, candlesticks, and any piece of silver in the house and bundled it up tightly. Then they closed the lid and nailed it shut. Late one night, my grandfather crawled into their tiny basement and buried it with a shovel. For all I know, that box is still there.

[19] I'm not sure what Renia meant by Buluś moving the house. Did my mum clear out the possessions she knew the Germans would take? The family photos, the cutlery, and the articles of clothing that reminded her of home? That had to be it. Hiding your possessions was one small act of control and defiance, and if my mother did anything in her life, she took charge of a situation.

My mum died in late 1969 from cancer. It had started in her breast, but they didn't have mammograms in those days, so she didn't find out till it had metastasised into her hip bone. She had been ill since about 1960, and she'd married a man named Clyde because she knew he could help take care of her. He was kind to her, but he wasn't fond of foreigners, even though he had immigrant friends, one of whom had introduced him to my mum.

That wasn't the only secret she'd kept. When I cleaned out her apartment, I found two small suitcases she'd hidden away in her cupboard. Inside one of them were two tiny silver spoons, a stack of faded family photographs, a pair of pearl earrings, a few gold bracelets, and a beaded chain made of coral. These were the treasures from my childhood, the memories I'd stored in my brain, too afraid to dig up because they might make me cry. In the other small suitcase, I found the embroidered, beaded traditional Polish vests that Renia and I had worn at the harvest festival in Zaleszczyki. They were *strój krakowski*, meaning the traditional garb from the Krakow region. Right there in those suitcases sat my childhood. Right there was Poland. And I have no idea how my mother carried

443

all of it from our estate to Przemyśl to Warsaw to Austria to all the dozen other places we'd lived after the war, without me knowing.

[20] The news about my father and Lila living in a ghetto is one of the few solid pieces of evidence I have about where my dad was at the end of 1941. Unfortunately, what Renia wrote doesn't give much away. I don't know which ghetto my dad and Lila were living in, though it was probably in Horodenka, where they'd fled when they were forced out of our estate. The Germans created the ghetto in Horodenka around April 1941, establishing it in a part of the city that was one third the size of the area where most Jews had previously lived.

If my dad and Lila were there, I'm sure they didn't make it out. That's because, on 5 December, the Nazis executed their 'First Action' in Horodenka, assembling a murder squad to wipe out the ghetto. They lured out 2,500 Jews – which was half of the ghetto's population – telling them that they'd be receiving a typhus vaccine. Instead, everyone was murdered in the nearby forest. Those that were left in the ghetto were sealed off in a four-block stretch, living practically on top of each other until 2 September 1942, when almost all of them were shipped to the concentration camp at Majdanek, about 400 kilometres north-west.

The Nazis kept meticulous records in the camps, but we don't have my dad's birth date, so we don't know if he was there. The same goes for Lila.

[21] On 26 December 1941, the Nazis announced that Jews had to hand over their furs because the German troops needed them on the battlefield. German and Polish police officers – like the one we'd paid off months before – entered homes and seized furs, and on the streets, German police stopped Jewish men and women, ripped out the fur linings of their hats or coats, and moved on. In some cases, women on the street were also ordered to remove their shoes. They took them off and walked home along the cobblestones in their stockings.

My grandma had hired a tailor to make our coats. My sister's coat was fully lined with a fur collar, my grandpa's went to below his knees and was entirely fur-lined, and my grandmother's was just the same. Mine was a smaller version of Renia's, and we always wore them out with tights and hats in the winter. We had other coats, but these were our best – what we wore on special occasions and when winter was at its worst.

When Grandpa heard that the Germans had sent out an edict about our furs, he didn't panic. Some hopeful part of him decided that the war would be over soon. He'd survive. He might lose his family's furs now, but he could get them back when everything was all said and done and the Germans had retreated.

So he made a plan and asked a friend for a favour.

My grandpa sometimes worked with a Ukrainian man who had a business making keys. They liked and trusted each other, so Grandpa gathered together all our furs, placed them in a suitcase, and walked to the Ukrainian man's shop, which was nearby.

'Take these coats,' he said. 'Please save them for me. I'll be back for them after the war's over.'

I imagine I don't have to tell you that we never got those coats back. Everyone except for me and maybe the locksmith was dead before the next winter.

[22] When you were shut into your quarter, it wasn't with walls or barbed wire, like we'd soon be in the ghetto. Instead, you couldn't leave your neighbourhood without special permission from the Germans. My grandparents' house was on the main street of the city, and while I know Norka lived in a different quarter from the one we lived in, I don't remember which it was. I know she lived on a small street – not one of the main ones – but our town was small, so Renia could walk there easily. In any case, my sister's chances of seeing Norka every day, the way she always had, were slim because she didn't have the right papers.

Around that time, though, even worse things were happening near where the main road made its way toward the suburbs. Przemyśl's Jewish cemetery is located just off Słowackiego and was built on a hill around 1860, when the old cemetery became full. I've heard it's still beautiful today: hilly, wooded, and overgrown in the middle where the oldest graves are, some of which have toppled a little bit to their sides over time. The newer graves are towards the outside, and you can usually find flowers or photos sitting at their bases.

This was one of the places where Gestapo officials decided to execute Jews starting in the spring of 1942, when Renia realised she'd never see Norka again. It was also where Maciek's mum was taken on 3 September 1943, after she'd been found hiding in a bunker in the ghetto with thirty other Jews. Before the Gestapo took her to the cemetery, where they'd force her to strip naked and dig her own grave, she looked at one of the guards and said, 'Yes, you may have me, you bastards, but you will not catch my son and my husband.'

[23] I never understood my parents' relationship in the way that Renia did. In my earliest memories, my parents were separated because my mother was managing my career in Warsaw, and my father had his business on the estate. Was anything wrong? Not that I knew, but I was a busy little girl who'd never really had a relationship with my dad. What was there to understand? Renia was almost a teenager by the time my mum and I moved to Warsaw, so she had years and years before me to see things I didn't and feel things I never did. I think that's why my mum told her she was going to ask for a divorce. She knew Renia would understand it, even if it was hard for her to accept.

Renia didn't tell me anything, but that was like her. Even though she complained about me being too flirtatious, annoying or big-mouthed, I was her baby sister, and she wanted to protect me. I also never asked my mum what made her want the divorce. Of course, she hadn't seen my father in years as far as I knew, but divorce was a major decision that would change her life. Women didn't do that in those days.

As for my dad … it breaks my heart to say it, but the letter Renia mentions was the last we heard from him. The war killed most of my wonderful family. God rest your soul, Bernard Spiegel, my Ticio. You were a man of few words, who tended to your fields, your leather boots shiny and green eyes sparkling under the summer sun. I wish I had known you longer and better.

[24] There's a quarter in Przemyśl called Zasanie, and, before the war, it had one synagogue. During the war, the Germans turned the synagogue into a power station, and they forced the Jewish residents of the quarter to live together in one building. I've read there were about forty-five to sixty occupants, packed together like sardines.

On 3 June 1942, Germans murdered forty-five of these people. Just like so many others before them, they were loaded onto trucks, taken to a fort in the suburbs of Przemyśl, and shot, one by one in the nape of the neck. Just before they died, many of them – just like Maciek's mum – had been forced to strip naked and dig their own graves.

I don't remember this, but other Jews – both in Zasanie and throughout Przemyśl – were beaten on the street for trying to steal a piece of bread. Others were chased by dogs while the guards – some of whom had their children with them – laughed. Then they were hanged, a public spectacle that the children watched, too.

Writing this makes me sick. Renia had the full, open emotions to describe what she lived through, but most of the time now, I don't. When people ask me about the war, I just don't want to talk about it.

[25] In the early summer of 1942, news spread that there had been a series of anti-Jewish riots in the towns of Tarnów and Rzeszów, which lay along the road between Przemyśl and Krakow. Communication wasn't reliable between cities during the war, so the Przemyśl Judenrat decided they needed to investigate, to work out if the rumours about the riots were true. They were.

'This can't happen here to us,' the Judenrat told the Gestapo. 'We're going through enough without the whole community coming after us, too.'

The Judenrat and the Germans worked together in two ways. The Judenrat was administered by the Nazi government, so they performed services for them like registering Jews and reporting those numbers. They also worked to protect the Jewish community, organising food distribution, helping the elderly, and trying to simplify life in the ghetto. It wasn't unusual for them to come to the Gestapo with a concern; they knew the Jewish community needed protection, and they thought the Gestapo might offer it.

The Gestapo officials listened and nodded, seeming sympathetic. Then they told them they'd come up with a plan. A few days later, they announced it.

'If you behave well, we'll protect you,' a Gestapo official said.

'But how is that?' the head of the Judenrat asked.

The Gestapo chief, whose name was Benthin, cleared his throat.

'If you provide me with one thousand young people for work at the Janowska camp in Lwów, they'll be safe. Nothing will happen to them.'

On 18 June 1942 – the horrible night Renia describes, which was also her birthday – 1,260 Jews were loaded into cattle cars and transported to forced labour at Janowska. There, most of them slaved away doing carpentry or metalwork for the Nazis. To make things worse, the Gestapo shot many of their relatives right there on the tracks as they waved goodbye. The families that weren't killed were later charged the cost of their loved ones' transportation to the camps.

The Gestapo's words had all been lies, and they'd betrayed the trust of the Judenrat to help them with their dirty work.

Acknowledgements

I would like to dedicate this book to the memory of my cherished sister, Renia. She was a mother figure to me during the war. Through this book, her memory will not be lost to history.

I am grateful to the renowned Holocaust scholar Deborah Lipstadt for writing the introduction to my sister's diary. I appreciate her insight into my sister's poetry, love and humanity.

To *moja mamusia*, Bulczyk. You were the most beautiful, well-educated, elegant and resourceful woman I have ever met. You knew how to manoeuvre through life. You knew how to survive. You gave me life. You gave me courage. You gave me hope. You gave me a life in America.

There are certain people to whom I owe my very existence. Their bravery is the reason I am alive today: Ludomir Leszczyński, a righteous Pole who, under threat of the death penalty, saved my life and took me from Przemyśl to my mother in Warsaw; the Bereda family, who welcomed me in Warsaw, reunited me with my mother, whom I had not seen in two long years, helped me to obtain papers, and basically saved my life – again; Zygmunt Schwarzer, who risked his life and took me out of the ghetto in Przemyśl to safety. He saved my life. Again. He brought the last remnants of my sister in the form of the diary and miraculously found my mother in the United States. I am forever indebted to them for my life.

My deepest appreciation to Tomasz Magierski. Tomasz unearthed press clippings, film reels, photographs, and countless other documents about Renia and me. He was captivated by Renia's story, and without his tireless efforts, her story would not have been brought to life. *Dziękuję bardzo.*

I would like to acknowledge with gratitude the support and love of my family: my son, Andrew Bellak, and daughter-in-law, Susan. My beautiful grandchildren, Theo, Nicholas and Julian.

A special note of gratitude to Anna Blasiak and Marta Dziurosz, who had the painful and arduous task of translating over seven hundred handwritten pages of my sister's work, including sixty poems.

Thank you to Jennifer Weis of St Martin's Press for taking an interest in this story and believing wholeheartedly that it needed to be told!

To my recently departed husband of fifty-three years, George Bellak, I miss you dearly. You understood me implicitly. George was my Viennese-born wunderkind, who showed unwavering support and love and devotion to me and our children.

I would like to thank all those whose assistance proved to be a milestone in the accomplishment of my end goal: to tell the world what happened.

I would also like to pay tribute to my extended family, who were not as lucky and perished in the Holocaust.

But there is one person more than any other whose never-failing dedication and perseverance in bringing this story to light allows my sister's legacy to continue, and have ensured that her words would not be lost to history.

That person is my beloved daughter Alexandra Renata.

Renia's spirit lives on through her and it is to her that generations of future readers will be indebted.

– Elizabeth Bellak

CELTIC WARRIORS

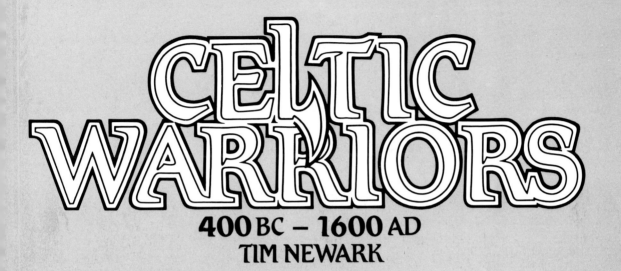

CELTIC WARRIORS

400 BC – 1600 AD

TIM NEWARK

COLOUR ILLUSTRATIONS
BY ANGUS McBRIDE

BLANDFORD PRESS
POOLE · NEW YORK · SYDNEY

For my mother

First published in the UK 1986 by Blandford Press
Link House, West Street, Poole, Dorset BH15 1LL

Copyright © 1986 Tim Newark

Distributed in the United States by
Sterling Publishing Co, Inc,
2 Park Avenue, New York, NY 10016

Distributed in Australia by
Capricorn Link (Australia) Pty Ltd
PO Box 665, Lane Cove, NSW 2066

British Library Cataloguing in Publication Data

Newark, Tim
  Celtic warriors: 400 BC–1600.
  1. Celts—History
  2. Europe—History, Military
  I. Title
  940′.04916   D25.5

ISBN 0-7137-1690-8

Typeset by Graphicraft Hong Kong
Printed in Great Britian by Butler and Tanner, Frome
Colour printing by Friary Press Dorchester.

Contents

Preface

At one time, the Celts dominated the ancient world from Spain to Turkey. They sacked Rome and invaded Greece. Their war chariots devastated all adversaries. But then it all went wrong. They were crushed by the Roman Empire. Their legendary kingdoms in Europe were no more. Only Britain remained a Celtic stronghold. And even there, the Scots, the Welsh, and the Irish were forced to fight for their independence against waves of Anglo-Saxons, Vikings, and Anglo-Normans.

This book tells the heroic story of two thousand years of Celtic warfare. From four centuries before Christ to the sixteenth century, it describes the dramatic, hard-fought withdrawal before succeeding military powers and the times when the Celts struck back. It celebrates the persistent struggle of the Celtic-speaking people to retain their independence and their way of life. The occasions of unity and the defeat brought by division.

As a survey, this book serves as an introduction to Celtic military culture and it is hoped will encourage reading in depth to discover further the true character of the Celtic warrior.

Tim Newark 1985

The Golden Age

When Alexander the Great asked an envoy of Celtic warriors what they feared most, he expected them to say 'You, my lord.' Instead they replied: 'We fear only that the sky fall and crush us, or the earth open and swallow us, or the sea rise and overwhelm us.' A peace was made, but Alexander was furious. How dare a tribe of insignificant barbarians fear the fantastic more than his realistic military might. Fifty years later, this same confident people devastated Alexander's homeland of Macedonia.

The raiding campaign of 279 BC was an ambitious one for the Celts. Living north of the Danube, they had pillaged Thrace and Macedonia before. But this time they had killed the King of Macedonia, heir to the glory of Alexander and Philip. A fever of adventure gripped the army of raiders. This expedition would be different. Brennus, their chieftain, described the rich townships of Greece. He told his followers of the sacred sanctuaries crammed with gold and silver offerings to the Greek gods. He knew it was a good time to embark on such a campaign. The Macedonian Empire had broken up: the Greeks were a divided people. The Celts mounted their horses and rode south.

Tales of Celtic atrocities in Thessaly gradually convinced many Greeks to forget their wrangling and combine their forces. They chose to confront the Celtic warriors at Thermopylae. Almost exactly two hundred years earlier, a Greek army had fought a bitter last stand at this mountain pass against Persian invaders. The tragic outcome of that gallant defence of their homeland cannot have escaped those Greeks now guarding the narrow mountain roads. In order to prevent the Celts even reaching Thermopylae, Callippus, the Athenian commander of the Greek force, sent a detachment of horsemen to the river Spercheius. There they broke down all the bridges across the fast-running waters.

Unhindered by any major resistance, Brennus had led his warriors along the coast. Having come so far, the Celts would not be denied their booty. That same night as the Greeks camped on the bankside, a group of Celtic raiders crossed the Spercheius lower down, in slower waters. Swimming in the dark, they used their long shields as rafts. Next morning, the Greeks dashed back to Thermopylae while Brennus forced the local population to rebuild the bridges. Needing food and supplies and in no rush to confront the Greek army, the Celts were content to plunder the countryside around Heracleia. They did not even bother to attack the town. But the Greek army mustering at Thermopylae could not be avoided indefinitely. Celtic scouts and Greek deserters warned Brennus that it increased day by day.

On the day of conflict, it was the Greeks who began the battle. At sunrise they advanced quietly and in good order. Because of the rough terrain and the many streams that hurtled down the mountainside, horsemen proved useless and the majority of fighting was on foot. Despite being unarmoured except for their shields, the Celts fought with impressive ferocity. Some drew out from their wounds the spears by which they had been hit and threw them back at the Greeks. As the battle for the pass raged, the Athenian contingent rowed their triremes along the coast of Thermopylae: a coastline slowly silting up and becoming a salt-marsh. They attacked the flank of the Celts with arrows and slingshot. The Celts were hard pressed and many fell into the swamp, sinking beneath the mud. The first day of battle ended with many losses.

After a week's rest, Brennus decided to split his enemy's ranks. He sent horsemen off to the neighbouring region of Aetolia. Their plundering soon reached the ears of the Aetolian warriors camped at Thermopylae. Desperately worried by this assault on their homeland, they immediately left their Greek allies and pursued the Celtic raiders. Brennus now capitalised on the resentment of local Greeks. Fed up with the freebooters on their soil, local herdsmen were happy to see the Celts clear off along the many remote mountain paths. Acting as guides, they led Brennus and his warriors along the same tracks that had allowed the Persians to outflank the Greeks.

Obscured by a morning mist, Celtic warriors suddenly descended on the Greek guards of the mountain pass. Fighting a fierce rear-guard, the majority of the Greeks managed to clamber into Athenian ships and were evacuated from certain disaster. Thermopylae, however, belonged to the Celts and they now pressed on southwards through the mountains. The Celts had been promised the treasures of the Greek temples. But, as they approached the sacred territory of Delphi, it seemed that the very gods of the Greeks had finally rallied to protect their own people. Earthquakes shuddered beneath the raiders. Great rocks tumbled down from Mount

Bronze spearhead found in a burial mound at Snowshill, Gloucestershire, England. Early Bronze Age. The makers of this blade were a proto-Celtic people from central Europe who used their metal-working skills to spread their areas of influence and trade throughout western Europe. Their established routes of conquest were followed by later Celtic communities.

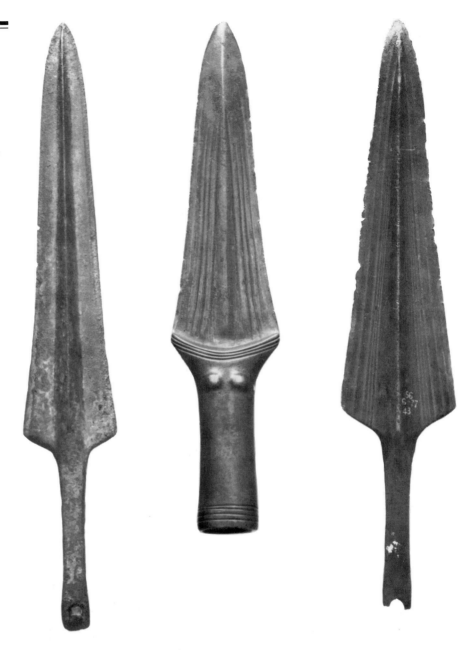

Bronze tanged and socketed spearheads found at Arreton Down, Isle of Wight, England. Early Bronze Age, 1600–1400 BC, now in the British Museum, London. Such keen-bladed weapons gave these warriors a significant advantage over the prehistoric natives of the lands they dominated.

Parnassus and bottomless crags ripped open. Thunder crashed all around. Lightning bolts engulfed individual warriors in heavenly fire. Amidst the chaos, the weird shapes of the ghosts of past Greek heroes arose.

As Delphi came within view, the supernatural forces were joined by the very real strength of a Greek army. To this were added the guerilla assaults of the local Phocians, haunting the snow-covered slopes of Mount Parnassus and pouring arrows and javelins into the Celtic ranks. In the face of all this, the Celtic warriors fought remarkably well. But that night, battered

11

and exhausted, a panic spread through their camp. In the dark, thinking they were being attacked by the Greeks, Celt killed Celt. The next day, Greek reinforcements chased the Celts back to Heracleia. During the long retreat, Brennus, already wounded, took his own life. Harried throughout Thessaly, few of the Celtic raiders returned home.

This then is the legend of the Celtic raid on Greece in 279 BC as recorded by Pausanias, a Greek historian of the second century AD. Analysing his account, one is immediately aware of several discrepancies and clichés. The Celtic raid on Delphi did not fall short of the city and end in a dismal rout. The Roman historian Livy writes several times of the pillage of Delphi while Strabo even suggests that treasure found in the sacred Celtic lake at Toulouse originated from Delphi. Moreover, after satisfying themselves in Greece, the Celts advanced back along the coast to the wealthy port of Byzantium where they crossed into Asia Minor. There they fought as mercenaries for the King of Bithynia. They then advanced further into Turkey and established themselves in territory belonging to the Phrygians, around present-day Ankara. The lands became known as Galatia and the descendants of those Celtic warriors continued to terrorise Asia Minor for over a hundred years, extracting tributes from rulers as far away as Syria.

Pausanias is guilty also of cultural cliché. His vision of the Celts is one of badly-armed, near-naked savages. Of course, he admits, they fight courageously but it is the ferocity of animals. When confronted by the cool discipline of Greek warriors, these yelping, charging wildmen have to resort to the sneaky subterfuge of the barbarian Persians: a stratagem facilitated by Greek traitors. However, even Pausanias has to admit that Brennus—for a barbarian—handled the crossing of the river Spercheius with efficiency and success. But, like all Imperialist correspondents, Pausanias greatly exaggerates the numbers of the raging savages: 200,000 Celts against 25,000 Greeks.

In reality, the Celtic force that invaded Greece was probably little stronger than those raiding parties which frequently crossed the Danube. Along the way, it may have been joined by Greek bandits but it cannot have been more than a few thousand. It would also have been divided up into numerous plundering gangs, scattered across the countryside, not at all suited to a pitched battle. Such warriors were professional raiders and augmented their own arms with a variety of stolen armour and weapons. They were better equipped and of a higher morale than the hastily assembled Greek forces that confronted them. The oldest specimen of interlinked mail yet found has been excavated from a third-century BC Celtic grave in Romania and this was probably developed from protective garments made up of rings threaded onto cords, like netting; a fragment of which has been found in an eighth-century Halstatt grave in Bohemia.

The renowned ferocity of the Celts was not all Greek myth. Livy puts a vivid description of the Galatians into the speech of Gnaeus Manlius Volso, a consul sent to crush the Asian Celts in 189 BC. 'They sing as they advance into battle,' the consul warns his troops, 'they yell and leap in the air, clashing their weapons against their shields. The Greeks and Phrygians are scared by this display, but the Romans are used to such wildness. We have learned that if you can bear up to their first onslaught—that initial charge of blind passion—then their limbs will grow weary with the effort and when their passion subsides, they are overcome by sun, dust, and thirst. And anyway, these Celts we face are of a mixed blood, part Greek. Not the Gauls our forefathers fought.' Despite references to the 'degeneracy' of the Galatians, such a description of the Galatians differs little from other

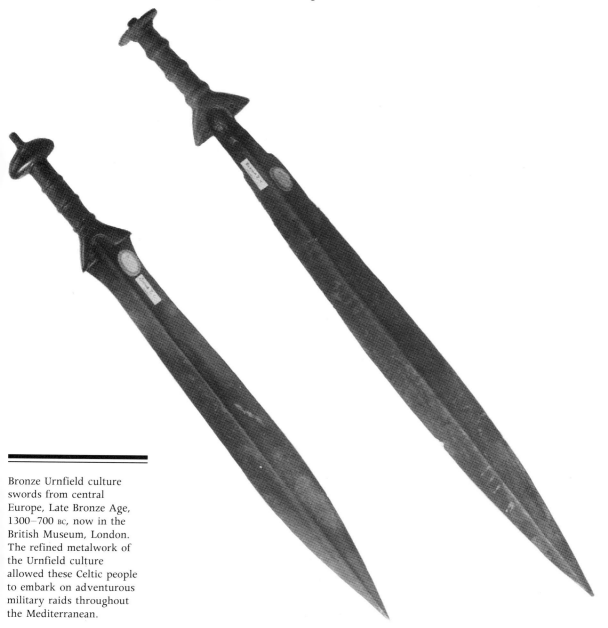

Bronze Urnfield culture swords from central Europe, Late Bronze Age, 1300–700 BC, now in the British Museum, London. The refined metalwork of the Urnfield culture allowed these Celtic people to embark on adventurous military raids throughout the Mediterranean.

13

accounts of Celtic and Germanic warriors in Europe. Here again, the ferocity of the Celts is respected, but it is undermined by a lack of discipline and staying power which the Romans can turn to their advantage.

Such a vision of the Celts as ferocious barbarians has endured over the centuries. In the culture war of projected images, the Celts have come off second best to Graeco-Roman propaganda. This is largely because the Celtic peoples of central Europe maintained a culture without writing. The only written accounts we have of them in the thousand years until the fifth century AD are Greek and Latin. We see the Celts through the eyes of their enemies: it is like writing a history of twentieth-century America based on Russian chronicles. Aspects of the Celts were admired, but at best they are represented as noble savages cowed by the might of classical civilization. It is a tradition mirrored in Mediterranean art. When King Attalus I of Pergamum defeated a force of Galatians in around 230 BC, he commemorated his victory with a series of sculpture. In actual fact, the victory was short-lived and the Galatians continued powerful until the next century, but the Pergamene sculptures of defeated Gauls were copied throughout the Greek and Roman world.

The most famous of these images, *The Dying Gaul*, shows a naked Celtic warrior kneeling wounded and subdued on his shield. Only the Celtic torque round his neck suggests the strength that had to be conquered to render this figure pathetic. A Roman marble copy of this sculpture now stands in the Capitoline Museum in Rome to remind us all continually of the defeated Celtic people: supposedly a naked, savage race inevitably overwhelmed by the higher civilization of the Mediterranean. Another sculpture copied from the Pergamum group, now also in Rome, shows again a Celt with characteristic wild hair and moustache (Romans and Greeks never wore moustaches without beards). This time the figure has slain his wife and is stabbing himself in the chest rather than be taken alive. A gallant and brave but eventual loser. Just as the Romans wanted them.

The true standing and culture of the pre-literate Celts can only be deduced from archaelogical discoveries. That they emerge as a recognisable collection of tribes in the first millenium BC is revealed by a series of finds in central Europe. These consist predominantly of bronze and iron metalwork and their famous hill-fort settlements. The people were called *Keltoi* by the Greeks and *Galli* by the Romans. That all these peoples of central Europe were called Celts is because from the fifth century BC onwards they were identified as speaking variations of the same Celtic tongue: an Indo-European language distinct from that of the Germans and the people of the Mediterranean, and now surviving only in the language of the Gaelic Irish and Scots, the Welsh and the Bretons.

The ancient Celts were not a unified people. They did not rule an All-Celtic Empire. Their many hill-forts attest to the fact that Celtic tribes throughout Europe fought and raided against each other as much as they did against the Romans, Greeks and Germans. Nevertheless, archaeological finds maintain that they did share a similar culture as well as a common language. That they did not develop the art of writing does not mean that this culture was any inferior to that of the Romans or Greeks. Technologically and economically, they were equal to their southern neighbours and in peace a thriving trade was continued between them. As an alternative to literature, the Celts developed highly skilled patterns of speech. Their verbal eloquence was valued and respected not only by themselves but also by the Romans and other literate races. Without doubt, however, it was the Celtic lack of written records that contributed to their apparent and real decline in influence and power from the third century BC onwards. Indeed, it is remarkable that the Celts retained any of their potent presence in European history in the face of Latin culture and warfare.

Before the Roman war-machine reached its zenith, the Celts enjoyed a golden age of martial prowess. From a heartland in central Europe, Celtic warriors carried their culture and influence into France, Spain, and Britain. Native tribesmen were unable to resist their long iron swords. By the fifth century BC, the Celts had overcome the Etruscans in northern Italy and settled the land of the river Po. In 390 BC Rome was sacked and several Roman armies humbled. Why were these Celtic warriors so successful? We are told they were fierce fighters. But, above everything else, they were horse-warriors—superb horse-warriors. So renowned were they that they were employed as mercenary cavalry by Greeks and Romans throughout antiquity. Strabo states that the Celts were better horsemen than foot-soldiers and the best mercenary cavalry the Romans ever employed: a recommendation echoed by Caesar, who almost exclusively used Celtic horsemen in his Gallic campaigns.

One of the earliest accounts of Celtic horsemanship to survive is recorded by Xenophon, a Greek historian and cavalry officer of the fourth century BC. In the war between Sparta and Thebes, he records, mercenary troops were sent by Dionysius of Syracuse to aid the Spartans. Xenophon's text makes a distinction between the Celts, Iberians, and horsemen sent, but this seems a later manuscript error and they are all one and the same: Celtic or Celtiberian horse-warriors. Xenophon describes their performance against a Theban army plundering a plain near Corinth. 'Few though they were,' he wrote, 'they were scattered here and there. They charged towards the Thebans, threw their javelins, and then dashed away as the enemy moved towards them, often turning around and throwing more javelins. While pursuing these tactics, they sometimes dismounted for a rest. But if anyone charged upon them while they were resting, they would easily leap onto their horses and retreat. If enemy warriors pursued them far from the Theban army, these horsemen would then turn around and wrack them with their javelins. Thus they manipulated the entire Theban army, compelling it to advance or fall back at their will.' Xenophon is a trustworthy chronicler of military horsemanship as he was himself a cavalry officer and wrote a treatise on the subject. Later, in his account of

Bronze ornamented mace-heads from southern Germany, now in the State Prehistorical Collection, Munich. Urnfield culture, late Bronze Age, 1250–750 BC.

Greek wars of the 360s, he gives an example of how horsemen are best used in battle. As a force of Arcadians give way to the Spartans, a group of Celtic horsemen are sent after the fleeing Greeks, cutting down the running foot-soldiers.

Five hundred years later, Pausanias gave an equally vivid and interesting account of Celtic horsemen. 'To each horseman were attached two servants, he wrote. 'These were themselves skilled riders and each had a horse. When the horse-warriors were engaged in combat, the servants remained behind. However, should a horse fall, then a servant brought a new horse for the warrior to mount. And if the warrior were killed, a servant mounted the horse in his master's place. If both rider and horse were hurt then one servant would ride out to replace him, while another led the wounded warrior back to camp. Thus the Celts kept up their strength throughout a battle.' This description may have been based on earlier chroniclers nearer the time of the Celtic invasion of Greece, or it may have been inspired by contemporary Celtic horsemanship in the second century AD. Whatever its source, it clearly demonstrates a sophisticated use of cavalry. It shows that Celtic horsemen possessed a high social and economic status like that of a medieval knight in relation to his squire and attendants. It suggests that Celtic horsemen fought in military units similar to the medieval 'lance' in which a heavily armed horse-warrior was supported by lighter cavalrymen who were also grooms.

The power and importance of the Celtic horse and rider is dynamically represented in Celtic art. From the great white horses carved into the chalk slopes of southern England to the tiny representations of horse-warriors on Celtic gold coins: both are symbols of dominance over the native population and the means by which it was achieved. As to the horse equipment itself, much ingenuity and craftsmanship was lavished on it. Sophisticated flexible iron horse bits from France have been dated from the fifth to the third centuries BC. In Scotland is preserved a fascinating piece of bronze armour for a horse's head. It is magnificently decorated with swirling patterns and has two curved horns attached to it. As in most societies, it appears that horsemanship was predominantly the preserve of aristocratic, wealthy warriors. An intriguing glimpse of what an ancient Celtic horse-warrior may have looked like in all his finery is provided by a relief on the Gundestrup Cauldron.

Found in a Danish peat-bog and dated to the second century BC, the cauldron depicts Celtic warriors of central Europe. The horsemen wear short, tight-fitting linen tunics. Some may also have worn the knee-length trousers of the foot-soldiers lined up beneath them. On their heads, the horsemen wear iron helmets with elaborate bird and boar crests. According to the head decorations on the Aylesford bucket, some helmets also had huge curled horns. The horsemen wear spurs but, of course, no stirrups. Bridle and harness are decorated with metal plates. Chieftains and noble soldiers probably also wore torques around their necks and shirts of mail.

On the Gundestrup Cauldron, the horse-warriors are clearly in command, wearing the most expensive arms. Beneath them are foot-soldiers armed only with spears and large rectangular shields. They wear no helmets. At the end of the line of foot-soldiers is a warrior wearing a helmet with boar's head crest. He presumably belongs to the same class as the horse-warriors and is some kind of officer. Behind him are three foot-soldiers blowing on long trumpets shaped like a horse's head. This is the clearest Celtic record we have of the composition of an ancient Celtic army.

The excellence of Celtic horsemanship extended to their famous use of chariots. 'The chariots of the Britons,' wrote Julius Caesar, 'begin the fighting by charging over the battlefield. From them they hurl javelins; although the noise of the wheels and chariot teams are enough to throw any enemy into panic. The charioteers are very skilled. They can drive their teams down very steep slopes without losing control. Some warriors can run along the chariot pole, stand on the yoke and then dart back into the chariot.' Primarily, it seems, Celtic chariots were for display, intended to overawe and enemy in the prelude to battle. Once involved in combat—according to Caesar and Diodorus of Sicily—a chariot team would dismount to fight, using it more as a means of fast retreat or advance rather than as a weapon. However, those noble warriors who rode in a chariot probably did not fight on foot but mounted their horses and fought with their usual retinue of horsemen. The chariot therefore was used only for a spectacular arrival on the battlefield and was driven away when fighting commenced.

That Celtic chariots ever possessed scythes attached to their wheels seems a myth suggested by the addition of these blades to the hubs and yokes of Persian and Syrian chariots. No archaeological evidence has been discovered of scythed wheels. Although, curiously, an early medieval Irish epic tale, featuring the hero Cuchullain, does refer to a war chariot with 'iron sickles, thin blades, hooks and hard spikes. Its stinging nails fastened to the poles and thongs and bows and lines of the chariot, lacerating heads and bones and bodies.' Most Latin references to Celtic chariots mention them only as a speciality of the Britons, but the remains of chariots have been found in Celtic tombs throughout Europe.

Light, elegant two-wheeled chariots, like those that impressed Caesar, developed from heavier, four-wheeled carts found in Celtic tombs dating from before the fifth century BC. The later two-wheeled vehicles were expertly made. Their spoken wooden wheels were bound with iron tyres. The hubs were also bound with iron bands while the wheels were held on the axle by iron linch-pins. The platform was of wood, usually with curved wood or wicker sides. Two horses pulled the chariot, linked by a yoke to a wooden pole. To these basics were added splendidly crafted rein-rings, flexible bridle-bits, and harness fittings, many decorated with red, yellow and blue enamel. The best contemporary illustrations of Celtic chariots occur on Celtic coins. In the British Museum a chariot is depicted on a tiny bronze coin of the Remi tribe in northern France of the first century BC.

Such images were usually based on the chariots appearing on the reverse of Greek coins, the model for most Gallic coinage. But, in this case, the Celtic craftsman has chosen not to reproduce slavishly the realism of Greek art, but to reduce the chariot to its most vital elements. The horses are portrayed as a series of dynamic balls: muscular thighs, flaring nostrils, and plaited mane. The chariot is represented by one wheel and its semi-circular side, while the driver has been abstracted to arms holding a whip, a head, and three curved rays springing from his back, that is, his cloak flying in the wind.

The evolution of Celtic cavalry and chariotry suggests an origin for this culture in the plains of eastern Europe and Russia, the traditional home of chariot burials and excellent horsemanship. Like all Indo-European speaking people, the Celts were originally from the Eurasian steppes. That the Celts did not lose their talent for riding over their centuries of settlement in central Europe is no doubt due to their close contact with the Cimmerian and Scythian tribes that dominated eastern Europe. It is interesting to note, however, that as with the eastern German tribes of later centuries, the Celts did not adopt the deadly horse-archery characteristic of the steppe tribes. Perhaps they, like the Germans, considered it unmanly for a noble horse-warrior to kill an enemy from afar. Celtic mastery of the horse in battle is a

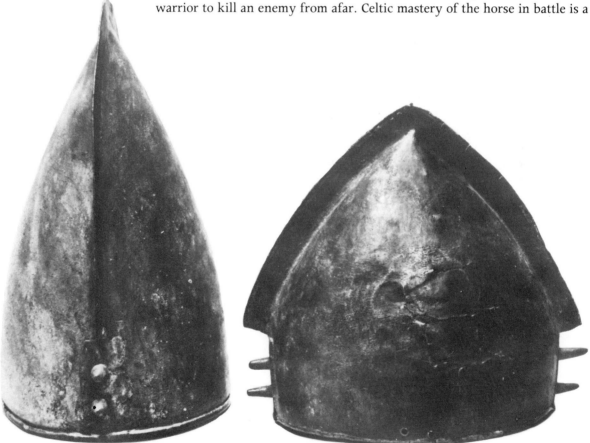

19

potent thread throughout the history of Celtic warfare, from antiquity to sixteenth-century Ireland. It was this horsemanship that gave the Celts the military power to establish themselves so firmly in European civilization.

For a further fifty years after that raid on Greece, Celtic warriors held absolute control over central Europe, France, Spain and Britain. It was a golden age for the Celts in which their civilization clearly rivalled that of the Greeks and Romans. But then it started to go wrong. Gradually, an ever more confident, ever more united and ambitious Roman Republic made inroads into Celtic territory. The first region to be lost was northern Italy. By 200 BC, after a fierce campaign, virtually all the Italian Celtic tribes had submitted. The Roman war-machine had not only proved superior, but the Romans had even beaten the Celts at their own game. Challenged to single

The Dying Gaul, a Roman copy of one of a series of sculptures commissioned by king Attalus I of Pergamum to celebrate his victory over the Celtic Galatians around 230 BC. Reproduced ever since, it has become a symbol of Celtic defeat. This version is an engraving from Duruy's *History of Rome*, 1883.

combat by the chieftain of the Insubres, M. Claudius Marcellus accepted. In the killing ground between the assembled armies, the Roman general rode forward with his shield, spear and sword. Virdomarus, the north Italian Celtic leader, bellowed that he had been born from the waters of the Rhine and would make quick work of the Roman usurper. He dashed in front of his warriors, hurling his spear. But both their spears missed and the chieftains clashed. As each side cheered his leader on, the duel came to a sudden end. A Roman sword slit the Celtic throat and his bent golden torque fell to the ground.

The next Celtic realm to lost control of its own destiny was Spain. Here, many powers converged. Celtic tribesmen had been established in Spain by the fifth century BC. They could not overwhelm the whole native population of this vast country but appear to have made themselves a ruling class over the Iberians in northern and western Spain. Over the years their cultures fused, and ancient historians generally refer to these people as Celtiberians. Along the Mediterranean coast, rivalry between Rome and Carthage over the Spanish ports exploded in war. By the start of the Second Punic War, the Carthaginians controlled most of Spain bar the north-west and Celtiberian mercenaries provided some of their fiercest warriors. However, there were other Celtiberians who resented Carthaginian exploitation of their land and welcomed the intervention of the Romans in Spain. They fought together to rid the land of the Punic invaders. It was an alliance the Celts would regret.

Although their triumphs in the Punic Wars left the Romans with unparalleled power in the Mediterranean, it also left them with many problems. The Celts of northern Italy, ignored during Hannibal's invasion, now rebelled. It took ten years to reconquer them. In Spain, the Celtiberians retained their independence and would not enter into any contract of obedience with the victorious Romans. They had not seen the back of one master merely to submit to another. If the Romans wanted the whole of Spain, they would have to conquer it by arms and not diplomacy. 'This war between the Romans and Celtiberians is called the fiery war,' wrote the contemporary historian Polybius, 'for while wars in Greece or Asia are settled with one or two pitched battles, the battles there dragged on, only brought to a temporary end by the darkness of night. Both sides refused to let their courage flag or their bodies tire.'

The war in Spain was a succession of vicious, indecisive campaigns enduring through most of the second century BC. Roman military incompetence and cruelty was particularly marked and provoked controversy among the politicians in Rome. At the siege of the Celtiberian hill-fort at Pallantia in 136, a Roman commander allowed his supplies to run out. He evacuated his position at night, but, in the hurry, wounded and sick soldiers were left behind. Retreat turned into rout when the Pallantines emerged from their fortress and chased the Romans relentlessly. This general, like many others during the wars, was recalled and deprived of his command. Failure encouraged desperate savagery. Titus Didius set about his suppression of Celtiberian independence with ruthless efficiency. One tribe claimed it had been reduced to banditry because of poverty caused by the war. Didius offered them the lands of a neighbouring Celtic settlement. They agreed, having received similar booty when fighting for the Romans against the Lusitanians. They were invited to the Roman camp where Didius would apportion the land. Once disarmed and inside the stockade, Didius secured the gates and sent in his soldiers to massacre the assembled Celtic men and their families. 'For this,' remarked a disgusted and astonished Roman historian, Appian, 'Didius was actually honoured with a triumph.' Such massacres were matched by numerous military disasters and both served only to stiffen the resistance of the Celtiberians.

'They are no better than bandits,' grumbled the Roman general Scipio Africanus, frustrated yet again by their deception and treachery. 'They may be brave when devastating neighbouring fields, burning villages, and rustling cattle, but are worth nothing in a regular army. They fight with greater confidence in flight than in their weapons.' In truth, the Celtiberians were supreme guerilla warriors. Masters of their own hilly, forested landscape, they exhausted their enemies with relentless skirmishing and raids. Never hanging around long enough for a major confrontation, they humbled the reputation of many Roman generals. After half a century of indecisive conflict, few Roman officers could be found to fill the vacant command posts in Spain. It was a make or break war. But in 134, Publius Cornelius Scipio, the grandson of Scipio Africanus, rose to the challenge. When he arrived in Spain as overall commander, he found a Roman army profoundly demoralized. Discipline was non-existent. Prostitutes and traders, along with fortune-tellers, had to be expelled from the army camps. The soldiers had been reduced to astrology for any signs of a victory. While Scipio retrained his warriors, he surveyed the territory of the Celtiberians. He observed that the town of Numantia in northern, central Spain was a key position and resolved to crush it.

Numantia was a formidable Celtic hill-fort. Set high on a mountain ridge, it was surrounded by dense forest and two fast-flowing rivers cutting through deep ravines. Behind its massive earthen ditches and ramparts, its wood and stone stockade, lay a town with paved streets, blocks of houses, and 8,000 warriors. It had withstood many sieges. In 153, the Romans had employed elephants in their assault. The animals had certainly frightened the Celtic warriors and their horses back into the town, but once the elephants approached the walls the defenders dropped rocks on them. A rock crashed onto the head of one elephant, driving him mad with fury. The great beast let out a terrible scream and turned round, trampling and gouging his own side. The rest of the elephants panicked and soon the Roman army was in tatters as the raging beasts were joined by the Numantines.

Scipio knew well the reputation of Numantia and confined his opening

Brennus receives tribute from the Romans in 390 BC. At the height of their continental power, Celtic warriors shattered a Roman army at Allia and then sacked Rome. Legend has it that when the Romans complained of the weights used by the Celts to measure their tribute gold, the Celtic chieftain Brennus threw his sword onto the scales with the words 'woe to the conquered'.

22

manoeuvres to plundering the surrounding countryside. His troops harvested the fields, stored what was of immediate use and then burnt everything else. Their activities did not go unheeded and they were constantly ambushed. With losses mounting Scipio decided it was time to deal directly with Numantia. But, rather than attempting to scale its awesome natural and man-made defences, he erected seven forts around the town and linked them with a ditch and palisade. As the Romans laboured, they were joined by neighbouring Celtiberian tribesmen who valued their independence less than the destruction of a powerful rival. Scipio expected the Numantines to disrupt his siege preparations and organised special task forces. If a section of the earthworks was attacked, a red flag should be raised or a fire lit at night so reinforcements could come to their aid. When this first ring was completed another ditch was dug and a palisade built behind it upon an earthern mound eight feet wide and ten feet high. The Numantines, however, still managed to receive provisions from the river Duero. Scipio responded by building a tower each side of the river. To the towers he attached by rope heavy logs studded with knives and spear-heads. The tree-trunks bobbed up and down in the furious mountain stream and prevented anyone sailing past. With ballistae and catapults mounted on the towers of his walls, Scipio now waited for starvation to do the rest.

Restless and frustrated, the Numantines led several forays against their besiegers. Emerging out of the night, they clambered over the palisades. They fought with spears and knives, but, above all, they wielded the *falcata*, a heavy cleaver-like cutlass used throughout Spain. According to Livy, the *falcata* could 'cut off arms at the shoulder and sever heads with one chop.' Carthaginian and Greek influences were strong amongst the Celtiberians and it seems likely that, in addition to simple shirts of mail, professional warriors may also have worn horsehair crested helmets and breastplates of strips or scales of metal and leather. They used massive oblong shields and small bucklers, and sometimes a round, concave shield called a *caetra*. In their night attacks, the Numantines probably also used javelins whose three-foot iron blades were tied with rags soaked in pitch. The rags were ignited and the spear flung at an enemy's shield.

Flexible Celtic bridle-bit found in London, now in the British Museum. The Celts were powerful horsemen and the craftsmanship of their cavalry equipment reflects this excellence.

25

These sorties proved unable to break the Roman ring and Rhetogenes, one of the leading Numantine warriors, decided to ride out for help. One cloudy night, with a few comrades and servants, he crossed the no-man's-land between the two earthworks. Carrying a folding scaling-ladder, the Celts scrambled up the first wall and silenced the guards. They then hauled up their horses and dashed along the palisade to freedom. They rode off to the hill-fort of the Arevaci, entreating them as blood relations to come to their aid. The Arevaci feared the retaliation of the Romans and refused. Rhetogenes rode onto a town called Lutia. There, the young men sympathised with the Numantines and prepared to join them. But older citizens doubted the wisdom of this and informed the Romans. Scipio reacted immediately. He surrounded Lutia the next day and demanded to see the

young warriors. Under threat of attack, the young Celts emerged from the town. Scipio seized the 400 and had their hands cut off. That night he was back at Numantia.

As the weeks passed, hunger made the Numantines consider a negotiated surrender. Avarus, their leader, approached Scipio with terms of settlement. But Scipio was not interested. He would accept only absolute capitulation. The Numantines were furious and murdered Avarus and his envoys, thinking they may have made private terms for themselves with the Romans. Within the town, the situation became desperate. With no food at all, some citizens resorted to cannibalism. Finally, famine and disease broke their spirit. They surrendered, but many took their own lives. Appian, the Roman chronicler of these events, was moved by the valiant endurance of the Numantines. He wondered at how 8,000 Celtiberians could only be brought to heel by 60,000 Romans; and not even in a pitched battle, but through the prolonged agony of a siege. The survivors of the conflict were a strange and pathetic sight. 'Their bodies were foul, their hair and nails long, and they were smeared with dirt,' wrote Appian. 'In their eyes there was a fearful expression: an expression of anger, pain, weariness, and the awareness of having eaten human flesh.' Scipio was untouched by the spectacle. Having chosen fifty warriors for his triumph, he sold the rest of the Numantines into slavery and set fire to their town. Their territory was divided among neighbouring tribes, ensuring bitter feuds for years to come. The heartland of Celtiberian resistance had been devastated and 133 BC is generally accepted as the end of the Spanish war.

There were many rebellions, but essentially Celtiberian independence had been smothered by the Roman Empire. That said, there was no extensive Roman colonisation of Spain. Only a few legionary veterans settled around the prosperous coastal towns. Most of the Spanish interior remained under the direct control of Celtiberian warlords, even though they now did homage to Rome. Their culture continued strong, as did their warriors. At the end of the second century BC, when the wandering Germanic tribesmen of the Cimbri turned away from Italy and rode into Spain, it was Celtiberian warbands who confronted them. The Cimbri, allied with the Teutones, had already devastated three Roman armies. In Spain they met warriors of their own kind and after two years of raiding, their rough reception form the Celtiberians forced them back upon Italy. United again with the Teutones, who had received a similarly tough time from the Celts of northern France, they advanced to defeat at the hands of a reformed Roman army in 102.

It has been suggested that the Cimbri and Teutones were not Germans but Celts. Many ancient historians saw little difference between the two barbarian peoples and it is more than likely that this horde consisted of many Celtic freebooters from France and central Europe. Certainly, the plundering movements of these tribes were typical of the intertribal warfare that wracked non-Roman Europe. The immediate effect of these

Model of a reconstructed Celtic chariot. Such chariots were mainly used for the spectacular arrival of chief warriors on the battlefield: intended to overawe the enemy.

raiders in southern Europe was to stir up other Celtic tribes against the Romans. Only a decade earlier, the lands of Mediterranean Gaul had been annexed by the Romans. Now these tribesmen rebelled. In the Balkans, the Germans had been prevented from advancing any further by the Scordisci of Yugoslavia. Once they rolled back the Teutones, these tribesmen took advantage of Roman weakness and invaded their territory in Greece. Emboldened by their strength against the Cimbri, the Celtiberians again threw off Roman Imperialism. Eventually, after a disastrous start, the Romans took control of the situation, but it was a profound crisis that reminded them of the force of the Celts.

Realising that a successful military career was the best way to political power, the young Julius Caesar placed himself in the forefront of the border wars with the Celts. His first military experience was won against the Celtiberians. He then placed himself in command of the provinces of Cisalpine Gaul (northern Italy) and Provence. The ambition of this one man was to bring the Celtic warlords of France to their knees. But conquests are not won by brilliant leaders alone. As Caesar himself admitted: 'Fortune, which has great influence on affairs generally and especially in war, produces by a slight disturbance of balance important changes in human affairs.' In Gaul, the Roman's good fortune was to be the same that had dogged the independence of the Celtiberian chieftains. In this case, the threat of the Carthaginians was replaced by a German invasion of Gaul, but, as before, those Celtic chieftains who applied to the Romans for help were to find that they had played into the hands of a more ruthless master.

From 65 to 60 BC, a confederation of German tribes known as the Suebi were led by a dynamic warlord called Ariovistus. Recognising his power, Gallic chieftains employed the Suebi to defeat their Celtic rivals, but Ariovistus demanded in payment the land of his allies. Soon, Celtic warlords were asking the Romans to intervene against the German invaders. But the Senate did not like to back losers, entering into friendly relations with Ariovistus. One of the principal architects of this agreement was Caesar. The disarray of the Celtic tribes encouraged Caesar to move his legions westwards from Aquileia to the Rhone. He had planned to build a reputation for himself against the Dacians, but the inter-tribal conflict of the Gauls and their fear of the Germans seemed a golden opportunity. Events came to a head when the Helvetii of Switzerland wished to move out of the

Reverse of a British coin showing a horse and wheel of a chariot. Many Celtic coins were based on Greek or Roman prototypes, but on this one Celtic craftsmanship predominates and the chariot has been abstracted to its powerful essentials. Found in the south of England near Silchester, now in the British Museum, London.

Iron Celtiberian falcata, fourth to first century BC, now in the National Archaelogical Museum, Madrid. The iron scabbard frames of this sword remain to show how it was usually carried in a leather sheath hung from a baldric.

Hilt of an iron and damascened bronze Celtiberian falcata, fourth or third century BC, found near Cordoba, now in the National Archaeological Museum, Madrid. The total length of this sword, characteristic of the Spanish Celts, is 57 cm (22 in).

way of the Suebi and cross through the neighbouring Celtic territory of the Aedui to western France. The Aedui asked Caesar for assistance. With an army of Roman legionaries and Gallic cavalry he complied. The Helvetii gave him a tough time, using their wagon laager as a strong defensive position, but eventually they were subdued. Caesar massacred 6,000 of them and sent the rest back to Switzerland. Such ruthless strength clearly impressed the Celts and they redoubled their requests for his help against Ariovistus.

These facts we know from Caesar's own chronicle of the events. In his account he emphasises the Gallic fear of the Germans, their disunity, and their desperate plea for Roman assistance. The Celts are portrayed as a once mighty nation, now less brave than the Germans and in need of outside warriors to fight their battles. Such a view, of course, makes Caesar appear as the protector of the Gauls, whose entry into their territory is not an invasion, but in response to their repeated invitations. This begs cynicism. Celtic tribes had been determined and daring enough to defeat both Roman and Teutonic armies only fifty years earlier. And yet this is an eye-witness account: why should Caesar write of the Gauls with barely disguised contempt when it is in his own interest to make them seem a mighty, bold people, so as to make his own victory over them even greater? This he does do, but later in his account when describing their noble last-stand at Alesia. Caesar has his cake and eats it. In the meantime, Caesar reneged on Rome's friendship with Ariovistus and threw the Germans back across the Rhine. He now exploited his strong position in Gaul and annexed the land of the Aedui and the Sequani. Their weakness and supposed invitation is his excuse.

The Belgic tribes of northern France saw the error of their Celtic kinsmen and combined to confront Caesar's legions. The Belgae were a notoriously

Iberian dagger found near Cordoba, now in the National Archaelogical Museum, Madrid. The blade is 8 cm broad at the base and 19 cm (7½ in) long.

fierce confederation, hardened by years of border conflict with the Germans. They were part German themselves. On receiving this news, Caesar raised two more legions to add to his six already quartered in Gaul, and rapidly advanced on Belgic territory. His speed surprised the Remi, the nearest of the Belgic tribes, and they immediately caved in, offering him hostages and military intelligence. Caesar dispatched his Aeduan auxiliaries to plunder Belgic land, while he sat tight. The ferocious reputation of the Belgae discouraged Caesar from meeting them in a pitched battle, so he tested their stamina with numerous cavalry skirmishes. The main Roman army remained in a camp protected by marshes and entrenchments. The Belgae tried to entice the Romans into a full-scale confrontation, but Caesar's Gallic horsemen continued to keep them at a distance. As the skirmishing endured, the supplies of the Belgae began to run out. Like most barbarian armies, it appears they did not organise a proper supply train, so unless they gained sufficient food from their plundering their campaigns lacked staying power. When reports of Aeduan raids on their own territory added to their frustration, the Belgic horde retreated with the Gallo-Roman horsemen in hot pursuit. Thus the Belgic confederation was reduced tribe by tribe by a Romano-Gallic force in which the Celtic auxiliaries of Caesar played a vital part. Without doubt, the Celts could be their own worst enemy. And yet, to impose such concepts of a national identity on all Celts is misplaced, for the Belgae were as different and alien to the Celtic tribes to the south of them as they were to the Romans, even though they spoke a similar language. A shared culture never stopped the Romans or Greeks from ripping themselves to pieces.

A Gallic horseman proudly drawn by Alphonse de Neuville on the eve of the Franco-Prussian War. From Guizot's 1870 L'Histoire de France, it reflects a nationalistic pride in the Celtic roots of French culture.

Throughout the campaigns in Gaul, Diviciacus, chieftain of the Aedui, was constantly at Caesar's side, urging his Celtic confederates to submit peacefully to Roman domination. As the Roman war-machine rolled on, more and more Gallic warriors joined its legions. So far, in his march through Gaul, Caesar had had good excuses for his agression: the invitations of the Aedui, the attacks of the Belgae. But in 57 BC he sent a detachment under the command of a subordinate to the lands of the Atlantic coast. Their subsequent reduction of this peaceful area was unprovoked and patently revealed Caesar's intention to conquer the whole of Gaul. The next year, recovering from the shock of Roman occupation, the Celts of Brittany, led by the Veneti, took up arms. The Veneti were a maritime power, deriving much wealth from their shipping of British tin from Cornwall to Gallic traders. Their strongholds stood on headlands or islands in tidal estuaries which were cut off from the land for most of the time by the sea.

As the Romans approached the Atlantic coast, the Veneti strengthened their fleet and gathered fellow tribesmen, including many warriors from Britain. Caesar was secure in his excuse this time: the quelling of a tribe who had already submitted and the punishment of a terrorist kidnapping of Roman envoys. He again employed the assistance of friendly Celts who supplied him with Gallic ships built along the Loire. With his land forces he tried to capture the Breton strongholds. Using all the ingenuity of Roman siegecraft, he had huge dykes constructed to the island fortresses. But no sooner had these been completed than the defenders simply evacuated into awaiting ships and moved to another fortress. The lack of natural harbours and the rough ocean weather made Roman assaults by sea difficult. The considerable advantage of knowing the local seaways lay very much with the Veneti. But, as elsewhere, there was no shortage of Celts ready to assist the Romans.

Local Gauls presented the Romans with a rapidly-built fleet which cannot have been very different from that of the Veneti. 'They have flat bottoms.' wrote Caesar of the Gallic ships, 'which enables them to sail in shallow coastal water. Their high bows and sterns protect them from heavy seas and violent storms, as do their strong hulls made entirely from oak. The cross-timbers—beams a foot wide—are secured with iron nails as thick as a man's thumb. Their anchors are secured with chains not ropes, while their sails are made of raw hide or thin leather, so as to stand up to the violent Atlantic winds.'

When Caesar's fleet was ready, he confronted the Veneti in the Loire estuary. As the boats crashed into each other, legionaries and their Gallic allies watched the battle from the cliff-tops. The Romans in the boats—all land soldiers—were at a loss as to how to tackle the Gallic seamen. They improvised with scythes attached to long poles and used them to cut the Celtic rigging. With their sails fluttering uselessly and apparently no oars to assist them, the Celtic ships soon lost control. Several Roman boats then locked onto individual Celtic ships and boarded them. The Celtic sailors were overwhelmed by the armoured Romans and the fleet of the Veneti broke up. A fall in the wind prevented many from escaping and the majority of the Gallic force was captured. This seems a particularly miserable defeat for the Celts. A fleet of expert seamen shattered by landlubber Romans making do with scythes. Caesar's account doesn't ring true. It seems more likely that the fighting on the Roman side was conducted wholly by Gallic auxiliaries used to sailing. Whatever the actual details, this defeat of 56 BC was a crushing one for the Atlantic Gauls. Caesar had many of his prisoners executed and the rest sold as slaves to his legionaries and allied Celtic tribes.

Over the next couple of years, Caesar suppressed local rebellions in northern Gaul. An expedition was made to Britain on the pretext of quelling those tribes who had assisted the Veneti. At this time, south-east England had been overrun by Belgic immigrants. Their warlord Cassivellaunus was gradually extending his control over the native Celts. Again, it seemed as if Celtic dissension might aid Caesar, but on this occasion the Celts put up a stiff guerilla resistance and Britain remained an independent Celtic realm. Throughout his campaigns so far, Caesar had restricted himself to securing a ring of conquests around central Gaul without venturing into the interior. But as he consolidated this position, perhaps preparing for that next stage of his conquest, the Celts sprang out at Caesar with a vengeance.

Bronze anthropoid hilt of an iron sword from Salon in France, around the second century BC, now in the British Museum, London.

The Celtic warriors were led by an Arvernian chieftain called Vercingetorix. A powerful personality, he instilled a strict discipline into his warrior retinue. Neighbouring tribes were asked to submit hostages to him and disaffection was punished with death. No waverers would be tolerated. Equally determined, Caesar plunged straight into the heartland of the Arverni. Initially successful, he was savaged by the Gauls at the hill-fort of Gergovia. At one stage, the Romans were surprised by the arrival of their own Gallic cavalry, for these auxiliaries were clad identically to other Celtic horsemen. According to Caesar, friendly troops usually 'left their right shoulders uncovered as an agreed sign.' With this defeat, Caesar's aura of invincibility was broken and Celtic tribes throughout Gaul joined the independence fighters. Even the Aedui threw in their lot with Vercingetorix. Caesar was shaken. He had to reinforce his cavalry with German horsemen.

The final confrontation was enacted at the siege of Alesia in 52 BC. It may have been that Vercingetorix hoped to hold Caesar outside the hill-fort until Gallic reinforcements arrived to crush the Romans between both forces. But Caesar employed Roman siegecraft to good effect and protected his rear with a second chain of earthworks. When the massive relief army arrived, the Roman force was strained to its limits but eventually fought them off. Alesia was then starved into surrender. With the capture of Vercingetorix, Gallic independence broke up and was eventually snuffed out. An overall peace was made and Caesar withdrew the majority of his troops from Gaul. Not only was the siege of Alesia the last major battle of the Gallic wars, it

symbolized the extinction of Celtic liberty in Europe. Rebellions would come and go, but never again would a warlord independent of Rome rule a continental Celtic realm. Celtic independence remained only in Britain and Ireland.

This then is the story of Celtic defeat in Europe, an account based on the legends of Greece and Rome. For the chronicles describing these events are frequently the work of Romans and Greeks writing hundreds of years after the action they recount. Pausanias compiled his account of the Celtic invasion of Greece, the fullest we have, almost 500 years afterwards. It may have been based on earlier records but essentially it is a classical view of the Celts as inferior barbarians cowed by the civilization of Greece. Appian is a more realistic historian, cynical of his Empire's disgraceful conduct in Spain, but still his accounts of the Celtiberians are 400 years later and laced with hackneyed descriptions of noble but vanquished Celts. Caesar's memoirs are, of course, based on eye-witness experience but a calculating bias ensures that the inherent weakness of the Gauls is emphasised to excuse Roman intervention. This is the Mediterranean myth of the Celts. From now on, as Britain fights to maintain itself as the last Celtic bastion, we begin to see the struggle of the Celts through their own culture, through their own legends.

The Battle for Britain

Cuchulainn—ancient Irish warlord, Hound of Ulster—slept for three days. The men of Connacht had pushed a cattle raid deep into his territory. Short of warriors, he had had to restrain himself to brief, surprise attacks on the plunderers. Many of the enemy had been killed, but he was wounded and exhausted. In the delirium of his pain and fatigue, a heavenly phantom advised him to rest. After three days, Cuchulainn awoke. An excitement possessed him. Blood quickly pulsed through his body and his face turned red. He felt good. He felt fit for a feast, fit for fighting. He instructed a retainer to prepare his chariot.

The charioteer donned a tunic of supple stitched deers' leather. He wore an iron battle-cap and daubed a circle of yellow on his forehead to distinguish him from his master. Over his two horses he secured a harness studded with iron plates, spikes and barbs. Every surface of the chariot bristled with blades. Every inch had a ripping hook or a tearing nail. Finally the driver cast a protecting spell over the chariot and grabbed his iron-shod goad.

With the chariot ready, Cuchulainn prepared himself for battle. His followers strapped on his armour. A tunic of waxed skin plates, several layers thick, was tied securely with rope so it would not burst at the onset of his fighting rage. Over this, the warlord wore a thick, wide battle-belt of tanned leather from the choicest hides of his prize cattle. This covered him from his waist to his armpits. Around his stomach was a silk apron embroidered with gold, over which a battle apron of the darkest leather was

36

Roman horseman riding over northern British warriors. Detail of a second-century dedication slab from the eastern end of the Antonine Wall where it meets the Firth of Forth.

strapped. On his head was placed a crested helmet. Within the iron, his long battle cry echoed so as to cause the demons of the air and glen to scream back. Cuchulainn now reached for his weapons: an ivory hilted sword, several short swords, throwing and stabbing spears, a five-pronged trident, and a dark red curved shield. He held a shield stout enough to keep a wild boar in its hollow, with a rim so razor sharp that it could cut a single hair— a shield as deadly as his spear or sword.

Loaded and reinforced with all his battle gear, Cuchulainn began to work himself up into a fighting fury. A spasm tore through his body. It distorted him, made him a monstrous thing. Every bone and organ shook like a tree in a storm. His insides made a twist within his skin. His shins filled with the

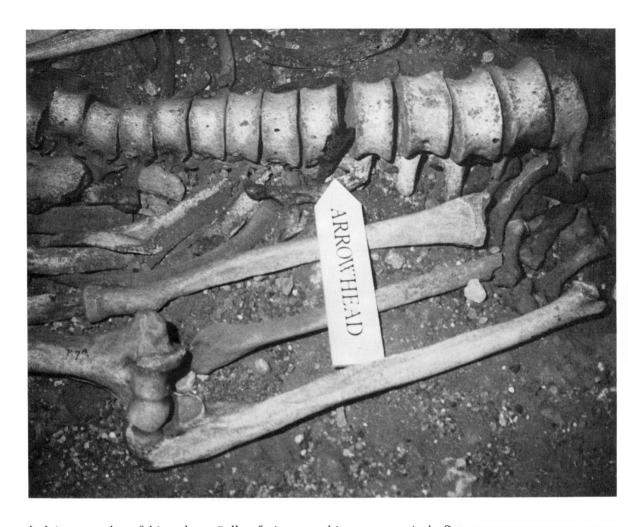

ARROWHEAD

bulging muscles of his calves. Balls of sinew as big as a warrior's fist pumped up his body. His head swelled and throbbed. Veins dilated. Suddenly, he gulped one eye deep into his head so not even a wild crane could pull it out from his skull. The skin of his cheeks then peeled back from his jaws to reveal the gristle and bone of his gullet. His jaws crashed together and foam oozed up out of his throat. His hair twisted and bristled like a red thornbush. Dazzling lights and thick black smoke rose above his head. A broad halo emerged over his brow. With the transformation completed, Cuchulainn leaped onto his chariot. He had no fear. He was a mad man. A hero.

Cuchulainn burst upon his enemies like a thunder storm. His chariot wheeled furiously in the mud: its iron tyres dug up earth tracks high enough for a fortress rampart. At the end of the day, the warlord had slain hundreds of his enemies. Nothing was too great or too insignificant to be spared Cuchulainn's blades. Chieftains and warriors, horses and dogs, women and children. All were slaughtered.

Roman ballista bolt-head lodged in the spine of a Celtic warrior. A victim of the assault on Maiden Castle by Vespasian in AD 43, his bones now lie in the Dorset County Museum, Dorchester.

38

The next morning, Cuchulainn arose to display himself to his followers. He paraded in front of his women and poets, reassuring them that his hideous battle form was now replaced by a handsome image, a youthful man whose hair was brown at its roots, rising through blood-red to a golden yellow at its tips. This hair fell luxuriantly in three coils over his shoulders. Around him was wrapped a purple cloak secured with a brooch of light gold and silver. Beneath he wore a fretted silk tunic and a warrior's apron of deep red royal silk. To his back was attached a gold-rimmed shield with five discs on a crimson background. From his belt hung a sword with a guard of ivory and gold. In his hands, he gripped nineteen human heads and shook them at his followers. All his people crowded forward to marvel at the hero.

This account of the Ulster warlord Cuchulainn comes from the *Tain Bo Cuailnge*: The Cattle Raid on Cuailnge. An Irish epic tale dated to the eighth century AD, it is believed to be centuries older, perhaps even pre-Christian. It is a terrifying vision of the ritual and glamour of violence. To his followers, this savage executioner is a hero of supernatural stature. For him, psychopathic aggression is physical strength. The epic tale is our deepest insight to the psychology of Celtic warriors: the importance of display and parade; the working up into a fighting rage. The belief in a hero's halo was widespread throughout the Celtic world and sometimes even exploited by non-Celtic adversaries. According to L. Annaeus Florus, around 130 AD, a Roman centurion struck terror into the Moesi by carrying a flaming brazier on his helmet. Other supernatural qualities ascribed to Celtic warriors in battle are elaborated in the Tain. Cuchulainn repeatedly leaps high in the air to come down heavily on his opponent's shield. Strange weapons are referred to, such as the legendary *gae bolga*, 'the lightning spear': a javelin that enters the body as one blade, but then bursts open into thirty barbs. Only by cutting away chunks of flesh could it be removed. The Tain also demonstrates that though there might be a sense of respect, even fair play, between two renowned warriors meeting in single combat, all other living things in a battle zone were vulnerable to brutal slaughter.

That such an epic tale as the Tain could be woven out of a relatively minor cattle raid should not be surprising. This is the stuff of Celtic warfare. Major campaigns against foreign enemies involving armies of united tribes—thousands of warriors strong—were rare. Most conflict was centred around the pursuit and prevention of plundering expeditions by a martial elite of warlords and their retainers, separate from the great body of tribesmen. However, to look upon the Tain as a war fought over the mere material gain of a few prize cattle is to miss the point. The rustling of cattle from an opponent's territory was simply an excuse to test that rival's strength. If a warlord allowed such a challenge to his authority without retaliation, he risked losing the respect of his own warriors as well as that of outsiders. This revelation of weakness could encourage an outsider to embark on a full-scale campaign in the belief that the victim was vulnerable. It might even encourage a coup d'état within the clan as a more able warlord arose to avenge the insult to his people. For Celtic warlords—as with all men of authority—a lack of respect means an actual lack of power. A cattle raid, therefore, had to be met with forceful retribution, otherwise worse could follow.

This endemic intertribal combat may have produced a hardened, highly experienced class of professional fighters but it also lay Celtic realms open to determined, strategically-wise foreigners. In 43 AD, the Atrebates of southern Britain fell back before the dominant Catuvellauni. The chieftain of the Atrebates asked the Romans for help and the Roman invasion began. Roman conquests in Britain were aided by further tribal dissension as well as friendly Celtic auxiliaries hoping for favours in the new regime. In just over fifty years, all England and most of Wales and Scotland had been absorbed into the Latin Empire. It is little wonder then that Gildas, a northern Briton, complained around 540 AD that 'It has always been true of this people that we are weak in beating off the weapons of the outside enemy but strong in fighting amongst each other.'

The plight of the Celts under Roman rule was not one of only abject slavery or bold revolts. More often than not, in the Roman provinces of Spain, France and Britain, Celtic chieftains continued to rule over their tribes and territory. These warlords might have Latin names, live in Roman villas, and fight alongside legionary armies, but they were still Celts. In a curious way, Roman Imperialism did not totally destroy Celtic power. It may even have strengthened it. Celtic warlords accepted the material luxuries, military sophistication, Christian religion and Latin literature of the Romans, but they still remained in control of their own land. Indeed, the military back-up of the Romans enabled them to keep their land free of Germanic raiders. Celtic chieftains would have to make tribute to their Imperial overlords, but essentially it was they who were there in the field to defend their own territory against all marauders. They maintained the Roman way of life because they liked it. But, beneath it all, it was Celtic tribal loyalties and customs that kept the ordinary man in order, not Roman citizenship. Thus, the Roman Empire in western Europe can be seen not so much as a defeated Celtic people under the yoke of Roman Imperialism, but a confederation of tribes held together by Romanized Celtic warlords paying feudal homage to a supreme, but absentee landlord.

This state of affairs became obvious when the agents of the Emperor, with their mercenary retinues, cleared out of Britain at the beginning of the fifth century to concentrate on the defence of Italy. Britain did not suddenly revert to a purely Celtic realm, naked without its Roman defenders. Of course, the warlords of Britain could always do with continental reinforcements, but they could also see to their own defence. For centuries they had dealt with Irish and German pirates and the plundering of the Picts. This was nothing new, but typical of old scores yet to be settled. Around the hard core of their retainers, the British warlords did as the Romans did. They supplemented their forces with mercenary

Northern ramparts and ditches of Maiden Castle, an Iron Age hillfort of the first century BC, near Dorchester, south-west Britain. The massive earth ramparts were originally surmounted by a wood palisade.

recruits from the coastal tribes of Germany. In the early years of the fifth century, it was Vortigern—overlord of the Romano-Celts in south-eastern England—who invited three shiploads of Saxons to assist him. Just like other provincial governors of Roman Europe, he settled these warriors along his borders as a buffer against raiders.

The Celts relished their inheritance of *romanitas*. In future centuries, they wrote about the Roman Empire as a time of greatness. In the Welsh saga of the *Mabinogion*—a fourteenth-century manuscript whose stories are much older—a Roman warlord Magnus Maximus is idealised. 'The ruler Maxen was Emperor of Rome,' it recalls, 'and he was handsomer and wiser and better suited to be an Emperor than any of his predecessors.' A senior officer in the Romano-Celtic army of Britain—probably stationed at Caerleon in South Wales—Magnus was a Spaniard, perhaps a Celtiberian. It may even have been the dream of establishing a truly Romano-Celtic Empire that excited his ambition. Whatever the spur, he was acclaimed Emperor by his followers in 383 AD. Leading a Romano-Celtic band of adventurers across

41

Iron and bronze decorated spearhead uncovered from the Thames, first century BC, now in the British Museum, London.

the Channel, he defeated the Emperor Gratian in Gaul and proclaimed himself lord of all the ancient Celtic realms of Britain, France and Spain. He had a precedent: a century earlier the Roman general Postumus had similarly ruled an *imperium Galliarum* for ten years. In events such as this, it is difficult to know whether to see Magnus as a rebel against the Roman Emperor, or simply one of many warlords pushing a little far the flexibility of Romano-Celtic command of western Europe. According to the tale in the *Mabinogion*, it is British warriors who storm the very walls of Rome and give the city to Magnus. Many of these Celtic warriors then settled in Brittany. In truth, Magnus never made it to Rome but was assassinated in Aquileia in 388. In Britain his legend lived on and many Welsh kings claimed him as their forefather.

Magnus was one of several Romano-Celtic warlords who assumed political as well as military control over their territories. Carausis was a Gaul from the coast of Belgium. Because of his profound sea-knowledge, he was given a naval command in the Channel with orders to crush the North Sea pirates. It was the late third century and Saxon raids on Britain and France were increasingly ferocious. From his bases in northern Gaul, Carausis successfully countered the freebooters; almost too successfully, for he was suspected of waiting for the priates to carry out their raids and only then, on their way back, would he pounce and confiscate their treasure for himself. But, before he could be arrested, he sailed to Britain and there proclaimed himself Emperor. Wild seas and the expertise of his Celtic fleet prevented the Romans from any immediate action.

For ten years Carausis prospered and built a string of forts along the coast of eastern England. These were massive fortifications, earthworks and stone walls, and intended as much to repel Roman invaders as Saxon raiders. But the Imperial Caesar Constantius was determined to end this Celtic break-

42

away state and set about blockading the Gaul's main continental base at Boulogne. While the French base succumbed to siege, Carausis was murdered by one of his retainers and in 296 a final assault brought eastern Britain back under direct Imperial control. During his reign, Carausis had done much to strengthen Britain's naval defences. In the next century, these were further improved by the introduction of camouflaged scouting craft. According to Vegetius, these boats had their sails and rigging dyed blue. With the sailors similarly disguised in blue tunics and painted faces, the craft acted as an early warning system against pirates.

The break-up of the western Roman Empire was not so much a sudden onslaught of Barbarian savages upon the Imperial frontiers as a gradual realisation among Germanic auxiliaries that it was they who wielded real power in the Romano-Celtic provinces. They arose from their frontier military settlements to assume political control. This happened in Britain. The Romano-Celtic overlord Vortigern had many problems. Irish and Pict raiders impinged on British land in Wales and northern England. Within Romano-British ranks, Vortigern contended with Ambrosius for the Emperorship of Britain. Added to this was the fear that Ambrosius might capitalise on continental Catholic fears of heresy in Britain and bring a Romano-Gallic army across the Channel. To strengthen his military position within and without, Vortigern invited Saxon mercenaries into his country and settled them on the island of Thanet in the river Thames. Initially they were welcome and proved useful, but the situation deteriorated.

Bronze helmet crest in the form of a wild boar. Found at Gaer Fawr, Welshpool, Powys, north-east Wales, now in the National Museum of Wales, Cardiff.

Hengist, the leading Saxon chieftain, was a shrewd warlord. He exploited Vortigern's weaknesses, his bitter rivalry with Ambrosius and other magnates. 'We are few,' he told the British overlord, 'but if you wish, we can send home for more men to fight for you and your people.' Across the Channel came nineteen more ships packed with Saxon adventurers. As Hengist amassed his warriors, tensions grew between them and the British. The Saxons complained that their monthly payments were inadequate. If they were to continue propping up Vortigern, then he would have to give them more supplies. Vortigern granted them land in Kent, but soon the Saxons were plundering further afield. By the 440s, the Saxons had openly turned against their paymasters and stormed several British towns.

'In this devastation by the pagans,' wrote the Romano-British Gildas, 'there was no burial to be had except in the ruins of houses or the bellies of beasts and birds.' But, as the Saxons consolidated their conquests in Kent and East Anglia, the British gathered their native troops and counter-attacked. Surprised perhaps by the strength of the Britons, the Saxons were shaken in two battles by Vortimer, son of Vortigern. On the banks of the river Darenth and again at Horseford or Aylesford, the Saxons suffered heavy losses. Horsa, one of their chieftains, was killed. In a third battle, according to the British chronicler Nennius, 'in the open country by the Inscribed Stone on the shore of the Gallic Sea, the barbarians were beaten. They fled to their ships and many were drowned as they clambered aboard them like women.' The Saxons fell back on their stronghold at Thanet where they were besieged three times.

Sending for reinforcements from the continent, the Saxons eventually broke out of Thanet and the war against the British ebbed and flowed, with the ordinary peasant Briton suffering most from the plundering of both sides. Upon the death of Vortimer, the Saxons resorted to negotiations to better their position. The ageing Vortigern could not maintain a state of war against the Saxons indefinitely without the political and financial support of all Britain's warlords. This was not forthcoming and old rivalries forced Vortigern to accept Hengist's suggestions of an armistice. The two sides agreed to meet, unarmed, to conclude a treaty. But Hengist ordered his men to hide their daggers in their boots. As the noblemen gathered, the Saxons sprang their trap and slaughtered 300 leading British aristocrats. Vortigern was spared his life on condition he handed over Essex and Sussex to the Germans. With Hengist now riding high, many more German warriors sailed to Britain. Over the next fifty years, Saxons, Angles and Jutes secured their hold over southern and eastern England.

The Anglo-Saxon wars in Britain were part of a broader conflict across north-west Europe. In France, the Romano-Gauls had long protected the coasts of Brittany against Saxon pirates with their river-mouth forts. During the fifth century, the Romano-Gallic warlords were joined by British immigrants. These were the cream of Romano-British aristocracy from Cornwall: some fleeing before Irish raiders, others hoping for closer

Iron spear heads from Llyn Cerrig Bach, Anglesey, north-west Wales, now in the National Museum of Wales, Cardiff.

associations with Imperial Roman culture. Allied sometimes with the Franks, it was this Romano-Gallo-British amalgam—the Bretons—who fought most ferociously against the Saxons of the North Sea and the Goths settled in central France. And then, in later centuries, when the Franks had established themselves as a separate kingdom, it was the Bretons who maintained Brittany as an independent Celtic state against the Merovingian and Carolingian dynasties. In the sixth century, Gregory of Tours records their damaging raids on the cities of Nantes and Rennes. Two hundred years later, the Bretons were still resisting and Charlemagne had to devote an entire campaign to their conquest. Even then this proved fragile and during his reign they were in constant rebellion.

Back in the fifth century, the security of the Bretons depended on the efforts of independent Romano-Gallic warlords like Ecdicius. With only his

'The Free Northern Britons surprising the Roman Wall between the Tyne and the Solway'. An engraving from a drawing by William B. Scott in the *Illustrated London News* of 1843. Chosen by the newspaper from a national competition of cartoons by history painters, it reveals a burgeoning British interest in their Celtic past.

private income to fund him and no assistance from other magnates, Ecdicius gathered together a·small force of horse-warriors. He then set about ambushing the local plundering expeditions of the Goths of central France. So hard did the Gallic horsemen harass the Goth raiders that, according to the account of Sidonius, the bandits had no time to retrieve their dead. Instead, the raiders preferred to cut the heads off their comrades so that at least Ecdicius would not know how many Goths he had slain by the hairstyle of the corpses. When this private band of man-hunters relieved the town of Clermont from Goth bandits, Ecdicius was received rapturously by the townspeople. 'What tears and rejoicing greeted you!' wrote Sidonius, brother-in-law of Ecdicius. 'Some townspeople kissed away the dust that covered you. Others caught hold of your bridle, thick with blood and foam. When you wished to take off your helmet, the clamouring citizens unclasped the bands of iron. Some entangled themselves in the straps of your greaves. Some counted the dents along the edges of your sword blunted by slaughter. While others fingered the holes made by blade and point amid your shirt of mail. You bore all these stupidities of your welcome with good grace.'

These Gallic guerilla actions took place around 471 AD and may well have been inspired by stories of the successful resistance of the Britons led by Ambrosius Aurelianus. Ten years earlier, Ambrosius had commanded a similar task force of horse-warriors against the Saxons. Raised from the Romano-Celtic estates of the West Country and Wales, these swift-moving, professional, largely aristocratic horsemen hammered the Saxons in a series of confrontations. The Celtic warriors called each other *Combrogi*, 'fellow countrymen', a word probably derived from the Latin *cives*. It is the origin of *Cymry* and *Cumbri*, names still used by the Welsh and north-west British to denote their Celtic separateness from the Germanic English. For a hundred years, the British and Saxons fought their border wars. At sometime during the conflict Ambrosius died. He was replaced by an equally competent warlord, a major Romano-British land-owner and expert leader of horsemen: Arthur.

All we truly know about Arthur is a list of twelve battles he fought throughout Britain. Many of these have been traced to sites in northern England and may have been conflicts not with the Germans but again t the Celtic warrior tribes of Scotland who were as much of a problem. Arthur probably commanded a flexible force of aristocratic young horse-warriors, riding from Roman fort to Roman fort across Celtic Britain. His stronghold in southern Wales may well have been Caerleon: a stalwart Roman fortress of earthwork ramparts and timber-laced stone walls, long in use after the last foreign Imperial garrison left. Was this Camelot? The British chronicler Nennius states that 'Arthur carried the image of the Holy Mary, the Everlasting Virgin, on his shield,' while the Welsh Annals declare that he wore 'the Cross of Our Lord Jesus Christ across his shoulders.' It seems likely that the Christian Romano-Britons considered their campaign against the pagan Saxons a Crusade and carried out their warfare with an outraged fervour: avenging the sight of their churches burnt and sacked by the Germanic barbarians.

At the end of the fifth century, Arthur's string of victories culminated in the battle of Badon Hill. Nennius describes the hot water that bubbled up at the natural springs of Badon as one of the wonders of Britain. It therefore seems likely that Badon was the Roman settlement of Bath and the battle took place on the hills overlooking its villas, temples, and hot-water bathing complex. It was a city worth fighting for and it was probably the Saxons of Wessex and Sussex who wished to claim it. The general conflict may have been a siege as Gildas describes it, for the Welsh Annals say that the battle lasted three days and three nights. But, in the event, it seems to have been decided by a grand cavalry charge in which Arthur slaughtered many of the enemy. So decisive was this victory that no other major battles are mentioned for two decades. Arthur appears to have successfully blocked the Saxon advance into the West Country.

Germanic desire proved relentless, however, and around 515 the British defence of the West was shattered. In the battle of Camlann, perhaps a siege of Caerleon, Arthur was killed. Nevertheless, Celtic resistance remained persistent enough to deny the Saxons part of the West Country for a further fifty years and most of Wales and Cornwall for centuries. In the wake of Germanic supremacy in Europe, it could be said that this part of Britain was the last independent Romano-Celtic province. But its defenders were not Roman legionaries but Celtic horsemen. It was these Celtic warriors who called the Saxons 'barbari' and preserved Latin culture. This is Arthur's success and the origin of his legend as the supreme Christian knight.

The conversion of the Anglo-Saxons to Christianity at the end of the sixth century brought no immediate softening of hostilities, but provided yet more causes for conflict. Around 603, St Augustine, the first Archbishop of Saxon Canterbury, set about bringing the British of the Celtic Church into line with Catholicism, altering their customs and rites in accordance with the Church of Rome. The Britons referred to their holy men and received the following advice. 'If Augustine is a humble man and rises as you approach, then he is a man of God and you may follow him. If he does not, but despises you, then you may despise him.' In the taut atmosphere of a synod on the Welsh border, the Celts approached Augustine. The saint remained in his seat. The Britons refused to join with the Catholic Church. Augustine was furious and threatened them with a prophecy that if they refused to worship as the English did, then they would fall victim to English swords.

Augustine's promise was fulfilled at the battle of Chester. As the Northumbrians prepared to assault the Romano-British city, their Anglo-Saxon warlord observed a large group of Celtic monks from a monastery in Bangor. The holy men had gathered to offer up prayers for the British warriors. They were guaranteed protection by a Welsh warrior called

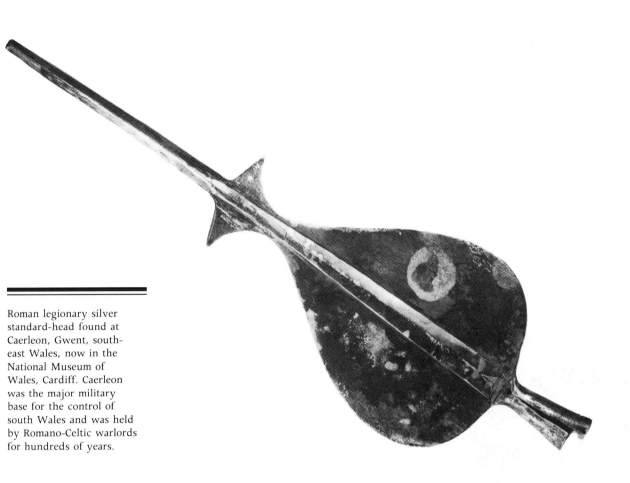

Roman legionary silver standard-head found at Caerleon, Gwent, south-east Wales, now in the National Museum of Wales, Cardiff. Caerleon was the major military base for the control of south Wales and was held by Romano-Celtic warlords for hundreds of years.

Brocmail. Their Celtic chants irritated the Northumbrians beyond endurance. 'Though they carry no arms,' the Angle warlord announced, 'those monks, by crying to their God, still fight against us.' Full of the righteous fury of a Catholic charging down a heretic, the Anglo-Saxons spurred on their horses and ploughed into the crowded monks. Brocmail had already fled at the sight of the onrushing Northumbrians. Twelve hundred holy men were massacred. 'Thus was fulfilled the prediction of the holy bishop Augustine,' concludes the Anglo-Saxon chronicler Bede.

Campaigns against the Anglo-Saxons in the sixth and seventh centuries were not the only battles the British had to fight. Romano-British warlords along the coasts of the West Country, Wales, and north-west England had to contend with the sea-borne raids of the Irish. These Celtic adventurers were called *Scotti*: a name probably derived from the Irish verb 'to plunder'. The kidnapping of St. Patrick was the most notable of their hit-and-run exploits. In earlier centuries, Roman forts had been raised against the pirates and much Roman bullion has been uncovered in Ireland. Some of it includes elaborate metalwork that has been chopped up, suggesting a booty divided to pay a marauding gang. However, it is just as likely that the Irish were such a problem that the Romans gave them silver and gold as a protection payment to keep them away from their coasts. Perhaps also Irish warbands were hired by Romano-British warlords as auxiliaries.

In later centuries, the Irish were settled on coastal territories by the British as a buffer against further raids. But, like the Saxons in eastern England, they exploited the agreement and expanded their authority over British land until in the fifth century there were strong Irish realms in south-west and north-west Wales. Some British legends report that Romano-British warlords were able to expel the Scots from Anglesey and Pembrokeshire at around the same time as Arthur battled against the Saxons. But Irish presence remained potent in south Wales for some time. In Llangors Lake at Brecon, there are remains of a lake-dwelling similar to those found throughout Ireland. These crannogs were fortified settlements built upon man-made islands in the middle of swamps and lakes. Nowhere, however, was the influence of the Irish stronger than in Scotland. There they settled the craggy north-west peninsulas and imposed their language and culture on the native Britons and Picts until the very land bore their name.

Facsimile drawings of Romano-Celtic soldiers illustrated in the fifth-century manuscript of Prudentius in the National Library of Paris. Warriors such as these defended the Romano-Celtic provinces of western Europe against the Germanic barbarians.

50

Booty from the Anglo-Saxon wars against the Britons. A ceremonial whetstone surmounted by a bronze stag, thought to be a sceptre from the Celtic regions of north west Britain. Found in the Seventh century tomb of the Anglo-Saxon warlord of Sutton Hoo, perhaps included as a symbol of Anglo-Saxon triumph over the Celts.

The Irish, like all coastal Celts, were excellent seamen. The Irish Sea was not so much a barrier as a great lake across which trading and raiding was effectively carried. Indeed, before the establishment of a road system in Britain, communications were more efficient across water than across land. The most characteristic Celtic boat is the curach. In its simplest form, this consists of a wicker framework over which hides are stretched. That these were sea-worthy is attested by Gildas, who writes of the Picts and Scots using them to raid southern Britain. Fleets of fifty curachs are also mentioned by ancient annals. In 891, the *Anglo-Saxon Chronicle* states that 'three Irishmen came to King Alfred in a boat without a rudder, from Ireland whence they had made their way secretly because they wished for the love of God to be in a foreign land. It was made of two and a half hides and they carried with them food for seven days. And after seven days they came to land in Cornwall and went immediately to King Alfred.' Such accounts probably exaggerate the fragility of Celtic voyages, as most Celtic sea-going boats would have been more sophisticated craft like those of the Bretons, furnished with sails and steering oars. For raiding, the Irish may also have employed narrow-beamed, oak clinker-built rowing boats similar to those of the North Sea pirates.

The Irish settlement in north west Scotland was called Dalriada. At first, it was ruled by kings living in northern Ireland, but then in the fifth century Ulster warlords sailed over to Dalriada and founded an independent line of Scots kings. These Irish warriors spoke Gaelic. Dunadd became a principal stronghold. Sited on a rocky outcrop and surrounded by bogland, it recalled the hillforts of ancient times. It consisted of an inner citadel, almost a keep, in which lived the Dalriadic warlords with their retainers. Outside, in a series of courtyards formed by the rock, sheltered the labourers, peasants and animals. For centuries, the Scots and Picts battled over the highlands, often employing Britons from the lowlands against each other. The Picts were an ancient race. They spoke a language combining Celtic with an older aboriginal tongue. Their name derives from the Latin meaning 'the painted people' and refers to their custom of daubing or tattooing their bodies with woad, a blue plant dye. By the fifth century, however, this custom appears to have been neglected. The Picts were the descendants of those Caledonian tribes defeated by the Roman governor Agricola at Mons Graupius in the first century. Nevertheless, after this show of strength, the Picts remained untamed enough to prevent the Romans ever again subduing them and the province of Britain never extended into highland Scotland. Their realm survived uncontested until the arrival of the Scots.

Though their literature remains largely indecipherable, there are many Pict remains demonstrating their military might. Inscribed stone monuments show that, like all Celts, they were keen horsemen. Battlefield encounters began with horse-warriors raining javelins upon each other. They then closed in with long stout lances. Foot-soldiers fought with spears

and square shields and one cross-slab in Angus suggests they countered horsemen with a kind of phalanx in which warriors holding pikes stood behind shield-carriers. Some of the formidable fortresses of the Picts have been uncovered. Early in their history, they probably made use of brochs, circular towers of dry stone-work. These brochs lacked any apertures apart from the entrance and were probably solely defensive refuges against Irish pirates and Romano-British slave-raiders who could not afford a long siege. More aggressive are the major Pict fortresses with timber-laced stone walls. These possessed defendable parapets and were centres of power from which raids could be led. Curiously, these stone and timber forts resulted in the vitrification of their silica-rich foundations. For whenever they were set alight by enemies the intense heat produced by the draught channels of the timber constructions turned the stone to glass. As these forts were used over and over again, the vitrified walls no doubt formed a strong part of the defences.

The border conflicts between the Picts and the Scots of Dalriada raged for centuries. Sometimes it was the Picts who were victorious. In 740, the *Annals of Ulster* shudder at a devastating attack on Dalriada by Angus mac Fergus. He captured their strongholds and drowned a Scots warlord in triumphant execution, forcing others to row back to Ireland. But then, under a fresh generation of warriors, the Scots struck back deep into Pictland. Hoping to exploit the dissension amongst the highland Celts, the Angles of north-east England pushed up past the Britons of Strathclyde. At Nechtansmere in 685, they were met by a Pict army and so soundly thrashed that the Angles never again ventured into the Celtic highlands. Eventually, however, it was the Scots who triumphed: partly in peace, partly in war. Ever since Angus mac Fergus plunged into Dalriada, it seems that Pictish noblemen were active in Scots circles and vice versa. There were Dalriadic kings with Pictish names in the late eighth century and through such aristocratic contacts and intermarriage, the Scots King Kenneth mac Alpin succeeded to the Pictish throne around 843. No doubt it was not wholly peaceful and one tradition maintains that it was a bloody coup d'état in which the Scots wiped out Pict warbands weakened by fighting against the Vikings. Whatever the truth, from this time on the two people were united, with the Scots predominating and the Picts becoming a people of the past.

In lowland Scotland, between the rambling remains of the Antonine Wall and Hadrian's Wall, lived the Britons of Strathclyde. In former times, when the Roman walls were patrolled by warriors from all over Europe, the native Celts were allowed to rule their own territory. Only partly subdued by the Romans, it was hoped they would absorb Pict raids before they touched any Roman citizens. With the breakdown of a centralized Roman military command, the defence of the walls and their many forts was assumed by tribal warlords who had served with the Romans and ruled the surrounding territory. Rival families controlled opposite ends of the walls. At the beginning of the fifth century, it was a Romano-British warlord Coel Hen—the Old King Cole of the nursery rhymes—who dominated the eastern end of the walls down to York. Combating the ever more ambitious raids of the Picts, Coel Hen followed Roman practice and employed Anglian warriors from across the North Sea. Their military settlements probably pre-date those of the Saxons. From this time on, it was not so much the crumbling Roman walls that divided enemies, but the natural bulwark of the Pennines that separated the major western and eastern powers of northern Britain. By the late sixth century, the Angles had asserted themselves and challenged the north-eastern Britons. One clash in this struggle is recorded in a Welsh poem by Aneirin. It recalls the heroes of the Gododdin.

The Romano-British Gododdin controlled the eastern end of the Antonine Wall and their power-base may have been at Edinburgh. At the time of Aneirin's poem, around 600, they were ruled by a warlord called Mynydogg. For a year before his campaign against the Angles, Mynydogg feasted his followers on mead and wine. This probably refers to a time of preparation and recruitment. For, throughout the poem, the fighting services of his men are said to be given in payment for mead. The mead and wine that a warrior received from his lord becomes a symbol of the material bond and obligation between the two. 'The war-band of Mynydogg, famous in battle,' proclaims Aneirin, 'they paid for their mead-feast with their lives.' Later the poet recalls the action of one particular hero: 'In return for mead in the hall and drink of wine, he hurled his spears between the armies.' It may be that these warriors even drank a draught of mead before battle, both to fortify themselves for conflict and to signify their loyalty to their lord. Such drinking, however, may have affected their performance in battle, as one translation suggests:

> To Nudd, the son of Ceido.
> I loved him who fell at the onset of battle,
> The result of mead in the hall and the beverage of wine.
> I loved him who blasphemed not upon the blade
> Before he was slain by Uffin.
> I loved to praise him who fed the bloodstains.
> He used his sword with animation.
> We do not speak of heroism before the Gododdin
> Without praising the son of Ceido, as one of the heroes
> of conflict.

Aneirin's poem is not a narrative but a series of panegyrics praising individual heroes who fell at the battle of Cattraeth in Yorkshire. Myny-dogg assembled three hundred horse-warriors from noble families through-out northern Britain and rode them south against the Angles of North-umbria. Some of the horsemen may even have been professional freelance warriors from the highlands and north Wales. They were well equipped, mail-clad, and wore gold torques around their necks. Wealthy as they were,

T·B·J·

each warrior would have been accompanied by several retainers on spare horses. The entire war-band was therefore considerably larger than the three hundred named warriors. Whatever its strength, however, it came to grief at the battle of Cattraeth. Virtually all the three hundred leading Celtic warriors were slaughtered.

With the Gododdin shattered, north-east England and lowland Scotland were absorbed into Northumbria. Across the Pennines, however, the Britons of Cumbria and Strathclyde proved stubborn, and bitterly contested any further conquests. Around Carlisle, in the territory of the Rheged, arose an Arthur of the north-west. Urien was a warlord of the sixth century and is featured in a cycle of Welsh poems. They tell of his fight against the Angles and culminate with his death in battle. The poet Llywarch Hen imagines himself a warrior carrying away Urien's head:

> A head I carry at my side:
> The head of Urien, a generous leader of his war-band.
> On his white chest now, a black raven is perched.
> A head I carry in my cloak:
> The head of Urien, generous ruler of his court.
> On his white chest ravens glut themselves.
> A head I carry in my hand:
> He was the shepherd of Erechwydd
> Noble in heart, a spender of spears.
> A head I carry on my thigh:
> He was a shield to his land, a wheel in battle.
> He was a pillar in conflict, a snare for the enemy.
> A head I carry from the land of Pennog:
> Far reaching was his fighting.
> The head of Urien, eloquent and famous.
> A head I carry from my arm:
> He made a pile of biers out of the Angles of Bernicia.
> A head I carry in my hand:
> The head of the pillar of Britain has been toppled.
> My arm has become numb.
> My breast beats.
> My heart has broken.
> I carry the head of one that supported me.
> A head I carry on my shoulder.
> Disgrace did not overawe me.
> But woe to my hand for striking the head off my lord.

Part of a hoard of gold-alloy torques discovered in Ipswich, south-east England, now in the British Museum, London. Torques may have been the badge of the free-born male and were still being worn by Celtic warlords in the sixth century, according to Aneirin.

The Celtic warrior had cut the head off his slain lord so as to prevent the Angles from mutilating it.

Carlisle was a Roman city near the western end of Hadrian's Wall. It remained an important centre of Romano-British culture and would have been a focus for much Celtic resistance. A seventh-century poem announ-

ced that its original walls were still standing and it boasted a marvellous Roman fountain. But this was recorded by an Anglo-Saxon and it was in this century that Anglo-Saxon expansion reached its zenith, impinging yet further on the border lands. Their conquests were strengthened by a series of dynamic kings and there was little hope of a Celtic counter-attack. But still the Britons held on. In the eighth century remained the Celtic realms of Cornwall, Wales, Cumbria, Strathclyde, and Scotland. Ireland was untouched. The battle for Britain had ended in stale-mate. Half the country belonged to Germanic warlords, the rest to Celtic warlords. That the Anglo-Saxons possessed the most desirable lowland territory is significant of their

Bronze penannular brooch, originally enamelled, sixth or seventh century. From Navan Fort, County Armagh, northern Ireland, now in the British Museum, London.

upper hand in the conflict and aided the development of their culture. A lowland cereal-based output is capable of supporting a strong church, a money economy, and centralised royal authority. Amongst the herdsmen of the Celtic highlands—where a man's wealth was measured in cattle and sheep—tribal institutions prevailed. Had the Celts already lost the economic war? It certainly seems that the Anglo-Saxons were content with their conquests and under Offa, King of Mercia, the boundary with Wales was given physical permanence. He erected a great length of earthworks, longer than Hadrian's Wall, stretching from Treuddyn to Chepstow. Not so much a fortified wall, Offa's Dyke was intended more as a boundary marker and a discouragement to cattle raiders.

Behind the ramparts of Offa's Dyke, the warlords of Wales coalesced into several regions of power. In the north, incorporating the fecund island of Anglesey, emerged the land of Gwynedd, the dominant realm of Wales. Sometimes it allied with the Mercians against the Northumbrians and a victory of the Gwynedd warlord Cadwallon was remembered as one of the Three Pollutions of the Severn as the blood of the defeated Saxons reddened

58

the river from source to estuary. In the north-east, on the border with Mercia, was Powys. Since the Saxons had conquered the land around Chester in the seventh century, direct links between the Welsh and the Welsh-speaking Britons of Cumbria had been broken. In the south of Wales there were several principalities, such as Gwent in the south-east and Dyfed in Pembroke, whose aristocratic families claimed descent from Magnus Maximus.

By the end of the eighth century, the British status quo was shaken. The Anglo-Saxon enjoyment of their conquests was cut short by the arrival of another sea-borne invader. This was a force that would absorb half the Anglo-Saxon kingdoms, ravage the Celtic realms of Britain, and achieve what no other continental power had so far managed: the invasion of Ireland. These warriors were the Vikings.

The Northern Menace

At first the pagan Vikings came as raiders. The *Annals of Ulster* chart their progress:

AD **793.** Devastation of all the islands of Britain by gentiles.

AD **794.** The burning of Rathlin by the gentiles. The Isle of Skye was pillaged and wasted.

AD **797.** The burning of the Isle of Man by gentiles. They carried off plunder from the district. The shrine of Dochonna was broken into and other great devastations were committed by them in Ireland and Scotland.

AD **801.** Iona was burnt by gentiles.

AD **805.** The monastic community of Iona slain by gentiles, that is, sixty eight monks.

AD **806.** The gentiles burn Inishmurray and invade Roscommon.

AD **810.** A slaughter of the gentiles by the men of Antrim and Down.

AD **811.** A slaughter of the men of Connemara by the gentiles. A slaughter of the gentiles by the men of Owles and Munster.

AD **812.** A slaughter of the men of Owles by the gentiles in which was slain the king of Owles.

AD **820.** Plundering of Howth by the gentiles. A great booty of women being taken.

AD **822.** The gentiles invade Bangor in County Down.

AD **823.** The plundering of Bangor by the Foreigners and the destruction of its places of worship. The relics of Comghall were shaken out of their shrine.

Etgal, monk of the Isle of Skellig, was carried off by the gentiles and died soon after of hunger and thirst.

AD **824.** Plundering of Downpatrick by the gentiles. Burning of Moville and its places of worship. A victory of the men of Antrim and Down over the gentiles in which a great many were slain. A victory over the men of Leinster by gentiles. The martyrdom of Blamacc, son of Flann, by gentiles.

AD **826.** The plundering and burning of Lusk. The destruction of Derry to Ochta-Ugan. The destruction of the camp of the Leinstermen by gentiles, where Conall, son of Cuchongult, king of the Forthuatha, and others innumerable, were slain. A royal meeting at Birr between the king of Munster and the high king of all Ireland.

. . . and so on, from raids on coastal islands to full-scale invasions of the mainland. With each new assault, the Vikings gained more knowledge of their victims' homeland and plunged ever deeper. When their longboats could travel no further along rivers or lochs, the sea-wolves took to horses to ravage the land. Ireland was the last Celtic realm to be invaded from the continent, the last to reel before the iron blades of professional warrior-pirates. As the Vikings grew bolder, so did the size of their expeditions, until vast invading armies—intent on permanent settlement—sailed into the Irish Sea.

'There were countless sea-vomitings of ships and boats,' wrote the chronicler of the Wars of the Gaedhil (the Irish) with the Gaill (the Vikings) in the early tenth century. 'Not one harbour or landing-port or fortress in all of Munster was without fleets of Danes and pirates. There came the fleet of Oiberd and the fleet of Oduinn, and the fleets of Griffin, Snuatgar, Lagmann, Erolf, Sitriuc, Buidnin, Birndin, Liagrislach, Toirberdach, Eoan Barun, Milid Buu, Suimin, Suainin, and lastly the fleet of the Inghen Ruaidh. All the evil Ireland had so far suffered was as nothing compared to the evil inflicted by these men. The whole of Munster was plundered. They built fortresses and landing-ports all over Ireland. They made spoil-land and sword-land. They ravaged Ireland's churches and sanctuaries and destroyed her reliquaries and books. They killed Ireland's kings and chieftains and champion warriors. They enslaved our blooming, lively women, taking them over the broad green sea.'

Elsewhere in Celtic Britain, the Vikings proved equally rapacious. Scandinavian interest was first shown in the northern islands of Scotland. 'Picts and Gaelic priests were the original inhabitants of these islands,' wrote a Norwegian chronicler. 'The Picts were scarcely more than pygmies in stature, labouring strongly in the morning and evening at building their towns, but at midday they lost all their strength and out of sheer terror hid themselves in subterranean dwellings.' These dwellings may well have been the windowless stone brochs erected by Scottish natives against sea-raiders. By 800, the Norse were in firm control of the Orkneys and Shetland and sailing southwards. Though mainland Scotland was assaulted, it was largely

the Western Isles down to Man that were favoured as Viking haunts. Not all Norwegian settlement was violent and many Scandinavian farmer-fishermen lived alongside the native Celts. But, that said, it was the Vikings that dominated the Irish Sea. From their island bases, the Norse and the Danes ravaged north-west Britain and Wales. The Britons of Strathclyde and Cumbria were defeated and the Vikings tried to link their conquests around York to their bases in Ireland. On the north-west coast of England, a fierce combination of Norse and Irish set up the Viking kingdom of Galloway. In Wales, however, the Vikings bit off more than they could chew. Their raids in the 790s were repelled with heavy losses.

At this time, Wales was an assembly of little Celtic kingdoms, but it had the good fortune to be ruled by several effective warlords. In the north swelled the kingdom of Gwynedd. Its royal line claimed connections with Urien of Rheged and Coel Hen. Around the middle of the ninth century arose a warrior-lord the equal of his forefathers: Rhodri Mawr—Rhodri the Great. In 855 the Vikings made a powerful attack on the island of Anglesey, long admired as the granary of north Wales. This was to be no pushover. Rhodri responded with strength and assurance and threw the pirates out of Anglesey in a great battle. The Danish chieftain was killed. So momentus was this victory—the first major reversal of the Vikings in Britain—that it was recorded in the *Annals of Ulster* and celebrated in the court of the

'They made spoil-land and sword-land. They enslaved our blooming, lively women, taking them over the broad green sea.' A plundering expedition by Vikings. From Ward Lock's *Illustrated History of the World*, 1885.

62

Carolingians, also hard pressed by the Danes. Later though, Rhodri was savaged by the Vikings and fled to Ireland.

Welsh resistance remained defiant and there were no Scandinavian settlements in Wales. In the tenth century, Rhodri's grandson, Hywel Dda, maintained the family's dominance of Wales and emerged as its overlord. But, unlike Rhodri, Hywel was not anti-English. He knew strength derived from alliance. Thus, by doing homage to the Saxon Athelstan he kept his borderlands free of conflict and could concentrate on protecting the coastland. So successful was the Welsh defence that its general effect was to encourage the Vikings to swerve southwards and northwards to raid England. Asserting his authority over south Wales, Hywel then co-operated fully with the Anglo-Saxons of Wessex in their battle against the pagan pirates. This Christian unity seems to have worked, shielding south-west Britain from the terrible invasions that afflicted eastern England.

Scotland was similarly blessed with stout defenders and, though its islands fell completely to the Vikings, the majority of the Scottish mainland remained free of Scandinavian colonies. It was Ireland, the Celtic realm that had remained for so long free of invasion, that suffered the most. As in Anglo-Saxon England, the Viking presence was long and influential. They erected fortifications at river mouths and these developed into towns. Dublin, Waterford, Wexford, Cork and Limerick were the key Scandinavian settlements. From them, expeditions were led by land and water into the hinterland. Up until the ninth century, Ireland was roughly divided into four great spheres of power. Ulster in the north, Connacht in the west, Leinster in the east, and Munster in the south. Dominance shifted between these regions and men owed allegiances to a variety of clans within the provinces. The arrival of the ambitious Scandinavians added another element to the internecine warfare of the Celts. Irishmen allied with Danes to fight against Irishmen allied with the Norse. Throughout, the Vikings were regarded as the superior warriors. 'Not one of the champions of the Irish was able to deliver us from the tyranny of the foreign hordes,' wrote the Irish chronicler of the *Wars of the Gaedhil with the Gaill*. 'This is because of the excellence of the foreigners' polished, treble-plaited, heavy coats of mail, their hard, strong swords, their well-rivetted long spears, and because of the greatness of their bravery and ferocity and their hunger for the pure, sweet grassland of Ireland.'

That the Vikings did not conquer the whole of Ireland was probably due to the fact that it suited them just fine to extract tribute from the inland Irish through regular raiding campaigns rather than permanent conquest. The Vikings preferred to consolidate their hold on the coastline and build up their fortified ports, frequently using them to launch raids on England and Wales. Danish and Norwegian rivalry in Ireland was intense in the ninth and tenth centuries and often the only way the Irish could damage at least one of their conquerors. But, here again, as with the Romans, the Viking invasion was far from a complete disaster for the Celts. Irish

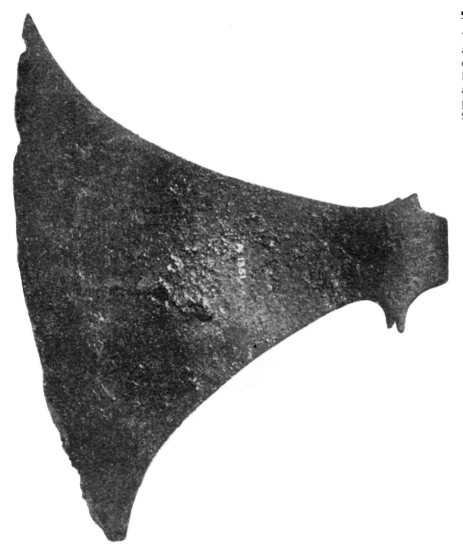

warlords still ruled the interior and they gained much materially from the coastal settlements. Not least was a great improvement in trading and first-hand experience of Viking military craft. It was from this time that the Irish are supposed to have adopted the axe as a principal weapon. This was also adopted by the Scots and may have led to the development of the long-hafted battle-axe. In Ireland, Viking swords were copied, bought, and stolen. There were Irish resistance movements and one in 902 succeeded in throwing the Norse out of Dublin. But the Vikings returned and the Irish seemed content to use them in their own political intrigues, just as the Vikings employed the Irish against each other and against the kingdoms of Britain. Typical of this Celto-Scandinavian warfare was the battle of

Celtic raiders fall upon Greek guards at the pass of Thermopylae, 279 BC.

Celtiberian chieftain and warrior break through Roman siege-works surrounding their hill-fort. Numantia, northern Spain, 133 BC.

A Belgic chariot and horse-warrior harass Roman legionaries during Caesar's expedition to Britain. South-east England, 54 BC.

A sailing ship of the Veneti is boarded by Romano–Gallic auxiliaries from the Aedui. Morbihan Bay, the Atlantic coast of France, 56 BC.

Cuchulainn of Ulster rides his legendary scythed chariot against Connacht raiders, described in the pre-Christian Irish saga *Táin Bo Cuailnge*.

An Arthurian Romano-British landlord clashes with a Saxon raider on the outskirts of Bath, Britain, in the late fifth century.

Pict horse-warriors chase an isolated Scot into a deserted broch. Dalriada, north-west Scotland, seventh century.

Murchad, the son of Brian Boru, High King of all Ireland, tackles a Viking at the battle of Clontarf, Dublin, 1014.

A Norman Breton landlord is ambushed by Welsh herdsmen. The Marches of northern Wales, late eleventh century.

Dermot MacMurrogh, warlord of Leinster, is backed up by a Norman Welsh knight and a Welsh archer. Ossory, south-east Ireland, 1169.

Scots highlanders in a schiltron hold their ground against English knight Sir William Deyncourt. The battle of Bannockburn, 1314.

Edward Bruce attacked by Anglo-Irish warriors at Moiry Pass in Armagh, Ulster, 1315.

Owain Glyndŵr and his Welsh followers are attacked by the English garrison of Caernarfon Castle, 1401.

James IV, King of Scotland, is cut down by English billmen, and longbowmen. The battle of Flodden, Northumberland, 1513.

A galloglas and his kern attendants await their Irish lord, Shane O'Neill, during his visit to the court of Elizabeth I, London, 1562.

Irish warriors of the army of Hugh O'Neill charge upon the English at the battle of the Yellow Ford, Ulster, 1598.

Clontarf at the beginning of the eleventh century—a campaign that made Brian Boru's reputation as one of the greatest warlords of Ireland.

As chieftain of the Dal Cais at the mouth of the river Shannon, Brian Boru established himself through a series of guerilla attacks on the Scandinavian settlers around Limerick. 'However small the injury he might be able to do to the foreigners,' wrote the chronicler of the Gaedhil, 'Brian preferred it to peace. From the forests and wastelands, he emerged to plunder and kill the foreigners. If he did not destroy them during the day, then he was sure to do so at night. Moreover, his followers set up temporary dwellings rather than settled camps as they moved through the woods and solitudes laying waste to northern Munster. The foreigners of Tratraighe raised great fortified banks around their settlements and prepared to conquer northern Munster. But Brian killed many of the foreigners of the garrison. Great were the hardships that Brian endured: bad food and bad bedding on the wet, knotty roots of his own country. It is said that the foreigners killed many of his followers so that only 15 survived.' But, with reinforcements from other Irish warlords, Brian continued his hammering of the Vikings.

At the age of 26, Brian Boru stormed the Viking city of Limerick. The campaign had begun with the battle of Sulcoit. There, the Vikings had assembled a force of Danes and Irish. The chronicler of the *Wars of the Gaedhil* says that these Irishmen were brought under tribute, and when some Munster chieftains refused to join the Danes they were murdered. In truth, many warlords of Munster were probably only too willing to side with the powerful Vikings against the upstart Brian. The Dal Cais and Brian's fellow chieftains were none too keen to confront the superior force in open conflict, but with the arrival of a renowned Irish champion, a freelance warrior with a hundred retainers all armed and bearing large shields, they decided to fight a 'manly battle on the open part of the plain.' The Vikings were mounted and wore mail. It is likely that Brian and his chief retainers were also so armed. This was, after all, a battle between professional warriors. Numbers were not large and few unarmoured peasants would have been involved. From sunrise to midday, the warriors struck and slaughtered each other. Finally, it was the Vikings who broke and were chased by the Dal Cais 'who killed and beheaded from that time until evening.'

Brian and his warriors overran Limerick, slaughtering and plundering. 'They carried off the foreigners' jewels and their best property: their saddles beautiful and foreign; their gold and silver; their satins and silken cloth, pleasing and variegated, both scarlet and green. They carried away their soft, youthful girls, their silk-clad women, and their large and well-formed boys. The fortress and the good town they reduced to a cloud of smoke and red fire. All the captives were assembled. Every one fit for war was killed and every one else enslaved.' It seems that many of the Danish women were then ritually raped. Brian's sack of Limerick, though barbaric, showed him as a man of power. He now consolidated his success. Local

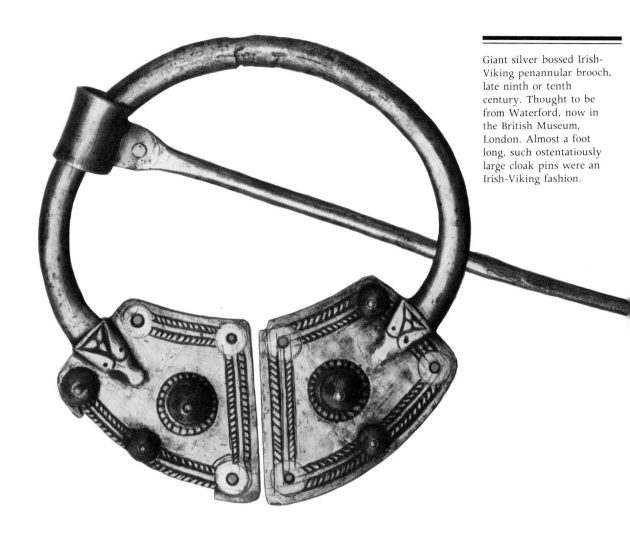

Giant silver bossed Irish-Viking penannular brooch, late ninth or tenth century. Thought to be from Waterford, now in the British Museum, London. Almost a foot long, such ostentatiously large cloak pins were an Irish-Viking fashion.

opposing chieftains were slain. His warriors kept fit and fed by numerous cattle raids. He built a fleet upon the Shannon and sailed as far as Loch Ree where he plundered the territory of Connacht and Meath. With his hold over Munster secure, Brian then moved against the men of Leinster.

The lords of Leinster appreciated the benefits of Viking colonies on their land and allied with the Vikings of Dublin against Brian. The two forces met around the year 1000 and the men of Munster were triumphant. Dublin was ransacked and the Vikings forced to submit to Brian's authority. They were allowed back into their settlement on acknowledging Brian's overlordship and no doubt ensuring he received a goodly part of their trading profits. As lord of Munster, Leinster and the Viking communities, Brian's ambitions were now focused on the north. Mustering a war-band of Irish and Danes, he rode to Tara and challenged the high king of Ireland to battle. For centuries, the clans of the north had been the dominant force in Ireland.

The O'Neills had ruled Ulster and from them descended a line of high kings of all Ireland. Now, around the year 1002, Mael Sechnaill, lord of Meath and holder of the high kingship, sent requests to all the warlords of Ulster and Connacht to counter the usurper. But the head of the northern O'Neills recognised true power and replied to Mael Sechnaill: 'Whoever possesses Tara, let them defend its freedom. It is not right that one man should risk his life against the Dal Cais in defence of sovereignty for another man.'

Mael Sechnaill offered his crown to the O'Neills. 'I would rather give thee hostages,' he told them, 'than be dependent on Brian Boru.' But they refused. Even the men of Meath, Mael Sechnaill's homeland, would not take up arms to defend him. The overawed north chose a relatively peaceful submission rather than war. At Tara, Brian assumed the high kingship of all Ireland. He followed this up with raids on all the northern estates of Ulster and Connacht, principally to obtain noble hostages but also to fill his coffers and strengthen his army. As was becoming obvious, Brian Boru's conquest of Ireland was not a nationalistic battle of Celt against Viking. It was a personal struggle to supreme power in which Irishmen fought Irishmen with the Vikings helping as auxiliaries and hoping to hang on to their colonies. Despite regular rebellions, Brian ruled as overlord of Ireland for over a decade. He even sent expeditions across the Irish Sea to levy tributes from the Scots, Welsh and Anglo-Saxons.

As Brian grew older, so his grip on Ireland weakened. In 1013, the lords of Leinster and the Vikings of Dublin threw off their allegiance to him. After a series of probing raids on each other, Brian and his son led warriors from Munster and Connacht to Dublin and set siege to it. A lack of provisions forced Brian to retire, but in the next year he returned. Plundering through Leinster, he closed on Dublin. The Vikings sent messengers throughout their territories and across the Irish Sea to gather an army. On receiving the call, fleets of adventurers set sail. The Viking warlords of Orkney and the Isle of Man arrived with their followers. They were joined by Danish and Celtic Cumbrian mercenaries. The Irishmen of north Leinster were ready for the fight, but those of the south lost their nerve and backed away.

Brian's army relied principally on the men of Munster and the Dal Cais, the heartland of his support. There were some warriors from Connacht and Meath, but Brian knew these were not to be trusted, being likely to desert in the first onslaught. There were no men from Ulster. At the last moment, Brian was joined by a group of Vikings from the Isle of Man who had hastily converted to Christianity to assure him of their support. As his forces gathered beneath striped banners of red, green and yellow, Brian sent horsemen forward to plunder all round Dublin. He thanked the warlords who had brought him men and cursed those who did not.

To stop the Irish plundering, the men of Dublin rode out from their settlement, crossed the rivers Liffey and Tolka, and set upon Brian's warriors to the north of the town in an area called Clontarf. The Vikings were brilliantly garbed in mail-coats of iron decorated with brass rings. According to the chronicler of the *Wars of the Gaedhil*, these mail-coats were triple layered. The Danes opened the fighting with their bows and arrows. 'Poisoned arrows, covered in the blood of dragons, toads, and the water-snakes of hell.' They then set to with dark spears and stout swords. According to the chronicler of the *Wars of the Gaedhil*, the Irish warriors of Brian did not wear mail, but fought in long, many-coloured tunics with shields with bronze bosses. The chieftains wore crested helmets studded with precious stones, and sound like heroes from the *Tain Bo Cuailnge*. In reality, both sides probably looked very similar, clad in mail with swords, axes and spears. Brian placed his most dependable warriors of the Dal Cais in the forefront of the battle, led by his son Murchad. Behind these were the other men of Munster. On their flanks were Brian's Viking mercenaries and Irish auxiliaries. The men of Meath, led by Mael Sechnaill, were said to have made secret contact with the Vikings of Dublin and sat out the battle behind earthworks. The Vikings of Dublin, led by the warlord Sitric, and the warriors of Leinster, led by Maelmore, placed their Danish and Norwegian auxiliaries in the front of their army. The Vikings from Orkney were led by Sigurd and those from Man by Brodar.

'The two sides made a furious, smashing onset on each other. And there arose a frightful screaming and fluttering above their heads as birds and demons awaited their prey.' At first, Brian's flank of Irish auxiliaries clashed with the Leinstermen. The Leinstermen broke and were chased off by mail-clad horsemen. It was then that the Dal Cais and the Vikings hacked at each other with axe and sword. A strong wind hampered the throwing of spears. From their walls and towers, the inhabitants of Dublin watched the men of Connacht play a key role in bloodying the Vikings. But, above all, the battle of Clontarf was a combat of individuals. A fight in which warriors could make a name for themselves: become heroes recalled in epic poems. As the crowds surged—men flailing their limbs and weapons excited by fear and violence—the sagas isolated individual combats.

Murchad, son of Brian, wielded two swords, one in his right hand and one in his left: he had equal power in striking. Enraged by the Viking slaughter of his fellow Dal Cais, Murchad rushed at the Danes like a furious ox. He made a hero's breach in the enemy. Fifty foreigners fell to his right hand; fifty foreigners fell to his left hand. One blow was sufficient to kill them. Neither shield nor mail stood up to his blades. Murchad's retainers followed their master into the heart of the battle. Such feats cowed the Vikings: many turned and ran. But Sigurd of Orkney refused to flee. Slaughtering and mutilating the Dal Cais, no point or blade seemed to harm the Norseman. Murchad rushed upon him and dealt with his right hand a crushing blow to his neck that cut the mail and straps of his helmet. Murchad then brought his left-hand sword down on the Viking's exposed neck, felling the warrior with these two blows.

Still Murchad was not finished. Fury urged his body on and he charged

Welsh iron stirrups found in Glamorgan, south Wales, late tenth century, now in the National Museum of Wales, Cardiff. Welsh warriors kept Wales relatively free of the Vikings.

68

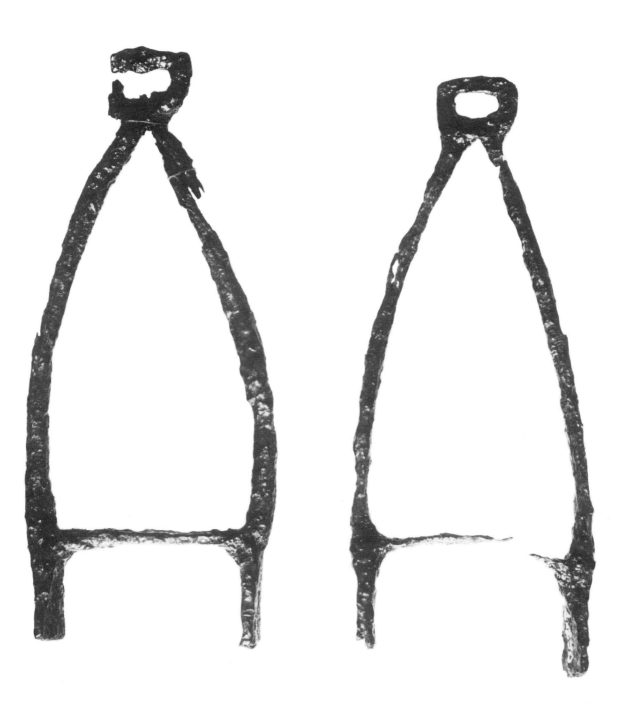

upon another Viking warlord. This time, the inlaid ornament of Murchad's sword began to melt with the heat of his striking. Throwing the burning blade away, the Irish hero gripped hold of the foreigner's armour and wrenched the mail over his head. The two warriors fell to the ground and wrestled. Murchad thrust the Viking's own sword into his ribs. But the foreigner drew his knife and ripped a gash in Murchad's guts. Exhaustion and pain overcame both warriors. They lay beside each other. But before he fainted, Murchad is said to have cut off the Viking's head. Murchad survived the night, but died the next day after taking communion and making his confession and will.

Throughout the battle, Brian took no active role in the fighting. He stayed at the rear protected by the shield-wall of his retainers, issuing orders and praying. It was there he received news of the eventual rout of the enemy and their desparate dash to the sea. But the victory was not clear-cut. Brian's army had lost many men, and in the chaos at the end of the day

Welsh horseman at the base of the Cross of Irbic. Cast of the tenth century cross in Llandough churchyard, near Penarth, south Wales. Such warriors fought alongside the Anglo-Saxons against the sea-wolves.

Viking bands still roamed around the battlefield. One, led by Brodar of Man, rode through the relaxing Irish ranks toward Brian's camp. At the height of victory, Brodar's sudden attack was unexpected and the Viking succeeded in reaching Brian himself. Brian unsheathed his sword and gave the foreigner such a blow that he cut the Viking's leg off at the knee. The Viking then dealt Brian a stroke that cleft his head in half. Thus Brian died at the moment of his greatest victory.

For a victory, the battle of Clontarf seemed like a defeat. Ireland's greatest overlord was dead and his retinue devastated. In the aftermath, Ireland reverted to a disunity of warring clans. Nevertheless, it was a decisive defeat of the Vikings: keeping Ireland free of any further Scandinavian invasions. Of course, the Vikings of Dublin and Leinster continued to live in their coastal settlements, but they operated alongside the Irish and did not dominate them. They became Christians and intermarried with the Irish noble families. Vikings from abroad still harried the coasts in search of plunder but they could expect an equally ferocious reaction from the Irish. The Heimskringla Saga of the thirteenth century recalls raids by King Magnus of Norway on the Irish coast a century earlier. Sailing from Norway to the Orkneys to the Hebrides, Magnus then harried Ireland. Along the coast of Ulster, he demanded a shore-killing of cattle to provide his warriors with fresh meat. The Irish refused: Magnus and his followers disembarked. As they penetrated inland, they readied themselves for ambush. 'King Magnus wore his helm,' wrote the chronicler, 'and a red shield displaying a lion in gold. Strapped to his side was a sword called Leg-Biter: the best of weapons. Its hilt was of walrus tooth and the handle covered in gold. Over his shirt he wore a red silk jacket with a lion sewn in gold silk on its back and front. He carried a spear.'

Apparently, the Vikings found the slaughtered cattle, but as they returned through the coastal marshes, the Irish broke cover. In the confusion, the Vikings were separated and many fell to Irish arrows. Magnus ordered a shield-wall around his standard. The Viking retreat was hindered by a dyke. Magnus was wounded: stabbed with a spear through both legs beneath the knee. He grabbed the spear and broke it off, bellowing 'Here's how we break every spear shaft, my lads!' Some of his comrades clambered over the dyke in an attempt to cover the rest, but they panicked and ran for their ships. Magnus was wounded again: a mortal blow on the neck with an Irish axe. Around him his closest retainers fell. One, called Vidkunn, managed to escape the carnage, picking up his lord's sword and standard. The Vikings sailed immediately back to Norway. At home, Vidkunn managed to avoid the terrible disgrace of surviving his lord, by showing his many wounds and insisting that he had slain all Magnus' killers. Only then did the sons of Magnus receive him with love.

Although the Vikings established enduring colonies along the coast of Ireland and in the northern and western islands of Scotland, it remains a remarkable fact that mainland Ireland, Scotland, and Wales remained relatively free of Scandinavian settlement, whereas a good half of Anglo-Saxon England was absorbed by the Danes and Norse. This may be due to the land of the Anglo-Saxons being richer and more attractive, but it must also attest to the fierce independence of the leading Celtic warlords. Such was the power of these Celtic warlords that Viking adventurers frequently found it more profitable to intervene on their side in the endless little wars of the Dark Ages. Macbeth, a Gaelic warrior from Moray, was assisted by the Vikings of Orkney in his assault upon Duncan, king of the Scots.

Macbeth has suffered badly from history. Shakespeare transformed him into an archetype of murderous medieval anarchy. In reality, it seems he was no worse and may have been better than other contemporary warlords. On seizing the crown of Scotland in 1040, he ruled the land for a prosperous 17 years. So settled was the country that he felt secure enough to leave and journey to Rome on a pilgrimage. As for Duncan: he had led his countrymen into a string of defeats. When Macbeth proclaimed himself king at Scone, few chroniclers protested. Indeed, later historians have even regarded his success as a highland Celtic reaction against the excessive English influence encouraged by Duncan. Besides, Macbeth, like Duncan, was a grandson of Malcolm II and had a legitimate claim to the throne. In Celtic clan law, election was the method of obtaining power. A more capable and popular warlord could legally oust an elder relative.

The Scotland that Macbeth ruled was a greatly extended country. In 1018, the Northumbrian Angles had been shattered at Carham by Malcolm II and he rode on to claim the lowlands as far as Hadrian's Wall. That same year, the king of the Britons of Strathclyde and Cumbria died without an heir and the triumphant Scots immediately placed Malcolm's grandson Duncan on their throne. In 1034, Duncan became King of Scotland. Six years later, he was killed by Macbeth in battle near Burghead on the Moray Firth. In that combat, Macbeth rode in an army of northern Gaelic clansmen allied with Norse warriors led by Thorfinn Sigurdsson, lord of Caithness and Orkney. It was the Vikings who took the lead in the battle, as it was they who Duncan had come to humble. Duncan fought alongside southern clansmen and Irish mercenaries. The *Orkneyinga Saga* evokes some of the conflict: 'After the crashing of spears, the Orkney warlord raised high his helmet. He exulted in battle and reddened spear point and sword edge with Irish blood. With stout arm, the gracious lord kinsman of Hlodver bore up his Welsh shield and rushed upon the enemy.' With his Irish auxiliaries routed, Duncan managed a counter-charge, but the Norse held firm and Duncan was slain amidst the fighting.

Duncan's son, Malcolm, lived as an exile in England and was brought up on that court's concepts of heredity. As Duncan's eldest son, he was convinced he was entitled to be king and not Macbeth. But Macbeth was strong and Malcolm had to bide his time. Malcolm's ambition and revenge suited the English just fine, for here was a man they could control. As soon as he reclaimed the throne, the Scottish monarchs would have to do homage

Welsh warrior with mace and dagger on the Cross of Briamail Fou. Cast of the restored tenth-century stone from Llandyfaelog Fach churchyard, Powys, north-east Wales.

to the Anglo-Saxon king and thus admit the feudal superiority of England over Scotland. It would also secure their northern borders. So, in 1054, backed up by an army of Anglo-Saxons and Danes, the 21-year-old Malcolm advanced on Scotland by land and by sea. His army was led by a Northumbrian-Danish warlord called Siward. The English met little resistance from the Scots in the lowlands and were confronted by Macbeth just outside Scone, the Scottish capital. This was the famous battle in which supposedly 'Birnam Wood do come to Dunsinane'. No doubt accompanied by his Norse allies—the lord of Orkney was his cousin—Macbeth put up a stiff fight. But the *Annals of Ulster* maintain that 3,000 Scots were killed and 1,500 English and Danes slain. Still, it was far from a victory and Siward had to withdraw his troops from Scotland, Malcolm having to be content with lordship over Cumbria.

The next year, Siward died and in 1057 Malcolm alone had to lead the battle against Macbeth. With the full support of the Northumbrians, Malcolm cornered the King of Scotland in his homeland of Moray. Macbeth and his retainers charged Malcolm's warriors but were overcome and killed. Even then, Malcolm did not immediately succeed to the throne but had to avoid the avenging highlanders and back off southwards to safety. The next year, Malcolm had to slaughter Macbeth's stepson, his legally elected successor, before the anglicised Malcolm could crown himself at Scone. With his accession came closer ties with England and a retreat in the influence of the Gaelic clansmen. Far from being a tyrant, Macbeth could be called the last of the truly Celtic kings of Scotland.

With the acceptance of Viking spheres of influence in the islands of Scotland and the cities of Ireland, there followed a short period of consolidation beneficial to both Celt and Scandinavian. This status quo was overturned at the end of the eleventh century with the arrival of another wave of North Men. This time, they did not come direct from Scandinavia, but were the French descendants of that aggressive colony of Vikings in north-west France: the Normans. In the years following their great victory of 1066, they successfully subdued the whole of England. It was not long before they then overran the borders of the British Celtic realms. In this adventure, the Normans were joined by other French warriors. Not least amongst them were the Celtic warlords of Brittany.

The Bretons had managed to hold on to their Celtic identity despite the power of the Franks. In the ninth century, they made large gains in Normandy and though beaten back, Rennes remained Breton. When Harold of England stayed with William of Normandy, he accompanied the Duke on expeditions against the Bretons. With the submission of several Breton warlords, William then included them as an important contingent in his invasion of England. At the battle of Hastings, they formed an entire flank. Highly regarded by the Normans and fighting in a similar manner, the Bretons did well out of the conquest and received extensive estates. Some were settled in the south-west and on the Welsh border where their Celtic language, similar to that of the Welsh, was of considerable help in dealing with the natives.

The Norman conquest of Wales was piecemeal. It took a long time and was never completed. Much of this difficulty has been ascribed to the rough Welsh countryside. The mountainous interior covered with forests. Heavy rainfall ensuring that the clay soil was marshy for much of the year. Above all, however, it was the quality of Welsh resistance. 'They make fine use of light arms, which do not impede their agility,' observed the twelve-century Welsh Norman writer, Giraldus Cambrensis. 'They wear short coats of mail, helmets and shields, and sometimes greaves plated with iron. They carry bundles of arrows and long spears. Their nobles ride into battle, but the majority fight on foot. In time of peace, young men learn to endure the fatigue of war by penetrating deep into the forests and climbing the mountains.' In short, the Welsh were excellent guerilla warriors. Giraldus, therefore, recommended that the Normans should also employ lightly armoured foot-soldiers, and when possible the Normans incorporated Welshmen into their own forces. But, before this, a conqueror of Wales must prepare his victim. Giraldus suggests the Normans divide the Welsh with bribes and treaties, then blockade the coasts and the English border so that few provisions reached them. In the event, the Normans chose their path of conquest carefully and exploited the Welsh geography by sticking to the wide coastal plains.

Led by adventurers hungry for land of their own, the Normans first settled Gwent in south Wales. Whenever possible, William preferred to admit the homage of native Welsh warlords, but the desire of his landless followers ensured that a slow advance began around the coasts of Wales. As always, foreign influence was aided by Celtic power-play and Welsh exiles from Ireland fought alongside the Norman knights. Bit by bit, the Norman lords of the Marches—a French word meaning frontier—encroached on Welsh territory. The Marcher lords were used by successive English kings as a means of creating buffer states between themselves and the Welsh. They were offered absolute power over any frontier land they could subdue. It was an offer the warrior families of the Fitzalans, Gilberts, Clares, Mortimers and Laceys could not refuse. At the head of their war-bands, supported by the border garrisons of Chester, Shrewsbury, Hereford and Bristol, they carved out private kingdoms where their word was law.

Fierce resistance rocked the invaders from the end of the eleventh century. Woodcutting pioneers had to advance before Norman war-bands, clearing away undergrowth that might hide Welsh guerillas. The Marcher lords managed to hold onto many of their conquests and even north-west Wales, the heartland of the powerful dynasty of Gwynedd, lay at times in their hands. But, recovering from the shock of the Norman war-machine, the Welsh had begun to fight back and much of northern and central Wales remained solidly Celtic. Two centuries of raid and counter-raid now followed: the borders becoming a wilderness of slaughter. In a constant

Celtic Bretons fought alongside the Normans at the battle of Hastings and gained much from the share-out. Hand-coloured engraving from Charles Stothard's *Bayeux Tapestry* published in 1819.

state of war, the Marcher lords grew in power and frequently had to be quelled by their own king. The Welsh in their turn became hardened and Gwynedd was re-established from Anglesey down the west coast. By 1137, Gwynedd was recognised by the Norman English as the chief Celtic realm of Wales, so Welshmen could proclaim: 'No other language but Welsh shall answer for this land on the day of Judgement.' The Welsh had defied the initial onslaught of the mighty Normans.

Scotland became the home for many English refugees of the Norman conquest. Malcolm III married the sister of Edgar Aetheling, the only surviving claimant to the Anglo-Saxon throne after Harold. Again, this brought increased anglicisation and the Celtic Church of Scotland fell in line with the Church of Rome. Malcolm was persuaded to support Saxon claims to the English throne and four times he invaded Northumbria. By 1072, William tired of this aggression and led an army north. He forced Malcolm to accept him as overlord. But, with William's death, the Scots again ravaged Northumbria. The Conqueror's son, William Rufus, countered swift and hard. In the fighting, he took Cumbria as far as Carlisle, thus establishing Scotland's frontier as it has remained ever after. It was in another raid across the border that Malcolm was killed by a Norman knight. His death encouraged a Gaelic backlash and a warlord from the Hebrides was elected king of Scotland at Scone. The English followers of Malcolm were expelled.

The Normans could not rest with such a state of affairs. Over the next stormy years, Norman-backed claimants proclaimed their crowning as an hereditary right against the old Celtic system of election. Eventually the Anglo-Norman kings triumphed and the Celtic way of life retreated to the highlands. Scots sympathetic to England and new Norman landlords infiltrated the lowlands. In peace, the Normans gained much more Scottish territory than they would have won from battle. Gaelic was still spoken by the common people of Scotland, especially the almost independent clanlords of the north, but Norman-French became the dominant language of the Scottish aristocracy. Some refugees of the old regime fled to Ireland. There they joined with the Vikings of Dublin in raids against the west coasts of Britain. It may have been such conflict that encouraged certain Welsh Norman warlords to look across the Irish channel with ambition.

No one likes to commit to history the fact that his people have invaded another country out of sheer lust for conquest. Caesar justified his invasion of Celtic France as an intervention on behalf of the Gauls against the Germans. When Giraldus Cambrensis came to write his history of the Norman expedition to Ireland, he too opened his account with an invitation. The unity to be expected from the great victory at Clontarf in 1014 had come to nothing with the death of Brian. Ireland in the twelfth century was divided by bitter dynastic feuds. Leinster, always ready to do business with foreigners, was led by Dermot MacMurrough. Now Dermot had abducted the wife of Tiernan O'Rourke and in a revenge worthy of the Trojan War, O'Rourke and Rory O'Connor of Connacht, high king of Ireland, was coming to get him.

In 1166, Dermot sailed for help to the Norman court of Henry II. The king agreed to aid the Irishman as 'vassal and liegeman', but could not afford to send his own troops. Instead, Dermot was allowed permission to recruit the support of the Marcher lords of south Wales. Frustrated by the resurgence of the Welsh, many warriors were keen to join Dermot. They were led by the half-Norman, half-Welsh Robert FitzStephen who agreed to help Dermot in return for the town of Wexford as payment. By 1169, FitzStephen had disembarked at Bannow Bay in Leinster with thirty fully-armoured retainers, sixty half-armoured horsemen, and three hundred archers and foot-soldiers, all from south Wales. A force more Celtic than Norman, although the Annals of Tighernach say that the majority of soldiers were Flemish immigrants from settlements in Wales. Wishing to secure his promised land, FitzStephen wasted no time and made straight for Wexford. One of the major Viking settlements, Wexford was still ruled by Norse-Irish and considered itself independent from Leinster. The townsmen resolved to battle it out and advanced to meet the Norman army now joined by Irish warriors sent by Dermot. But the men of Wexford were overawed by the Norman horsemen and their armour, and retreated back into their town, burning all the outlying buildings.

The English defeat at Hastings in 1066 had profound repercussions for all of Celtic Britain. The death of king Harold engraved for Cassell's *History of England*, 1875.

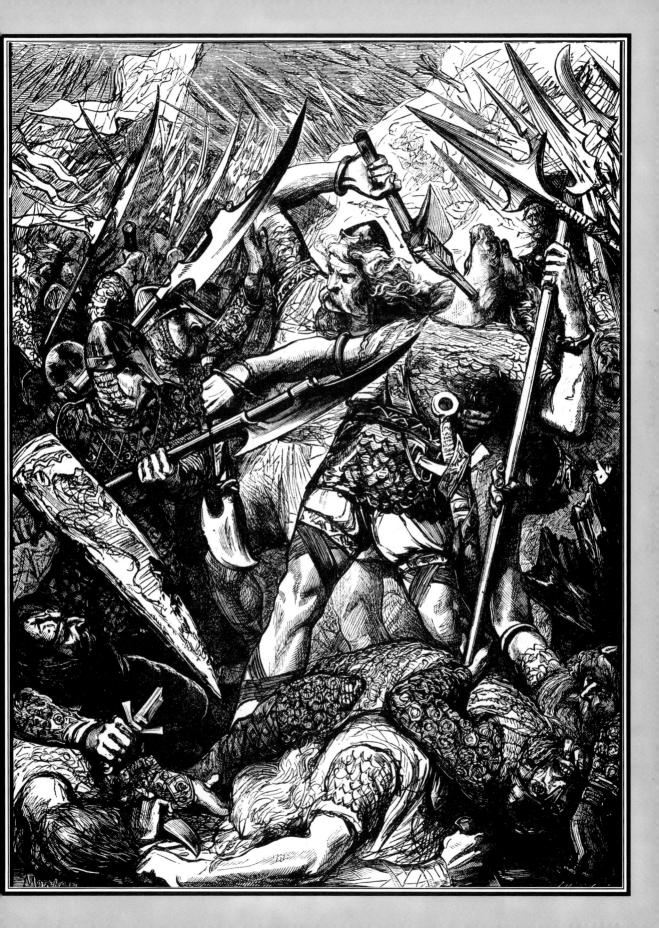

Throughout his account, Giraldus Cambrensis emphasises the military primitiveness of the Irish. 'They go to battle without armour,' he writes, 'considering it a burden and esteeming it brave to fight without it. They are armed with three kinds of weapons: short spears, light darts, and heavy battle-axes of iron, exceedingly well wrought and tempered. These they borrowed from the Norwegians. In striking with the battle-axe they use only one hand, instead of both. When all other weapons fail, they hurl stones against the enemy. In riding, they use neither saddles, nor boots, nor spurs, but carry only a rod in their hand with which they urge forward their horses.' Latin propaganda seems uppermost here, for in reality, the Irish nobility and certainly the Scandinavian Irish were as well equipped as the Normans and wore similar long coats of mail, iron helmets with nasal, and kite-shaped shields. And always, the Celtic Irish were excellent horsemen.

It is in Giraldus' contemptuous descriptions that we see the origin of the English prejudice against the Irish and their belief in the inferiority of Irish culture. 'Their clothes are made after a barbarous fashion,' he continues. 'Their custom is to wear small close-fitting hoods, hanging below the shoulders. Under this they use woollen rugs instead of cloaks, with breeches and hose of one piece, usually dyed. The Irish are a rude people, subsisting on the produce of their cattle only and living like beasts. This people, then, is truly barbarous, being not only barbarous in their dress, but suffering their hair and beards to grow enormously in an uncouth manner.'

FitzStephen lost no time in preparing for his assault on Wexford. His armoured warriors moved into the dry trenches around the city, while his archers covered them by raking the wall-towers. The Normans then heaved their siege ladders against the walls and clambered to the top with loud cries. The men of Wexford cast down large stones and wooden beams and managed to repulse the attack. With only a few hundred men under his command, FitzStephen called off the assault and withdrew to the harbour where he set fire to all the ships. Undeterred, the next morning, after celebrating mass, the Normans assaulted the walls again. This time, the townsmen despaired of holding the battlements and preferred to make a peaceful settlement. With bishops acting as mediators, the town did homage to Dermot and he in turn gave the town and its surrounding countryside to FitzStephen. The townsmen now joined the Normans and Leinstermen on their freebooting and ravaged the territory of Ossory. At the end of this raiding campaign, fought by horsemen amid woods and bogs, two hundred heads were laid at the feet of Dermot. He turned the heads one by one, raising his hands in joy as he recognised those of his enemies. 'Among them was one he hated above all others,' wrote Giraldus, 'and taking it up by the ears and hair, he tore the nostrils and lips with his teeth in a most savage and inhuman way.'

Receiving the homage of the lord of Ossory, Dermot was now perceived as a threat by Rory O'Connor, the high king. As the men of Connacht rode out against Dermot, he, under FitzStephen's direction, prepared a defensive position among the thick woods and bogs of Leinster. Trees were felled, underwood cut and woven into hedges, level ground broken up with holes and trenches, and secret passages cut through thickets. Hidden away thus, Dermot avoided a major conflict and instead offered to reassert his submission to Rory and give him hostages. The Normans would be sent away as soon as they helped Dermot secure Leinster. This apparently assured Rory and there was peace. But no sooner had the high king retreated than Maurice FitzGerald landed at Wexford with 140 Norman-Welsh warriors. While FitzStephen erected a fort of earth ramparts and wood stockade at Wexford, Dermot and FitzGerald marched on Dublin. They ravaged and burned the territory around Dublin so the Norse governors were compelled to accept Dermot's lordship. Dermot now sent

FitzStephen to the aid of the lord of Limerick and north Munster and they raided the land of Rory O'Connor. This was reckless indeed, but, with his Norman allies, Dermot now entertained thoughts of snatching the high kingship. On the advice of FitzStephen and FitzGerald, Dermot sent to England for more warriors. Above all, he requested the help of Richard FitzGilbert, a powerful Norman warlord of south Wales nicknamed Strongbow.

The special character of warfare in medieval Ireland is described fully by Giraldus Cambrensis. 'The Normans may be very good soldiers in their own country,' he wrote, 'expert in the use of arms and armour in the French manner, but every one knows how much that differs from the way of war in Ireland and Wales. In France, war is carried out across open plains; here, you find dense woods and mountainous terrain. In France, it is counted an honour to wear armour; here, it is a burden. There, victories are won by close fighting ranks; here, by the charges of lightly armed warriors. There, quarter is given and prisoners offered for ransom; here, heads are chopped off as trophies and no one escapes. Therefore, in all expeditions in Ireland and Wales, the Welshmen bred in the Marches make the best troops. They are good horsemen and light on foot. They can bear hunger and thirst well when provisions are not to be had. These are the men who took the lead in the conquest of Ireland and will be needed to complete it. For when you have to deal with a race naturally agile and whose haunts are in rocky places, you need lightly armed troops. In addition, in the Irish wars, particular care should be taken to include archers for they can counter the Irishmen who rush forward and throw stones at our heavily armoured warriors and then retreat.' It may be said that the Normans in England by the twelfth century should properly be called English for they were long descended from those Normans of 1066. This is true, but what is clear from Giraldus' passage above is that these warriors still considered themselves fighting in a Norman French manner different from that of the native Celts of Britain. Hence their dependence on Welsh auxiliaries.

In 1170, Strongbow arrived in Ireland. He brought with him 200 armoured horsemen and 1,000 Welsh archers and other soldiers. He had already sent an advance group of warriors and they had set up a beach-head near Waterford. The Viking-Irish townsmen savaged this advance guard and when Strongbow landed he made straight for them. Surveying the walls of Waterford, the Normans spotted a little wooden house on the outside attached to the stockade. This in turn was being supported by a single post. Under cover of their archers, armoured warriors rushed into the house and chopped down the pole. As the house collapsed, it brought with it part of the town wall. The Normans clambered over the wreckage and burst into the town. Some of the leading citizens held out in a tall stone tower but eventually they were overcome. Joined by Dermot, FitzStephen and FitzGerald, Strongbow now rode on Dublin. They descended unexpectedly by a mountain track and the Viking lord of Dublin immediately entered into lengthy peace negotiations. While they talked, a group of Normans stormed the walls.

Heady with success, Dermot raided the territory of his greatest enemy: Tiernan O'Rourke. Rory O'Connor reminded Dermot of his peace agreement but not even the execution of his own son, kept hostage by Rory, could prevent Dermot's ambition and he now claimed the high kingship. But Dermot's luck had run out. A few months later he died, leaving Strongbow in command of Leinster and the Viking towns. This did not please king Henry II of England who feared a warlord grown too powerful. He ordered the Normans to return on penalty of losing their lands in England and refused to allow any ship to sail to Ireland. This loss of reinforcements and supplies fell hard on Strongbow but he held his conquered territories.

In the meantime, Haskulf, the Viking lord of Dublin, returned to his city with sixty ships full of Northmen from the Isle of Man and the Scottish Isles. 'They were under the command of John the Mad,' reported Giraldus. 'Some wore long breastplates, others shirts of mail. Their shields were round, coloured red, and bound with iron. They were lion-hearted and iron-armed men. A member of the garrison had his leg cut off by a single stroke of one of their battle-axes.' The Normans were bundled back into Dublin. They regrouped, however, and a contingent moved out unobserved and pounced upon the rear of the besieging Vikings. The Northmen were thrown into confusion and routed. In order to calm the still largely Scandinavian townspeople, Haskulf, though a prisoner, was brought back in triumph to Dublin. Before the Norman lord of the city, he did not thank him for his mercy but insisted: 'We came as a small band, but if my life is spared, we will follow up with a much more formidable assault.' Haskulf was beheaded.

Hoping to exploit Strongbow's isolated situation, the Irish now besieged Dublin. While a Viking fleet blockaded the port of the city, Rory O'Connor assembled his men of Connacht and Meath, and supporters from Leinster and Ulster. Even worse for Strongbow was the fact that FitzStephen was surrounded in his castle by the men of Wexford. For two months the siege of Dublin persisted. With food running low and no prospect of relief, the Normans decided to bring the struggle to a head. 'What are we waiting for?' asked FitzGerald of his comrades. 'Do we expect help from our homeland? No. Such is our situation that to the Irish, we are English, and to the English, we are Irish.' The Normans rode out in three groups. The first contingent of twenty knights, the second of thirty knights, and the last of forty knights led by FitzGerald and Strongbow. They were supported by other less well-armed horsemen, archers, and some of the Norse-Irish townsmen. The Normans charged upon the retainers of Rory O'Connor, hoping to discourage the rest of his army. Rory was surprised, and as his men collapsed before the Normans, he escaped just in time to lead the Irish retreat.

From Dublin, Strongbow rode to Wexford. It was too late. Thinking that

Line drawing of a warrior from a miniature in the Dialogues of Saint Gregory, from a manuscript in the National Library of France, Paris. The coat of mail and nasal helmet was an international style of war-gear worn by almost all European knights of the eleventh century, including Celts.

Dublin had fallen to the Irish, FitzStephen had agreed to sail back to England. As his retainers gave up their arms, the men of Wexford threw FitzStephen into their dungeon and threatened to cut his head off if Strongbow should advance against them. Receiving a summons from his king, Strongbow returned to Britain. In south Wales, he reaffirmed his loyalty to Henry II and agreed to give up the conquered towns of Ireland in return for keeping Leinster as a fief. From a Welsh-Norman adventure, the assault on Gaelic Ireland had now developed into an Anglo-Norman invasion headed by the king of England.

Landing at Waterford with 500 knights and many more archers and light horsemen, Henry was greeted by the men of Wexford. Hoping to curry favour with the king, they offered him FitzStephen so he could be punished for invading Ireland without royal licence. This Henry did and FitzStephen was kept in chains as a royal prisoner until it was felt safe to pardon him. Henry paraded throughout Leinster. The lords of Cork, Limerick and many other southern Irish estates all did homage to him. They gave him hostages and agreed to pay a yearly tribute. At Dublin, Henry received the submission of Rory O'Connor and all the northern Irish lords except those of Ulster. He then convoked a synod of all the clergy of Ireland and tried to bring them in line with the English church. It seemed that the conquest of Ireland had been achieved with ease and only trouble at home forced Henry back to England. He was not to return to Ireland.

The submission of Rory O'Connor, lord of Connacht and high king of all Ireland, though attested by Giraldus, is not recorded by any other chronicler. With Henry gone and only Dublin and Leinster ruled by his governors, the north and west of Ireland remained Gaelic. Strongbow reasserted his hold over Leinster and led an attack against Munster. His first raid was successful, but his second met with complete defeat and he was pushed back to Waterford. Rory O'Connor led a force across the Shannon and ravaged the Normans in Meath. Strongbow struck back and by 1175 Meath was under Norman control. It was then that O'Connor made a formal submission to Henry II. It was acknowledged that Dublin, Meath and Leinster were to be ruled directly by the Normans, while the other Irish lords could rule their own lands in return for a yearly tribute of one hide for every ten animals slain. O'Connor remained Irish overlord. A year later, Strongbow was dead. His lands were held by the king and then divided among trusted vassals.

According to Giraldus, it would seem that the Celts of Ireland had been dealt a profound blow. Behind a rough diagonal from Cork and southern Munster to the eastern coast of Ulster, the Normans ruled from their stone-built castles. But how did the Irish see this invasion? Throughout the period described by Giraldus, the *Annals of Ulster* are very much concerned with the wars of the Celtic clans. The Normans—called Saxons in the *Annals*—are hardly mentioned and only then as a minor back-up force to Dermot MacMurrough: sometimes successful, sometimes not. 'They inflicted

In 1169, 30 Norman knights, 60 men-at-arms, and 300 archers landed at Bannow Bay in Leinster. A drawing by Alphonse de Neuville for Guizot's *L'Histoire de France*, 1870.

slaughter upon the Vikings of Dublin and Waterford and, on the other hand, many slaughters were inflicted upon themselves.' But, all the time, it is the Irish who are in control: conducting their own politics, their own wars. The only occasion the English are seen as a superior force is when King Henry lands with 240 ships. The Irish do homage to him, but the king soon leaves and the Irish lords continue their feuding. In the *Annals of Ulster*, the English—on the few occasions they are considered worthy of mention—are quickly absorbed into the Celtic world of raid and counter-raid.

To encounter such a perspective of the Normans in Ireland after reading that of Giraldus, encourages the view that Giraldus was engaged in the business of legend-making. His chronicle of the Normans in Ireland is a saga full of bold personalities and daring exploits. We are shown the Norman

84

invasion from the point of view of a handful of conquistadors, cutting their way into virgin territory held only by easily outwitted natives. Of course, this is how the English wished to view their first assault on the Irish. To them it was a heroic tale. Little did they realise, however, that the Irish considered the 'invasion' little more than a pinprick. The power-play of the Irish warlords remained, with the Normans now playing that role of opportunist auxiliaries formerly fulfilled by the Vikings. In time, both the Vikings and Normans were to be absorbed in the Irish way of war. Against the English, the North Men may have gained significant victories, but against Celtic warriors it had been a far longer, harder struggle: with no victors.

Celtic Counter-attack

WELSH
AND SCOTS
AGAINST THE
EDWARDIAN
KINGS
1200–1450

'To his most excellent lord, Philip, the illustrious king of the French . . .'. Llywelyn, lord of north Wales, supervised the composition of a letter of alliance. 'How am I to repay the excellence of your nobility,' the scribes continued, 'for the singular honour and priceless gift of sending me your knight with letter sealed in gold in testimony of the treaty between the kingdom of the French and the principality of north Wales. This letter I will keep in the church as if it were a sacred relic. An inviolable witness that I and my heirs will be friends to your friends and enemies to your enemies.'

There was more: the demand. 'Having summoned the council of my chief men and having obtained the common assent of all the princes of Wales, I promise that I will be faithful to you for ever. From the time I received your highness's letter, I have made neither truce nor peace with the English. By God's Grace, I and all the princes of Wales have manfully resisted our, and your, enemies. With God's Help we have by force of arms recovered from their tyranny a large part of the land and strong defended castles which by fraud they have occupied. Therefore, all the princes of Wales request that you make no truce with the English without us, knowing that we will not for any terms bind ourselves to them without your approval.'

When Llywelyn ab Iorwerth sent this treaty of alliance to the King of France in 1212, Celtic Wales was in a far stronger position than it had ever been since the Normans first surged into their land. In the previous century, the Welsh had made the most of crises in the English monarchy: the civil war of Stephen's reign; the unpopularity following Henry II's assassination of Thomas à Becket; the absence of Richard I on crusade in the Holy Land. Re-establishing themselves, the Welsh also adopted the castle-building of the Normans.

By the early thirteenth century, Llywelyn ab Iorwerth—Llywelyn the Great—had built a string of castles around Gwynedd. At Dolbadarn, dominating the mountain pass to Conwy, is a fully developed, strongly-fortified round stone keep, the match of any fortress built by the Marcher lords. In the heartland of the mountains of central Wales, stands Castell-y-Bere. Founded in 1221, the castle follows the shape of its base rock. Towers command each angle with the entrance protected by another tower and ditches cut in the rock. The towers are of the D-shaped type characteristic of Welsh castle-building. One served as the keep, while another was decorated with sculpture and probably contained a chapel. The high standard of stonework suggests this was one of Llywelyn's principal strongholds.

It was at the age of 21 in 1194 that Llywelyn claimed the throne of Gwynedd. He married the daughter of King John of England and gained a useful insight to the English way of power. He observed that a greater degree of centralisation was important to the maintenance of strength. Subsequently he cut across the native rivalry of the Welsh clans. Improvements in administration were coupled with the annexation of neighbouring Welsh estates. He did not lack for enemies among his own people. But, when King John set about cutting him down to size, it was Llywelyn's strength that encouraged the other Celtic warlords to join in his successful defence of Gwynedd. By 1215, baronial discord had undermined John's plans for Wales and the *Magna Carta* recognised that Celtic Wales, the Marches and English land in Wales were each ruled independently by the law of their own lords. Following hard on this victory, Llywelyn rode into south Wales at the head of a powerful array of united Welsh chieftains, leaving the English with few remaining footholds. Llywelyn was now overlord of Wales. He never actually called himself Prince of Wales, but preferred to honour himself as Prince of Aberffraw and Lord of Snowdon, to whom all other Welsh lords did homage. Even the Marcher lords were cowed.

Aside from their political strength, the Welsh were notably hardy fighters. 'In a certain part of this island, there is a people called the Welsh,' wrote King Henry II to the Emperor of Constantinople. 'They are so bold and so ferocious that even when unarmed, they do not fear to confront an armed force. Ready to shed their blood in defence of their country and to sacrifice their lives for renown. Even when the beasts of that land became calmed, these desperate men remained untamed.' Such hyperbole was probably intended as an excuse for Henry's lack of military success against the Welsh. But it is supported by Giraldus Cambrensis' description of their fighting spirit. 'The English fight in order to expel the natural inhabitants from the island and secure it all for themselves. The Welsh, who have for so

Drawing of a Welsh archer from the famous Register, Liber 'A', which includes the text of the Treaty of Montgomery, 1267, agreed between Llywelyn ap Gruffydd and Henry III. Correctly, the archer does not carry a 'longbow', supposedly characteristic of the Welsh, but an ordinary wooden bow probably more suited to the close-range archery praised by Giraldus Cambrensis.

long been sovereign over their land, maintain the conflict so that they may at least find a hiding place in the worst corner of it, among woods and marshes. The English fight for power, the Welsh for liberty. The English fight for money, the Welsh for their country.'

The Welsh warlords and their retainers were armed very much like their Norman-English enemies. They were mail-clad horse-warriors wielding sword and lance. It was their foot-soldiers, however, the common tribes-men, who seem to have contributed a particular Welshness to border warfare. 'The men of Gwent,' remarked Giraldus, 'are more used to war, more famous for their courage, and more expert in archery, than those of any other part of Wales. In an assault on the castle of Abergavenny, for example, two knights were passing over a bridge to take refuge in a tower built on a mound of earth. The Welsh, taking them in the rear, fired arrows that penetrated the oak door of the tower to a depth of four fingers. In memory of that feat, the arrows were preserved in the gate. William de Braose also testifies that one of his warriors was wounded by a Welsh arrow which passed through his mail clad thigh, his saddle, and penetrated his horse. Another knight had his armoured hip pierced by an arrow to the saddle. When he turned round, he received another arrow through his leg which fixed him to his horse. Yet the bows used by the Welsh are not made of horn, ivory, or yew, but of wild elm. They are unpolished and rough, yet stout. They are not intended to shoot an arrow at a great distance, but to inflict severe wounds in close fighting.'

It is generally assumed that it was amongst these talented Welsh archers that the celebrated longbow developed. In truth, there was no such weapon as the 'longbow' in the middle ages. It was referred to only as a 'bow', and the simple wooden bow used by the Welsh was common throughout Europe. What is significant, however, is that the English were so impressed by the forceful use of the bow by Welsh woodsmen, that they rapidly learned to employ large contingents of Welsh archers in their battles against the Irish, the Scots and each other. It was this deployment of large bodies of archers on the battlefield that was novel for the period. From this, of course, derived the tradition of massed Anglo-Welsh bowmen set against cavalry, culminating in the legendary archery triumphs of the Hundred Years War. What is surprising is that according to Giraldus the Welsh did not use their bows as the English were to—as a long-range shock weapon against organised formations of horsemen or foot-soldiers—but employed it as a precise close-range weapon in their guerilla wars of ambush.

Llywelyn ap Gruffyd maintained the strong, independent Wales that his grandfather, Llywelyn the Great, had built up. He exploited English weakness. The civil war between Henry III and his barons encouraged Llywelyn, under the guise of supporting Simon de Montfort, to attack the royalist Marcher lords. In 1265, this opportunism was transformed into a formal alliance. Simon recognised Llywelyn as Prince of Wales. Later that year, the wheel of fortune revolved, and Simon was killed at the battle of

Evesham by King Henry's son, Edward. In the fighting, the defeated Welsh auxiliaries of Simon were treated ruthlessly. They fled to a church for sanctuary. Undaunted, Edward and his warriors set about slaughtering the Welshmen, both inside and outside the church. Llywelyn now stood alone against the royalists, but his power was such that the war could only be brought to an end by treaty. In 1267, Henry III signed the Treaty of Montgomery, confirming Llywelyn as Prince of Wales and giving him the homage of all other Welsh chieftains. Llywelyn ap Gruffyd was riding high.

With King Henry's death in 1272, Edward claimed the throne. He was to be a formidable, unforgiving monarch. Llywelyn misjudged his character and immediately relations between the two warriors broke down. Although Edward's overlordship was never in doubt, Llywelyn nevertheless refused to attend the king's coronation. He refused to pay tribute and he refused to do homage. It now seemed as if Wales might break away completely as a separate state. In 1273, Edward sent a letter to Llywelyn, forbidding him to build a castle at Abermule near Montgomery. 'We have received a letter written in the king's name,' replied Llywelyn ironically. 'It forbids us to build a castle on our own land. We are sure it was not written with your

Welsh warrior with spear and sword, also illustrated in the Liber 'A' manuscript now in the Public Record Office, London. Alongside Welsh archers, Giraldus noted the fighting skill of the spearmen from north Wales. It has been suggested the one foot left naked was to enable a better grip on soggy terrain.

Welsh arrow-heads of various types from the castles of Caerleon, Cardiff, Castell-y-bere, and Dyserth, twelfth to fourteenth centuries, now in the National Museum of Wales, Cardiff.

knowledge and would not have been sent if you had been in the country, for you know well that the rights of our principality are totally separate from the rights of your kingdom. We and our ancestors have long had the power within our boundaries to build castles without prohibition by any one.' Today the walls of Dorforwyn castle near Abermule still stand.

Edward harboured Llywelyn's disrespect until he was secure in his new crown. As for Llywelyn, it was not wholly his proud independence that repeatedly prevented him from paying homage. Many of Llywelyn's fiercest Welsh enemies had fled to the English court and the Welsh prince would be risking his life to ignore their presence. In 1276, Edward's patience snapped. He was an exceptionally able warlord and personally commanded all his armies. For the first two years of his reign he had fought in the Holy Land and defeated the Saracens at Haifa. For his first royal campaign on British soil, he assembled a powerful army of his own retainers and those of the Marcher lords. Overawed by Llywelyn, the Marcher lords were keen to reinstate their power. They spear-headed the invasion with two strikes against central Wales. In 1277, Edward took the field and advanced into northern Wales.

Llywelyn was unused to such English unity. He believed they were still divided by the split loyalties of the Barons' War. Instead, it was the Welsh who cracked up. Llywelyn's former Welsh allies broke away and marched alongside the English. Unprepared for such a rapid collapse of his power structure, there was little the Welsh prince could do. Literally cutting a path through the Welsh forests, Edward rode through the north of Wales, initiating the construction of a castle wherever he camped. Employing ships from the Cinque Ports, Edward cut off Llywelyn's supply lines from the grain-rich island of Anglesey. With only his faithful men of Gwynedd to protect him, Llywelyn was forced through hunger and the sheer size of Edward's campaign to admit a humiliating defeat. Llywelyn now not only paid homage to Edward, but lost much of the land he had conquered over the previous years. He lost also the homage of all his former Welsh vassals. He remained Prince of Wales, but this was now a meaningless title.

Retreating to his mountain castles, Llywelyn waited for events to overtake him. The English victory bit deep, and in 1282 it was Llywelyn's brother David who expressed Welsh resentment. Llywelyn had learned his lesson and repeated his homage to Edward, but, seeing his brother burn and loot English settlements, vengeance overcame caution. The rapidity of the uprising surprised Edward. Throughout Wales, Celtic warlords joined in an assault on the castles of the Marcher lords. Edward felt he had been generous in the first conflict, allowing the Welsh chieftains to keep their lands. Now he resolved to crush them. Gathering an army of feudal retainers and paid companies of crossbowmen and archers, he repeated his many-pronged campaign. Loyal Marcher lords rode into southern and central Wales, while the king's major force advanced from Chester. Edward again utilised ships to capture Anglesey. But this time, rather than waiting to starve out Llywelyn, one of his vassals, Luke de Tany, constructed a pontoon bridge across the Menai Strait to Bangor. Thus, Edward hoped to draw the net tight on Llywelyn and his followers in the mountains of Snowdon.

Carefully and efficiently, Edward captured castles on the mainland. But Luke was impatient. His warriors charged over the bridge. Ambushed by the Welsh, they rushed back to Anglesey. In the panic many were drowned. This victory temporarily bolstered the Welsh, who believed it a sign that, according to the prophecy of the legendary Merlin, Llywelyn would soon receive the crown of the Britons. The Welsh prince left his mountain lair to David and rode south. In a skirmish near Orewin bridge where the river Yrfor joins the Wye, he was confonted by the Marcher lord Roger Lestrange. Archers pelted the Welsh and then the mail-clad knights charged. In the fighting, Llywelyn was run through. His head was cut off and sent to Edward in north Wales. He in turn sent it to his warriors in Anglesey and then had it conveyed to London where it was stuck upon a spear and displayed at the Tower of London.

The Welsh were shattered. His own countrymen handed David over to the English. Wales was now under direct English control for the first time in its history. The Celtic heartland of Gwynedd became English crown lands. Edward's son, born at Caernarfon, was proclaimed Prince of Wales. A crown supposedly belonging to the legendary King Arthur was fortuitously uncovered and presented to Edward. He had become King of the Britons. This meant much to Edward: the Anglo-Normans had adopted Arthur as the leading hero of their cycle of chivalric tales. For had not Arthur defeated Saxons, just as the Normans had done? The Celts were furious that their national hero had been taken up by their enemies. Welsh propaganda maintained that Arthur was still alive in the mountains of Wales, awaiting his time to triumph over the enemies of his people. The English responded by uncovering the bones of the dead Arthur on English soil at Glastonbury. During his fighting in Wales, Edward deemed it important to interrupt his campaign to witness the disinterring of what were believed to be Arthur's bones and their reburial in a grander English tomb. Not only had the English taken the land of the Celts, they had stolen their legends.

The collapse of Celtic Wales cannot be wholly blamed on Llywelyn's over-confidence. It was Welsh misfortune to choose a fight with one of England's most powerful and effective rulers. Like other medieval kings, Edward had problems to settle in France, but throughout his reign these were overruled by his determination to increase English influence in Britain. Such a focus of attention, backed up by high military expertise, was bad news for the island's Celtic realms. For, after Wales, Edward set his sights on Scotland. In 1286, Alexander III, king of the Scots, went for a midnight ramble. 'Neither storm nor floods nor rocky cliffs, would prevent him from visiting matrons and nuns, virgins and widows, by day or by night as the fancy seized him.' On one of these adventures, Alexander

Gruffydd, son of Llywelyn the Great and father of Llywelyn the Last, tries to escape from the Tower of London. The rope snaps and he breaks his neck. After a drawing by Matthew Paris in his *Chronica Majora* of the thirteenth century in Corpus Christi College, Cambridge.

plunged over a cliff and was found with a broken neck. His only direct heir was his grand-daughter. Edward proposed a marriage between her and his son, the Prince of Wales. But she too met an untimely death. The competition for the Scots throne was now flung wide open.

Acknowledging his feudal and military superiority, the Scots regents allowed Edward to decide who should rule Scotland. The front runners were John Balliol and Robert the Bruce the Elder. Both these lords were descendants of the knights of William the Conqueror. For, by this time, Scotland, especially the lowlands, was dominated by Anglo-Norman landowners ruling estates throughout the realm. John Balliol ran vast estates in France; Robert the Bruce the Younger owned land in Essex. This conquest of Celtic Scotland had been achieved through court politics, intermarriage, and peaceful settlement. In the north, there were some Scots landowners and clansmen who were of direct Celtic descent, but increasingly the politics of the day was handled by warlords of Norman blood. The ensuing Anglo-Scots war can therefore be more clearly seen as a power struggle between Anglo-Norman dynasties and not an international war of Scots versus English or Celts against Normans, as was more true in Wales and Ireland. That said, the common people of Scotland and many of the lower aristocracy, the clansmen, were Celtic and still spoke Gaelic. It was these people, rallying to the cause of their Scots Norman masters, who may have envisaged their battle against the English invader as a national or Celtic struggle for independence.

Edward wanted to dominate Scotland. If he could not become its king, then he would choose the most malleable contender. He selected John Balliol as his puppet monarch. The elderly Robert the Bruce passed his family's claim onto his son, also called Robert the Bruce. They refused to do homage to the new king. Tiring of his humiliating role as frontman for Edward's ambitions, John Balliol renounced his allegiance to the English king and prepared for war. Robert the Bruce ignored his call to arms. Loyal to king Edward, it seemed now that Balliol might be displaced in favour of the Bruce claim.

Although embroiled in war in France and Wales, king Edward rode north with an army of English knights and Welsh archers. It may, incidentally, be thought remarkable that the Welsh should form such a major part of Edward's army so soon after their own defeat at his hands. But the defeat was against the Welsh Celtic nobility, whereas the ordinary Welshman was happy to fight for money and food on any side. For many of the Celtic nobility, however, Wales had ceased to be their homeland and several served abroad as mercenaries. Froissart, for instance, mentions an Owen of Wales who offered his services to the King of France during the Hundred Years War.

Berwick at once fell to Edward. His lieutenant, John de Warenne, shattered the Scots at Dunbar. Parading in triumph through Scotland, Edward demanded the abdication of Balliol. At Montrose, the two kings confronted each other. In front of both English and Scots courtiers, Balliol's coat of arms was ripped from him and thrown on the floor. His humiliation was complete. But Edward's arrogance had further heights to reach. Through fear alone, he received the homage of the Scots magnates. At Perth, he commanded that the sacred stone of Scone—upon which generations of Scots kings had been crowned—be removed and delivered to Westminster Abbey. Ignoring the Bruce claim, Edward appointed an English viceroy over the Scots. Scotland it seemed was now part of an English Empire. As Edward returned over the border, a chronicler recorded his concluding remarks on the campaign: 'It is a good job to be shot of shit.'

Recovering from Edward's blitzkrieg, a few Scots warlords set about reclaiming their dignity. Foremost among these was the Gaelic-speaking William Wallace. A man of low status and called by some a bandit, it may have been that Wallace was used by more powerful Scots aristocrats as a cover for their rebellion so they would be seen not to break their feudal vows of homage to Edward. In the *Lanercost Chronicle*, Wallace is called 'Willelmus Wallensis'—Welsh William—perhaps a reference to his Celtic tongue or his descent from the Britons of Strathclyde. Harassed by English tax collectors and hiding in the forest of Selkirk, Wallace gathered around him a band of outlaw warriors. One evening, he made a dash to see his lover. Surprised by an English patrol, he retreated into his woman's house and disappeared out the back door. The frustrated Englishmen set fire to the house and slaughtered Wallace's lover and family. The tall, angry Scotsman vowed vengeance. He had little time to wait. He and his retainers caught up with the English patrol and cut them to pieces.

This blow against the English encouraged several Scots aristocrats to raise their banners in rebellion. Among them were Sir William Douglas, the former commander of Berwick, and James Stewart, a major Scots landowner. King Edward hoped to settle the insurrection with his Scots allies and sent Robert Bruce from his base in Carlisle to capture the Douglas castle. But Robert was none too sure of the righteousness of his order. His mother was Celtic and his deep feelings for the country of Scotland ran contrary to his family's political friendship. Besides, the Bruces had been used before with the promise of kingship and Edward had failed to deliver. At the castle of Douglas, Robert made the vital decision. He would fight with his countrymen, not against them.

In the meanwhile, William Wallace fought in the name of the deposed king, John Balliol. He readied his followers for a decisive clash with the English invaders. Committed to continental politics in 1297, king Edward sent John de Warenne to sort out the Scots. Wallace positioned his men in the hills around a bridge crossing the river Forth north of Sterling. Not all the Scots felt confident about the confrontation. James Stewart approached the English warlord with an offer of peace. Warenne refused and his knights began to advance across the bridge. With half the English over the river, it was then that Wallace pounced. Half his warriors fell upon the leading English, while the rest set about chopping down the bridge. The English knights across the bridge floundered in the waterlogged fields of the river-bank. Scots spearmen pierced and prodded them off their horses. Scots axes rent the rings of English mail. With the bridge destroyed, the English vanguard was isolated. Their comrades on the south side of the river could only watch as the Scots wiped out the beleaguered knights. Among the dead was Hugh de Cressingham, chief tax collector of Edward's

The mighty four-towered gatehouse of Harlech Castle. Built by Edward I between 1283 and 1290 to prevent Snowdonia from ever becoming a region of stiff Welsh resistance.

regime in Scotland. His body was flayed and Wallace had a broad strip of his skin from head to heel made into a baldric for his sword. John de Warenne and the rest of the English fled back to Berwick. James Stewart captured their baggage train on the way.

In the forest of Selkirk, William Wallace was proclaimed Guardian of the Kingdom of Scotland and knighted by Robert Bruce. The Earl of Carrick, Bruce had himself roused the men of his own estate and Galloway to the

Reconstruction of the seal of king Edward I, showing the scourge of the Celts in full knightly panoply.

common cause, but had yet to meet the English in battle. Throughout the rest of 1297, Wallace ravaged the border land of England for corn and cattle. Such a turn of events wrenched Edward back from his adventuring in Europe. He transferred his headquarters to York. Now he would hammer the Scots. Feudal dues were called upon. Gascon crossbowmen and Welsh archers were recruited. A vast supply train of wagons and ships was assembled. By the summer of 1298, 2,500 horse-warriors and 12,000 foot-soldiers marched into Scotland. The Scots retreated before the mighty army. But the further the English advanced, the more their supplies began to break down. Their ships brought no food, only wine. Fighting broke out between the Welsh and the English. With his expedition on the brink of collapse, Edward suddenly caught wind of the Scots. The action would take place on hills near Falkirk.

William Wallace feared the greater numbers of the English horsemen. To counter them, he positioned his spear-carrying foot-soldiers behind boggy land, with woodland and rough terrain guarding their flanks. The spears of the Scots were long pikes and they stood in crowded phalanx formations— schiltrons—presenting the enemy with a forest of iron points. In front of the spearmen, stakes were hammered into the ground with ropes joining them. Groups of archers gathered between the schiltrons. The few Scots horsemen waited in reserve, hoping to exploit any break in the enemy. King Edward realised his superiority in horse-warriors and sent his knights in on the first wave of the attack. Galloping into the marshland, the horses slowed down. The majority of the English horsemen then wheeled to the left and right and rode round the swamp, hitting the Scots in the rear.

The shock of battle scattered the Scots horsemen and the English now plunged amid their foot-soldiers. The bows of the Scots had little penetrating power against the mail of the English and soon they too had joined the routed horsemen. But the Scots spearmen held firm. Their rope and stake entanglements tripped up the English horses: knights crashed to the ground. The English men at arms could not break the relentless rows of pikes. The Master of the Templars rushed too recklessly on the spear forest, flailing madly with his sword, hoping to break it with his animal strength. He and his five retainers were impaled. By this time, Edward and his foot-soldiers had caught up with his knights and called off their rash attacks. With no enemy horse or archers to harry him, Edward gathered his Welsh bowmen in front of the Scots schiltrons. They fired hail after hail into the standing targets. The stalwart Scots could only take so much. Men fell and gaps appeared in the once formidable spear wall. It was then that Edward sent his knights in among the broken formations. With war hammer, mace and sword, the horse-warriors hacked at the Gaelic underlings. William Wallace escaped the slaughter, but his power perished with his army.

Edward's victory at Falkirk was not complete. The countryside remained hostile and he was desperately short of supplies, forcing him to retreat to the border. In Carlisle, he sent out summonses for warriors for yet further

campaigns. His obsession turned the lowlands into a devastated killing ground. Among the Scots, William Wallace returned to his raiding: there would be no key role for him. In 1305, he was betrayed by demoralised countrymen, dragged through the streets of London, half hanged and then dismembered. The next year, Robert Bruce eliminated his only serious rival to the Scots throne and had himself crowned Robert I. The English fell upon him with a vengeance. His retainers were smashed at the battle of Methven. Members of his family were executed. His lover and sister held like animals in cages on the battlements of Berwick and Roxburghe castles. Robert was reduced to the life of a fugitive, hunted by Scotsmen eager for the bounty placed on his head by Edward.

Caernarfon Castle, begun in 1283 and built by Edward I to command the entrance of the Menai Strait. These castles are still regarded by many Welshmen as unacceptable symbols of English domination.

When Robert emerged from hiding in 1307, the harsh retribution of the English had provided Bruce with many fresh supporters. But his greatest break was yet to come. As the elderly king Edward prepared to launch another assault, the veteran warrior died. The aura of inevitable victory that seemed always to follow the English when led by Edward was at last at an end. But Edward's determination to subdue the Scots lived on. He had extracted from his son two promises: first, that the Prince of Wales should carry on the fight against Bruce; and, second, that Edward's coffin be carried ahead of his army into Scotland.

Edward II could not hope to be the supreme warlord his father had been. It was not until 1310 that this king of England crossed the border. In the meantime, Robert's guerilla warfare had undermined his enemies in Scotland and he had regained his leadership of the Scots. In 1308, it is said, he held a parliament at St Modan's Priory, Ardchattan, at which the business was conducted in Gaelic: perhaps an acknowledgement to the loyal support of the clansmen and the lower Scots classes. Eventually, Edward II did march against Bruce. But Robert avoided confrontation, devastated the land before him, and the English had to turn back. Robert now took the war across the border and ravaged Northumberland. In Scotland, he reduced resistant castles one by one, until only Sterling held out. The revival of Robert's power was remarkable. From a fugitive to chief Scots warlord in just over two years: a clear sign of his popular support.

In 1314, Edward II gathered a great army outside Berwick to raise the siege of Sterling: 500 knights accompanied by 2,000 mounted retainers;

Battle axe discovered in the Thames, thirteenth or fourteenth century, now in the London Museum. The breadth of the cutting edge is 17 cm (7 in).

3,000 Welsh archers and 15,000 foot-soldiers armed with spear, pole-axe, dagger and shield. In his eagerness to finish off Bruce, Edward marched his men into the ground. By the time they reached a little stream called Bannock, north of Falkirk, they were exhausted. It was then that Robert brought his men out of his lair in the forest of Torwood and confronted the English. His army was around a quarter of the numbers of Edward's. His warriors came from all over Scotland. His 5,000 massed spearmen consisted of lowlanders and highlanders, with some soldiers coming from the Western Isles. Bruce himself commanded a phalanx of Gaelic clans. These were led into battle by their own clan chieftains. The following claim to have been represented: Cameron, Campbell, Chisholm, Fraser, Gordon, Grant, Gunn, MacKay, MacIntosh, Macpherson, Macquarrie, Maclean, MacDonald, MacFarlane, MacGregor, MacKenzie, Menzies, Munro, Robertson, Ross, Sinclair and Sutherland. Among the bristling schiltrons, there were a few archers and about 500 lightly clad horsemen. This was the same battle formation that had been devastated at Falkirk.

Although short in numbers, Robert hoped to make up for this deficiency by training his men hard. The Scots knew how to wield their 12-foot spears, stand tight in their formations, and resist the temptation to run wildly into the conflict. Bruce prepared the ground around the burn of Bannock carefully. Pits were dug and then covered with brushwood. Tree trunks were built into barricades across forest paths. The time of combat was getting nearer. Robert dispatched his camp followers to a nearby valley.

On the morning of the battle, the Scots celebrated mass. By midday, the English had ridden into view. The first warriors on the field were the vanguard of English knights. They expected to overawe the Scots with their brilliant armour and streaming pennons. In the open ground between the two armies they came across a few Scots scouting out the land. Among them was Robert Bruce. One of the leading English knights, Sir Humphry de Bohun, recognized the Scots king, couched his lance, and spurred his horse into a gallop. Seeing the English knight powering towards him, the sensible reaction for Robert would have been to fall back. His death would mean the end of the battle. But to turn now, in front of his own men, would be equally disastrous. Besides, Robert had a particular loathing for the knight de Bohun. When he had been on the run, Edward I had handed his estates in Annandale and Carrick over to the de Bohuns. Later, Edward II gave the Bruce's estates in Essex to the same family. Robert urged his grey palfrey on towards the duel. Henry de Bohun's lance charge was deflected. Robert stood in his stirrups, raised his battleaxe high and brought it crashing down on the knight's helmet, splitting it and breaking open his head, shattering the axe shaft. A great cry went up from the highlanders. They clambered over their earthworks and ran on towards the English horsemen. Thrown into a panic by the hidden pits and charging Celts, the English backed off.

Elsewhere on the battlefield, another group of English knights rode upon the Scots. This time they were confronted by a schiltron of spearmen. Of the

The abbot of Inchaffray
blesses the Scots
highlanders of the
schiltron before the battle
of Bannockburn, 1314.
From Cassell's *Illustrated
Universal History*, 1884.

two leading English knights, one was killed immediately, the other captured, his horse being impaled on the pikes. The rest rode more cautiously around the circle of spears. Out of desperation, some threw their knives, lances and maces at the Scots. The spearmen thrust at the horses. Eventually, the intense summer heat proved decisive, and the humbled, sweating Englishmen rode off. That night, the Scots were convinced they had done enough to claim victory and were ready to decamp. Certainly, across the battleground, panic had swept through the English ranks; so much so that king Edward had to send heralds around his camp to assure the men that the conflicts so far had been mere skirmishes, the main battle was yet to come. In the meanwhile, English deserters reassured Robert of his success and encouraged him to stay with the promise of an absolute victory the next day.

During that short summer night, the English knights had taken the best ground around Bannockburn for their brief rest. Their archers and foot-soldiers had been forced to lie on the soggy, marshy land near the stream. In the dawn light, the English knights impatiently mounted their horses, keen

101

to avenge the humiliation they had suffered the previous day. They expected Robert to remain in his defensive position, awaiting their attack. Instead, the Scots took the offensive, rolling down the hillside in three densely-packed schiltrons. Foot-soldiers daring to attack horsemen! The English could not believe their luck. The Earl of Gloucester was among the first of the knights to charge upon the Scots. Spears cracked and splintered, but the Scots held firm. No matter how many knights hurled themselves on the forest of points, the schiltrons rolled on.

With their knights already immersed in the fighting, the Welsh and English archers had little opportunity to break the Scots with their arrow storm. The battle was now a hand-to-hand struggle. Axe against sword. Spears thrust through visors. The lightly-armoured Scots leaped among the fallen mail-clad knights, hammering them mercilessly. The Scots crushed the English towards the marshy river bank. Despite the chaos of the crowded

Robert Bruce commanding his Highland warriors at the Battle of Bannockburn. After having routed an enemy, warriors of the schiltron would often jump on horses and thus drive home their victory. From Cassell's *History of England*, 1905.

fighting, English arrows still fell hard and these Robert feared most. He therefore ordered his small band of 500 horsemen forward against the archers, cutting them down. The schiltrons pressed on. Robert sent in his reserves. Scotsmen leaned on their comrades in front, pushing and heaving forward. English knights trampled their fellow warriors into the mud in desperation to escape. Horses and men fell into the stream, drowning. Realising the battle was over, English noblemen grabbed the reins of their king and led him away. With victory safe, the Scots camp followers, women and children, joined in the final struggle, looting and slaughtering. With their make-shift banners held high, it appeared to the English that a second Scots army had arrived and their rout was completed.

Bannockburn was a devastating defeat for the English. The Earl of Gloucester, thirty-four barons, and two hundred knights were among the dead. Nearly a hundred other knights had been captured, to be ransomed over the next year. Robert Bruce was undisputed king of Scotland. In the aftermath, the Scots paid back the English for all those years of invasion. They swept south and raided northern England as far as Durham and Richmond in Yorkshire. They drove back herds of cattle and wagons of loot. The English dared not confront the Scots and Northumberland was left to fend for itself. But the victory of Bannockburn also allowed Robert to consider a grander strategy. He sent his brother, Edward, to Ireland. Some said this was merely an excuse to rid Scotland of a strong rival to Robert's throne, providing Edward with the chance to win a crown of his own. However, it also made good strategic sense. The English estates in Ireland had been a source of warriors and supplies for the armies of both Edward I and Edward II. It was also part of a general Scots determination to master the Irish Sea. For, as soon as Edward had landed in Ireland, his fleet was returned to Robert who used it to secure the homage of the Norse-Scots lords of the Western Isles.

In Ireland, Robert Bruce hoped to arouse a sense of Celtic brotherhood. He sent before Edward a remarkable letter addressed to all the Irish chieftains. 'We and our people and you and your people,' he proclaimed, 'free since ancient times, share the same national ancestry and are urged to come together more eagerly and joyfully in friendship by a common language and by common custom. We have sent to you our beloved kinsman, the bearer of this letter, to negotiate with you in our name about permanently maintaining and strengthening the special friendship between us and you, so that with God's will your nation may be able to recover her ancient liberty.' Clearly, the medieval Scots were aware of their Irish ancestry and now wished to call upon that valued Gaelic aspect of their nationhood to overthrow the Norman-Saxon English. In the wake of Bannockburn, the Irish were indeed tempted by the successful independence of the Scots. The O'Neills of Ulster were particularly keen to hit back at the English and offered Edward Bruce their kingship.

Donal O'Neill called upon fellow Irishmen to support Edward against the 'sacrilegious and accursed English who, worse than the inhuman Danes, are busy heaping injuries of every kind upon the inhabitants of this country.' He noted that their past disunity had made the Irish vulnerable: 'we, being weakened by wounding one another, have easily yielded ourselves a prey to them. Hence it is that we owe to ourselves the miseries with which we are afflicted, manifestly unworthy of our ancestors, by whose valour and splendid deeds the Irish race in all past ages has retained its liberty.'

Landing at Lough Larne in Ulster, Edward Bruce led an army of 6,000. A small force, it nevertheless comprised veteran warriors of the war of independence and soon defeated the local Anglo-Irish barons. A few Irish chieftains immediately allied themselves with Bruce, but others had to be beaten into submission. Despite a call for Celtic unity, this would become a campaign as much against the native Irish as against the English. The Scots' progress through the country sent out ripples of mayhem. An army from Connacht arose to confront him, but was split by Edward playing off one clan against another so that Connacht was itself plunged into civil war. In 1316, in Dundalk, Edward Bruce was crowned High King of all Ireland. He now invited his brother to survey his newly conquered territory. Robert Bruce arrived with a powerful force of galloglas, notoriously ferocious Norse Gaelic mercenaries from the Hebrides. So far, Robert's masterplan had worked well. With Edward in Ireland, the Western Isles under Robert's control, rumours soon spread that the Bruces were to land in Wales and restore their ancient liberty. An all-Celtic movement seemed imminent, unifying the Celts against Edwardian England. Encouraged by such thoughts, the Welsh rose in revolt under Llywelyn Bren. Edward II could not even trust his Welsh archers and all ideas of a counter-attack against Scotland had to be forgotten as he defended his lands in Wales and Ireland.

In Ireland, it was customary that a High King parade all round the country to secure his homage and respect. Early in 1317, Edward Bruce set out with his brother on just such an expedition. They received a rough welcome. The earl of Ulster set an ambush. Allowing Edward's vanguard to proceed through forestland, he then set his archers on Robert's rear. Robert was not provoked and maintained his warriors in good order—except for his nephew Sir Colin Campbell: he spurred his horse on towards the Irish despite the likelihood of a trap. Robert dashed after him and stunned him with a blunt weapon before he could be surrounded. At that moment, more warriors emerged from the forest and a fierce struggle ensued. Only the discipline and military expertise of the Scots saved them from the superior numbers of the Irish.

The people of Dublin, fearing that Edward would march on them next, demolished and set fire to the suburban buildings outside their walls so as to deprive the Scot's army of any cover. It was a decision they were later to regret, for they destroyed many important buildings in their panic, including the king of England's Irish manor. And, anyway, Edward had little time for a siege and had decided to bypass the stout defences of the

city. The Bruces advanced into Munster, for here Irish clansmen promised that the entire countryside would rise to their side. But mutual suspicions overrode these ambitious plans and famine prevented any successful campaigning. Edward was forced to turn back and consolidate his base in Ulster. After such an anti-climax, Robert returned to Scotland. The shock-waves of Bannockburn had begun to recede and Edward II was able to act with more confidence in the support of his barons. A small force of Genoese crossbowmen was sent to Ireland to encourage the cause of the English. Through a generous attitude to enemies and a consolidation of feudal privileges, king Edward managed to increase his influence among the Anglo-Irish. A royal mission to the Pope had also brought benefits. Archiepiscopal vacancies in Ireland were filled by men favourable to king Edward and all supporters of both Bruces were excommunicated. It appeared that Edward II was far more astute at politics than warfare.

Donal O'Neill, self-styled king of Ulster and 'true heir by hereditary right of all Ireland', wrote to Pope John XXII with the Irish point of view. He detailed how the English dominated his land and treated the Irish as inferior

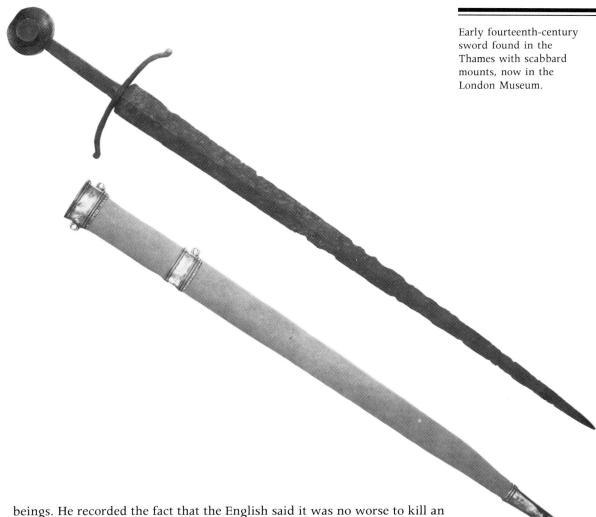

Early fourteenth-century sword found in the Thames with scabbard mounts, now in the London Museum.

beings. He recorded the fact that the English said it was no worse to kill an Irishman than a dog. But there were few other Irish who saw the Bruce invasion as a welcome blow against the English. Many Irish viewed Edward as yet another alien adventurer and preferred to do business with the English simply because they had been longer established. A chronicler of Connacht summed up Bruce's army as: 'Scottish foreigners less noble than our own foreigners.' As for the ideal that both Irish and Scots should unite under a common Gaelic banner, this seems to have been soon forgotten by both sides in the powerplay that followed invasion. Among the remote tribesmen of the Irish mountains who did join Edward Bruce, the prospect may have appealed of fighting alongside warriors speaking a similar Celtic language. But, by 1318, Edward Bruce still only had the support of a few Ulster opportunists. The action of English privateers in the Irish Sea had broken the dominance of the Scots and reinforcements from Scotland could not be depended on. Nevertheless, Edward Bruce was a potent political force and, supported by the de Lacy family, he rode southwards at the head of an Irish-Scots army over two thousand strong. An Anglo-Irish force under Richard Clare, Lord Lieutenant of Ireland, met him at Faughart, just north of Dundalk.

Bruce was heavily outnumbered and his senior knights advised him to wait for reinforcements. But Bruce was impatient for a victory that would give him greater political control. His Irish allies refused to join in the foolhardiness and suggested they harry the English with raids while Bruce awaited the extra men that were expected. Again Edward ignored this sound advice and sent his warriors into battle. The vanguard and mainguard became spread out, their thin numbers annihilated piecemeal by the Anglo-Irish. Loyal to death, Edward's knightly retainers charged alongside their leader as the rearguard rumbled forward. Having belated thoughts of mortality, Edward exchanged his conspicuous royal armour for the plainer garb of a lowly knight. The Scots fought bravely, but inevitably were overwhelmed. According to legend, the English found the body of the lowly knight clad in royal armour and presumed it to be Edward Bruce. His head was cut off, salted in a bucket, and sent to Edward II. But the Bruce

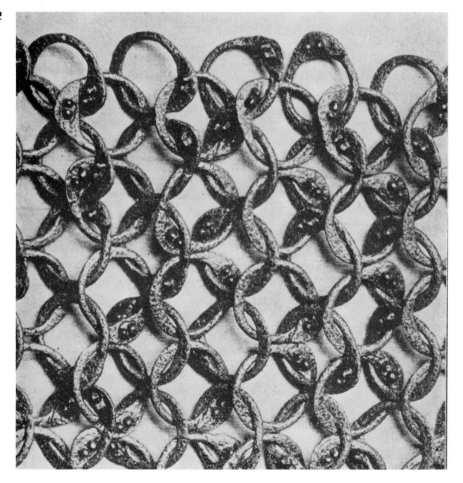

Section of early fourteenth-century mail. By this period, plate armour had become more important and the ubiquitous mail coat shortened.

had not escaped the slaughter. His body lay elsewhere on the battlefield. As the Gaelic prisoners were led away, a Scots knight Sir Philip Mowbray regained consciousness and broke away with other captives. They carried the heavy news of Edward Bruce's death to Scotland.

In that second decade of the fourteenth century, it seemed as if the Celtic realms of Britain and Ireland might rise together and throw back the descendants of the Normans and Saxons. In the event such a dream did not come true, and the English held onto many of their Celtic possessions. But the struggle had not been in vain. In Ireland, English control had been further weakened. Irish chieftains contested the land as strongly as the Anglo-Irish barons. Although some admitted the overlordship of the English king, all were united in their determination not to be ruled by a middle strata of Anglo-Irish adventurers.

Norman dynasties were bundled out of several Irish estates. A Gaelic revival was under way that would eventually reduce the power of the English to the Pale—the royal territory around Dublin. The authority of the great Irish lordships emerged intact from the Celtic highlands. Already, in 1258, an attempt had been made to restore the high kingship of all Ireland. In 1327, Leinster—the heartland of Anglo-Irish support—had thrown itself behind the MacMurroughs and elected one of them king of Leinster, the first since the Norman conquest. Military victories were paralleled by a resurgence of Gaelic culture that engulfed the Anglo-Irish and ensured that the Celtic tongue and law were dominant in Ireland until the coming of the Tudors.

In Scotland, the struggle had been decisive. The Scots had powerfully secured their border. No Englishman dared set foot on Scots land in the years following Bannockburn. In battle, Gaelic-speaking, spear-wielding common foot-soldiers had shown they were the equal of any lance-carrying, knightly horse-warrior. Above all, the Scots had a king from their own country. Robert Bruce was an intelligent and ingenious warlord and repelled all attacks on his kingdom by Edward II until the unpopular English monarch was murdered in 1327. In 1328, the young Edward III acknowledged at last Robert's title of king and a 13-year truce was agreed. A year later the Bruce was dead. Hostilities recommenced, but a legend of Scots independence had been established.

In Wales, the mere rumour of a Bruce invasion had been enough to encourage the Welsh to rebel. Throughout the rest of the fourteenth century, the English managed to control the principality, but such Celtic anger could not be stemmed forever. When it burst in 1400, it was not in the form of a nationalist uprising; there were very few such movements in the Middle Ages. It broke as a feud between Marcher lords. That it then developed into a popular strike for independence is a tribute to the charisma of its leader: Owain Glyndwr. Here was a Welsh warlord who satisfied both the English and the Celtic qualifications of leadership. Descended from the royal family of Llywelyn, he could rightfully claim to be

Scots footsoldier armed with pike and sword as he might have fought in the famed schiltron. From the thirteenth-century Liber 'A' manuscript now in the Public Record Office, London.

108

Reconstruction of the seal
of Robert Bruce, king of
Scotland, now in the
National Library of France,
Paris.

Prince of North Wales. But he also satisfied the older Celtic tradition of a warrior accepted by his peers as chieftain because of his military prowess and because he was the most competent figure to fill the role.

Although of Welsh blood, Glyndwr was a perfect English knight. He fought loyally and bravely for the king of England against the Scots and was a respected member of the English court. In 1400, he was a middle-aged man when he returned to his family estate in north Wales. He probably considered himself to be in retirement. He was an unlikely hero of what was to follow. When a border dispute with his neighbour, Lord Grey of Ruthin, irritated him beyond endurance, he did not immediately take to arms, but chose to settle the argument through the English parliament. The mood at Westminster was far from sympathetic to the Welsh. A civil war had rent the kingdom. Henry IV had defeated Richard II. The Welsh had supported Richard's claim. Eager to demonstrate their loyalty to the new king, English lords were far from keen to support the cause of a Welshman. Owain's case was dismissed. He accepted the decision, but events would not leave him alone.

The siege of Carlisle by the Scots in 1315. Line drawing of the initial letter from the charter granted to the city by Edward II in recognition of their successful defence. The Scots' siege engines were not used to good effect in the assault.

Lord Grey, as chief Marcher lord, was entrusted by king Henry to raise warriors in north Wales for a campaign against the Scots. He sent notice to all the king's subjects, demanding their presence in the royal retinue. If subjects did not respond to this duty then their lands could be taken away from them, for they received them only on condition of their service to the king. Whether by chance or ploy, the summons to arms arrived too late at the estate of Owain for him to gather his forces and join the king. His absence was noticed, and in the ensuing defeat at the hands of the Scots a furious king empowered Lord Grey to arrest Glyndwr. According to tradition, Glyndwr escaped from the trap set by Grey and began raising forces against the Marcher chief. On the banks of the Dee at Carrog, he was crowned Prince of Wales. Bards spread it far and wide that the stream in which the decapitated head of Llywelyn the Last had been washed now ran with blood.

Glyndwr's followers struck back at Ruthin, Grey's town. They then raided Denbigh, Flint, Hawarden, Holt, Rhuddlan, Oswestry and Welshpool. Glyndwr was declared an outlaw and his estates confiscated. In turn, he set up a mountain stronghold in Snowdonia on the shores of Lake Peris. Support was growing for Glyndwr, but his immediate military power was undercut by royal pardons issued to all Welsh rebels apart from their leader. The Marcher lords required sterner measures to protect their interests. A state of emergency was declared which effectively took all power of administration and law away from native Welshmen and handed it over to the English. Even the Welsh students ensconced in English universities were outraged and there were skirmishes with the citizens of Oxford. The situation deteriorated into open warfare. In 1401, the Tudor brothers from Anglesey captured the castle at Conwy. A year later, the rumour that the deposed king Richard was still alive stiffened opposition to Henry IV.

Avoiding confrontation, Glyndwr's warriors spread the rebellion from the north of Wales to the south. In a mountain glen in the Hyddgen valley, near Llanidloes, Glyndwr's guerilla band of 400 men was surrounded by 1500 Flemish immigrants and merchants of south Wales, fiercely determined to protect their newly-established colonies. For Owain, it was death or surrender. But the Welsh rebels were hardened fighters and they savaged the Flemish civilians. It was Glyndwr's first victory in a pitched battle and it increased his following overnight. Such a force, however, could not hope to survive the mighty army that Henry IV now assembled to finish off the Welsh. In desperation, Glyndwr wrote to both the kings of Ireland and Scotland. 'So long as we shall wage manfully this war on our borders,' he told the Gaelic high king of Ireland, 'so you and all other chieftains of your parts of Ireland will in the meantime have welcome peace and quiet repose.' Unfortunately, both letters were intercepted by king Henry. There would be no union of the Celtic realms.

Henry's army burned and ransacked monasteries and villages. It took

Irishmen fighting with axes. After the illustrations in Giraldus Cambrensis' early thirteenth-century *Topographia Hibernica & Expugnatio Hiberniae*, now in the National Library of Ireland, Dublin.

prisoner the children of suspected rebels. But it came nowhere near to ending Welsh independence. Glyndwr emerged from his mountain lair to capture Lord Grey of Ruthin. By 1404, he was at the height of his power. He summoned a national Welsh parliament which all the leading Welsh magnates attended. His unity was greater even than that of Llywelyn, for Powys had always remained aloof: now Powys did homage to Glyndwr. He planned to establish a separate Welsh church and university. He made individual treaties with France and Scotland. It seemed that Welsh independence would again become reality.

In 1405, the French invaded Britain. Almost 3,000 French warriors landed at Milford Haven. They were met by an army of 10,000 Welshmen. Together they would smash the English. At Caerleon, the French marvelled at the Roman amphitheatre. They were told it was the original Round Table of the Arthurian knights and that, of course, Arthur was the warrior hero of the Celtic Britons and not the English. Worcester, the first major English town in their path, was devastated. At Woodbury Hill, they set up camp.

Kidney daggers, fourteenth to fifteenth centuries, now in the London Museum. Commonly a civilian weapon, but also carried by archers in battle.

They were confronted by an English army led by king Henry's son, the
future Henry V. Apparently, with their minds full of Arthurian legend, the
Franco-Welsh challenged the English not to battle but to a tournament. For
eight days, knights of both sides hurtled towards each other with lance and
sword. Two hundred died in the sporting combat. Eventually Prince Henry
tired of the game. He retired to Worcester and then turned on the retreating
French, harrying their rearguard. Some French sailed home, others stayed
with the Welsh. The ambitious expedition had run out of steam and the tide
now turned for Glyndwr.

From 1406 onwards, Prince Henry and the English tightened the ring
around Glyndwr's principality. The Marches were won back slowly and the
Welsh retreated to the mountains of central Wales. As always, the superior
economic and logistical back-up of the English was beginning to dominate

114

the struggle. But the Glyndwr was far from finished. In 1415, Henry V sent an envoy to offer a pardon to the Welshman. Owain refused. It was then that Glyndwr became swathed in legend. His whereabouts were unknown. The chronicles are silent. The date and site of his death are a mystery. Many Welshmen were convinced that like Arthur, Glyndwr was asleep in a cave in the heart of Wales awaiting the right time to lead his people to freedom. The inspiration of Celtic liberty remained. But increasingly, despite the action of heroic warlords, the future of all the Celtic realms of Britain and Ireland was haunted by the English. In the next century, Celtic warriors would face the final challenge to their independence. It came from a dynasty of Celtic ancestry: the Tudors.

The Final Challenge

For two hundred years, English influence in Ireland declined. From the invasion of Edward Bruce to the rise of the Tudor dynasty, the power of the English crown had been so reduced that in 1465 the Pale included only the four home counties of Dublin, Kildare, Meath and Louth: a frontier of not even 150 miles. Civil war and continental conflict had undermined English control, but it was also the independent Celtic spirit of the Irish warlords. The majority of Anglo-Irish lords, descendants of the Normans, had gone native. Their language, appearance and law was Gaelic. Militarily, the Irish were no longer cowed by English or Welsh mercenaries. They had fierce mercenaries of their own. Emerging from the ancient relationship between Ulster and the Scots Isles and Western Highlands, a potent military force had developed over the two centuries since Edward Bruce. Scots adventurers and families of professional warriors sailed to Ireland intent on hiring themselves out to the highest bidder. These were the galloglas, a fiery mixture of Scots, Irish and Norse.

Galloglas means 'foreign young warrior' and probably refers to their Viking blood. But, essentially, these warriors were Gaelic in tongue and custom. Some had accompanied Edward Bruce and many fought for the Ulster chieftains. As their notoriety grew, they were hired by other Irish warlords. Such business enabled generations of galloglas families to prosper from Gaelic feuds. The principal mercenary dynasties were the MacDonalds, MacSwineys, MacSheehys, MacDowells, MacRorys and MacCabes. It was only a matter of time before the English felt the need to employ them as well. In between bouts of fighting, the galloglas set up their own settlements on Irish territory. By the sixteenth century they had become an institution and were the elite of every Irish army. John Dymmok in the late sixteenth century captured their basic image: 'The galloglas are picked and select men of great and mighty bodies, cruel without compassion. The greatest force of the battle consisteth in them, choosing rather to die than to yield, so that when it cometh to bandy blows, they are quickly slain or win the field.' Such a description of the short bursts of fighting energy of Celtic warriors could have come from the pens of Latin writers of the first centuries AD. Perhaps the English saw themselves as the new Romans and so inflicted such classical imagery on their Celtic opponents. 'They are armed with a shirt of mail, a skull [*close-fitting iron helmet*], and a skean [*long knife*],' continued Dymmok. 'The weapon which they most use is a battle-axe or halberd, six foot long, the blade whereof is somewhat like a shoemaker's knife, but broader and longer without pike [*that is, spike*], the stroke whereof is deadly where it lighteth. And being thus armed, reckoning to him a man for his harness bearer, and a boy to carry his provisions, he is named a spare [*spear? or 'sparre' meaning a long-handled axe*] of his weapon so called, 80 of which spares make a battle of galloglas.' Although frequently from noble families and regarded as gentlemen soldiers by the English, the galloglas did not fight on horseback, but assembled in bodies of heavily-armoured foot-soldiers.

On an equal ranking were Irish horse-warriors. 'Their horsemen are all gentlemen (I mean of great septs or names, how base soever otherwise),' noted Fynes Moryson in 1600 with a pertinent afterthought. Like the galloglas, many were professional soldiers of fortune. 'These horsemen,' wrote Rochard Stanihurst in 1577, 'when they have no stay of their own [*that is, are not retained by any lord*], gad and range from house to house like errant knights of the Round Table, and they never dismount until they ride into the hall and as far as the table.' They were highly respected as light cavalry by the English. Sir Anthony St Leger remarked on them in a letter to Henry VIII in 1543: 'I think for their feat of war, which is for light scourers, there are no properer horsemen in Christian ground, nor more hardy, nor yet that can better endure hardness.' Later in the century, Edmund Spenser concurred: 'I have heard some great warriors say that in all the services which they had seen abroad in foreign countries they never saw a more comely horseman than the Irishman, nor that cometh on more bravely in his charge.'

It seems the high skill of Celtic horsemanship had not deserted the Irish. And yet, in other descriptions of Irish cavalry we have a clear picture of a military primitivism that is supposed to have been characteristic of Irish warfare. 'The horsemen are armed with head-pieces, shirts of mail or jacks [*leather quilted coats sometimes plated with iron*], a sword, a skein, and a spear. They ride upon pads [*stuffed saddles*] or pillons without stirrups, and in this differ from ours; that in joining with the enemy, they bear not their

An Irish kern and old man with two women in old English dress. From a water-colour drawing by Lucas de Heere, c. 1575, after a lost drawing by an anonymous artist showing Irishmen from earlier in the century.

staves or lances under arm, and so put it to rest, but taking it by the middle, bear it above arm, and so encounter.' Contemporary engravings reinforce this image of stirrupless riders, while Edmund Spenser states that among the Irish 'the stirrup was called so in scorn as it were a stair to get up'. It is baffling that, alone among all Europe's horse-warriors, the Irish chose to ride without stirrups or good saddles. It seems more likely that such primitivism was an invention of the English to play up their barbarity. Yet it is mentioned and illustrated by several sources, not all of them wholly uncomplimentary to the Irish. There seems little point either to focus on this detail when the general character of the Irish was found sufficient by the English to condemn them. In an earlier time, a French manuscript of the fourteenth century shows an Irish noble horseman clad in archaic coat of mail with no stirrups and bare feet. That Irish cavalry held their spears overarm rather than couched underarm is also a primitive military custom, reminiscent of ancient Celtic horsemen hurling spears before their initial contact. This, however, is the most effective tactic of light cavalrymen determined to harass and avoid confrontation.

In battle, records John Dymmok, 'every horseman hath two or three horses, and to every horse a knave; his horse of service is always led spare, and his knave, which carrieth his harness [*armour*] and spear [*presumably spears*], rideth upon the other, or else upon a hackney.' The lowest in status of the three main contingents of Irish armies was the kern. 'The kern is a kind of footman, slightly armed with a sword, a target of wood [*shield*], or a bow and sheaf of arrows with barbed heads, or else three darts [*javelins*], which they cast with wonderful facility and nearness, a weapon more noisome to the enemy, especially horsemen, than it is deadly; within these few years they have practised the musket and caliver, and are grown good and ready shot.' Earlier, Sir Anthony St Leger described these light foot-soldiers as 'naked men, but only for their shirts and small coats. And they have darts and short bows; which sort of people be both hardy and active to search woods or morasses, in the which they be hard to be beaten.'

The ferocity of the kerns left deep impressions on many veterans of the Irish wars. In 1600, Gervase Markham wrote a poem in which he imagined the town of Kerne as an Irish Sodom. Because of the licentious behaviour of its inhabitants, it is drowned beneath the waters of Lough Erne and the citizens transformed into wolves.

> The kerns sprung thus from this prodigious brood
> Are still as lewd as when their city stood.
> Fraught with all vice, replete with villainy,
> They still rebel and that most treacherously.
> Like brutish Indians these wild Irish live;
> Their quiet neighbours they delight to grieve.
> Cruel and bloody, barbarous and rude,
> Dire vengeance at their heels hath them pursued.
> They are the savagest of all the nation;
> Amongst them out I made my peregrination,
> Where many wicked customs I did see
> Such as all honest hearts I hope will flee.

From the verse above, it can be seen that by the sixteenth century the gulf in understanding between Irish and English cultures had become irreconcilable. The disdain of Giraldus had been succeeded by the invective of Tudor conquest.

The Irish of the sixteenth century were as adept at guerilla warfare as their forefathers. 'Because they are only trained to skirmish upon bogs and difficult passes or passages of woods,' observed Fynes Moryson in 1600, 'and not to stand or fight in a firm body upon the plains, they think it no shame to fly or run off from fighting, as they advantage.' 'A flying enemy,' is how Edmund Spencer chose to describe the Irish warrior's tactics. 'Hiding himself in woods and bogs, from whence he will not draw forth but into some strait passage or perilous ford where he knows the army [*of the enemy*] must needs pass, there will he lie in wait, and if he find advantage fit, will dangerously hazard the troubled soldier.' Right into the sixteenth century, the Irish maintained a particularly Celtic manner of warfare: light cavalry and guerilla tactics. It was to prove relentless and costly for the English.

Gaelic culture was predominant among the native Irish and the Anglo-Irish, more so than in any other Celtic realm. The language was spoken throughout the land and even in the Pale, while Gaelic law was still an institution difficult for the English to comprehend. 'For whereas by the just and honourable law of England, murder, manslaughter, rape, robbery, and theft are punished with death, by the Irish custom, or Brehon Law, the highest of these offences was punished only by fine, which they called an ericke.' Such humanity was not appreciated by the English and featured little in their savage dealings with the Irish in war. Leading Irishmen continued to elect their leaders in the time-honoured Celtic manner. 'It is a custom amongst all the Irish that presently after the death of any of their chief Lords or Captains, they do presently assemble themselves to a place generally appointed and known unto them, to choose another in his stead: where they do nominate and elect for the most part not the eldest son nor any of the children of their Lord deceased, but the next to him of blood that is the eldest and worthiest.' Again, such good sense was not appreciated by the English who had fought many wars over the rights of the elder son to claim his father's throne.

Once the English had reconstructed royal authority after the Wars of the Roses, the Tudor dynasty set about curbing the prevailing Gaelic culture of Ireland. In 1494, Henry VII issued Poyning's Law which dictated that the Irish Parliament could only pass bills approved by the Privy Council in London. It ensured a subordinate, colonial role for the Irish government and was only repealed in 1782. Next was an attack on Irish customs. Henry VIII struck at the very heart of Gaelic identity when he recommended a ban on native appearance. 'No person or persons shall be shorn, or shaven above the ears, or use the wearing of hair called glibes [*a thick fringe of hair on the forehead that frequently covered the eyes and was characteristic of Irish warriors*], or have to use any hair growing upon their upper lips, called or named a crommeal [*an attack on the moustache, the quintessence of Celtic manhood for so long*], or to use or wear any shirt, kerchief, of linen cap, coloured or dyed with saffron [*the traditional colour of Irish noblemen*], nor yet to use or wear in any of their shirts or smocks above 7 yards of cloth. Be it enacted that every person or persons, the King's true subjects, in habiting this land of Ireland, of what estate, condition or degree he or they be, or shall be, to the uttermost of their power, cunning, and knowledge, shall use and speak commonly the English tongue and language.'

The prohibition of Irish manners and customs was made law in the reign of Queen Elizabeth in 1571. 'The sons of all husbandmen and ploughmen shall follow the same occupation as their fathers. If the son of a husbandman or ploughman will become a kern, galloglas, or horseboy, or will take any other idle trade of life, he shall be imprisoned for a twelve month and fined.' Private armies were banned. 'For avoiding of robberies and idleness, no lords or any others shall keep more horsemen or footmen than they are able to maintain upon their own costs. They shall present the names of such men as they keep in a book to the justices of the peace in the country where they dwell.' Failure to do so brought death. 'All Irish law called the Brehon Law to be of no force, and all persons taking upon them to adjudge causes according to the said law, to have a twelve months' imprisonment and to forfeit all their goods and chattels.' The wearing of Irish clothes and the Gaelic hairstyle known as the glib was to be punished with a £100 fine. Such measures may seem silly or impossible to maintain, but it was a law against Irishness and meant that every Irishman had been declared an outlaw. This was a convenient weapon against rebels, if no other crime could be proved.

Gaelic discontent with the Tudor anglicisation of Ireland was strongest in western Ulster. Beyond the river Bann and Lough Neagh was a land ringed by mountains and deep cut waterways, a land the Normans had never penetrated. Gaelic clans ruled the territory as they had for centuries and the

An Irish lord, probably a MacSwiney of a galloglas dynasty, prepares to set out on a cattle-raid. From a woodcut, probably by John Derricke, for his book *The Image of Irelande*, published in London in 1581.

121

English counter-attack against the cattle-raiders and the Irish chieftain is wounded. From John Derricke's *The Image of Irelande*.

O'Neills were, as always, the dominant family. But, even there, the foreign policy of Henry VIII cracked open splits in the Celtic society. The head of the O'Donnels of Donegal submitted to the English king and he was followed by Con O'Neill who pledged the loyalty of Tyrone, forsook the title of The O'Neill, and agreed to pursue English customs and language. Such submission meant that Con O'Neill's eldest son, Matthew, was his successor according to the English law of primogeniture. This was too much for another of Con O'Neill's sons, Shane. He had been elected successor by the senior members of the clan according to Brehon law and the principle of tanistry. He set about proving he was the more effective man. Matthew was proclaimed a bastard son, ambushed and murdered. Con O'Neill was thrown out of Tyrone, dying shortly after in the Pale. Fifteen thousand Scots mercenaries were invited over from Kintyre and Islay: the Campbells, McLeans, MacLeods and McKays. In addition, Shane broke with the tradition that only freemen could carry weapons: all the peasants on his estates were armed. The Anglo-Irish army in the Pale barely numbered 2,000 and were clearly over-awed, preferring to sit tight and observe Shane consolidate his power.

In 1561, Shane O'Neill moved against his biggest rivals in Ulster. Calvach O'Donnel was betrayed by his wife to Shane. He kept O'Donnel in chains and his woman as a mistress. All of Ulster was now under his direct control. The Earl of Sussex, Lord Lieutenant of Ireland, had to act. But Shane was in no need of a confrontation. Sussex advanced to Armagh in south east Ulster and Shane's lightly armed warriors kept out of his way. The English army paraded on through Tyrone to Lough Foyle. They captured 4,000 cattle but not even this traditional challenge could bring O'Neill into the field. Eventually, achieving nothing, the English force wearied of the guerilla response and backed off to Newry. Tyrone had been ravaged but the hearts and minds of the Ulstermen were with O'Neill. In order to put his case fairly to Queen Elizabeth, Shane accepted an offer of safe conduct and travelled to London.

To the English, Ireland was one of the frontiers of Europe, a land on the edge of their world, full of barbarians. It is little surprising then that the courtiers of Elizabethan London observed O'Neill's retainers with 'as much wonder as if they had come from China or America,' according to a contemporary chronicler. Indeed, the Celtic party, headed by The O'Neill, presented a fantastic sight. In defiance of previous Tudor legislation, his warriors were wholly Gaelic in appearance. Their hair was long: fringes hanging down to cover their eyes. They wore shirts with large sleeves dyed with saffron, short tunics and shaggy cloaks. Some walked with bare feet, others wore leather sandals. The galloglas carried battle-axes and wore long coats of mail. O'Neill was himself a man of fearsome reputation. He could not abide anything English. He is said to have hanged a warrior for eating an English biscuit and called a stronghold 'Fuath-na-Gall', 'hatred of the Englishmen'.

Though bold and confident, O'Neill was not foolish. In front of Elizabeth, he begged for forgiveness for his alleged rebellion and explained his case. Matthew O'Neill had been a mere bastard, so, according to both English and Celtic laws of succession, Shane was entitled to be The O'Neill. Above all, the O'Neills had run Ulster as long as anyone could remember. But Shane was willing to admit Elizabeth's overlordship and help her in any way possible. The Queen held back her anger and invited him to clear eastern Ulster of the 'robbers of Hebrides': the military Scots families who had settled in Antrim. Thus, O'Neill returned to Ireland with his status enhanced, his position recognised, and carte blanche to acquire further territory in north-east Ireland.

The MacDonalds were the chief galloglas family of Antrim. They were the sons of the Lord of Islay and Kintyre and great-great-grandsons of John MacDonald of the Isles. Arming his warriors with matchlock handguns, O'Neill saw no need to employ the hit-and-run tactics he had against the English, but chose confrontation. The MacDonalds in their turn raised the alarm for reinforcements from the Western Isles by lighting beacons on the coastal cliffs of Antrim. They clashed a few miles south of Ballycastle. The battle was ferocious and long. By nightfall, it was clear that the O'Neills were victorious. The leading MacDonalds were made prisoner and thirteen clan banners captured. Queen Elizabeth rejoiced at the breaking of the Scots foothold in Ireland, but now she faced an independent Irish warlord of even greater strength. O'Neill followed up his military victories with political strategy. He wrote to the king of France requesting 6,000 troops 'to assist in expelling the English'. O'Neill was under no illusions. He played along with Elizabeth's efforts to set one Gaelic faction against another, but he knew that in the end it was the English who were his greatest enemy.

In 1566, Sir Henry Sidney, a new English Lord Deputy of Ireland, set about curbing the power of The O'Neill. 'Lucifer was never more puffed up with pride and ambition than O'Neill is,' he wrote to Elizabeth. 'He continually keepeth six hundred armed men about him and is able to bring into the field one thousand horsemen and four thousand foot. He is the only strong man of Ireland.' Marching to the mouth of the river Blackwater, Sidney captured O'Neill's Coney Island stronghold in Lough Neagh. A stone tower 30 feet high and surrounded by sharpened stakes, a thick hedge, ditch, and stone rampart, it was the Ulsterman's treasury. Sidney then progressed through Tyrone, again demonstrating English power, and again being avoided by O'Neill's men who had reverted to their guerilla tactics. Such a parade of strength, however, had damaged Shane's pride and purse and restored the O'Donnells in Donegal. With little money to pay his followers and a dent in his control of the land, O'Neill had to act decisively or he would lose the support of his warriors. He decided to regain his reputation as a winner by attacking the O'Donnells.

In the spring of 1567, the O'Neills rode into view of the O'Donnells at Farsetmore, a sandy ford across the river Swilly. At first, the horsemen of both vanguards exchanged blows. Spears were thrown over-arm in the traditional Celtic manner. But the clatter of javelins was joined by the crack of gun-fire as the arquebusiers of each side joined in. The O'Donnells were pushed back to their prepared positions on boggy ground. Reinforced by galloglas of the clan MacSwiney, they then counter-attacked. Galloglas of the MacDonalds fought alongside the O'Neills. 'Fierce and desperate were the grim and terrible looks that each cast at the other out of their starlike eyes,' recorded the *Annals of the Four Masters*. 'They raised the battle-cry aloud and their united shouting when rushing together was sufficient to strike with dismay and turn to flight the feeble and unwarlike. They proceeded to strike and cut down one another for a long time, so that men were soon laid low, youths slain, and robust heroes mangled in the slaughter.' The galloglas of both sides, axes swinging, were engaged in a struggle fuelled not by the animosity of their pay-masters but by deeply inbred clan rivalry. Exhaustion brought the battle to its crisis and the O'Neills were the first to break. Many tried to cross the river Swilly, but the waters had risen since they first crossed and many were drowned.

Shane O'Neill's forces were routed and with them disappeared his power. His judgement shaken by the defeat, Shane sought shelter among the MacDonalds of Antrim. Although politics had united them while Shane was riding high, the Scots clan could not forget the damage he had done to their people on behalf of Elizabeth. Initially, they welcomed him and helped him forget his sorrows with a drinking party. But, whether it was the drink or a prepared trap, fighting broke out. Shane and his bodyguard were cut to pieces. A few days later, O'Neill's head was presented to Sir Henry Sidney. Where the English had failed, Celtic warriors had succeeded in destroying the one Irish warlord who could have kept at least one part of Ireland wholly Gaelic. In 1569, the title of O'Neill and the sovereignty of the dynasty was abolished. The Elizabethan conquest had begun in earnest.

Frontier warfare brings out the worst in its warriors. Both sides consider each other alien and inhuman, so savagery prevails. Beyond the Pale, English conquistadors suspended any humanity they possessed and treated the Irish as they would the Indians of America: natives to be dispossessed and exterminated. The Irish responded with equal ferocity. The English spearheaded their campaigns with warlords of barbaric renown. In 1570, Humphrey Gilbert was made commander of the English army of Munster. Any visitor to his camp was compelled to walk between two lines of severed Irish heads leading to his tent. Largely due to the efforts of Gilbert, resistance in Munster was crushed and the land divided into English plantations. Similar ruthlessness ensured the English conquest of Connacht. Only Ulster remained a Celtic realm. And yet its leading Gaelic heir of The O'Neill had been educated in England as a potential weapon against the Irish.

Hugh O'Neill was the son of Matthew, the son of Con O'Neill. After the

Homage by the citizens of Dublin to Sir Henry Sidney, Lord Deputy of Ireland, after he returns from a victory over the Gaelic Irish in 1575. From John Derricke's *The Image of Irelande*.

O Sydney worthy of tryple renowne,
For plagyng the traytours that troubled the crowne. 1581.

murder of his father by Shane O'Neill, Hugh was brought up in England as a royal ward. Attached to the household of the Earl of Leicester, he learned lessons in England, both political and military, which were to prove highly useful. Returning to Ireland in the year after Shane O'Neill's death, he served with the government forces. He was considered safe enough to be rewarded with the title of Earl of Tyrone. The English now had a puppet ruler of Ulster through whom they could further exploit the country; or so they thought. Once settled in his homeland, Hugh's Gaelic blood rose. He consolidated his native power base. 'All men of rank within the province are become his men,' it was observed, 'they receive his wages and promise him service according to the usual manner of that country.' In 1593, Hugh O'Neill was elected by his clan to the title of The O'Neill. It was a slap in the face of English law. Drawn between both the role of an English peer and that of a Gaelic chieftain, it was to the latter that Hugh finally dedicated his life. Such a turn of events was encouraged by the presence of Red Hugh O'Donnell. Having dramatically escaped from Dublin castle, O'Donnell gathered his forces, including 3,000 Scots mercenaries, and took his revenge on the English colonists in Connacht: 'sparing no male between fifteen and sixty years old who was unable to speak Irish.'

O'Neill was ordered to attack O'Donnell, which he did, but he also dragged his feet. Observing the English hard-pressed, he continued to build up his own forces. Queen Elizabeth had permitted him 600 troops, trained by English captains. These were then used to train further recruits: Irish

Spanish morion helmet of around 1580. The Irish obtained much arms and armour from abroad, usually smuggled through English ports and sometimes direct from Spain.

and Scots mercenaries called bonaghts. The institution of the galloglas had declined since the heroic days of the early sixteenth century. Many of the Scots adventurer families had long since become a part of the Irish community. They were landowners and no longer needed to fight for their living. Effective English fleets in the Irish Sea prevented any frequent forays from the Western Isles. Besides, the traditional arms of the galloglas, the sword and pole-axe, had been supplanted by the pike and musket as the universal instruments of death. Those Scots warriors who now fought with the Irish mainly served under the name of bonaghts and wielded pike or musket. Organised in companies of 100 men and armed with the latest weapons imported from Scotland and Spain, or smuggled from English ports, there was little to distinguish them from their English adversaries, apart from the drone of the bagpipe that urged them on into battle.

By 1595, O'Neill had recruited and trained some 1,000 pikemen, 4,000 musketeers, and 1,000 cavalry. He was strong enough to declare his Gaelic interests and was forthwith proclaimed a traitor. An English policing force was mauled at Clontibret. The O'Donnells captured Sligo, thus securing the south-west approach to Ulster against English reinforcements. But, before all-out war could break, a truce was called. In the meantime, O'Neill asked for assistance from England's arch enemy—Spain. In his correspondence, he allied the survival of Gaelic Ireland with the re-establishing of the Catholic religion against the Protestant regime of Elizabeth. He received a friendly ear but effective military aid was not forthcoming. No agreement was reached between O'Neill and the English and, in 1597, a three-pronged campaign was launched against Ulster. Each element was repulsed and O'Neill and O'Donnell were forced ever closer in the common defence of their land.

In 1598, Sir Henry Bagenal of Newry was instructed to relieve an English fortress on the banks of the river Blackwater besieged by the Ulstermen. He commanded an army of around 4,000 foot and 300 horse. Almost 2,000 of these were raw recruits, barely a couple of months in Ireland and poorly equipped. 'The want of the men's apparel is such,' wrote Captain Francis Stafford, 'that if they be not speedily relieved, many will march without shoes or stockings.' Irish clothing was recommended for the English soldiers as being cheaper and more durable than the clothing imported from England, but Lord Burgh, Lord Deputy of Ireland, could not accept this because such clothing was made by the Irish who would thus receive 'her Majesty's good coin, wherewith they buy out of Denmark, Scotland and other parts, powder and munition to maintain their rebellion.' The rest of Bagenal's army, however, were veterans of the Irish war, half of which were probably native Irishmen, including many cavalry.

The English force marched from Armagh to the Blackwater across 'hard and hilly ground, within caliver shot of wood and bog on both sides, which was wholly possessed by the enemy continually playing upon us.' Charles Montague, Lieutenant-General of the English, was correct in this account.

O'Neill and O'Donnell had invested some 5,000 warriors in the densely-forested countryside. The English marched in battle order, returning the skirmishing fire, but inevitably the advancing line became strung out and soon it was to be every man for himself. The English pressed on; the fort on the Blackwater was now nearer than Armagh. But O'Neill had carefully prepared the territory. Brushwood and undergrowth had been weaved together to create living fences. Pits had been dug to ensnare the unweary and impede cavalry action. Finally, boggy land was linked by a trench some five feet deep and four feet over, with a thorny hedge on the other side.

The English tried to break through. Their formations were scattered. The first half of the English vanguard was isolated beyond the trench, within sight of the beleaguered garrison of the Blackwater. The garrison threw up their caps in joy and dashed out to meet the English relief force. But O'Neill was well in command of the situation and pulled the noose tight. His skirmishers pummelled the English ranks further. Then horsemen surged forward and foot-soldiers armed with sword and shield. This was not a time for orthodox pike and shot tactics. Irish blades cut in among the English. The recent recruits broke before the Irish war cries. The vanguard was cut to pieces.

Realising the danger of his vanguard, Bagenal rode forward to support them. At the trench, he raised the visor of his helmet to gain a better view. Gun shot shattered his face and killed him instantly. The other English commanders decided on retreat, but this was easier said than done. A loud explosion ripped through the chaos. An English musketeer had gone to replenish his powder-flask: his lighted match carelessly sparked over the open powder barrels and the contents blew up, throwing a black cloud over the disintegrating army. Confusion tore the English apart. Some had not received the orders of retreat and pressed on to the killing ground of the trench. Others threw down their arms and deserted into the woods. At the end of the day, a shocked and bewildered English army reached Armagh. O'Neill had won a great victory. He did not follow it up: the remnants of the English army were allowed to escape. But Ulster remained resolutely Gaelic until the end of the century.

The strength of Hugh O'Neill's military leadership lay in his combination of professional training and the latest weapons with a traditional Celtic talent for guerilla warfare. In his victory he showed that Gaelic warriors, given the arms and training, were more than a match for any contemporary army. This is worth stressing, as much has been written about the archaic nature of Irish warfare and Celtic warfare in general. Certainly, it was a hard fact realised by English officers at the time. 'The Irish are most ready, well disciplined,' said one, 'and as good marksmen as France, Flanders, or Spain can show.' The Elizabethan invasion of Ireland was not so much an act of colonial discipline as a full-blown continental war, and one in which the Gaelic Irish won much success.

In the next century, the Irish were joined by Spanish soldiers landed at

Kinsale. Drawn out of their strong defensive situation in Ulster, the Gaelic Irish advanced to support the Spanish on the soutern coast of Munster. The English were besieging Kinsale, and O'Neill hoped to crush them against the Spanish. Advancing in the most contemporary tactical formations—the *tercio* of pike and shot—O'Neill led a formidable force. But his Celtic warriors were far away from familiar territory and were now being drawn into a confrontation on open ground. Confusion and panic broke the army. The Spanish and Irish did not act together. The English triumphed and O'Neill dismally dragged his forces back to Ulster. The Spanish capitulated and sailed home. A great opportunity had been lost. The Gaelic Irish had taken the offensive in what could have been a final shattering blow to English occupation. Instead, it proved the downfall of the Gaelic regime.

The English pressed hard on O'Neill and a harsh winter in 1603 finally compelled the Celtic warlord to surrender. Queen Elizabeth was dead but James I continued the anglicization of Ireland. O'Neill was allowed to return to his Ulster estates, but it was no longer a Celtic realm. English law predominated. Gaelic laws and customs were illegal. English government effectively reduced the power of the Gaelic chieftains; so much so that O'Neill and O'Donnell felt the land had now become alien and they preferred to sail into exile. O'Neill died in Rome in 1616. There would be further uprisings against the English and the O'Neill dynasty was far from finished, but essentially Gaelic power had been broken. The culture remained, but the military potential of Celtic warriors to maintain an independent realm was over. The same was true of other Celtic regions.

In Wales, the fiery independence of the Celtic Welsh was paradoxically undermined by the victory of one of its warlords. In 1485, Henry Tudor, a

Caricatured Irish soldiers in the service of Gustavus Aldolphus, 1631. From a contemporary German Broadside now in the British Museum, London. After the Elizabethan conquest, many Irish warriors sort a better life abroad.

In folchem Habit Gehen die 800 In Stettin angekommen Irrlander oder Irren.

member of the Anglesey dynasty, sailed to England under the red dragon standard. He advanced with a Welsh army to the battle of Bosworth. There, he smashed an English army, killed an English king, and assumed the English crown. At the time, a Venetian ambassador proclaimed that the Welsh had at last regained their liberty. But, in reality, this was not a Welsh victory, it was a Tudor triumph. The Tudor dynasty could not afford to tolerate any independent powers that might threaten its security. So Wales was incorporated into a union under the English crown. The old tripartite Wales of Celtic, Marcher and Royal estates was reorganised as English counties. The Welsh language was banned from public life. It was relegated to the language of the common people: no longer spoken by ambitious intelligentsia or the ruling classes. That this Celtic cultural defeat was delivered by an English monarch with Welsh blood in his veins seems to have softened the blow, for there were no more armed uprisings. Perhaps the Welsh felt they could claim with satisfaction that they were now ruled by a Welshman. Certainly, the Tudors rewarded their Welsh followers and could depend on their support.

In Scotland, English was also the language of the rulers, with Celtic the tongue of the ruled. However, after centuries of fighting the English for their independence, Scots aristocrats were far from happy to be told they were speaking the language of their enemy. Therefore, in the fifteenth century, the northern English spoken by the Scots ruling class became known as Scots, while the previously Scots Gaelic language was termed Irish. A wedge was again hammered between the anglicized Scots and the Gaelic Scots during the Reformation. Scots rulers accepted Protestant ideas and were urged to crush old Gaelic affinities to the Catholic faith, thus further lessening the presence of Celtic culture in Scotland. By 1521, the divide between the Gaelic Highlands and the Scots of the Lowlands was crystallised in a characterisation that has lingered on ever since.

'Just as among the Scots we find two distinct tongues,' wrote John Major in his *History of Greater Britain*,' so we likewise find two different ways of life and conduct. For some are born in the forests and mountains of the north, and these we call men of the Highland, but the others men of the Lowland. By foreigners the former are called Wild Scots, the latter householding Scots. One half of Scotland speaks Irish and all of these as well as the Islanders we reckon to belong to the Wild Scots. In dress, in the manner of their outward life, and in good morals, for example, these come behind the householding Scots—yet they are not less, but rather much more, prompt to fight. It is, however, with the householding Scots that the government and direction of the kingdom is to be found. One part of the Wild Scots have a wealth of cattle, sheep, and horses, and these with a thought for the possible loss of their possessions yield more willing obedience to the courts of law and the king. The other part of these people delight in the chase and a life of indolence. Their chieftains eagerly follow bad men if only they may not have the need to labour. They are full of mutual dissensions and war rather than peace is their normal condition. The Scottish kings have with difficulty been able to withstand the inroads of these men. These men hate our householding Scots, on account of their differing speech, as much as they do the English.'

Although this description of the Gaelic Scots by an outsider is a typical example of anti-Celtic propaganda, it nevertheless demonstrates the independent lifestyle maintained by the Gaelic clans and their clashes with Lowland kings. For, throughout the fifteenth century, the Gaelic lords of the Western Isles and Highlands were as much a danger to the kings of Scotland as the English. Indeed, many of the island chieftains used alliances with English factions to pursue their clan ambitions. The leading dynasty throughout this period was the MacDonalds. All other island clans did homage to them: the MacLeans of Mull, the MacLeods of Skye, the MacNeils of Barra, the MacIntoshes and the MacKinnons. In 1411, Donald, Lord of the Isles, led a formidable army to within a few miles of Aberdeen. In 1429, Alexander, Lord of the Isles, sacked Inverness. In 1451, John, Lord of the Isles, seized the royal castles of Urquhart, Inverness and Ruthven, and ravaged the islands in the Firth of Clyde. In 1491, Alexander, a nephew of the Lord of the Isles, invaded Ross and destroyed the castle of Inverness. It is little wonder, then, that when James IV ascended the throne in 1488 his immediate attention was directed towards the Islands and Highlands.

'The king is of noble stature, neither tall nor short, and as handsome in complexion and shape as a man can be.' So wrote Don Pedro de Ayala, Spanish ambassador, of James IV. 'He speaks the following foreign languages: Latin very well; French, German, Flemish, Italian, and Spanish. The king speaks besides, the language of the savages who live in some parts of Scotland and on the islands. He is courageous, even more so than a king should be. I have seen him often undertake most dangerous things in the last wars. He is not a good captain, because he begins to fight before he has given his orders.' Armed thus with both an aggressive nature and a working knowledge of Gaelic, James sailed to the island strongholds of the clans and commanded their respect. James was the last monarch to speak Gaelic and he used it to good effect. He treated the Highland chieftains with friendship and granted them land. In return, the clansmen acknowledged his overlordship. James even extended his influence over the Irish Sea, receiving the submission of Hugh O'Donnell of western Ulster.

The Celtic warriors confronted by James on his expeditions to the Western Isles have been described by John Major. 'From the mid-leg to the foot, they go uncovered. Their dress, for an over-garment, is a loose plaid and a shirt dyed with saffron. They are armed with bow and arrows, a broadsword, and a small halberd. They always carry in their belt a stout dagger, single-edged, but of the sharpest. In time of war they cover the whole body with a coat of mail, made of iron rings, and in it they fight. The common folk among the Wild Scots go out to battle with the whole body clad in a linen garment sewed together in patchwork, well daubed with wax or with pitch, and with an over-coat of deerskin.' After a few years of settlement, it was inevitable that the clansmen should kick against royal authority.

At the age of 25, James revoked all the charters he had granted the lords of the Isles. It was a constitutional act, but it now meant that the clansmen were tenants at the king's pleasure. To secure this relationship he appointed several deputies over the region once ruled by the Lord of the Isles. Displeased by this increased supervision of their traditional spheres of power, the clansmen became restless; particularly so when one of the king's deputies, the Earl of Argyll, was noted to grant favours to his own clan members. In the tenseness of the situation, James imprisoned Donald Owre, the generally acknowledged successor to the last Lord of the Isles. Later, James relented and released him. It was to be a costly generosity. At once, Donald set about claiming his true right of lordship. Many disaffected chieftains joined his banner, including MacLean of Lochbuie, MacLean of Duart, and Ewen Allanson of Lochiel. Supporters of the king in the Isles were killed and clansmen ravaged Bute.

In retaliation, the Scots parliament enacted several laws against the independent Celtic warriors. The king's muscle was supplied by one of his deputies, the Earl of Huntly, who assaulted clan strongholds on the mainland, and the king's ships which sailed for the remote castle of Cairn na Burgh to the west of Mull. Little is known of the action in this confrontation, but it is clear the Highlanders were not quelled. Further ships were equipped with cannons and German gunners from Edinburgh Castle and these patrolled the Western Isles. By 1507, however, the last rebel stronghold was besieged by the royal fleet and Donald Owre had been captured. Relationships between the clansmen and the king became more friendly, but the extent of James' trust of the Highlanders is demonstrated by his strengthening of several castles at strategic points throughout the Highlands. It might seem that James had maintained his authority, but in reality little had been achieved against the Gaelic Scots. The clansmen remained semi-independent warlords ready to prove a major threat to Scots kings in the future.

By 1511, James had other enemies to consider. Scotland was enmeshed in continental affairs. Her Auld Alliance with the king of France was tested as the Pope, the king of Spain, the Doge, the Emperor, and the king of England all prepared to divide France. The Scots stood by their traditional ally and in 1513 James demanded Henry VIII withdraw from his invasion of France. Henry refused, adding that he was 'the very owner of Scotland' which James 'held of him by homage', thus evoking the claims of English kings before the war of Independence. Outraged, James responded by recruiting a great army and marching across the Tweed. Raiders rode ahead, clashing with the border landlords and their retinues. In the main body of the army, seventeen cannon were dragged forward by four hundred oxen. Three

English castles fell to James, but many Scotsmen had already lost the stomach for fighting and desertion plagued the king's army. To march on York was now considered foolhardy and unnecessary. The invasion slowed down. An English army was reported to be advancing northwards. Led by the Earl of Surrey, it numbered about 20,000. The Scots army cannot have differed greatly in strength as neither side was daunted by the numbers of the other. James prepared a secure position on Flodden Hill and awaited confrontation.

The rain rushed down the hillsides around Flodden, overflowing streams and transforming fields into swamps. James felt content with the situation. If the English attacked, his cannon and schiltrons would hurl them back down the slippery slopes of Flodden Hill. If they did not, then he could retreat to the frontier and reinforce his army for whatever move he considered prudent. Surrey tried to draw James off the hill with a challenge to come down from his fortress-like position and fight on the plain of Milfield. But, though a lover of the tournament and the chivalric duel, James refused: 'Show to the Earl of Surrey that it beseemeth him not, being an Earl, so largely to attempt a great prince. His Grace will take and hold his ground at his own pleasure.' James was a cooler general than Ayala had credited him for. Surrey, however, was no fool either. He commanded his troops to march northwards and then wheel round so as to stand between the Scots and Scotland. The next day, James awoke to this danger. He had to get to Branxton Hill, to the north-west of Flodden, before the English, otherwise they would possess a similarly impregnable position. The alarm was sounded. The camp was stripped down and burnt: a great cloud of smoke hung over the land. Teams of oxen heaved the Scots' cannon across to Branxton Hill. Battle was approaching and the Scots assembled in their familiar schiltrons. Four massive squares took shape: the king commanded the right centre while the majority of Gaelic warriors in the army—the Highlanders and Islanders—formed the right wing. A further body of soldiers were placed in reserve. They now all looked down the muddy slopes of Branxton Hill at the advancing English.

The Earl of Surrey felt distinctly uneasy. The Scots had moved quicker than anticipated, leaving the English vanguard in the deadground at the base of the hill awaiting the rest of the army. If the Scots had attacked then, they could have destroyed the English piecemeal. Instead, time passed, and the English rearguard joined its fellow soldiers. At last, the Scots' cannon opened fire, hurling balls of stone among the enemy. The English replied with their guns. Apparently, the English gunners were more accurate and their shot crashed into James' division, mowing down his armour-plated comrades. It was then that James' bold recklessness finally took over from his strategic prudence and he led his warriors forward. Before the advancing schiltrons, the English right flank just ran away. But the English counter-attacked and both backed off. The king of Scotland's division surged on towards the Earl of Surrey. It was in this combat in the centre

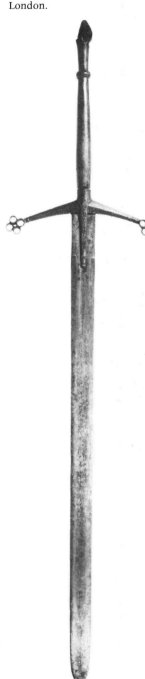

Scots sword of the type known as a claymore, or claidheanih-mor. Early sixteenth-century, now in the British Museum, London.

that the battle was won and lost. Thomas Ruthall, the bishop of Durham, described the crucial conflict only a few weeks later. 'The Scots were so surely harnessed that the shot of arrows did them no harm and when it came to hand strokes of bills and halberds, they were so mighty that they would not fall when struck by four or five bills all at once. But our bills did us more good that day than bows for they soon disappointed the Scots of their long spears. And when they came to hand strike, the Scots fought valiantly with their swords yet were unable to resist the bills which alighted on them so thickly.' From contemporary accounts, it appears the English soldiers armed with 8-foot bills, a kind of pole-arm, were at an advantage in close combat as the Scots' 15-foot spears were too unwieldly to be effective. Yet when the Scots threw them down and drew their swords, they were outreached by the bills.

In the struggling crowd, James also threw aside his pike, slashing and hacking at the English with his sword. He got within a spear's length of Surrey, but a series of bill blows cut him down. It might be thought that the death of a commander would go unnoticed in the chaos of fighting, but unless he is always on show, urging his warriors forward, the loss is soon clear and the fight drains from soldiers only there because of him. At the foot of Branxton Hill, the death of James broke his army. A further surprise appearance of an English force around the hillside shattered the High-landers who had yet to prove themselves but saw little reason for standing in the dusk with no king to note their loyalty. In the fading light, the surviving Scots made their way home, pursued relentlessly by the victorious English.

The death of James IV, the last Gaelic-speaking monarch, did not particularly harm the Celtic cause in Scotland. Indeed, his death initiated a century of uncertainty and weakness for the Scots monarchy that allowed the Highland warlords to increase their power and liberty. Again they allied themselves with the Tudors, but in the end victory for the English could mean only ultimate defeat for all Scots. For with the increasing influence of English Protestantism on Scotland and its eventual success, the Catholic-orientated culture of Gaelic Scotland was dealt a severe blow. Yet, in 1603, it was the Scots' king James VI who became James I of England and succeeded Elizabeth, that scourge of Celtic society. Like the Welsh, over a century earlier, all Scots could at least claim that Britain was ruled by one of their own. But here again, as with the Tudors, dynastic survival overcame national loyalty and James VI came down hard on the clans.

In the year of James I's accession, a bloody incident at Glenfruin encouraged a stern anti-Gaelic stance. In a pitched battle between the Macgregors and the Colquhouns of Luss, two hundred of the Colquhouns and several spectating citizens from Dumbarton were slaughtered, Immedi-ately, James passed an act outlawing the entire Macgregor clan. A few years later in 1609, James enacted further statutes against the Highlanders intended to bring them in line with the Lowlanders. One of the statutes

prohibited the importation of whisky, known as *aqua vitae*, to the Western Isles. It was claimed that 'one of the special causes of the great poverty of the Isles and of the great cruelty and inhuman barbarity which has been practised by sundry of the inhabitants upon their natural friends and neighbours has been their extraordinary drinking of strong wines and aqua vitae brought in among them, partly by merchants of the mainland and partly by traffickers among themselves.' Another statute hit harder at Gaelic identity. 'The Irish language which is one of the chief and principal causes of the continuance of barbarity and incivility among the inhabitants of the Isles and Highlands may be abolished and removed.' It was decreed that every gentleman must send his eldest son or daughter to the Lowlands to learn to speak, read and write English. It was clear the English and Lowland government were intent on extinguishing the Gaelic culture of Scotland as far as it could be seen to be a political threat.

The importance of language to the identity of a people cannot be overestimated. In the ancient world, it was only the common Celtic tongue that gave unity to an otherwise varied and often divided people. The Celt existed through his language. Without it, he ceased to be truly Celtic. Thus, by ensuring Celtic was spoken only by the common people and not by their leaders, it effectively struck away at Celtic power. The destruction of their language was the greatest blow Celtic warriors could ever receive. It denied their very existence.

Bibliography

THIS IS, OF NECESSITY, A SELECT BIBLIOGRAPHY OF
BOTH PRIMARY AND SECONDARY REFERENCES

PRIMARY SOURCES

ALL THESE TEXTS ARE AVAILABLE IN ENGLISH TRANSLATIONS IN SEVERAL EDITIONS.

Annals of Ulster: Medieval Irish history from the earliest times.

Appian, *Roman History*: principal source for Roman conquest of Spain by a Graeco-Roman of the second century AD.

John Barbour, *The Bruce*: fourteenth-century poem about Robert Bruce written by the Archdeacon of Aberdeen.

Brut Y Tywysogion—Chronicle of the Princes: Welsh history of Wales from the seventh to thirteenth centuries. There are two other versions of this chronicle, *The Red Book of Hergest* and *The Kings of the Saxons*.

Caesar, *The Gallic War*: first century BC autobiography of campaigns against the Celts of France.

Four Ancient Books of Wales: nineteenth-century compilation of the major early medieval British sagas, including the Urien cycle.

Wars of the Gaedhil with the Gaill: twelfth-century Irish account of the invasion of Ireland by the Vikings.

Gildas, *The Ruin of Britain*: sixth-century chronicle of the Anglo-Saxon wars by a Romano-Briton from the northern kingdom of Clyde.

Giraldus Cambrensis, *Historical Works*, including a geography of Wales and Ireland and an account of the Norman invasion of Ireland: twelfth-century chronicles by a Norman-Welsh ecclesiastic in touch with eye-witnesses of the events he describes.

138

The Gododdin: sixth-century poem attributed to Aneirin, a northern Briton, recounting war against the Angles.

Lanercost Chronicle: fourteenth-century chronicle by an anonymous English historian at Lanercost near Carlisle.

The Mabinogion: thirteenth-century compilation of Welsh tales and history of ancient times.

Nennius, *The History of the British*: ninth-century chronicle by a Briton.

Pausanias, *Description of Greece*: principal source for Celtic invasion of Greece by a Greek geographer of the second century AD.

Scalacronica: fourteenth-century history of the Edwardian wars in Scotland by Sir Thomas Gray, an English knight held prisoner in Edinburgh castle during the wars of Edward III.

Edmund Spenser, *A View of the Present State of Ireland*: first published in 1633, but written at the end of the sixteenth century by a Tudor Englishman.

Tain Bo Cuailnge: Irish epic tale dated to the eighth century but believed to be centuries older, perhaps pre-Christian.

SECONDARY WORKS

Alcock, L., *Arthur's Britain*, London, 1971.

Arribas, A., *The Iberians*, London, 1964.

Bannerman, J., *Studies In The History of Dalriada*, Edinburgh, 1974.

Canny, N.P., *The Elizabethan Conquest of Ireland*, Hassocks, Sussex, 1976.

Carr, A.D., 'Welshmen and the Hundred Years' War', *The Welsh History Review*, Vol. 4, p.21, Cardiff, 1968.

Chadwick, H.M., *Early Scotland*, Cambridge, 1949.

Chadwick, N.K., *Early Brittany*, Cardiff, 1969.

Chadwick, N.K., *The British Heroic Age*, Cardiff, 1976.

Davies, W., *Wales In The Early Middle Ages*, Leicester, 1982.

Drinkwater, J.F., *Roman Gaul*, London, 1983.

Edwards, O.D. (editor), *Celtic Nationalism*, London, 1968.

Ellis, P.B., *Macbeth*, London, 1980.

Falls, C., *Elizabeth's Irish Wars*, London, 1950.

Filip, J., *Celtic Civilization and Its Heritage*, Prague, 1977.

Frame, R., 'The Bruces In Ireland', *Irish Historical Studies*, Vol. 19, p. 3, Dublin, 1975.

Harding, D. (editor), *Hillforts*, London, 1976.

Hatt, J-J., *Celts and Gallo-Romans*, Geneva, 1970.

Hayes-McCoy, G.A., *Irish Battles*, London, 1969.

Hogan, J., 'Shane O'Neill comes to the court of Elizabeth', *Essays and Studies presented to Professor Tadhg Ua Donnchadha*, Cork, 1947.

Hogg, A.H.A., *Hillforts of Britain*, London, 1976.

Laing, L., *The Archaeology of Late Celtic Britain and Ireland*, London, 1975.

Loyn, H.R., *The Vikings In Britain*, London, 1977.

Lydon, J., *The Lordship of Ireland In The Middle Ages*, Dublin, 1972.

Lydon, J., and MacCurtain, M., (editors), *The Gill History of Ireland* (several volumes), Dublin, 1972.

Mackie, R.L., *James IV of Scotland*, Edinburgh, 1958.

Maxwell, C., (editor), *Irish History From Contemporary Sources*, London, 1923.

McKerral, A., 'West Highland Mercenaries in Ireland', *Scottish Historical Review*, Vol. 30 p. 1, Edinburgh.

Morris, J., *The Age of Arthur*, London, 1973.

Myers, J.P. (editor), *Elizabethan Ireland: A Selection of Writings by Elizabethan Writers*, Connecticut, 1983.

Nicholson, R., *Edward III and the Scots*, Oxford, 1965.

Otway-Ruthven, A.J., *A History of Medieval Ireland*, London, 1968.

Pine, L.G., *The Highland Clans*, Newton Abbot, 1972.

Powell, T.G.E., *The Celts*, London, 1958.

Quinn, D.B., *The Elizabethans and the Irish*, Ithaca, 1966.

Rees, W., *South Wales and the March 1280–1415*, Oxford, 1924.

Sandars, H., 'The Weapons of the Iberians', *Archaeologia*, Vol. 64 p. 205, Oxford, 1913.

Scott, R.M., *Robert the Bruce*, London, 1982.

Shetelig, H., (editor) *Viking Antiquities in Great Britain and Ireland*, Oslo, 1940.

Thompson, E.A., *Saint Germanus of Auxerre and the End of Roman Britain*, Woodbridge, 1984.

Wheeler, M. and Richardson, K.M., *Hillforts of Northern France*, Oxford, 1957.

Wightman, E.M., *Gallia Belgica*, London, 1985.

Williams, A.H., *The History of Wales: The Middle Ages*, Cardiff, 1948.

PICTURE CREDITS

Index

Page numbers in *italics* refer to illustrations.